SLAVERY
AND THE
Scottish Enlightenment

SLAVERY
~AND THE~
Scottish Enlightenment

[signature: John D O Fulton]

JOHN D. O. FULTON

Fonthill Media Language Policy

Fonthill Media publishes in the international English language market. One language edition is published worldwide. As there are minor differences in spelling and presentation, especially with regard to American English and British English, a policy is necessary to define which form of English to use. The Fonthill Policy is to use the form of English native to the author. John Fulton was born and educated in Scotland and now lives in Edinburgh, therefore British English has been adopted in this publication.

www.fonthill.media
office@fonthillmedia.com

First published in the United Kingdom
and the United States of America 2024

British Library Cataloguing in Publication Data:
A catalogue record for this book is available from the British Library

Copyright © John D. O. Fulton 2024

ISBN 978-1-78155-934-5

The right of John Fulton to be identified as the author of this work has been asserted by him in accordance with the Copyright, Designs and Patents Act 1988.

All rights reserved. No part of this publication may be reproduced, stored in a retrieval system or transmitted in any form or by any means, electronic, mechanical, photocopying, recording or otherwise, without prior permission in writing from Fonthill Media Limited

Typeset in 10.5pt on 13pt Sabon
Printed and bound in England

I dedicate this book to

*my mother, Anna Christian (Kirsty) Orchard or Fulton,
5 August 1923–7 July 2022*

and to

*Kristina, David, Sophie, Doug, Alice, Pietro, Charles, Raphael, Rose,
Leo and Angus*

Foreword

With this book, the distinguished documentary historiographer John Fulton has added a powerful volume to the library of books on one of humanity's greatest evils, the Atlantic slave trade. During the centuries it pursued its vile transactions, it transported millions of West Africans to labour in the plantations of the Southern states of the USA. President Obama described the slave trade as America's original sin, and its repercussions continue to reverberate in US politics today.

The distressing fact is that for centuries, slavery was simply taken for granted everywhere, and dour, puritan old Scotland was far from immune to the disease. Professor Sir Geoffrey Palmer pointed out in a lecture that the phone directories of the West Indian nations are full of Scottish names, testimony to Scotland's enthusiastic involvement in the vile business, and other historians have amplified the point. I remember a lecture at the Edinburgh Book Festival a few years ago, in which we were told that if purple plaques identifying the addresses of previous slave owners were to be added to buildings in Edinburgh, the Georgian streets of the New Town would be smothered in them.

Mind you, one would have had to be exceptionally independent-minded and intellectually awkward to face up to the consensus of every philosopher in the ancient world, who all took slavery for granted, and that includes the writers of the Bible. The Book of Exodus records God's instruction to Moses on the subject.

> When you buy a Hebrew slave, six years shall he serve; and in the seventh shall he go out free, for nothing. If he came in by himself, he shall go out by himself: if he were married, then his wife shall go out with him. If his

master has given him a wife, and she has borne him sons or daughters, the wife and her children shall be her master's.

Even the first Christians did not challenge the existence of this vile institution, though some scholars believe that was because they were expecting the End of the World soon, so why bother challenging an evil that would soon be wiped away with everything else? Certainly, in the Apostle Paul's Epistle to Philemon, Paul asks his correspondent to allow him the continued services of Philemon's slave Onesimus, which is why it has been described as a Christian foundation document in the justification of slavery.

Given that long backstory, who first found the courage to challenge the authority of the Bible and the academy of ancient scholars and denounce slavery as evil? The Pennsylvanian Quakers of 1688 were the first in the game; and what is significant is how they went about it. Quakers believed in the prime authority of the 'inner light'.

Many of their earliest activists, through their critique of the problems of the scriptural text, pioneered the modern discipline of biblical criticism. Their disrespect for the established conventions of biblical authority was the reason they could take a fresh perspective on biblical authority and reject it. For them slavery was wrong, even if the Bible appeared to justify it, the implication being that the Bible was a human not a divine creation. That was the beginning of the process that led to the Enlightenment, when light bulbs switched on in people's heads and they looked at religion's sacred books and said to themselves, why should we bind ourselves to what these ancient texts tell us, when our own sense of justice is outraged by what they say? And that's still a question we should go on asking.

RICHARD HOLLOWAY
Author and broadcaster,
and former bishop of Edinburgh and primus of the
Scottish Episcopal Church

Preface

The twin issues of slavery and racism remain highly topical in both Britain and America today, and their history is subject to ongoing revision by academics and activists alike. This involves an examination of the past which centres on the exploitation and mistreatment of the black slaves whose forced labour played a crucial role in initiating and financing the industrial development of both Britain and America—a sacrifice which, in the minds of many, remains unacknowledged. These issues are explored in the context of why the legacy of slavery matters in both countries today, and what might be done to provide a just society for all, regardless of colour or religion, in which our democracies and individual freedoms are secure from insinuation by this or other moral evils.

Set in Scotland, England, Africa, the Caribbean and North America between 1720 and 1865, this book tells, from a Scottish perspective, how Britain's trade with the New World developed on the back of slave labour. In fifteen stories, a diverse cast of characters is explored. The white men and women range from entrepreneurs, adventurers, slavers and plantation owners, to moral, religious and legal thinkers. Many of these people, to a greater or lesser extent, influenced the path which slavery took both at home and abroad, either through their words or deeds. The black men and women in these stories, the victims of slavery, chose to confront the cruelty of the institution, achieving personal triumph in contrasting ways. The stories illuminate the reasons that eventually brought slavery to an end in the British empire in 1833, and in the United States in 1865, although its corrosive bedfellow racism survived.

For many today, the time it took to emancipate the slaves was unforgivably slow. A point well made, but as this book highlights, during this period of huge geopolitical change, the rights of slaves, who were, in law, chattels, were largely unacknowledged or deemed unimportant. Britain and other European powers were preoccupied with establishing their empires in the modern world, pursuing wars on land and sea, financed in part by the profits of slavery, to secure economic, political and naval supremacy. This in no way absolves the perpetrators from the guilt of their crimes against humanity or their abject cruelty, but it allows the reader to understand why they were able to act as they did with impunity.

What emerges from the fifteen stories in this book are vivid narratives of how and why their central characters, at a point or points in their lives, had to choose between right and wrong, and how, for better or worse, their respective choices helped shape the world in which they lived. We may think that the time for such definitive moral decision-making lies in the distant past, but this book explores the notion that we are faced with decisions today that remain just as crucial, and that the choices we make will decide, now, as then, the values of the society in which we live.

Acknowledgements

I would like to thank Richard Holloway for so generously providing the foreword to this book, and for the time and careful consideration which that demanded. In like manner, many thanks are due to John Cairns, professor of civil law at the University of Edinburgh and an expert on eighteenth-century colonial slavery, for undertaking the substantial task of reading, reviewing and commenting on the history in this book. Also to Enda Delaney, professor of modern history at the University of Edinburgh, who provided sage support throughout my endeavour and helpful comments on my conclusion. Both Professors Cairns and Delaney are also to be thanked for sending me very helpful sources to research.

Huge thanks are due to James Hamilton, librarian of the WS Signet Library, Edinburgh, whose enthusiasm and knowledge were of enormous benefit as he consistently identified terrific sources of information. My son, David Fulton, similarly kept an eye out for me supplying me with articles and relevant books from time to time, which was much appreciated.

I would also like to thank my son-in-law, Pietro Pozzi, whose enormous patience, kindness and technical skills in computer formatting deserve a very large medal!

Others, who assuredly deserve a special mention in despatches, are my six chapter reviewers, Tim Orchard, Kay Hunter, Barbara Maier, Ailsa Loudon, Colette Grant and Susan MacLeod, whose opinions, encouragement and remarkable stamina for the entire journey were of substantial value to me. A very large thank you also to Jasper Hadman for his masterful editing.

I would like to record my appreciation to Donald R. MacLeod KC for his guidance on the legal aspects of the publication and to Alexander McCall Smith who so willingly gave me advice and support.

Finally, I would like to thank Kristina Taylor for her endless patience and vital support and advice, which she generously afforded me as the book progressed through its research and development to its final conclusion.

I could not have written this book without the immense support of those mentioned above and others not mentioned here, but it goes without saying that the responsibility for its contents are mine alone.

Contents

Foreword by Richard Holloway   7
Preface   9
Acknowledgements   11
Introduction: Medieval Scotland Searches for a Modern Future   15

1   The Dawning of Enlightenment:
Francis Hutcheson and Lord Kames   23

2   Justice for a Fellow Human Being:
Lord Mansfield and James Somerset   36

3   How to Value a Life: With Love or Money?
Lord Mansfield, Dido Lindsay and the *Zong* Massacre   48

4   Freedom of Choice: John Wedderburn and Joseph Knight   60

5   Rebel With a Cause: Robert Wedderburn   71

6   Passage to America: Peter Williamson   82

7   Slavery in West Africa: Archibald Monteith   97

8   Terrors of the Middle Passage: Sam Robinson and James Irving   113

9   The Findings of a Ship's Surgeon:
James Ramsay and Charles Middleton   131

10   The Abolition of the Slave Trade:
Henry Dundas, William Pitt and William Wilberforce   147

11   Glasgow and London: Richard Oswald,
Merchant and Entrepreneur   163

12   Slavery and a Battle for America's Soul: Fanny Wright   178

13	The Abolition of Slavery:	
	John Gladstone, Zachary Macaulay and Lord Brougham	196
14	Slavery in America and the Free Church of Scotland:	
	Frederick Douglass and Dr Thomas Chalmers	214
15	Two Men Who Changed America:	
	Allan Pinkerton and John Brown	234

Conclusion: Why It Matters Now	252
Notes and References	257
Bibliography	299
Index	307

INTRODUCTION

Medieval Scotland Searches for a Modern Future

Sam Robinson was fourteen years old when, in the winter of 1800, he boarded the aged sloop *Jean of Wigtown* at Garliestown in the Solway Firth, on the south-west coast of Scotland. His destination was Liverpool. As the lovely Isle of Whithorn slipped out of view and happy memories of his childhood home of Barglass, near Newtown Stewart, flooded into his lonely mind, Sam's mood of excitement turned to one of sadness. But such sentiments were soon banished when, despite departing on a sea 'as smooth as a milk-basin', an unexpected gale blew up that evening to threaten his journey. It was much to his relief that the ship found a safe mooring in the harbour of Ramsay on the Isle of Man. In time, with the gales abated, the *Jean of Wigtown* continued south, following England's west coast, and by the next morning was easing its way into the mouth of the River Mersey, towards the docks of Liverpool. The clear day and slow movement of the ship permitted an astonishing panorama to unfold gradually before Sam's naive eyes. He drew breath at the sight of the towering masts of ships and cranes resting in the docks before the backdrop of this booming commercial city. On disembarking, Sam was taken to his lodgings where he stayed pending the fitting for sail of his new ship, *Lady Neilson*, upon which he was to make his maiden voyage as a cabin boy.

The next day it was all hands on deck, where, as an apprentice, Sam was soon playing his part in preparing the ship for its journey to Africa. It was not long before the boat was 'painted and polished like a Dutch Doll [with] a row of black muzzles of eleven cannon, nine-pounders, peeping out of each side'. The ship's name and the nature of its cargo were emblazoned on its bow in large painted letters: 'Lady Neilson, of Liverpool allowed to carry 294 slaves.'[1]

Britain had been engaged in trading slaves since as early as the fifteenth century, and by the turn of the eighteenth, the trade was booming. To understand why Sam had chosen a slave ship for his first voyage begs the wider question of what was happening in his home country of Scotland and more widely, Britain, to make it his preferred option. Did he give any thought to his being complicit in a trade that would come to be universally regarded as evil?[2]

Of the Scots who follow in these stories, almost all were born in their homeland and had naturally absorbed the values and aspirations shaped by its history. Therefore, before taking their individual stories further, it is worthwhile to examine briefly the social, political and religious foundations upon which that history stood. What emerges is the story of how an impoverished, backward and medieval Scotland lying on the Atlantic fringes of Europe improbably managed to transform itself within a comparatively short time to a nation that would generate 'the basic institutions, ideas, attitudes and habits that characterise the modern age'.[3]

At first sight, an examination of these events might seem irrelevant to Scotland's relationship with slavery, but that is not the case. At the core of this relationship rests the tale of an underdeveloped country desperate to embrace the intellectual movement sweeping through seventeenth-century Europe. Had Scotland as a nation not been so forthright in this regard, it is possible that, due to its remote location, the Age of Enlightenment might have largely passed it by.

The changes sweeping Europe during this period were partly due to the advance of science, but this was only part 'of a much wider intellectual, social and cultural realignment, away from religion, deference to institutions and received wisdom and towards individual reason, scepticism, and the exchange of ideas'.[4] This tide of new liberal thinking called for religious toleration and legal rights in pursuit of 'knowledge, freedom and happiness', which understandably unsettled Europe's autocratic rulers.[5]

In Scotland, these ideas were to find fertile soil, due largely to John Knox who, beginning in 1559, single-handedly intimidated and bullied the country's aristocracy and urban classes into overthrowing the Catholic Church of their fathers and adopting the creed of John Calvin.[6] Knox wanted to turn Scotland into the New Jerusalem, expunging any vestiges of Catholicism and its links to the nation's past.[7] The rules of this new faith were harsh and unremitting, with traditional social pleasures stamped out, but it did offer one crucial benefit reflected in the stories that follow: direct access to God. Church governance now belonged to everybody, rich and poor, young and old, men and women. The congregation was at the centre of everything. It elected its elders and chose its minister. The elders cared for the sick and the poor; the church fed and clothed the community's orphans. Calvinism provided a community united by its commitment to God and its closeness.[8]

Imbued with the values of his faith, it was perhaps inevitable that Knox despised political authority and more specifically the power vested in monarchs. After his death in 1572, one of his followers, George Buchanan, shared these sentiments, asserting that 'all political authority belonged to the people, who came together to elect someone, whether a king or magistrates, to manage their affairs. The people were always more powerful than the rulers they created; and they were free to remove them at will.'[9] This was a powerful democratic formula which would resonate widely and later be found in the values of an emerging America: 'Government of the people and for the people.'[10]

Buchanan's doctrine of popular sovereignty, the first in Europe, was applied for the ensuing two decades but overturned by King James VI, who reasserted the power of the monarchy. While the concept of popular sovereignty faded, the reformed structure within the Kirk, the Church of Scotland, meant that members of its governing body were actually representatives of the people, as well as being the prosecutors of godly discipline and promulgators of the Word of God. A self-governing Kirk did not sit well with some monarchs, who claimed to rule by divine right; but for the people, the impact of the Reformation was long lasting and profound.[11] Its effect, and significance, was to imbue Scottish culture with egalitarian and democratic values. These values reverberate throughout the stories in this book, shaping the responses taken by many Presbyterians towards slavery and the enslaved.

To facilitate the promulgation of Christian principles, it was essential to the Kirk that its members could read the Bible. With this in mind, the Scottish parliament passed the Act of Setting Schools in 1696 to establish a school in every parish not already equipped with one. Within a generation, nearly every parish in Scotland had a school and regular teacher, albeit only providing a very basic education in some places.

The success of this act prompted Adam Smith to note in *The Wealth of Nations* (1776) that the parish school system had educated 'almost the whole common people to read and a very great proportion of them to write and account'.[12] Today, literacy and numeracy are taken for granted, but in the early eighteenth century, as Scotland prepared to enter the modern age, its literacy rates were the highest in Europe.[13] For example, by 1750, according to one estimate, male literacy stood at 75 per cent in Scotland, compared with only 53 per cent in England.[14] Greater levels of literacy increased the demand for a wider choice of books, which, in turn, fuelled the proliferation of printing and publishing. As the barriers of religious censorship fell, men and women alike were empowered to engage in debate and discuss new ideas and innovations with the intent of improving themselves and their society—an attitude shared and promoted by the five ancient Scottish universities. It resulted, as will become evident, in an educated workforce, a portion of which sought improvement for the common good, while others sought only to enrich themselves with little or no concern for moral scruple or even, in some cases, their own welfare.

The Kirk had empowered individuals to defy authority when that authority crossed a certain line, but despite such progressiveness, life was still hard for the average Scot. The country's economy in the mid-seventeenth century remained structurally medieval and highly vulnerable. The 1640s and '50s were particularly calamitous 'as war disrupted trade, bad harvests created misery and plague purged populations'.[15] The situation was no better by the late 1690s, when Scotland experienced 'starvation, population displacement, and mortality from disease'.

The root cause of this vulnerability was in the economy's dependence on the productivity of the land, which varied according to region. Scottish towns, handicapped by poor transport systems, remained dependent on harvests in the local area, with the potentially disastrous consequences of failed harvests always looming large.[16] The level of coal and salt production in the Lothians and Fife was only sufficient for domestic consumption, while small-scale 'cottage industries' which processed raw materials (including emerging textiles) did little to boost the economy. By the start of the eighteenth century, it was clear that, economically, Scotland was beginning to lag far behind its near neighbours, England and Holland.[17]

This economic situation was aggravated by political instability in Scotland. The Glorious Revolution of 1688, which saw James II and VII driven from his thrones in England and Scotland by his sister, Mary, and her Dutch husband, William, planted the first seeds of Jacobitism, which only ended in 1746 with the defeat of Bonnie Prince Charlie at Culloden. At the same time, England, bolstered by the Glorious Revolution, continued in pursuing its imperial ambitions, reaching west across the Atlantic to the New World, and east into Asia. It had expanded its navy to become the world's largest, able to protect its widening trade links, and there was clear consensus in the halls of power on the need to modernise the economy. Woollen cloth became a major export, and tobacco, cotton, molasses, pepper and sugar were imported from Asia and America. These commodities were then manufactured into profitable goods before being exported to the Continent. An infrastructure to support this burgeoning commercial development was created through the establishment of the Bank of England and the Board of Trade. The consequent growth of the economy created wealth and prosperity for businesses and the government, and provided a basis for political stability. While England was emerging as Europe's superpower, Scotland was in danger of being left behind.[18]

In the 1690s, it was clear to the Scottish parliament that innovative change was urgently needed. As well as political instability and the country's reliance upon exporting low-value primary goods such as fish and raw wool, there were three additional reasons for the economic malaise. One, the commercial damage inflicted by the wars William and Mary were waging on the Continent against France, Scotland's main trading partner; two, the English Navigation Acts which denied Scottish traders access to prospering markets in the English homeland and colonies; and, three, a series of disastrous harvests late in 1690s which killed an estimated 5–15 per cent of the population.[19, 20]

To address these problems, the Scots decided to copy the English model of creating an economy by legislation. The year 1695 saw the founding of the Bank of Scotland, closely modelled on the highly successful Bank of England, established the year before.[21] The Scottish parliament followed this by authorising a public chartered corporation, modelled on the British East India Company, to create a seaborne Scottish trading empire flowing both east and west. This effort backfired, however, when, in 1700, the Darien Company, which had been granted a permanent monopoly on Scottish trade, failed in its venture to establish a colony in Darien on the Isthmus of Panama. This disaster drained the country of an estimated 25 per cent of its liquid assets.[22] Supported by many in Scotland as a point of honour, families and businesses were ruined and the Bank of Scotland was broken.[23]

The Darien Company fiasco provided a clear message for those who chose to look. Without the help of the English, Scotland would never have the muscle to secure a new Atlantic trading economy, and under the existing arrangement of two sovereignties governed by a single monarch sitting in London, English interests would always be chosen above those of less prosperous Scotland.[24]

The idea of uniting the parliaments of the two nations, although unsuccessfully canvassed in the past, once more became an attractive prospect on both sides of the border, but for very different reasons. England stood to secure full political and fiscal union with Scotland and the Protestant succession to the throne, while Scotland took the great prize of forming a single economy with England and with it a common market, while negotiating provisions that enabled it to retain its nationhood, despite the ceding of its parliament. This was achieved first through the exemption of the Church of Scotland from the assimilation provisions of the Acts of Union of 1706 and 1707.

The deposition of James II and VII in 1688 had marked an end to his commitment to impose the Episcopalian establishment on Scotland as his father, Charles I, had done before him, alienating the previously influential Episcopalians, who were dispossessed of office. The Highland clan chiefs, who were deprived of the benefits they had enjoyed under the old regime, also lost out.[25] The Kirk, however, was able to regain its independence, free of interference from the crown—an independence that was further secured by the Acts of Union.

Secondly, Scotland retained its separate legal system and legal profession. Meanwhile, its universities, left free to encourage specialist teaching, attracted talented students and became, in the words of historian Arthur Herman, 'the crucible of the Enlightenment', built upon a 'faith in the improvability of the individual, and society through education, reason, and discussion'.[26]

This new drive for intellectual vigour was not restricted to the universities. Men and women, representatives of an increasingly urbanised middle class with time for leisure, met in taverns, dining clubs, reading societies, masonic lodges and theatres to engage in robust debate, often while enjoying food and drink. An important element common to all meetings, including those within the universities, was that they were conducted in a manner that promoted 'politeness'. The notion of politeness was more than good manners; it was a reaction, both in England and Scotland, to the narrow-minded bigotry and factional animosity that had polarised Britain's affairs during the previous century of civil war and revolution. It was part of a much broader wish to improve oneself and society for the common good.

While the intellectual ideas of the Scottish Enlightenment were bubbling away from the 1730s to the 1790s, the economic benefits of the Union were slow to come to fruition. A number of Scotland's domestic industries, which had relied on tariffs, were killed off by cheaper, more efficient competitors in England, and higher taxes, raised to match those in England, aggravated the situation, causing considerable resentment and, on occasion, violence.[27] In time, however, higher taxes generated better government, which provided stability and efficiency by enforcing the law. Transport infrastructure to London and outlying counties was improved, and overseas trade protected; the Union equipped a standing army and a navy to guard sea routes from Canada to England, while permitting Scottish ships access to English ports.[28] At the same time there were improvements in agriculture with the introduction of modern farming methods from Holland by enlightened landowners. Higher yields followed, which increased profitability, while mechanisation reduced the need for agricultural labour, fuelling an increase in the urban population from 1750.

One of the cities for which these major political, intellectual and economic events had huge implications was Glasgow. In 1667, a large deepwater harbour with warehouses and customs offices was constructed at Port Glasgow, which initiated further improvements to the Clyde's hinterland

and saw off competition from the city's small-town neighbours. Meanwhile, Scottish merchants, working from towns on the west coast, had from the 1650s already established effective trading links with the English colonies and had continued to trade covertly with Virginia, New Jersey and the Carolinas. Custom agents estimated that as many as twenty-four Scottish ships were operating illegally in the 1680s. They were used to transport criminals, indentured servants and political exiles to the New World, as well as forced emigrants, many of them Covenanters sent to Virginia and Maryland. These commercial links rapidly widened to Ulster and Europe.

At the time of the Union, Glasgow had a population of some 12–15,000 people. Trade had declined following the economic disasters of the 1690s, and for the first few years of the Union, the city's merchants had had no ships of their own capable of crossing the Atlantic. They were reliant instead upon chartering them from Whitehaven. But profits from the tobacco trade soon enabled them to start building their own fleet, with the first ship being registered in 1718. It was a trade they would soon come to dominate.

The merchants of Glasgow secured a contract to supply tobacco to the farmers-general of France. It was a contract so large that their English counterparts complained to the Treasury that Glasgow was evading tax and thereby cheating the government. The charge was dismissed, but it was only by the 1730s that the trade could be said to have been fairly and fully established. The tobacco lords became Scotland's first millionaires. As such, they invested in industrial ventures and founded banks which in due course created jobs and prosperity for others aside from themselves.[29]

Following the Union, the creation of free trade within the British Isles and unrestricted access for trade between the Scottish and English colonies in the West Indies and America enabled Glasgow to flourish, generating such wealth in the trade of tobacco and sugar that it would come to be known as 'the second city of the Empire'.[30] But this trade required labour on a vast scale. By the 1690s it had become clear that the demand for labour across the Atlantic could not be met by the transport of indentured workers. Indeed, the trend of using exclusively black slave labour had already begun in Barbados and Jamaica as far back as the 1680s.[31]

The stage is almost set to commence the stories that will show the history of Scotland's association with slavery, and how that past informs our present and frames our future. The first story shows the contributions made by two giants of the Scottish Enlightenment, who, with others, modernised its crucial institutions to enable Scotland to engage with the modern world. Francis Hutcheson, a Presbyterian minister, and Henry Home, Lord Kames, a judge, in their respective spheres of religion and law, formulated ideas and values that others followed. Although very different people, both developed the same theme in their ideas: that 'history' and 'man' were linked. It was a theme which allowed the Scottish Enlightenment to present man as a product of history: one whose fundamental character, even moral character, was constantly evolving and developing, shaped by a variety of forces over which we as individuals have little or no control. It meant that we are ultimately creatures of our environment. This innovative view remains pertinent to this day.[32]

It was recognised that the changes shaping man's intellectual development were not arbitrary or chaotic but formed of discernible patterns and fundamental principles. To enable these patterns and principles to be effectively refined required a scientific study of man. It led to a root-and-branch reorganisation of learning in Scotland by the division of the social sciences and the natural and other sciences into a series of separate disciplines that could be taught and passed onto future generations. The purveyors were teachers, professors and clergymen whose aim was to understand in order to teach others, to enable the next generation to learn and build on what they had mastered. In this way, human understanding would advance as an essential part of the ascent of man. It was a powerful message.

These enlightenment values elaborated by Adam Smith, David Hume and others, began to shape a new world, different to the medieval past. That past had been dominated by the fundamentalist values of the Reformation Kirk, but these new values no longer placed God at the centre, but man. In this way the notion was established that change was a process and not an event. Pertinent to this book, the Enlightenment also promoted the ideas of toleration and religiously inspired visions of a common humanity, an embodiment of which was expressed in the court of session judgment handed down in the case of Knight *v.* Wedderburn in 1778, in which it was decided that slavery was unsustainable in Scots Law.[33]

Conversely, the Enlightenment also produced educated and ambitious men who sought to make their fortunes in a country that, but for a few, lacked the economic muscle to deliver that outcome, at least initially. Other paths had to be found, which, for those unburdened by moral concern, led to the slave trade and the rich pickings derived therein. But before investigating that fertile, and at times, unexpected history, it is appropriate first to consider the contributions of Hutcheson and Kames. These two men recognised that Scotland was a nation on the verge of rapid change and thus in need of a new moral compass and set of laws by which to redefine and update its religious values and principles of law. Only then could the moral dilemmas faced by citizens like Sam Robinson, the young cabin boy aboard the slaver *Lady Neilson*, be addressed.

1

The Dawning of Enlightenment: Francis Hutcheson and Lord Kames

As Scotland rapidly emerged from its medieval past into the modern age, both its religion and its laws were in need of intellectual and moral reform in order for them to serve the country properly. Francis Hutcheson and Lord Kames were two men who responded to this need.[1,2] By advancing their respective disciplines of religion and law, they developed values and principles which created a platform upon which their followers would build. In so doing, they provided, among other outcomes, an enlightened intellectual basis from which to first challenge and then defeat slavery in the British empire. Yet despite this meeting of minds, as people they could not have been more different. Hutcheson, a clergyman and teacher, was softly spoken, diffident and thoughtful, while Kames, a judge and agricultural pioneer, was described as arrogant and brutish as well as energetic and kind.[3] To better understand the world into which these two men were born, we commence in 1707, the year Scotland entered the Union.

The economic advantages brought by the Act of Union—namely relief from tariffs imposed by England on foreign competitors and access to England's flourishing colonial markets—compensated for Scotland's underrepresentation in Westminster. Even so, things started badly in Scotland. On top of political instability generated by the Jacobite rebellions of 1708 and 1715, there was anger at the imposition of increased custom dues and excise payments (albeit matched by England's anger at rampant Scottish smuggling) and the unexpected abolition of Scotland's privy council, which reduced the Scottish government's effectiveness in managing periodic challenges. It took some forty years before the dividend of the Union would be widely felt by its people, by which time the political uncertainty presented by the Jacobite rebellions had ended on the battlefield of Culloden. Economic growth in Scotland created an emerging middle class which generated wealth progressively, thereby freeing its beneficiaries from the control of a repressive aristocracy and marking a profound change for the country as it broke away from its impoverished past.

A key aspect facilitating this change was a revision of religious values—the values by which society was directed—and their placement in law—the framework by which these values, if accepted, were implemented. This revision was therefore a central factor in regulating collective and individual behaviour in society, and in influencing how the nation was perceived abroad. In time, these revised values and laws, embodied within the religious and legal communities, would increasingly challenge the moral and legal legitimacy of the Scottish merchants who benefitted from slavery, either directly or indirectly via the tobacco and sugar trades. Indeed, the influence of Scotland's intellectual thinkers would spread to clergymen, politicians and lawmakers across the world.

In the religious sphere, the change began with a rise in liberal opinion within the Presbyterian Church. It sought to move away from the harsh 'fire and brimstone' dogma of John Knox and his followers, which was founded on the concept of original sin. Instead, the main object of this new brand of Presbyterianism was to focus on the moral questions that parishioners dealt with in everyday life, and thereby to uplift and inspire them.[4] In the legal sphere, there was a clear need to keep pace with the demands of an increasingly sophisticated commercial economy. Hutcheson and Lord Kames both played significant roles in establishing an intellectual and legal framework to bring about a more civil society in which all were equal. What followed would empower men of religion and the law to help bring slavery to an end.

Francis Hutcheson and Lord Kames shared a desire to create a new understanding (or world view) of human nature and society that would last through the generations.[5] Beyond this aim they were very different people. Hutcheson was a man whose strength lay in his personality: he was a preacher and not a system builder.

> His personal magnetism and method of lecturing were his main influences. The first brought him his audience and the second taught it.... His aim was not to give his students a system of morality which would bear the searchlight of keen logical scrutiny, but rather to saturate them with a code of ethics, by which they could live—or, if need be, die by.... He was primarily a 'maker' of moral men, not a constructive thinker.[6]

What may seem by some to be a weakness was made good by an ability to sell his ideas and values for others to pick up and develop. This approach was crucial while the country was not ready to accept a consistent and coherent system. Rather, incremental change was what was needed—something men like Adam Smith, one of Hutcheson's followers, would achieve for him by building on his principles. Indeed, Smith so admired his mentor that he described him as 'the never to be forgotten Hutcheson'.

Born in 1694, Francis Hutcheson was the son of a Presbyterian minister in County Down, Ireland, and a grandson of a minister who had moved from Monkwood in Ayrshire. Brought up in comfortable circumstances, both Francis and his brother, Hans, were given a good classical education under the tutelage of their grandfather, who favoured Francis over his less talented older brother. Such preferential treatment sat uneasily with Hutcheson, who expressed the wish to be treated in exactly the same way as his brother, a gesture which did much to sustain their loving relationship and mutual respect as grown men.[7] The death of their grandfather, much loved by Francis, in 1711 provided funds for their father, John, to pay for Francis's further education at Glasgow University, where he journeyed at the age of seventeen to prepare for the ministry.

Glasgow University had suffered from depleted revenue after the reinstatement of Episcopacy with the restoration of King Charles II in 1660. After the Glorious Revolution of 1688, which had freed the Church of Scotland of its bishops, it took many years for the university to recover from its financial malaise. That it was able to do so was largely due to King William III, who in exchange for recognising the authority of the general assembly of the Kirk, ruled that the harsh dogma of anti-monarchical covenant theology must end.[8] A more moderate path had to be found, and the best way of getting this message out to the parishes across the country was to start with the universities.

In 1703, shortly after the accession of Queen Anne, William Carstares was appointed principal of Edinburgh University, working in tandem with his brother-in-law, William Donlop, who had been principal at Glasgow University since 1690. Their strategy was to appoint a number of professorships to undermine the militants. They did so by introducing a series of new educational specialisms, including history, law, medicine and botany in place of the old school Calvinistic curriculum, which was abandoned. These reforms allowed the ideas of the 'new lights', a group gaining popularity among the ranks of the Scottish clergy in England, Holland and Ulster, to take root in Scotland.

The 'new lights' rejected the traditional harsh teachings of the clergy, that man was innately sinful, and adopted a new approach which asked 'what had happened to the notion of human beings being made in the image of God' and 'of changing one's life by accepting Jesus as Saviour'. It led a new generation of able men to shy away from the study of theology and instead focus on the natural and social sciences, which, among enlightened Scots, were regarded as equally important.[9]

Hutcheson's arrival in Glasgow in 1711 was well timed. A new and transformative wind was blowing through an increasingly educated Scotland in which science (including mathematics and engineering) and social sciences (such as literature, philosophy, history and the arts) were seen as natural bedfellows with the enlightened man, who was expected to understand both. These ideas resonated with Hutcheson as he settled into his theology course under John Simson, professor of divinity, who was then courageously challenging the harshest Calvinist doctrines by the application of reason. The world, as he saw it, was not the domain of the devil: 'Nature reveals a beneficent God,' he wrote, 'who watches over the fate of His creatures and provides for their needs and desires.'[10] It was a vision that was to provide the basis for Hutcheson's own teachings in an intellectual environment that had come a long way in a short time. Indeed, it was only in 1696 that repressive orthodoxy had led to the execution of Thomas Aikenhead for blasphemy.[11]

Hutcheson was appointed chair of moral philosophy at Glasgow University in 1730. He rapidly attracted large student audiences, breaking with tradition to lecture in English rather than Latin, and engaging his students with an interactive style unusual for the time. He stood before them dressed in gown and commodious wig, radiating a genial dignity from within his benevolent presence. His interest was to examine the mind with its reason and passions.[12]

In keeping with Whig thinkers such as Viscount Molesworth and the earl of Shaftesbury, Hutcheson believed that men were born with a desire to be free, and in consequence, held a 'just abhorrence of all slavish principles'.[13] In this his views were close to those of the old doctrines of right of resistance and popular sovereignty adopted by John Knox and his successor, George Buchanan. In the atmosphere of the Scottish Enlightenment, these ideas could be embraced in a more refined form. With the encouragement of Molesworth and Shaftesbury, Hutcheson asked a question that lies at the very heart of slavery: 'How do human beings become moral beings, who treat one another with kindness, regard and cooperation, rather than brutality and savagery?' The Scottish Presbyterian answer lay in the moral law of the Ten Commandments, but Hutcheson believed that all humans were born with an innate moral sense embedded in a fundamental understanding of the nature of right and wrong, which God gives to his own creatures in His own image.

> Moral reasoning ... is a natural human faculty ... expressed through our feelings and emotions. Love also proves man is not inherently selfish. Everyone's ultimate goal in life is happiness of which the highest form was making others happy.... Self interest and altruism are no longer at odds ... providing a contented mind and soul.[14]

Such views sound naive, and Hutcheson would have been aware of this. He knew only too well how rotten man could be, but in his view, by choosing to act in a rotten manner, man was electing to ignore his own conscience and the bonds of humanity that tie society together.

Hutcheson's enlightened views met stiff resistance from fundamentalists in the Church of Scotland, but his qualities as a potential leader for necessary change were recognised by his academic contemporaries, and more importantly, by Archibald Campbell, Lord Islay (and later 4th duke of Argyll). This formidable polymath and powerful Whig political operator had correctly identified in Hutcheson a man who was capable of completing the transformative changes in Scotland's universities which Carstares and Donlop had begun.[15] In time, Hutcheson's winning reforms would also serve as a model for academic change at other Scottish universities.

Hutcheson wanted Presbyterianism to present a more forgiving and encouraging face to the world: a Kirk which sought to engage with the moral questions faced by their parishioners from day to day—to listen rather than tell. The measure of Hutcheson's potential influence can be seen by the fact that, during his period of office, as many of one quarter of the Scottish clergy were thought to have studied at Glasgow.[16] They were thereafter free to carry and transmit Hutcheson's values and ideas to congregations throughout Scotland and abroad.

Hutcheson's ideas went further than the purely clerical. They were picked up by Adam Smith and others who would discover that the underlying principles of all human behaviour were part of an 'immense and connected' moral system governed by the dictates of natural law. This included economics and private law. As such, Hutcheson's ideas would serve to influence the political agenda of the American colonists before the War of Independence.[17] It follows that, for Hutcheson, liberty (or self-determination) was the critical element at the centre of this universe around which all other parts orbited.

> Human beings were born free and equal. The desire to be free survives, even in the face of the demands of cooperation with others in society. Society acknowledges it as a natural right which it must leave intact.... It applies to all human beings everywhere, regardless of their origin or status.[18]

In this, Hutcheson embraced both freedom of speech and freedom of religion and made no distinction between the rights of men and women. No less significant in this context was his view on slavery: 'Nothing can change a rational creature into a piece of goods void of all rights.'

Indeed, Hutcheson's lectures, published after his death under the title *A System of Moral Philosophy*, 'were an attack on all forms of slavery as well as a denial of any right to govern solely on superior abilities or riches'.[19] These sentiments would provide inspiration to anti-slavery campaigners in Scotland, England and North America. It was a vision of a free society. As one historian explains, '[Hutcheson] is Europe's first liberal in the classic sense: a believer in maximising personal liberty in the social, economic and intellectual spheres, as well as political. But the ultimate goal of this liberty was ... happiness.'[20]

On the one hand this meant self-gratification through a happy and contented life—something that Thomas Jefferson picked up when he added 'the pursuit of happiness' to the inalienable rights of man in the Declaration of Independence—but also altruistic in that no man stands alone. Hutcheson taught that 'the desire to be moral and virtuous and to treat others with kindness and compassion; the desire to be free, including political freedom; and the desire to enjoy our natural rights in society, as civil rights, are universal desires.'[21] These desires exist, taught Hutcheson, because they lead to human happiness.

But left unexplained was why, if these rights were universal, so many societies denied them of their people, and why, throughout human history, so few societies had delivered on Hutcheson's vision of a free society. It was a question he must have asked himself, but upon his death in 1746, he was yet to provide an answer. While on one level this outcome may seem unsatisfactory, on another it was not relevant. Hutcheson's teachings were not absolute; rather, they set out principles for others to take forward with the object of trying to answer the questions he could not. Lord Kames was one of those 'others', and to resolve Hutcheson's unanswered conundrum, he adopted a different, more pragmatic approach.

While Hutcheson argued that the most important instinct human beings have in common is their moral sense, and that men form governments in pursuit of the common good, Kames held a more sceptical view. Although he was prepared to accept the notion of innate moral sense and man's natural sociability, he saw the primary motivation for the establishment of society and government as one to provide an environment in which each person could enjoy what he had acquired by his own efforts without fear of challenge. It followed that the protection of property was paramount. For Kames, it was a principle of natural law 'and essential to the well being of society that men be secure in the possessions that they have honestly acquired'. This principle created the need for the individual to enter into a network of rights, obligations and duties with other individuals, because without this, he would never feel secure about what he owned.[22]

Kames also understood that there was a natural interplay between politics and the law, with one impinging upon the other. Law was organic, 'being founded on experience and common life'. It was therefore a fluid agency, and one that must change as society and man both develop with the purpose of yielding a sustainable framework for securing order and justice. Kames saw the law as a means to an end, and that end dependent on human desires and needs, which must vary with the nature of man and be refined as he refines. It meant 'to own possessions is to own myself'—a view that was shared by Lord Kames's protégé, David Hume.

Both Kames and Hume recognised that man's aspiration to acquire property was insatiable, and as such, directly destructive of society. Government and laws were necessary to put a check on people's voracious appetites for the personal goods of others. The law, through enforcement, could achieve this, and at the same time send out a clear message that by violating the rights of another, whether of property or life, the rights of all are threatened. Our innate moral view of the world is supplemented by our voice of conscience and of being one of a shared community. It forces the law to play catch up with man as his attitudes and society develop.[23]

Kames and Hutcheson both discerned the need to use reason to enable Scotland to break free from its violent and religiously repressive past—a past which, they thought, had constrained man's latent abilities—to enter into a new intellectual world in which man rather than God was placed at its centre. Only then, they claimed, could man achieve his full potential. This idea was founded on the premise that man and his moral character were constantly evolving and growing in response to influences beyond his control. Kames embraced this theory in his research on man's evolutionary development and the requirement of principles upon which law could progress in line with needs and aspirations.

Kames emerges as a man of huge energy and towering arrogance, a sharp wit who could be brutal and profane, not least on the bench, but also capable of great kindness and generosity. Most significantly, he had an endlessly curious mind. He shared with Hutcheson the desire to study history and the nature of man to create a better and kinder society for all, but elected to look to the sciences rather than God for the answers.

Born in 1696, Lord Kames's early years were a challenge. His grandfather, John Home of Renton, had been lord justice clerk in the reign of Charles II, but his father was a spendthrift who neglected his property, which fell into ruin. He assigned little or no importance to the education of his son, whom he placed under the charge of a harsh and incompetent tutor called Mr Wingate. But young Henry Home, the future Lord Kames, did not permit this setback to diminish his ambitions. At the age of fifteen, by his own determination, he secured for himself an apprenticeship with John Dickson, a writer to the signet (or solicitor), in Edinburgh.

Kames's journey in life had just begun, but his ambitions were accelerated when he was sent to an elegant townhouse in Bristo Street to have a meeting with Lord President Dalrymple. When he arrived, His Lordship was sitting comfortably reading a book in a spacious and attractive room while his daughter played on her harpsichord, singing a Scottish song. It was all in stark contrast to Henry's own gloomy and impecunious lodgings. Talk and tea followed, during which he was dazzled by the elegance, riches and prestige that the bar could offer a successful advocate. Henry's decision was made there and then, and after much scrimping and saving, he was called to the bar in 1724.[24] It would provide the platform for the burgeoning author, metaphysician, agricultural pioneer and party lover to blossom, and through his intellectual application, he would cultivate 'the flowering of disparate fields of knowledge during an age of profound change in Scotland'.[25]

Despite his lack of social connections, Henry Home gradually developed a practice at the bar. He proved to be a sound pleader, and in 1741, his career gained its required boost when he published two vast folios of court of session decisions, which served as important sources of reference for advocates and judges on the development of the law.[26] Until then, many judgements remained unclassified and unprinted. Lawyers were forced to search, often in despair, for old decisions in musty manuscripts. Judges looked anew 'upon the man who could drink with wits, dance with belles, and plod with lawyers'.[27]

In 1754, after becoming a senior examiner for the Faculty of Advocates and curator of the Advocates' Library (which, under his supervision, became one of the premier collections in Great Britain), Home took his place on the bench, thus acquiring the title of Lord Kames. By this stage he had a formidable reputation, and on the bench he joined men of variable character and ability.[28] Indeed, once he had identified those he could tease, he made them the butts of his jokes, and his pleaders were often the victims of his sarcasm.[29] His style could be vindictive, and in criminal cases, unnecessarily severe. When a former chess companion of his came before him on a charge of murder and was found guilty, Kames gave him the parting shot, 'That's checkmate for you, Matthew!'[34]

It was around this time that Kames was presented with an opportunity to take revenge on his old tutor, Mr Wingate, who had by then accumulated sufficient funds to have acquired title to some land. He asked Kames to check that the titles were in order. After closely examining the parchments,

Kames's air became increasingly serious, leading him to ask if the bargain had been concluded. 'Not only that, Sir, but the price paid,' responded Wingate. 'Oh, dear. How unfortunate!' replied Kames, before going on to highlight error after error in the papers before him, while sweat began to pour from Wingate's fearful brow. Having by now secured his retribution, Kames relented: 'Mr Wingate, you may remember how you made me smart in days of yore for very small offences. Now, I think our accounts are cleared.... You can go home with an easy mind, your title is good.'

These stories should not distract from Kames's ability to charm and entertain, whether in the taverns and oyster houses or at the theatre and prestigious dinners. Nor should it distract from the energy he invested in his legal career, in farming his estate, where he introduced several agricultural improvements, and in his publishing of many essays on a wide range of philosophical subjects. These essays placed him in the vanguard of a generation of intellectual giants, which included names such as Smith, Hume, William Robertson, John Millar and the admiring Benjamin Franklin, who stayed with Kames in Edinburgh in 1759 and communicated with him over many years on a wide range of subjects.

Before considering Kames's contribution to the principles of the law in Scotland, it is worth reflecting on the differences between the law in Scotland and that in England. Having developed in parallel through the early Middle Ages, in the twelfth century the respective systems began to diverge as England became more introspective, looking to precedent within England to resolve disputes and thus introducing the phrase 'common law', meaning common to the law of England, to the English lexicon. Scotland, meanwhile, followed a more international path, turning for its fundamental legal principles to the civil law of ancient Rome, which was being revived by medieval legal scholars in Europe. It meant that by the time of John Knox, Scotland's laws had more in common with those of France, where many young Scots completed their legal training, than England, and after the Reformation, with Holland.

While the English and Scottish systems shared common elements, once a case was before a judge, differences emerged. In Scotland, the prosecution makes no opening statement and the evidence against the defender must speak for itself. As Arthur Herman explains in his book, *The Scottish Enlightenment*, 'Unlike the English and American counterpart, the Scottish magistrate does not just ask what the evidence proves. He dares to pose the crucial question: what really happened?' It places a formidable responsibility on the judge and jury (in Kames's time, there were no civil juries). As such, a Scottish judge was required to look beyond the facts to the underlying principles of equity and fairness in order to make a judgement. His guide was reason, not precedent.[30]

Roman law was the source of reference when not in conflict with Scots law, and in the words of Lord Kames, 'The Roman Law is illustrious for its equitable rules, affording great scope for acute reasoning.' It placed the emphasis firmly on independence of thought; Judges were not to feel bound by what their predecessors had decided. But most importantly, it established in Scottish jurisprudence that 'no person, not even a monarch, stood above the law', once again echoing the fundamentalist values of Knox's successor, egalitarian George Buchanan, whose ideas had proved to be before their time.[31]

In the Act of Union of 1707, alongside the independence of its Kirk and universities, allowance was made for the retention of Scotland's legal system, with Parliament House transferring from being the seat of the country's politics to the home of its law courts. Before the great fire of 1824, the building presented an austere front of turrets and balustraded roofs 'on which their lordships could take the air, hidden from the vulgar gaze'.[32] It was to this building each morning that Kames could be seen progressing from his house in New Street in the Canongate, attended by Sinkum, his favourite caddy. The latter's stumpy figure, with one leg shorter than the other, causing him to duck at every step, was in stark contrast to the tall, thin, slouching lord, who would bend down to hear his companions' gossip of the morning.[33]

While Scotland's legal system was sound and well organised, its archaic feudal laws, which Kames had studied as an apprentice in John Dickson's chambers, were no longer fit for purpose. They needed to be adapted to the requirements of a rapidly emerging industrial society, but to do so threatened to create a conflict between the interests of the old landowners and the emerging business class. Reflecting Hutcheson's theme, a happy society for Kames was one in which laws and values were aligned, and since values were changing, the law had to change as well.[34]

To try to understand the genesis of societal evolution in Scotland and its relationship with the role of the law, Kames divided the history of human society into four identifiable stages, drawing on his voluminous reading of comparative history, law and geography. He then demonstrated how, in each stage, people were forced to change how they thought, acted and governed their lives.

The first of the four stages was categorised by 'hunting and fishing', essentially the pursuit of solitary activities undertaken with family in competition with others, who were avoided. The next stage, 'pastoral-nomadic', saw man domesticate animals into herds for his own use, fostering larger societies of clans and tribes, albeit limited and localised. During this stage, mutual benefits were secured by making the work profitable for others too. The third stage was centred on the cultivation of land, requiring a community endeavour to sow and reap the harvest, and the expansion of trades, with new workers such as ploughmen, farriers, blacksmiths, joiners and stonemasons. New relationships were developed between landlord and tenant, and tenant and labourer, and mutually supportive relationships also carried with them the tensions of potentially competing interests. The final stage saw the focus of activity move from an agrarian society to the seaport and market town, where the buying and selling of services and goods established a 'commercial (or capitalist) society'.[35]

In Kames's view, the first two stages did not require laws or government other than what was exercised by the heads of families over those under their charge. The third stage, however, did carry these requirements because of the unprecedented network of rights and obligations needed to make the relationships work. In support, laws needed to be introduced, and if necessary, with means of enforcement by sanction and punishment. Men of probity and substance were needed to judge and acquit. For Kames, the advance of government towards perfection within a society was in strict proportion to society's advance towards 'intimacy of union'.

'Intimacy' (or greater interdependence with others occasioned by deepening social and contractual engagement) began at the agricultural stage, but took a further step forward when activity switched from the village and farm to the seaport and market town. This called for a new society that had to cooperate to maximise commercial benefits and cope with the increased complexity brought by the trading of goods and property. These activities, better understood as capitalism, brought about the fourth stage for which new laws were required to bring enforceable rules into place, upon which businesses could rely to protect their contracts, their maritime agreements and their dealings in commodities and, in due course, manufacturing.

The introduction of laws encouraged a more conciliatory approach to business; it was understood that this would help establish consensus in trade and commerce, resulting in mutual satisfaction. The form of this approach was described as 'polite' (or polished) because it introduced a civilised tone between parties. It served to characterise the advance by social evolution of a society or nation towards what Kames and his followers chose to describe as civilisation. In so doing, a society could distinguish itself from others.

In relating this process to Scotland, Kames, in his *Essays Upon Several Subjects Concerning British Antiquities*, proved that the politics of the 'old' nation was not about loyalty and devotion to the crown as claimed by the Jacobites, but the power of patronage vested in the crown to grant royal lands in return for fealty. Its bedrock was feudalism—out of step with eighteenth-century society—under which Scotland's traditional laws did not uphold political freedom, but maintained a despotic status quo.[36]

As Europe emerged from the Middle Ages and the benefits of trade and manufacture spread, the prescriptions of feudalism ran contrary to 'the love of independence and property'. Custom and tradition increasingly made way for modern laws, which were needed to sustain markets based on the free circulation of goods and services. This commercial (or fourth) stage would deliver, as Smith and later economists were to confirm, the greatest change of all the four stages because it started to democratise power, and with that, change the form of government and the development of the law. This stage was one of continuous evolution, reflected in improvements in etiquette and manners and the way in which business was conducted. This democratisation, or empowerment, released a dynamic capitalist energy within society with 'its innate capacity for creative destruction'.[37] It was an outcome for all to see as the Industrial Revolution tightened its grip on Scotland.

The visibility of this 'capacity for creative destruction' allowed Kames to answer the question Hutcheson could not. Why, if everyone has the same desire to be free and happy, are there so few societies in which this has been achieved? Kames expounded that in certain primitive societies where resources are limited or in short supply, the rights of the individual must subordinate to the interests of the group. Under these severe circumstances, society sets aside individual choice or inclination, and instead, is guided by custom or the personal authority of those in a position of trust—the warrior chief or chiefs. Laws are strict and punishment harsh. However, as material conditions improve, and as man comes up with new ways of acquiring property, so the institutions improve in their wake. Awe-inspiring leaders are no longer needed to say what is right or wrong. Instead, as man acquires affluence from the beneficial union of a commercial society, he sees benefit in adopting a moral (or self-regulating) sense by which to live, and upon which laws are then founded.

To the contemporary eye, Kames's view of man's progression from a 'savage' to a civilised society might appear 'ethnocentric' or racist. Indeed, his ideas would play a part in anchoring nineteenth-century racial theories, but they should be assessed within the context of their time. His ideas enabled people to consider history and man's development as progressive and evolutionary, and they offered the prospect of change for the good. Importantly, in relation to race and the notion of supremacy, in Edinburgh during Kames's lifetime, countries like China and Persia were considered 'civilised', just as England was, while the Highland clans of Scotland were thought to be in the stuck in the 'savage' 'nomadic-pastoral' stage.[38] Thus, nurture, not nature in terms of race and skin colour explained human behaviour.

Upon reflection, Kames dismissed the idea that black Africans were inherently inferior to white Europeans. Instead he pondered on what African societies might have achieved and produced had they had the same opportunities as Europeans to exercise their powers of freedom.[39] Kames may have been making value judgements of other societies and peoples, but he was doing so without regard to colour. For him, the vital issue was not race but human freedom.

2

Justice for a Fellow Human Being: Lord Mansfield and James Somerset

When, on 22 June 1772, Lord Mansfield, lord chief justice of England and Wales, entered the crowded courtroom in Westminster Hall, bewigged and resplendent in his judicial gown, he found it buzzing with anticipation. At stake was the liberty of James Somerset, a black slave, the property of Charles Stewart, a Scottish merchant who lived and worked in America.[1] The decision Mansfield was to pronounce would serve not only to undermine the institution of slavery in Great Britain, but cause disquiet among merchants, financiers and plantation owners across the Atlantic.[2] At the same time, for abolitionists and slaves, it was a cause for celebration.

But who was Lord Mansfield and what drove his moral values? He served as England's most powerful jurist for thirty-two turbulent years of British history. He was a modernist and a central player in the Age of Enlightenment. He updated England's antiquated commercial laws, significantly helping the country to become an industrial and commercial world leader. As a humanitarian, he paved the way for the abolition of slavery in England. Yet he was not an Englishman but a Scot, born into a staunch Jacobite family.

Mansfield was born William Murray on 2 March 1705 at Scone Palace, near Perth, then in a ruinous state. He was the eleventh child and fourth son of the 5th Viscount Stormont, who enjoyed a life of genteel impecuniosity, not helped by the number of children he had to feed.[3] William was sent to the distinguished Perth Grammar School some two miles away from Scone Palace, to which, six days a week, he either walked or rode his pony. There he engaged in his studies with boys from all social backgrounds, many barefooted, gaining a lasting insight into how others less fortunate than himself lived. The shared language was lowland Scots, but William also learned Greek and Latin, becoming fluent in the latter, and English—a foreign language in Perth. The school placed special attention in reading and composition of English, with particular focus upon the rules of grammar.[4] In later life, Lord Mansfield reflected on the irony of how his grammatical education placed him at a substantial advantage over many eminent lawyers and statesman with whom he locked horns during his career in England, for they could not wield a pen or speak with the same grammatical precision as he who had learned his English in a local school in Scotland.[5]

Academia came easily to young William Murray; as dux of his class he was spared the tawse, a leather strap used to beat the boys less eloquent than him.[6] In 1713, at the age of eight, after his parents had moved to cheaper, more modest accommodation at Camlongan, Dumfrieshire, William and his brother Charles boarded with John Martin, headmaster of Perth Grammar School. Five years later, aged thirteen, his primary school education ended. Meanwhile, the Jacobite Rebellion of 1715 had occurred, and after it, the defeated James Stuart had been made welcome at Scone Palace. For this, William's elder brother James had had to flee with the prince into exile in France.[7]

These events influenced William's father, also a staunch Jacobite, to follow the advice of his elder son James in sending him to Westminster School instead of St Andrews University, as was previously intended, for his further education. Westminster was supervised by James's friend and avowed Jacobite, Bishop Atterbury, dean of Westminster. James harboured hopes that, in time, his brother might be persuaded to commit himself to the cause.[8] However, it was a cause for which the consequences for his family had been catastrophic. William had observed this, and it encouraged him in later years to develop a cautious nature and reluctance to challenge authority. He did not want to draw attention to the Achilles Heel of his family's political heritage.

On 15 March 1718, in an impressive display of independence, the thirteen-year-old William Murray went from Perth to Camlongan to bid farewell to his parents, whom he would never see again, and travelled down to London by pony. The journey took him forty-five days to complete.

Upon his arrival at Westminster School, Murray was the target of much ragging by his peers, who ridiculed his accent. However, they soon began to respect his academic ability. He secured a school scholarship, and by virtue of his attractive temperament, developed many permanent friendships. He was successful in anglicising his accent, but certain pronunciations such as 'bread' being 'brid' and 'Perth' being 'Parth', remained immutable throughout his life.[9]

Murray's academic and oratory powers at Westminster went unmatched. He was the school's highest achieving pupil before taking a scholarship place at Christ Church, Oxford, from where he graduated four years later. At this point the Church of England beckoned, offering a comfortable future if he was to be placed in a good college living. Fate stepped in, however, through his friendship with the son of Lord Foley, an enlightened industrialist, who learned that Murray's true ambition was to be called to the bar, though a lack of funds was preventing him. With the approval of Murray's father, Lord Foley provided him with a loan to see him through his studies, to be paid back with his future earnings at the bar. This kindness established a lasting friendship between Lord Foley and the young William Murray, despite their disparity in age.[10]

Murray prepared for the bar, staying clear of the two notorious evils: port, which ruined the health of many a young student, and prejudice. If he still nursed any latent Jacobite leanings, he kept them to himself. However, he was not afraid to express liberal views on religion and toleration, despite the prevailing high Tory dogma espoused by his companions, many of whom would gladly have enforced statutes against dissenters to deprive them of their civil rights. Reading exhaustively, he honed his knowledge and his powers as a speaker, developing a precocious understanding of 'how to work an audience' to advance one's argument.[11]

On graduation in 1727, Murray obtained chambers in Lincoln's Inn. The contrast between earning the right to practise before the bar in England and in Scotland could not have been starker. In the former, the barrister received no formal training at all. Rather, he learned his craft at the Inns of Court in London through 'hands on' experience, following what had gone before in practice and precedent. At the same time, to practice as an advocate in Scotland, one had to be a member of the Faculty of Advocates, which had strict rules of admission. It required from its members a university degree in philosophy and law, spanning at least two years, or seven years' formal experience. Furthermore, students were expected to be immersed in Roman legal theory, and since 1664, the faculty had insisted on private and public examinations on civil law and a public speech on a civil law text chosen by the dean of the faculty. Lastly, the Scottish advocate had typically studied at universities in Holland or France, stimulating a cosmopolitan air rarely matched by his English counterparts.[12]

But the comparatively undemanding nature of qualifying for the English bar did not inhibit Murray's thirst for knowledge. He read modern and ancient history, ethics, international law, the commercial codes of France (which he was keen to introduce to England), feudal law and, in particular, the law of property and English municipal law. Anticipating instructions from Scotland to appear before Britain's highest civil court, the House of Lords, Murray studied Scots law and especially the institutional writers Mackenzie and Stair. He supported some of the views expressed by Lord Kames in his *Principles of Equity*, published in 1760.[13] In a letter to Kames, Murray observed,

> I read everything that your Lordship writes with great Satisfaction.... Your Principles of Equity are very ingenious; but the Opposition to Equity to Law as now administered in England by different Courts, is not to be learnt from anything yet in print & not deducible from Reason.... I wish we had a Pen & Genius like yr Lordships do it.

Soon after being called to the bar in 1730, Murray had an opportunity to distinguish himself. In the case of Moncrieff *v*. Moncrieff, which in 1734 was referred on appeal from the court of session, Murray established himself as brilliant young talent. Many high profile cases followed, with work done for the City of Edinburgh in the aftermath of the famous murder of John Porteous, captain of the City Guard, who was lynched by an Edinburgh mob on 7 September 1736. For this, Murray was awarded the Freedom of the City and a diamond still in the family's possession.[14]

In 1738, Murray married Lady Elizabeth Finch, sister of the 1st marquess of Nottingham, a happy but childless union lasting forty-six years. His sister Mary married the 1st marquess of Rockingham, and both brothers-in-law were to prove valuable supporters in Murray's future career. Indeed, it was through Lord Rockingham that, in 1742, Murray became a member of parliament for Boroughbridge and immediately took office as solicitor general. Unlike many barristers of his day, Murray's ability as an orator in the House of Commons stood out alongside his logic and fluidity of speech, causing him to be described as 'beyond doubt [the House's] best speaker'.[15]

Although a comparatively junior legal appointment, the office of solicitor general opened the way, through custom, to the office of attorney general, and from there, to that of lord chief justice, which Murray achieved in 1756 In the same year he was created Baron Mansfield. This rise to high office was not, however, entirely smooth. In 1754, Murray's promotion to lord justice clerk was threatened when he was publicly accused of having toasted the health of the Old Pretender, James Stuart, twenty years before. He was duly called before cabinet, which, after an investigation, was satisfied of his innocence. But the experience, which Murray viewed as 'too much like an inquisition', left him infuriated; it was stark reminder that the risks posed by his Jacobite heritage were never far away.[16]

On the bench, Lord Mansfield was cordial and respectful of both junior judges and barristers. He 'strove, though a common law judge, to reach equitable solutions in cases that he tried,' as long as those solutions did not upset established legal principles or cause offence to a greater degree. This provoked claims from time to time that he was introducing ideas from other legal traditions.

His most important contribution in the legal sphere was as a founder of the commercial law of England, which was particularly evident in cases dealing with insurance and negotiable instruments. Both areas of commerce were under intense pressure due to England's maritime and mercantile expansion, and needed the law to catch up with what was required to service the economy. Mansfield's solution was to adapt and incorporate the common law principles long since adopted on the Continent with the object of providing stability and predictability. Central to his approach was a commitment to protect the needs of the mercantile economy and the interests of both the government and the crown. This was to be achieved while seeking, where possible, to keep common sense and legal principles aligned, though he was not always successful in doing this.[17]

Armed with these views and priorities, Mansfield found himself presiding over the case of Somerset *v.* Stewart in 1772. It was a case that called on his humanitarian rather than commercial principles, and in so doing, presented him with a moral conflict.

The facts relating to James Somerset are relatively straightforward. He was a slave brought from Africa to Jamaica, where he was bought by Charles Stewart.[18] The latter, born in Orkney, was the son of Orkney's sheriff clerk. His business centred on trading a broad selection of goods, including slaves, and he rose to become regarded as one of the most successful Scots in Virginia.[19]

By the late 1760s, Stewart had been appointed paymaster general of the American Board of Customs and lived primarily in Boston. It was in his role of paymaster general that, in 1769, he travelled to England, bringing with him his slave, Somerset, whom he had bought as a ten-year-old some twenty years earlier.[20] Stewart, who remained a bachelor with no children, effectively raised and educated Somerset, whom he valued and trusted. He allowed him considerable freedom so that Somerset often travelled on his own, and spoke of him with affection in correspondence with his brother, James, who was a lawyer in Edinburgh, and within his wider social and business circles.

In 1771, after a visit with his master to Edinburgh, Somerset, by then thirty years old, travelled to London where he was baptised in Holborn, with three abolitionists acting as godparents. It was then he took the forename James, with Somerset becoming his surname.[21]

On 1 October 1771, Somerset escaped his master. In his essay, 'After *Somerset*: The Scottish Experience', John Cairns suggests that his reason for absconding some two months after his baptism in August was 'perhaps influenced by this spiritual experience'.[22] Beyond this, no explanation is given, but there was a view held by some that baptism conferred freedom on slaves.

Somerset was recaptured two months later on 28 November by slave catchers in Stewart's employ. On Somerset's refusal to return to his service, Stewart had him placed against his will on the *Ann and Mary*, a ship anchored in the Thames. Shackled in irons, he awaited the ship's departure to Jamaica to be sold as a slave to a new master.[23] Help, however, was to arrive for Somerset. His godparents, on hearing of his detention, obtained a writ of habeas corpus from Lord Mansfield. This writ requires that any person who has detained another must bring the prisoner before a judge to justify his actions. If he cannot, the prisoner must be released. Thus, the ship's captain, John Knowles, was called before the court with Somerset to explain why the latter was being held captive and soon to be forced to leave the country against his will.[24]

So far, we have considered in general Lord Mansfield's values and his approach to law. However, before reviewing the approach he adopted in the Somerset case, it is worth considering how the moral issue of slavery had been developing in the case law in England.

The slave trade, which by the second half of the eighteenth century was transporting an average of 75,000 slaves a year, was bound by a series of complex business relationships fuelled by the demand for labour in sugar and tobacco plantations. The trade stretched from Britain to Africa and across to the British colonies in North America and the Caribbean. Within the network, aside from the African vendors of slaves, were plantation owners, merchants, financiers and ship owners, all aided significantly by subsidies provided by the British government.[25] The slaves were chattels of their owners and, as such, subject to the law of contract and property; their rights as individuals did not feature.

England was not a slave-based economy, but at the time of the Somerset case, Mansfield estimated there to be between 14,000 and 15,000 slaves resident in the country, many of whom were domestic slaves brought to England by their masters. There was an active market through advertisement for slaves to be either bought or sold, and rewards were proffered for the capture of those who had escaped. This was despite slavery having no legal basis in England. One justification for treating human beings as chattels was that slaves were not Christian. However, this would imply that if a slave was baptised, then they would be free. It was not a view supported by law, and Lord Chancellor Hardwicke had twice ruled that a slave did not become free merely by setting foot on English soil.[26] In short, the legal status of slaves in England, due to contradictory decisions made over many years, was unclear and conflicting.[27]

The issue became increasingly divisive as the anti-slavery lobby, led mainly by Quakers and Methodists, gained support from a better-informed public who were horrified by what was being revealed to them of the trade.[28] Within the other camp, bending ears in parliament, were those who saw their financial interests challenged, whether they were powerful merchants or ship owners with fortunes at stake, or members of supporting industries in cities such as Bristol and Liverpool, whose livelihoods depended on the trade. Another factor in the pro-slavery camp was the well-publicised fear that abolition would create a mass of unemployed black people, which would unleash a plethora of social problems.

Among the Quaker contingent was Granville Sharp, a member of a distinguished clerical family, whose father was archdeacon of Northumberland and grandfather archbishop of York.[29] Sharp became apprenticed to a Quaker linen draper in 1750 and was won over to Presbyterianism, or as he described it, independent persuasion. He completed his apprenticeship and became a member of the guild for linen drapers, but his business failed, leading him to accept a clerkship on ordnance at the Tower of London. He had an inquisitive mind and was drawn to biblical scholarship and evangelism.[30] His interest in slavery arose in the mid-1760s, and thereafter he worked tirelessly to end slavery and rescue individual slaves in England who had escaped from their masters and been recaptured. Somerset was one of those slaves.

The reformist lobby was a symptom of Enlightenment thinking, which challenged the accepted values of the mid- to late eighteenth century. Ideas of liberty and natural rights did not sit well with the principle of human bondage.[31] Lord Mansfield was influenced by some of the intellectual thinkers of that age as he strove to chart his own moral and ethical path. One who influenced him was John Locke, who wrote in 1690, 'slavery is so vile and miserable an estate of man, and so directly opposite to the generous temper and courage of our nation, that it is hardly to be conceived that "an Englishman", much less a "gentleman", should plead for it.'[32]

Meanwhile, in Scotland, in *The Theory of Moral Sentiments* first published in 1759, Adam Smith described slave owners as 'wretches who possess the virtues neither of the countries from which they come, nor those to which they go, and whose levity, brutality, and baseness, so justly expose them to the contempt of the vanquished'.[33] Aside from the views of Frances Hutcheson and Lord Kames, Lord Mansfield admired the work of poet and philosopher James Beattie, the son of a village shopkeeper in Kincardineshire who, in 1760, had been appointed professor of moral philosophy and logic at Marischal College, Aberdeen.

In *An Essay on the Nature and Immutability of Truth*, published in 1770, Beattie eloquently dissected the arguments of Scottish philosopher and historian David Hume, who had asserted that blacks were inherently inferior to whites.[34] Beattie argued that 'the apparent inferiority of Africans to Europeans [is] due to the absence of any civilising influence. Britons and Frenchmen were as savage 2,000 years ago, as Africans are now.'[35] He called on his countrymen to end slavery, saying, 'Never let it be said, that slavery is countenanced by the bravest and most generous people on earth; and by a people who are animated with that heroic passion, the love of liberty, beyond all nations ancient and modern.'[36]

Beattie's sentiments were well received in England, where he achieved celebrity status. In August 1771, Lord Mansfield invited Beattie to dine with him, and the two exchanged intellectual ideas over a six-hour period.[37] This was a matter of months before Mansfield was to hear the Somerset case in court, which strongly suggests that slavery was high on the list of topics discussed by the two men. Their mutual respect can best be judged by Mansfield's prevailing on King George III to grant Beattie a pension.[38] It also illustrates how porous the walls of enlightenment learning between Scotland and England were at this time, with the concept of reason and personal liberty at its very heart.

In 1771, a year before the Somerset case, Lord Mansfield heard a similar case involving a former slave named Thomas Lewis, formerly the property of English merchant Robert Stapylton. Lewis had been captured by Spanish privateers while travelling on a ship with his master, and was later released from slavery. He worked in paid employment in the American colonies before moving to England as a free man.[39] In London he was kidnapped by two watermen (workers who ferry passengers across the Thames) contracted by Stapylton. He was forcibly taken to a ship anchored in the Thames for transportation to Jamaica, where he was to be sold as a slave.

Granville Sharp, on learning of Lewis's situation, obtained his release by a writ of habeas corpus. At the same time he brought a criminal action against Stapylton and the two watermen for trying to take Lewis away from England without his consent. In this case, Lord Mansfield emphasised to the jury that when Lewis was captured by the Spaniards the contract between him and Stapylton had been broken; thus they had to decide whether Lewis remained Stapylton's property after he had gained his liberty. In saying this, Mansfield was assuming, though not saying outright, that a person could be legally held as a slave in England.

In the end, the jury found in favour of Lewis, finding no evidence that he was the property of Stapylton.[40] Although this was an outcome to be celebrated by abolitionists, Sharp was exasperated that Mansfield had managed to dodge passing judgement on the most critical issue of whether or not slavery was legal in England. For his part, Mansfield stated, 'I hope it never will be finally discussed. For I would have all masters think they [blacks] were free and all blacks think that they were not because then they would both behave better.'[41]

The problem for Lord Mansfield in the Somerset case was that, unlike in the Lewis case, the contract between the slave and his master had not been broken. Granville Sharp saw a second opportunity to push Mansfield into deciding on the legality of slavery in England, while Mansfield held out hope that the case would be settled privately and not come to trial. He suggested to the abolitionists that they buy out Somerset's contract, but this was refused. He then encouraged Stewart to free his slave, which likewise was refused. Tellingly, Stewart's legal costs were being met by West Indian planters and merchants on the basis that he did not settle.[42] Both sides were digging in for a clear decision to be made on the legality of slavery under English law.

To legalise slavery would have many consequences 'absolutely contrary to the municipal law of England', while to do the opposite would have 'disagreeable' outcomes too.[43] Among them would be the loss of more than £700,000 to slave owners in England, based on the average monetary value of £50 per slave. 'How would the law stand with respect to their [the former slaves] settlement; their wages?' the ever pragmatic Mansfield asked, before observing that the court 'cannot in any of these points direct the law'.

His predicament was that, on the one hand, he was loath to undermine the interests of the mercantile community, which he had represented many times over his long career and done so much to promote; on the other, he could not ignore his duty to deliver justice to a fellow human being. His predicament encouraged him to defer the case, citing various reasons, but this only heightened public interest in both England and America, where the newspapers discussed at length the implications of the case.

The trial eventually began on 7 February 1772, with Somerset's counsel arguing that in England no man could be a slave, nor could the laws of Virginia or of any other country apply in England. Stewart's counsel claimed that it was unjust to deprive his client of his property rights and highlighted the economic cost of releasing, in his assessment, the 14,000 slaves in England.[44] To this, Somerset's counsel responded by asserting that an immoral contract was unenforceable, a view to which Mansfield had subscribed in other cases.

Before adjourning the case for a month, Mansfield again urged the two sides to settle, though he conceded that 'if the parties will have it decided, we must give our opinion'. That opinion, he said, would be guided solely by the rule of law, not by empathy for Somerset or concern for Stewart's commercial interests or those of his fellow slave owners. But he was already shrewdly positioning himself for the approach he would take. He explained that since the case had been brought under a writ of habeas corpus, the object of the enquiry was 'the person of the slave himself' and not whether a contract for the sale of a slave was good in England, which he confirmed it was.[45]

On 22 June 1772, some seven months after John Knowles had brought Somerset before the court, Lord Mansfield delivered the court's unanimous decision. He opened by making it clear that the decision did not pertain to the legality of the slave trade, which was legitimised by the laws of Virginia and Jamaica. He tried to appease potentially threatened commercial interests by observing that slaves 'are goods and chattels; and as such, saleable and sold'.[45] As he had previously indicated, he narrowed down the subject upon which a decision would be based to the person of Somerset and not the contract under which he was bound. The question was whether the return to the writ of habeas corpus when the case was first brought before the court (that Somerset was the property of Stewart) was enough to permit Stewart to keep him in bondage and to remove him from the country against his will.[46]

'The only question before us is whether the cause on the return is sufficient,' said Mansfield. 'If it is, the [black] must be remanded; if it is not, he must be discharged.'

> Accordingly, the return states that the slave departed and refused to serve; whereupon he was kept to be sold abroad. So high an act of dominion must be recognised by the law of the country where it is used. The power of the master over his slave has been extremely different in different countries. The state of slavery is of such a nature, that it is incapable of being introduced on any reasons, moral or political; but only positive law, which preserves its force long after the reasons, occasion, and time itself from whence it was created is erased from memory. It's so odious, that nothing can be suffered to support it, but positive law. Whatever the inconveniences, therefore, that may follow from a decision, I cannot say this case is allowed or approved by the law of England; and therefore the black must be discharged.[47]

Already, a consortium of merchants had placed a bill before the House of Commons seeking to legalise the slave trade, which was rejected, as was their subsequent attempt to have the court's decision overruled.[48]

This decision on Somerset v. Stewart did not end slavery in England. Indeed the recapture and deportation of escaped slaves continued until the 1790s, and slaves continued to be bought and sold in England.[49] It did, however, lead many of those following the trial, including the large number of free blacks who attended the hearings, to believe that slavery had been abolished, and it added fuel to the abolitionist cause, which was to receive an altogether more resounding boost following the decision of Knight v. Wedderburn, heard in the court of session in 1777 after four years of litigation. It was there that the eighty-year-old Lord Kames declared 'We are here to enforce right; not to enforce wrong'—a view supported by the majority of the court leading to the landmark decision explored in Chapter 4. This time the decision was to be based on the principles of the law of Scotland and not England.

Lord Mansfield continued to walk a legal and moral tightrope in the years to come, demonstrated by his choice to stay silent in a case in 1782 which questioned whether a contract for the purchase of a slave was void on grounds of illegality or immorality.[50] And he continued to play down the implications of his decision in the Somerset case. In 1785 he commented that earlier court decisions went no further than ruling 'that the master cannot compel [the slave] to go out of the kingdom'.[51] He had, however, ruled that although slavery was not illegal, the court would not recognise the slave owner's mastery over a slave. This nuance was, perhaps, the inevitable outcome of Mansfield's attempt to lean in two directions at once.

But what Mansfield had done was to leave the door ajar for those following him to push open. Eventually, in 1793, Mansfield acknowledged to Granville Sharp that his decision had undermined British slavery.[52] In 'The Abolitionists' Debt to Lord Mansfield', published in *History Today*, Stephen Usherwood expressed the opinion that, without Mansfield's application of reason, taken in the context of the Enlightenment, to the long-established practice of slavery, which revealed it for the first time in precise legal terms, the abolitionists would have found it much harder to persuade parliament to declare slavery illegal in years to come.[53]

Not everyone shared that view at the time. Benjamin Franklin belittled the consequences of the Somerset case, attributing it to 'the hypocrisy of this country, which encourages such detestable commerce, while it piqued itself on its virtue, love of liberty, and the equity of its courts in setting free a single black.'[54]

Franklin was a resident in London for much if not all of the period of the Somerset case, and he cast an acerbic eye on it for good reason:

its implications on Britain's North American colonies. The decision was perceived as a threat to the practice of slavery, and, it has been claimed, contributed to spurring Virginia and other colonies into declaring independence from Britain in order to preserve their rights on the subject.[55] Within twelve months of the decision, slaves in Massachusetts started to challenge the tyranny imposed by their masters. The conflicting opinions provided a conundrum for the colonies rooted in the same dilemma faced by Mansfield: how could the 'Sons of Liberty' be slave owners? (It was an enigma reflected on some fifty years later by Fanny Wright, explored in Chapter 12.) Though taxation was the principal rallying point for the colonies in the outbreak of the American War of Independence in 1775, diverging attitudes towards slavery represented another strand feeding into the conflict.[56]

The slave trade continued to expand. It was not until 1807 that the trade was abolished in the British empire, and not until 1834, some sixty-two years after Mansfield's decision in the case of Somerset *v.* Stewart, that slavery itself was abolished. To this day, the consequences of the institution linger on in the form of racism. Yet Mansfield's decision was nonetheless a critical stepping stone on the long road towards abolition. As a pragmatist, he had tried to strike a balance, preserving the commercial status quo while refusing to neglect the civil rights of a fellow human being. His power and influence on the bench meant that people listened to his moral criticisms of the 'odious' state of slavery, and his ruling of 1772 fired fresh energy into those who thought the right to freedom should not be limited by the commercial interests of others.

3

How to Value a Life: With Love or Money? The Family Story of Lord Mansfield, Dido Lindsay and the *Zong* Massacre

On 19 August 1779, Thomas Hutchinson, an émigré from the American War of Independence, dined at Kenwood House as a guest of Lord Mansfield.[1,2] Afterwards, he recorded in his diary an incident that occurred during dinner. The interest lies not in the incident itself, but in Hutchinson's description of it, which offers a glimpse into both the prevailing attitude in England towards blacks and his host's private views on slavery. Writing in a judgemental tone, he said:

> A black came in after dinner and sat with the ladies, and after coffee, walked with the company in the gardens, one of the ladies having her arm within the other. She had a very high cap, and her wool was much frizzled in her neck, but not enough to answer the large curls now in fashion. She is neither handsome nor genteel—pert enough....[3]

Her unannounced presence provoked an explanation from Mansfield that Hutchinson had heard before and recorded as follows:

> Sir John Lindsay having taken her mother prisoner in a Spanish vessel, brought her to England, where she was delivered of this girl, of which she was then in child, and which was taken care of Lord M., and has been educated by his family. He calls her Dido, which I suppose is all the name she has. He knows he has been reproached for shewing a fondness for her—I dare say not criminal.[4]

This brief, derogatory account begs many questions, but the facts are clear: Mansfield had taken guardianship of a black baby to be brought up within his family as one of his own. In his professional life as lord chief justice of England, it was not uncommon for him, in proper application of the law, to place the interests of commerce—not least in the areas of mercantile and insurance law—before the ethical rights of the individual, presenting, now and then, a moral quandary in direct conflict with his domestic conduct. This chapter explores how Lord Mansfield came to adopt Dido and the apparent contradiction it sometimes created between his professional and private life.

The precise facts of Dido's early life are not certain. Her father, Sir John Lindsay, was Lord Mansfield's nephew, the younger son of Sir Alexander Lindsay of Evelix, near Dornoch in Easter Ross, Scotland, and Mansfield's sister Emilia, daughter of David Murray, 5th Viscount Stormont. Born in 1737, John Lindsay elected to pursue a life of adventure by joining the Royal Navy, becoming a lieutenant in command of the fireship HMS *Pluto* by the age of nineteen.[5] It was a modest but promising start to what would be an illustrious naval career, taking him across the world but mostly in and out of Caribbean ports.

The commencement of Lindsay's service coincided with the start of the Seven Years' War, increasing the joint prospects of glory, promotion and prize money, in addition to that of an untimely death. Service in the Royal Navy was tough, dangerous and poorly paid, and with the prevalence of press gangs, there was often no choice in it; but the sharing of bounties sweetened the pill for the sailors and spurred on officers (and privateers) to be zealous in going after merchant vessels (and naval ships) sailing under enemy colours. The British government, grateful for any disruption to the enemy's trade and military operations, imposed a statutory arrangement. For warships, the commander-in-chief and the captain each took a 1/8th share of the net amount taken for the sale of a captured ship and its cargo. The remainder was divided at different rates among the lower ranks, of which the seamen and marines took 3/8ths collectively.[6]

John Lindsay was promoted from the *Pluto* to take command of the 28-gun frigate HMS *Trent*, in which he served for the duration of the war with France.[7] After Britain declared war against Spain in 1762, Lindsay joined the fleet under Sir George Pocock in the expedition against Havana.[8] During the siege of Moro Fort, he gained 'distinction for his bravery', for which he was knighted—a rare honour for such a junior officer.[9] After this and other postings, he returned from the West Indies to England in 1765.[10]

It was during his time as commander of the *Trent*, a period of great risk and reward, that Lindsay met Dido's mother, Maria Belle (or later Bell), a black slave. In spite of Mansfield's story (reported by Hutchinson) of how they met, the precise facts remain uncertain. According to her baptismal registration, the estimated year of Dido's birth is 1760 or 1761, but the

Trent's logbook gives no mention of the seizure of a Spanish vessel during the period that she would have been conceived.[11] According to Mansfield's story, Dido was born in England, though the Murray family later claimed that Dido was born at sea.[12] Whatever the truth is, every scenario has at least one thing in common: that Maria Belle was on board the *Trent* with John Lindsay.

Before looking further into the timing and circumstances of Dido's birth, it is useful to consider the character of John Lindsay. He was only twenty years old when, in 1757, he took command of the *Trent*, bringing some 200 men, most with far greater experience of life and seafaring than he, under his direct command. At this young age he had already demonstrated outstanding bravery in battle, but another story shows how he used discipline to maintain control on board.

In or around late 1760, when the *Trent* was moored off Port Royal, Jamaica, for maintenance and the provision of fresh supplies, a midshipman was found guilty of embezzlement. Lindsay decided on a public punishment: nine lashes with a halter around the midshipman's neck, and with other ships alongside to bear witness. Punishment was often meted out with the entire crew assembled to view the spectacle, though for less serious offences, many officers used the cane, thus saving time and, to some degree, the honour of the offender.[13]

To avoid the necessity for punishment wherever possible, practical solutions had to be found to address the inevitable sexual demands of the crew. At a time when society considered homosexuality to be a mortal sin punishable by death, the Admiralty highly disapproved of homosexual behaviour. Documented cases are rare, and great care was taken to protect adolescent crew members from their older counterparts. In consequence, crews were granted licence to satisfy their sexual desires in what were regarded as more orthodox ways. With few ships out at sea for more than one or two months, prudent captains allowed their crews to take full advantage of the appealing opportunities offered in ports, while in wartime, when ports were off limits due to fears of desertion, women and moneylenders were permitted on board. Anything could be bought for a price. At the end of each day, upon calling 'shake a leg', petty officers would count the limbs protruding from hammocks to try to ensure that all who had come on board had left.

In the West Indies, naval officers made arrangements with plantation owners to supply large groups of slaves—female field hands—for their crews' pleasure. Whether John Lindsay made such arrangements for the crew of the *Trent* is not known.[14] Notwithstanding regulation to the contrary, which states that a captain 'is not to carry any woman to sea', officers often did as they pleased, and if a woman was brought on board and not returned to port, her name would most likely not appear on the ship's passenger or crew lists.[15, 16] Typically women who were kept on board were the wives of petty officers—usually more mature and unlikely to excite the passions of the crew. They often acted as nurses, or assisted with unpalatable chores such a cleaning decks or helping the cook. In times of battle they were no less exposed to danger than the sailors.

Precedent suggests that it would not have been untoward for Captain Lindsay to have taken a slave woman into his care on board the *Trent*, and it may be assumed that Maria Belle lived with him for a time in his cabin. The length of their relationship is not known, but that an attachment was formed is evidenced by the interest Lindsay took in the future welfare of their daughter, Dido. This attachment was sufficient for Lindsay, an unmarried man with a life at sea, to approach Lord and Lady Mansfield, his uncle and aunt, both by then well into middle age and childless, to take on the care of his child. Their acceptance of this request was a major commitment by any measure, and made all the greater because the infant was black.

History does not relate the emotions felt by Maria Belle, who had to surrender her child. One can only hope that her pain was ameliorated by the knowledge that Dido was going to be afforded a status rarely granted to an illegitimate child of a black slave. It suggests that blood ran deep for Sir John Lindsay and Lord Mansfield, both of whom decided to recognise Dido as their own—a product of the leading families of two of Scotland's great clans, the Lindsays and the Murrays.

Dido's formal introduction into the family took place on 20 November 1766 when she was christened at St George's church in Little Russell Street by Bloomsbury Square, London, where Mansfield had his townhouse. The entry in the baptismal register records 'Dido Elizabeth D [daughter] of Bell and Maria his Wife aged 5 y[ears].'[17] The use of the word 'Bell' as the surname of Maria's husband may simply have been a device used to hide the truth, it being a corruption of Maria's full name, Maria Belle. Whatever the explanation, it is worth noting that the choice of 'Elizabeth', Lady Mansfield's name and family name for the Murrays, as Dido's second given name further suggests Dido's inclusion within their fold.

Mansfield's marriage with Elizabeth, while long and happy, was childless. Aside from any personal disappointment, this created the need for him to choose a successor to his title and very substantial estate. Despite his physical separation from his family from an early age, Mansfield remained close to them, and decided to settle his estate on his nephew, David, eldest son of Viscount Stormont and Lord Scone. Mansfield's fondness for his nephew had developed during the latter's schooling at Westminster, Mansfield's former school, which he had overseen, and further education at Christ's College, Oxford, where Mansfield had also matriculated. The viscount, Mansfield's brother, died on 23 July 1748, leaving David, aged twenty, to inherit his father's title. In 1756, a contemporary of David's (by then Lord Stormont) noted that he was 'not only [Mansfield's] nephew but looked upon as his son'.[18]

The subsequent success of Lord Stormont's career was in no small part due to the Murray family's strategic integration into the fabric of the emerging British state. Mansfield played a crucial role in securing appointments for his intellectually gifted nephew, setting him up as a promising young diplomat, a career pursued overseas at a time when anti-Scottish prejudice ran high in England, dampening the prospect of finding a suitable job in London. Stormont recognised that 'with the dead weight of a Scotch title it would not be possible for me to make my way home'.[19]

His first appointment in June 1756 was as envoy-extraordinary to Saxony-Poland, a highly prestigious posting for a twenty-eight-year-old novice. Initially posted to Dresden, Stormont moved to Warsaw following the invasion of Saxony by Frederick the Great in late August 1756, during which Stormont made an ill-advised and unsuccessful attempt to mediate between the Prussian king and Augustus III, king of Poland and elector of Saxony. Following this unpromising start, in 1759 Stormont further damaged his prospects by ignoring his government's wishes and marrying Henrietta Frederica de Berargaard, daughter of an experienced Saxony diplomat and politician. It was a match led by love rather than calculation, and for a man with an eye on his career, inadvisable.

But the young Lord Stormont's qualities emerged nonetheless, and in concert with his family connections, led to his appointment to the distinguished post of ambassador to Austria in Vienna in 1763, at the end of the Seven Years' War. Stormont flourished as ambassador, his dour, serious manner forming the perfect foil for his wife's charm and liveliness. He held the post for a decade, and from the early years, with the help of Lady Stormont and his colleagues at the embassy, he restored a remarkable degree of harmony to Anglo-Austrian relations.

Lady Stormont gave birth to two children, a daughter, Elizabeth, in 1760, and a second daughter, Henrietta, who died in infancy. David was further bereft when, on 16 March 1766, at the age of twenty-nine, his wife died after suffering declining health. Traumatised and suffering something analogous to a nervous breakdown, he took a tour of southern Europe on an extended period of leave.[20]

It must have been recognised within the family that, whether because of his health or the demands of his overseas career, Lord Stormont was not going to be able to take care of his daughter Elizabeth. David's uncle and aunt, Lord and Lady Mansfield, took on the mantle of surrogate parents, and Elizabeth was welcomed into their care at Kenwood House. It was in

November of the same year, 1766, that Dido was christened in St George's, Bloomsbury. The Mansfields now had two young girls of much the same age under their care.

The evidence suggests that Lord Mansfield gave both children an equal share of his love and affection; skin colour was of no apparent consideration within the family unit. Dido was, however, subject to differing social conventions in recognition of her lower social standing to that of her adoptive sister Elizabeth, the daughter of Lord Stormont. Dido had a suite of rooms within the main house, and although she did not join the family for meals, she joined them for coffee afterwards, and was educated in like manner to Elizabeth.[21] She clearly developed a close and loving relationship with her adoptive parents and her sister, and in the opinion of Paula Byrne, author of *Belle: The True Story of Dido Belle*, it was Belle not Elizabeth who won the heart of Lord Mansfield.[22]

During the course of Dido's upbringing, the liberal values articulated in Mansfield's private life were outwardly at odds with certain decisions he handed down in his professional life, when presiding in highly sensitive cases involving the lives of black slaves. In conducting these cases, Mansfield applied the law strictly within a legal system that recognised slaves as the property of their owner—as goods, not people. A decision correct in law but denying fundamental human rights is a decision devoid of true justice, and as a man of compassion, Mansfield must have pondered, and indeed worried, long and hard over the wider equity of some of the decisions he felt compelled to make. One can only speculate whether he discussed such challenging issues with Dido. He knew that, had not fate intervened, she, being the daughter of a slave, would have been classed a slave, and therefore as much at risk to the injustices and brutality meted out to those less fortunate than herself. She was the physical embodiment of the contradictions Mansfield must have recognised and wrestled with continually. One case in particular, heard on 6 March 1783 when Dido was about twenty-two years old, brought this inner battle of conscience into sharp and distressing focus.

The case of Gregson *v.* Gilbert, commonly known as that of 'the *Zong* Massacre', was heard by Mansfield before a jury.[23] It related to the enforcement of an insurance claim for loss of goods at sea (the goods in question being human beings). The captain of the *Zong*, a slave ship sailing from Guinea to Jamaica, mistook the island of Hispaniola for Jamaica, which delayed the voyage to such an extent that there was not enough water on board for the crew and slaves.[24] Sixty slaves died of thirst and a further sixty threw themselves 'through thirst and frenzy' into the sea and were drowned.[25] Over a number of days commencing on 29 November 1781, 150 more slaves were thrown overboard, allegedly to save the limited supply of water for others on board. The action on a policy of insurance was to recover from the insurers the value of the lost goods (the slaves) thrown overboard due to a lack of water. The insurers had refused to honour the claim, but the jury found against them. The insurers immediately appealed on the grounds that 'a sufficient necessity did not exist for throwing the negroes overboard, and also that the loss was not within the terms of the policy'.[26]

On appeal, Lord Mansfield ordered a new trial which commenced before Justices Mansfield, Willes and Buller and a jury on 22 May 1783. Fresh information presented by the insurers claimed that there was still sufficient water on board when the first batch of slaves was thrown overboard, and the situation in fact improved after a fall of rain brought supplies up to level sufficient for a further eleven days on full rations. In his summary, Mansfield concluded that 'the ship was not foul and leaky' and therefore not the cause of the delay, and that, after the rainfall, there appeared to have been no need to have thrown the slaves overboard.

The relevance of these formal exchanges is better understood via the memoirs of Granville Sharp.[27] He explains that many of the slaves on the ship were ill and dying; if they died on board then no claim for their value could be made under the policy, but if they were 'cast overboard' to spare the remainder of the cargo, then a plea of necessity could be submitted and the financial loss recovered. However, the slaves' calamitous state of health was not due to the lack of water—that problem was only identified on the date when the first slaves were thrown overboard.[28] Rather, overcrowding, disease and malnutrition were the leading causes.[29]

Nonetheless, it can be deduced from Mansfield's decision that if the ship owner had been able to prove that there was a lack of water, it would have been legal to have thrown the slaves overboard within the terms of the insurance policy.[30] What is particularly chilling to the contemporary eye is that the trial did not relate to mass murder—the word was never mentioned—but to a claim for loss under insurance. What was done to these slaves was not illegal; under the applicable laws the slaves were deemed to be disposable goods owned by their masters and devoid of any human rights. It meant that whatever qualms Mansfield may have had in terms of addressing what was before him and the laws under which the case fell to be considered, under the law, no charges could be raised for these murders because the law did not recognise them as such.

Mansfield's personal opinions were never recorded, but he had made his views clear when he delivered his conclusion in the Somerset case of 1771, twelve years before. He had said then that slavery was 'so odious that nothing can be suffered to support it, but positive law'.[31] In this case, because positive law provided that support, Mansfield had no scope to address what might be regarded as the 'elephant in the room'. Rather, as Mansfield recorded, 'The matter left to the jury was, whether [the action of throwing the slaves overboard] was necessity; for [the crew] had no doubt [though it shocks one very much] that the case of slaves was the same as if horses or cattle had been thrown overboard. It is a very shocking case.'[32]

If something positive can be said to have emerged from such a dreadful case, it came in the form of Granville Sharp, who campaigned tirelessly to raise awareness of the massacre. The political and media responses at the time were muted, perhaps tellingly, but Sharp's efforts found traction with the Quakers, causing them to start their long campaign against slavery.[33] The lack of newspaper coverage of the trial suggests that Dido may never have been aware of the massacre aboard the *Zong*, and it is unlikely that Mansfield would have wished to burden her or the others in his family with the upsetting facts.

Nonetheless, Dido could not have been completely sheltered from events taking place in the outside world, even if Mansfield had wanted her to be. In June 1780, during what came to be known as 'the Gordon Riots' (an angry response to the passing of the Catholic Relief Act), a vicious mob attacked Mansfield's house in Bloomsbury Square. After tearing out the iron railings around its perimeter, they entered and ransacked the house before burning it to the ground. The personal shock to Mansfield's family who had to flee for their lives cannot be understated.[34] Lord Mansfield himself wanted to see out the attack, but underestimated the extent of its violence. As the threat to his life increased, he was forced to escape by the back door disguised in an old great coat. Furious that Mansfield had escaped, the rioters made for Kenwood House, but the militia was waiting for them and saw them off. It was never clear why Mansfield was a target for the rioters. Although he favoured religious toleration and no longer saw the need for Catholic repression, he had not actively supported the piece of legislation that had sparked the wrath of the mob.[35]

The razing of the house in Bloomsbury Square meant the total destruction of Mansfield's beloved library, and with it all his memoirs, manuscripts and writings. It amounted to the forfeiture of 'the whole work and labour of his life'.[36] It was also a great loss to historical research. Notwithstanding this disaster, Mansfield was still able to exercise ironic humour when he joked in a debate on the king's speech at the opening of parliament: 'I have not consulted my books; Indeed I have not books to consult!'

Prior to this distressing event, the Mansfields, with their servants, usually spent November to May at Bloomsbury Square and the remainder of the time at Kenwood. Their stay in London coincided with the height of the social season, and every Sunday Mansfield held a reception for 'the good and the great', comprising the powerful decision-makers of the time. His discreet nature, complemented by his high office, made him a natural choice to entertain visiting emissaries from abroad. Indeed, many of the dinners Mansfield hosted were arranged to discuss foreign and domestic politics, and it is likely that wives were not invited, unless the visiting guest chose to bring his spouse.[37] In any event, etiquette of the time did not require numbers of males and females to match.

As the eighteenth century progressed, however, the custom grew for dinners and other social events to include both genders.[38] Despite this social progression, Elizabeth and Dido would have been inducted as young ladies into what was essentially a man's world. Dido had ample skills for the role. She was well read, an accomplished musician, and able to mix with grace, elegance and intelligence among Lord Mansfield's guests.[39] She also had a semblance of independence, being provided with an annual allowance of £30 10s. It was less than the £100 received by Elizabeth, but Elizabeth enjoyed a higher social standing as the daughter of Lord Stormont. As has been mentioned already, in terms of the love and affection given by their adoptive parents, Elizabeth and Dido were equals, with Dido's mixed race never entering the equation.[40]

As Dido blossomed into womanhood, 'her amiable disposition and accomplishments ... gained her the highest respect from all her Lordship's relations and visitants'.[41] But change was on the horizon, coming with the death of Lady Mansfield in 1784.

Lady Mansfield had never recovered from the trauma of the sacking of her Bloomsbury home in the Gordon Riots four years earlier. Her husband, who was assiduous in tending to her as her health declined, was bereft at her loss. The next year, Elizabeth married her cousin, George Finch-Hatton, and Dido now shared Kenwood with a bereaved Lord Mansfield, now in his eighties, and two of his elderly nieces, Lady Anne and Lady Margery Murray. The loss of his wife and his own increasing infirmity saw Mansfield spend more time at Kenwood, which drew him closer to Dido.

During this period there is evidence that Mansfield used Dido as his personal secretary. In May 1786, he dictated a letter written in her hand on a point of law sent to Justice Buller, in which he concluded, tongue in cheek, 'This is wrote by Dido. I hope you will be able to read it.' (The joke being that Dido had an exceptionally clear hand.)[42] For Dido to be given such a role suggests that Mansfield not only had confidence in her discretion, but also respect for her intellectual and secretarial abilities. Lord Mansfield, who continued to entertain visitors and barristers after he stood down from the bench in 1786, died at Kenwood on 20 March 1793. He was buried at Westminster Abbey a week later.

Dido had to cope not only with the grief of losing her adoptive father, with whom she had enjoyed a loving relationship, but also with the loss of her home. Under Mansfield's will, the estate passed to his nephew, David, Lord Stormont. When last encountered in this story, Stormont had delivered his only daughter Elizabeth into the hands of Lord and Lady Mansfield to pursue his ambassadorial career. In 1772, after Vienna, he was posted to Paris, and there, on 5 May 1776, he married Louisa Cathcart, by whom he had three daughters and a son. He never reclaimed his first daughter, Elizabeth, who remained at Kenwood, probably because it suited all parties to continue the arrangement. Elizabeth, after her marriage to George Finch-Hatton in December 1785, moved to Eastwell, Kent, where she gave birth to five children, the eldest of whom, George, would become the 5th earl of Nottingham.

Dido's father, Sir John Lindsay, died on 4 June 1784 at the age of fifty-one, following a period of failing health.[43] In keeping with his father and uncle, he was buried at Westminster Abbey—no mean achievement for a family that only a generation before had been so closely connected to the Jacobite cause. This honour infers that, in view of the establishment, all traces of that connection had been washed clean.

Lindsay's private life had been altogether more unorthodox than his burial might suggest. On 19 September 1768, two years after Dido had been adopted by the Mansfields, he married Mary, daughter of Sir William Milner, MP for Aberdeen, but she did not bear him any children. However, recent research has established that before his marriage, Lindsay had a number of relationships with African women. Indeed, aside from Dido, Lindsay had four more illegitimate children, all by different mothers. John Edward was born to Mary Vallet, a mixed race woman in Jamaica, but died within a month of his birth on 19 February 1762, a year or two after Dido was born. On 15 November 1766, Ann was born of Sarah Gandwell, 'a free negro'. A month later, on 8 December 1766, another daughter, Elizabeth, was born to 'Martha G'. She lived a long life, dying in 1842. Finally, on 28 November 1767, John Lindsay was born to Frances Edwards, a free 'mulatto woman'.

Apart from Dido, all Lindsay's children were baptised in Port Royal, near Kingston, Jamaica, where the Royal Navy had ship repair yards. Only Elizabeth and John were provided for in Lindsay's will; both were taken to Scotland and raised and married there. In Elizabeth's case, she lived in Edinburgh in the 1780s, where she used the name 'Palmer'. On 3 May 1783, she married an Edinburgh bookseller, Peter Hill, a close friend of the poet Robert Burns. She died on 26 January 1842 and is buried in Canongate Kirk, Edinburgh, with her husband.

John, who remained in touch with his mother in Kingston throughout her life, joined the army of the East India Company on the Madras establishment in 1788, and during his eighteen years' service, rose to the rank of brevet colonel. He died in India in 1821, a wealthy man owning two properties and providing for his half-sister, Elizabeth, in his will. Elizabeth is believed to have surviving issue in Scotland to this day.[44]

It is believed that Dido's mother, Maria Belle, was supported by Lindsay for about ten years, after which, in 1774, she travelled from England to Pensacola, Florida. She took possession of a plot of land gifted her by Lindsay, which he had purchased in part or whole in 1765. There she built a home on the corner of Lindsay and Mansfield streets, in what was then a high-class area owned by the British.[45] It was also in Pensacola that on 22 August 1774 Maria finally secured her freedom from slavery in exchange for a payment by her of 250 Spanish dollars. The entry also records her age as 'about twenty eight years', which means she was only fifteen when Dido was born.

The full circle now returns to Dido, the beneficiary of a gift of rare acceptance into an aristocratic family as an illegitimate black child. It was an outcome only made possible by the Mansfields, who were open-minded enough to have faith in what she might achieve should she be embraced into their family. It was a faith that Dido demonstrably fulfilled. Inevitably, how it fell to be achieved was prescribed both by her gender and how her role within the family was distinguished from that of her adoptive sister, Elizabeth. That Mansfield saw in Dido the qualities of a personal secretary suggests she possessed a lively intellect founded on an excellent education, complemented by discretion and efficiency. At the same time her social skills as a hostess, which gained her the respect of her family and visitors, among them some of the leading luminaries of the time, indicate attributes of tact, grace, humour and wit.

Mansfield's commitment to Dido continued after his death. In his will he provided her with an annuity of £100 and a capital payment of £500.[46] It was a legacy that set her up as a single lady to enjoy a life of genteel comfort, albeit without the level of affluence she had experienced in Kenwood House. It would have been a welcome reassurance to her; as a woman of thirty-one or two when Mansfield died, she probably considered herself past the age of betrothal—a situation made more complex by her social position, colour and illegitimacy. These factors meant that marriage to a member of the peer group with whom she had mixed at Kenwood, albeit never on entirely equal terms, would be socially unacceptable.

Nonetheless, within nine months of Mansfield's death, Dido did get married. Her husband was John Devinier, and the match was made almost certainly following a family introduction. The probability of this rests on the fact that throughout this narrative, the Mansfield family had consistently done two things: they had found solutions to any issues they had been confronted with, and they had taken care of their own. Author Reyahn King convincingly suggests that it was David, Lord Stormont, who had come up with the answer, possibly having been coached on the matter by his uncle, who was concerned for Dido's future.[47] This proposition seems reasonable, and being the father of Dido's childhood companion and the man who had inherited Kenwood, Dido's home, he may, like Mansfield, have felt a strong sense of responsibility towards her.

John Devinier, a man of French extraction, was a steward, or 'a gentleman's gentleman', and in terms of social status, an appropriate suitor for Dido. He may have been employed by Stormont or indeed Mansfield, or he may have been recommended via one of Stormont's aristocratic connections in Scotland, England or France. As a steward, Devinier would have been the personal assistant to the master of the house, a highly privileged role that would have included handling his master's day-to-day finances. Such a position would have required Devinier to be well-educated, trustworthy and discreet.

Dido was married to John Devinier in the fashionable St George's church, Hanover Square, London, on 5 December 1793. It is recorded that both bride and groom were of that parish. It was also where, by either chance or circumstance, Stormont had his townhouse. The couple had three sons: twins, Charles and John, baptised in 1795 (of whom John did not survive infancy), and William, who was baptised in 1800. The children were educated at a private school in Pimlico where they lived. Charles entered the Madras Infantry, rising by 1855 to the rank of lieutenant colonel in the Indian Army, while William rose to become company secretary of the Hendre-Ddu Slate and Slab Quarry Company. Dido died in 1804, aged about forty-three, and was buried in St George's Fields. Her husband remarried and raised two more children.[48]

Devinier's income and Dido's annuity would have ensured them a comfortable life. It may have been humble in comparison to the lifestyle assumed by Elizabeth following her marriage to George Finch-Hatton, a landowner and member of parliament, but in those inequitable times, Dido's position was in stark contrast to most, if not all, illegitimate children born of an African slave mother.

Dido's last surviving direct descendent, her great-great-grandson, Harold Charles, died in 1975.[49] It is perhaps ironic that he lived in Johannesburg in apartheid South Africa. As for Lord Mansfield, he has gone down in history for his decision in the Somerset case of 1772. Although the legal implications of that decision were limited to England, they nonetheless reverberated around the world and carried enormous significance.

4
Freedom of Choice: John Wedderburn and Joseph Knight

Had you entered the inner house of the court of session, Edinburgh, from Parliament Hall late on the afternoon of 15 January 1778, you would have first been struck by the mingled stench of unwashed men and candle wax that pervaded the packed room as you jostled for a place to stand.[1] With the daylight fast retreating from the windows, your eye would have been drawn towards the twelve figures wearing red robes signalling the dignity of their legal office, crowded around a semicircular bench in the fashion of an amphitheatre, which faced into the room. The faces of these men, and the court papers scattered before them, would have been illuminated by the light of candelabras placed on the bench before them. Standing before the same bench, facing the red-robed judges, were six clerks. You might have spotted, through the assembled horde, a wooden bar erected diagonally across the room. This separated the judges not only from the public, but also from the advocates representing their clients. There was no seating provided for those on the near side of the bar, emphasising the judicial pecking order to all those present and generating an implied urgency to push on with the proceedings of the day. Those proceedings were conducted amidst an underlying hubbub of noise created by hacking coughs, the rumbling of low voices and the shuffling of feet on the bare stone floor. At times it was difficult for the judges to hear the voices of those appearing before them.

At this moment, your gaze would have been drawn to an advocate, previously hidden from view, rising to his feet from the only chair in the public area and moving confidently towards the bar to address the bench. It was none other than Henry Dundas, the lord advocate, who aside from enjoying the singular privilege of a chair to sit on, was the only advocate entitled to wear, as a symbol of office, a hat with his advocate's gown.[3] On this day, 15 January 1778, he was not acting for the crown, but rather for a private individual, Joseph Knight, in his action against a John Wedderburn. As for the cause Henry Dundas was representing, the central theme of the speech he was about to present to the court would have offered a clue: in that speech, Dundas challenged the right of one man to deny the right of liberty to another.

It was clearly a cause of great importance, emphasised by the presence behind the bench of the lord president, the lord justice clerk, and ten other judges, among them Lord Kames and James Boswell's father, Lord Auchinleck. The case had been in process for some weeks. Written and oral submissions had been presented and the case was reaching its climax, after which a decision would be handed down from the bench—one which, depending on the verdict, could have profound consequences not only for Joseph Knight, but for many others too. The substance of the debate and of the court's decision will be told later, but first we must understand who Joseph Knight and John Wedderburn were, what events had led their lives to intertwine, and why each had come to be aggrieved by the actions of the other.

At first sight, the two men could not have been more different: John Wedderburn was the son of a dispossessed and impoverished Jacobite nobleman, while Joseph Knight was a black man, sold into slavery as a boy off the coast of Guinea. They did, however, share a certain characteristic: the will to survive whatever life threw at them, and to improve their situation in spite of setbacks. It was to be expressed in very different ways due to their opposing positions in society and the differing nature of their ambitions. Both men were shaped by the world around them, which at the time was undergoing huge social, economic and political change. By chance, this drew the life of one of them into the orbit of the other, resulting in a collision of conflicting values and aspirations. This collision came to its climax before the inner court on that day in January 1778.

To begin to understand John Wedderburn, we must start with his relationship with his father, Sir John. The ambitions of the son were firmly shaped by the experiences (and their consequences) shared with the father. Sir John came from a distinguished line of gentry. His great-grandfather, Sir Alexander Wedderburn of Blackness, was one of eight Scottish commissioners to attend the Treaty of Ripon in 1640, which brought to an end the Bishops' Wars with the Scottish Covenanters.[2, 3] His reward, bestowed by Charles I in 1642, was a knighthood and a grant of the lands of Blackness in Forfarshire. It firmly identified him and his family as loyal subjects of the Stuart dynasty.

Two generations later, in 1715, by which time the Stuart monarchy was in exile, Sir Alexander's grandson, a man of the same name, joined the

Jacobite uprising led by the Old Pretender, James Francis Edward Stuart.[4,5] Upon its failure and James's flight to France, Sir Alexander Wedderburn was left to pay the price for his involvement: the forfeiture of his lucrative post of clerk in Dundee. It marked the beginning of his family's misery, during which various parts of their lands were sold off.[6]

The succession by Sir John to the baronetcy on his father's death in 1741 did not bring an end to the family's financial difficulties. Indeed, they appear to have become more chronic as further parts of the estate were sold to settle debts. His comparative impoverishment was made clear when, in 1744, he moved his family to a small farm, Mains of Nevay by Newtyle, Forfar. There they lived 'in a thatched hut with a clay floor with no light except what came through the doorway'.[7] Sir John worked his land hard to support his wife and nine children, all of whom went barefoot.

These hardships were duly suffered by the teenage John and his surviving siblings. All would have understood that the family's fall from grace had been triggered by the loss of political patronage. It had made them outsiders to the ruling Presbyterian elite. It was a situation they shared in common with a coterie of silent Jacobite sympathisers throughout Scotland and England. Each child would have coped with the adversity of their circumstances in their own way, but at the root of their shame, it is likely that all harboured an ambition to see the family's honour and fortune restored. These lofty ambitions were almost certainly beyond the scope of Sir John, whose energy was no doubt focused on the daily grind of putting food on his family's table. But whatever his feelings, an event beyond his control was about to intercede, flushing him, almost certainly unwillingly, from the cover of comparative obscurity and safety.

On 23 July 1745, Prince Charles Edward Stuart arrived unannounced from France on the Isle of Eriskay with seven of his companions. Charles's ambitious objective was to win back the thrones of England and Scotland for his father, James.

At first, possibly with the memory of his father's fall from grace still vivid in his mind, Sir John chose to cut a low profile. However, this was to prove impossible once Prince Charles's army, moving south, had occupied the nearby city of Perth. Sir John, with his established Jacobite pedigree, was soon called upon to collect dues and import taxes for the prince in an effort to raise much needed funds for the campaign.[8] Various accounts suggest that, undecided, Sir John faced threats of coercion to accept the post. But even if less than willing, he would have recognised that success offered an escape from his intractable impoverishment, albeit at great risk.[9] Whatever his motives, Sir John's eventual acceptance implied a commitment to a cause from which there would be no return. His son,

John, then only fifteen, in support of his father, shared that risk by taking arms for the prince.

Their commitment reached its denouement less than a year later on the battlefield of Culloden, after which Sir John, serving as a lifeguard to the prince, was captured and taken to Inverness. He was placed on board HMS *Exeter* and taken to London, arriving there on 20 May 1746. Imprisonment followed in Southwark Gaol, pending his trial. His younger son, James, only a sixteen-year-old boy, undertook the long and dangerous journey to London to try to persuade his father's remaining friends to secure his rescue and pardon. But it was to no avail.[10] Sir John was found guilty of high treason and both his estate of Ballindean and his title were forfeited to the crown. A few weeks after his trial, on 28 November 1746, he was dragged by a sledge to Kennington Common where he was hanged, disembowelled, decapitated and quartered.

At Culloden, James's elder brother John, who had served in Lord Ogilvy's regiment as a standard bearer for the Glen Proason company, had managed to flee the battlefield during the ensuing chaos. On the run and hiding in various houses, he arrived in Edinburgh where he adopted the name 'John Thompson'. It was from there that he made his way to London by working his passage on a Leith trading vessel.[11] Finding refuge with a family friend, Mr Paterson of Carpow, it proved too risky for him to see his father, then in Southwark Gaol, although correspondence did pass between them via Mr Paterson, in which Sir John, notwithstanding his impending doom, found time to rebuke his eldest son for parting with his money too easily in London and for not understanding the true value of a shilling.

After his father's execution, John Wedderburn returned to Scotland. In Glasgow, he persuaded a sea captain to allow him to work his passage, first to North America, and then to Jamaica, where he had arrived by May 1747.[12] In Jamaica he belatedly received a letter from his father, written the night before his execution. Wedderburn expressed his distress at this in a letter to his sister in Scotland: 'I am just as unhappy as if I were living among you as I have always an idea of your condition before my eyes.[13] I would have wrote to Mama and have begun to do it several times but on such an occasion as this I do not know what to write as it would be minding her of things which she may forget for her family's sake.'[14] Bearing the weight of his father's death and his family's destitution, Wedderburn, now eighteen years old, had to make his living in a strange land, but one he had chosen for a reason.

Jamaica had come under English rule in 1655 when the Spanish were expelled. In 1672, the Royal African Company was formed with a monopoly on the British slave trade, making Jamaica one of the world's busiest slave markets. African slaves soon outnumbered Europeans five to one, and the country emerged as one of Britain's most valuable colonies through the production of sugar, indigo, coffee and cotton. The failure of the Scottish Darien Company to establish an independent Caribbean empire in Panama saw the first Scots arrive in Jamaica from Argyll in around 1700 under the leadership of Colonel John Campbell. He sat at the centre of what would become, in time, a huge interdependent network for Scots, ultimately drawn from different clans, based on kinship and association. As profound economic change took place in the Scottish Highlands from the 1730s, land clearance, coinciding with population growth, led many to emigrate overseas.[15] In Jamaica, employment was offered in Scottish-managed plantations and by landowners who needed reliable men they could trust to manage their plantations and continue to generate profit in their absence when they had returned home to enjoy their fortunes.[16]

These adventurers, armed with ambition and a willingness to work hard, were joined by others from all over Scotland, including a host of exiled Jacobites. Later, they were also joined by loyalists from the rebellious American colonies, confident that there would be jobs to get them onto the ladder to possible riches.[17,18] It meant that in the twenty-five years after Wedderburn arrived in Jamaica, the number of estates owned by Scots rose from 20 to 30 per cent of the total, while by 1774, the number of resident Scots, often operating within their own networks, had increased to around 6,000, or one third of the white population.[19] (By comparison, by 1755 the number of slaves in Jamaica was 118,000.)[20] For the whites, life in Jamaica came with its perils. Yellow fever and other diseases were common, aggravated by general fast living and a common fatalism that, in itself, contributed to the callous disregard of slave owners for their slaves.[21]

It was into this scene that the teenage Wedderburn settled in Westmoreland on the west side of the island, where Dr James Paterson of Perthshire, a cousin of the family, took him under his wing, arranging an apprenticeship for him as an apothecary.[22] By 1752 John was practising as a surgeon despite his apparent lack of qualifications. Joined by his three brothers, James, Peter and Alexander, he started to accumulate capital, helped by a legacy from an uncle, David Wedderburn, which he inherited five years after his arrival.[23] It enabled him to purchase land and slaves for the cultivation of sugarcane, which in due course accrued him substantial wealth. It was during this period that Wedderburn bought a slave aged eleven or twelve named Joseph Knight.

The boy had acquired his name from Robert Knight, commander of the slaver *Phoenix*, who had bought the child as part of a cargo of slaves procured on the Guinea coast at Anoumaba and Cape Coast Castle. The *Phoenix*, departing for the Caribbean on 5 March 1765, arrived in Montego Bay, Jamaica, on 20 April 1765. There, Robert Knight sold the boy, by then known as Joseph Knight, by private sale to Wedderburn. Such sales were common practice for slave captains who were often allotted a number of slaves from the cargo as commission and allowed to sell them on their own account.[24]

Rather than work the boy in the fields, Wedderburn chose to make him his personal servant, suggesting that he had qualities of manners and intelligence. Three years later, in 1768, having made sufficient money, Wedderburn returned home to Scotland to restore his family's status and respectability, taking Joseph Knight with him.[25] In November of the following year John married Margaret, daughter of David Ogilvy, the commanding officer with whom he had fought at Culloden twenty-three years earlier. He also purchased Ballindean estate, Perthshire, near Dundee. The restoration of his prestige had begun in earnest, but what of Knight and his story?

History does not relate his feelings as a young boy during his six weeks aboard the *Phoenix*—his separation from his mother and the violence he might have witnessed or suffered as part of the human cargo.[26] As Wedderburn's property, he was spared an unremitting, dispiriting, and almost certainly short life of a field hand in the plantations, and compared to other slaves, he was fortunate when Wedderburn chose to bring him to Scotland as his personal servant. It suggests that an effective and trustful working relationship had been established between Knight and Wedderburn, albeit on the latter's terms.

The alien society, not to mention the weather, must have come as a rude shock to young Joseph, who for the first time in his life was part of a very small minority. He would have been regarded as a novelty. However, for Wedderburn it was business as usual. He clothed Knight and gave him an allowance of sixpence a week for pocket money. He paid a barber half a guinea in Dundee to show his servant how to cut his own hair. Knight acquired 'some little knowledge in reading and writing' with the assistance of fellow servants rather, as he later claimed, than his master, and after instruction by a Church of Scotland minister on the principles of Christian knowledge, he was christened. This was done with Wedderburn's support. It prompted him to promise Knight that he would one day have his freedom.[27] The promise was conditional on Knight's continued good behaviour and subject to a seven-year delay, after which time Wedderburn thought Knight would be of less use to him. He added that a further reason for delay was to spare him from starvation as nobody would employ him. After the seven years, Wedderburn promised to give him a house and some land in Jamaica 'where he might live comfortably all the days of his lifetime'.[28] Events, however, took an unexpected turn.

At twenty years old, Joseph Knight formed a relationship with a chambermaid, Anne Thompson, who was employed with him at Ballindean. She became pregnant with his child. On being made aware of the situation, Wedderburn dismissed Thompson, but because of her pregnancy, he gave Knight money to provide for her care and accommodation in Dundee. The child died and Wedderburn stopped the payment, hoping the relationship would end. It did not, and Knight married Thompson on 9 March 1773 before a minister of the Kirk in Edinburgh.[29]

So they could provide for themselves, Knight asked his master to reinstate Thompson and to provide them with an estate cottage to live in. The request was refused, placing Knight in an impossible situation. He wanted to honour his marriage and so decided to quit the service of his master without notice, packing his clothes and preparing for departure.[30] On discovering this, Wedderburn applied to the justices of the peace of the County of Perth for a warrant to prevent Knight's departure. It was issued on 13 November 1773. Two days later at Ballindean, Knight confirmed in a statement that he planned to seek work in Dundee with his wife. The justices concluded from this and other evidence that Knight must 'continue as formerly'.[31] This was perhaps no surprise as each of the justices had an interest in one way or another in slavery in the West Indies.

Significantly, in his deposition to the justices, Knight provided an important reason for unilaterally ending his bondage. He explained that, on 3 July 1772, he had read an article in the *Edinburgh Advertiser* which reported on the decision taken in London by Lord Mansfield in the Somerset case. Ignorant of the intricacies of the law, he concluded that the judgement 'enabled him to leave his master at pleasure'.[32] He had delayed in doing so until it suited him to change his personal circumstances, his reason for wanting to leave being based less on any bad treatment and more on his simple wish to be free of perpetual servitude. He wanted to make his own decisions and by doing so, support his wife.

The article in the *Edinburgh Advertiser* was incentive enough for Knight to challenge the decision of the justices, which he did by applying to Sheriff Principal Swinton in Perth, who was known to be sympathetic to the abolitionist cause. This proved true when Swinton gave the following judgment:

> The state of slavery in not recognised by the Laws of this Kingdom and is inconsistent with the principles thereof: and finds the regulations in Jamaica do not extend to this Kingdom; and repels the defender's claim to perpetual service.[33]

What Wedderburn thought of this is not recorded, but he may well have felt an element of betrayal. He would have also been very aware of the implications of a decision made in court to grant Knight his freedom. Aside from loss of face, it would threaten his credibility among like-minded friends and many others in Scotland, who would balk at the possible consequences of such a decision in relation to their own interests. Within a month, Wedderburn initiated a challenge in the court of session, which was heard before Lord Kennet in February 1775. He, in turn, referred the petition from the outer house to the court of appeal, the inner house. During the protracted litigation, full and detailed written submissions were presented by counsel on both sides (providing much graphic detail of the inequities and cruelties imposed on the slaves in the plantations). As part of a multi-layered argument, Allan MacConachie, Knight's counsel, chose to place emphasis on the views of a leading churchman, William Robertson, who claimed that slavery was 'inconsistent with the spirit and principles' of the Christian faith. Robertson also contended that 'the equality of all men under God flew in the face of slavery, and that Scottish law was not subject to Roman, let alone English or colonial law'. For Wedderburn, James Ferguson argued that acceptance into the Christian faith by baptism did not alter a man's state of servitude. He continued by finding authority in the Old Testament for divine sanction for slavery; something that neither Jesus nor St Paul had contradicted in any surviving records.[34]

A year later, on 20 February 1776, the stakes had risen so high that no less than the solicitor general for Wedderburn and Henry Dundas, the lord advocate, for Knight were weighing in with their oral pleadings before the court of appeal. The former referred to many authorities to prove that slavery was nothing new. It was not only understood by the Romans to be a good thing, he argued, but even in Scotland in 1258, when slaves and their children were sold 'from [one] master to another, as sheep and horses are now; that slavery was at this day authorised by the legislature of Great Britain, by various charters granted to the African Company; and that it was a lawful trade.' He argued if that the practice was stopped it would ruin the West Indies trade and if the blacks were granted their freedom it would 'produce a Code Sanguinaire'—a bloodbath in the colonies, with freed slaves taking revenge on their erstwhile masters.[35]

Dundas thought it was irrelevant to refer to the practices of ancient nations or even to earlier periods of Scottish history. As Christianity spread across nations, slavery was abolished, he said, and moreover, ancient customs had nothing to do with the present argument as there was now no slavery in Britain and nor could it be supported by its constitution.

The *Caledonian Mercury* reported that Dundas 'had nothing to say on the African trade; that it might be a very proper trade, but that he was conscious very great improprieties and even villainies were practiced in carrying it on; that children were often stolen from their parents'—an example of which was Joseph Knight. 'The presumption of law was in favour of liberty ... that every court of justice in Europe had rejected the claim of slavery with indignation;... and that Lord Mansfield had given the liberal decision in the famous case of Somerset.' Dundas 'hoped for the honour of Scotland that the supreme court of this country would not be the only court that would give its sanction to so barbarous a claim.'

Dundas continued by recounting that Knight had been told by his master that he would be looked after during his life and, should he die before his master, his master would meet the costs of his burial. Dundas quoted Knight's words that Wedderburn had 'not yet offered to give me any wages, to support me in old age, nor to bestow any expense in instructing me in principles of morality or religion; neither has he told me what is to become of my unoffending wife and helpless offspring.' Dundas concluded: 'Human nature ... spurns at the idea of slavery among any part of our species; and I am confident, that the decision now [to] be given will convince everyone of the rectitude of Judge Holt's opinion', in which he declared before an English court, 'that English air was too pure for a slave to breathe.'[36]

The case was continued for 'additional information' to be presented to the court for consideration when it next sat and a judgment was finally given. If Wedderburn won the day, Knight faced an uncertain future of permanent separation from his wife and child (she had given birth to a second child who had survived), and with the slender chain of trust between him and his disgruntled master broken, there was the likely prospect of his return to Jamaica and sale to another master. Wedderburn, for his part, if victorious, would have his intransigence justified, though at great cost and worry.

In the event, on 15 January 1778, the court, by a majority of eight to four, found in favour of Knight and affirmed Sheriff Principal Swinton's interlocutor (a judgment which, if appealed to a higher court, as proved in the case, was not final). Among those speaking in favour of Knight was the formidable Lord Braxfield:

> Mr Wedderburn's right of property depends altogether on the municipal law of Jamaica; but how came [Knight] to be subject to that law? Plainly by violence: for he was not of an age either to suffer slavery for offences, or as a prisoner of war, or through consent.

Lord Auchinleck agreed, declaring:

> Although in the plantations, they have laid hold of the poor blacks, and made slaves of them, I do not think that is agreeable to humanity, not to say to the Christian religion. Is man a slave because he is black? No. He is our brother; and he is a man, although not our colour; he is in a land of liberty, with his wife and his child: let him remain there.

Lord Kames was also in agreement:

> If the slave is the property of his master, he may use him as his property. If [the master] cannot use him as he will, which is certainly the case in Scotland, then his property [of the slave] is suspended: slavery is a forced state—for we are all naturally equal. It is a strange case for a man to bind himself during his life: but it is a much stranger for a man to bind all his descendants. Let the laws of Jamaica govern the inhabitants of Jamaica. *We* cannot enforce them; for we sit here to enforce right, not to enforce *wrong*.

The views of these men were enthusiastically shared by Edinburgh's *Caledonian Mercury* of 17 January 1778, which observed that 'the rights of humanity were weighed in the scales of justice; it must have given a very high satisfaction to the inhabitants of the United Kingdom, that the freedom of Negroes has obtained its first general determination in the Supreme Civil Court in Scotland.'[37]

James Boswell reported by letter to Samuel Johnston that the decision of the court, for those who held slavery as an abomination—of which he was not one—'should be remembered with a high respect, and to the credit of Scotland; for it was on a much broader principle than the case of Somerset … being truly the general question, whether a perpetual obligation of service to one master in any mode should be sanctified by the law of a free country.'[38]

The decision vindicated the long-held view of Lord Kames that what may have been suitable for ancient or primitive societies may not be now. It demonstrated that the law could evolve. Equally, it vindicated the different approach to the law in Scotland. The case was not decided on precedent but on the 'dictate of reason' in order to maintain the fundamental principles of equity and justice. By doing so, it delivered a verdict that echoed the views of Francis Hutcheson: that man's claim to liberty is universal.[39] The decision in the case was to carry weight among a later generation of educated Scots who were to petition for the abolition of slavery. As Iain Whyte observed in his book, *Scotland and the Abolition of Black Slavery*, 'The ground was therefore fertile in many a community for those who sought to evoke a natural sympathy for the victims of a horrific trade, once the facts about it were known.'[40]

But what of the protagonists? Knight, with his wife and son, was able to slip into anonymity after his freedom was secured. With his skills as a servant, there is no reason to conclude that he and his wife did not settle into a contented future; it is plausible that those who rallied around to meet his substantial legal costs, assuming they were not given gratis, introduced him into a social network, possibly through his church, of those sympathetic to his plight, facilitating a suitable position for both him and his wife. For Wedderburn, the decision must have come as a shock.[41] It coincided, as will be explored later, with a growing awareness within congregations of the Church of Scotland of the inequities of slavery. Inequities that congregations were more and more prepared to challenge publicly, while actively seeking to help men such as Knight. During the case, this moral support could only have served to embolden and stiffen Knight's resolve to fight the injustice of his slavery.

Notwithstanding the setback of the decision against him, Wedderburn's moral compass appeared to remain undisturbed. He elected to sell the slaves he still owned in Jamaica and otherwise continued his efforts to uphold the rights of slave owners, many of whom were his friends and business associates in Jamaica. It must be remembered, it was through slavery and the plantations, with the support of Scottish connections, that John Wedderburn had managed to restore his fortunes. It meant implicitly, however, that he elected to disregard the suffering of those less fortunate than Knight. By doing so, he cast his moral vote.

5

Rebel With a Cause: Robert Wedderburn

It may be recalled from the last chapter that, at sixteen years old, an impoverished and frightened James Wedderburn had travelled on his own from Perthshire to London to try to save his father, Sir John, from the gallows following his father's capture at Culloden in 1745. James had undertaken the journey by pony, spending the nights hiding in any byre or shed he could find. Twenty-seven years later, by then a wealthy man, he settled at Inveresk Lodge near Musselburgh, by Edinburgh, to raise his family of seven.[1] By then, the name and reputation of the Wedderburn family had been restored to its former place in Scottish society, but this is not a story of one of James's seven children by his wife Isabella; it is the story of his illegitimate son, Robert, whose mother, Rosanna, was his housekeeper on his Jamaican plantation.[2]

Contrary to the experiences of his half siblings, Robert, as a boy of mixed race, was afforded no privileges during his upbringing and young adulthood. From his earliest memories, he was a victim of racial prejudice, insecurity and hardship, but in coping with these challenges and seeking to come to terms with his identity and preconceived destiny, he emerged as a man of huge courage and moral strength. To understand Robert, we must examine his relationship with his father and the context in which that relationship was rooted.

In London on 28 November 1746, James, aged sixteen, having failed to secure his father's release from Southwark Gaol, watched as he was 'hanged by the neck ... cut down alive ... his bowels ... taken out and burnt before his face and ... his head... severed from his body... [which was then] divided into four quarters.'[3] As the son of a Jacobite traitor, James faced a bleak future in Scotland and England. In 1747, he followed his elder brother John to Jamaica, along with others fleeing the consequences of the Jacobite defeat.[4] It was to prove the making of him.

As with John, James's cousin, Dr James Paterson of Perthshire, arranged an apprenticeship for him to train as an apothecary; by 1752, like John, he was practising as 'a surgeon and practitioner in physick and chirurgery', despite his apparent lack of qualifications.[5] He settled in Westmoreland, in the west of the island, and began to accumulate wealth before expanding into the role of trader, slave owner, estate manager and finally, plantation owner. Having become rich, he and his brother purchased Bluecastle and Blackheath estates in Jamaica, among others.[6,7]

By 1755 there were around 118,000 black slaves in Jamaica, compared to a white population of about 18,000, of whom one third were Scots. Being outnumbered ten to one, and in fear of revolt, the white population, with the support of the courts, maintained control through fear. 'Terror, or naked power, was at the core of the institution of slavery. Jamaican slavery was especially brutal even by the elevated standards of New World brutality. Whites were encouraged to keep firm discipline and to punish slaves frequently and harshly.'[8] Beyond the death penalty, which was applied for relatively minor offences, sadistic practices were adopted to maintain discipline, including severe flogging, mutilation, and the shoving of faeces into slaves' mouths which were then clamped shut.[9] Slave owners and their overseers also regularly subjected their slaves to rape and sexual humiliation. James's neighbour, Thomas Thistlewood, was a well-known rapist of slaves.[10]

Upon his appointment as a plantation overseer, Thistlewood began his campaign. In a thirteen-year period, between 1751 and 1763, he recorded having intercourse 1,774 times with 109 black women and two white women. Professors Trevor Burnard and Richard Follett, in their paper 'Caribbean Slavery, British and the Cultural Politics of Venereal Disease', deduced that, alongside instructing savage beatings, such behaviour was calculated to demonstrate personal dominance. By acting in this manner, overseers such as Thistlewood 'stamped [their] authority over enslaved families ... [and] belittled slave men and women. These practices provided social constructs based on definitions of class, gender and nation [which] helped to define the slave holders' place as individuals within the political system and as masters on the plantations.'[11] One of the consequences of this abuse was the contraction of sexually transmitted diseases such as gonorrhoea, chlamydia and syphilis. In his diary on 17 June 1769, Thistlewood wrote, 'Dr [James] Wedderburn says, that of those who have been long on this Thomas island, he looks upon it 4/5ths die of the venereal disease or, one way or other, occasioned by it.'[12]

It was into this world that Robert Wedderburn was born. His account of his life starts with a description of the sexual tyranny suffered by his mother, Rosanna, who first met his father when, as a physician, James visited the neighbouring plantation of Lady Douglas, one of his patients and Rosanna's owner. James was instantly attracted to Rosanna, who was then, wrote Robert, 'chaste and virtuous', and by virtue of her education, well suited to her post as manager of Lady Douglas's household.[13] James wanted to purchase her, but Rosanna, who was only too aware of his lust, had no wish to be sold. In Jamaica, slaves who were valued by their owners usually had the right to withhold their consent to be sold; so James cunningly enlisted a respected friend, Mr Cruikshank, to act as his undisclosed agent in securing Rosanna's purchase from Lady Douglas. It was only once the contract was agreed that the identity of the true purchaser was disclosed to Rosanna, a deceit for which she never forgave him.

In the new household, Rosanna undertook similar duties of management, while also being forced to succumb to James's sexual desires. It was a household 'full of female slaves, all objects of his lusts: amongst whom [James] strutted like a bantam cock upon his own dunghill'. Rosanna had two sons by James, one of whom was to become a millwright on his estate. She was pregnant with a third child when his treatment of her became so 'brutal' that his brother, John, had to intervene, taking Rosanna into his protection. Only then did James consent to sell Rosanna, by now five months' pregnant, back to Lady Douglas, under whose roof Robert was born in 1762. An important condition of sale was imposed on James: Robert was to be born free of slavery. It was a condition that was honoured.

Lady Douglas was central to Robert's wellbeing in his early years, and became his godmother upon his baptism. Meanwhile, Rosanna's health was so badly damaged by her ill treatment from James, she had to place Robert into the care of her mother, Talkee Amy, a slave of Joseph Payne's. Talkee Amy sold sundry items of food and fabrics at her stall in Kingston, and also found time to peddle the goods of other merchants, taking a percentage of the sales. Ironically, she was appreciated for her honesty by those to whom she sold the smuggled goods. She was to have a marked influence over Robert who watched her live by her wits, with scant regard for the law, via her expressive and forceful personality. He would also have been aware of her position as 'a noted Kingston magic woman'.[14] It ignited in Robert a lifelong interest in magic and the supernatural.[15]

Robert only saw his father on one occasion, on a visit to Bluecastle accompanied by his grandmother, who went to find out if James 'meant to do anything' for his son. In answer she received a torrent of abuse, to which she retorted, '[I] have kept [Robert] hitherto and so [I] would yet, without [your] paltry assistance'.[16]

Robert loved his grandmother dearly, and grew to hate the condition of slavery under which she was trapped. He witnessed her, aged seventy, being tied up and flogged within an inch of her life by her slave master's nephew, whom she had brought up and treated as a son. A malicious female slave had accused her of cursing her slave master's ship, causing it and her slave master, who was on board, to be captured by the Spanish. He died shortly afterwards, and was, wrote Robert, 'thrown overboard to feed the fishes'. The slave woman lost her daughter soon after she had made the accusation, and seeing this as retribution, she sought forgiveness from Talkee Amy, whose assistance she sought with the burial of the child. Talkee Amy replied, 'I can forgive you but I can never forget the flogging.'

Lady Douglas had died when Robert was four, but her son had promised his mother, Rosanna, her freedom. He later reneged on this promise and she was sold to a succession of different masters who likewise treated her brutally. In one case she was able to force her sale in extremis by refusing food. Her master, fearful of her death and with it the loss of his investment, agreed to sell her before it was too late. Eventually, Rosanna was purchased by the Campbell family of Kingston, with whom she finally found kindness. Indeed, Robert would correspond with Miss Campbell in the decades to follow.

At the age of sixteen, with a stock of damaging boyhood experiences and in a state of near illiteracy, Robert Wedderburn sought escape from the capricious cruelties of his society by joining the Royal Navy.[17] This choice was also a consequence of his fear that his right to freedom could be revoked at any time. Although unfounded, this fear never left him, and kept him from ever returning to Jamaica again. For the rest of his life, while himself free of bondage, he remained burdened with a simmering anger rooted in the injustices he had witnessed.

In the Royal Navy, Wedderburn would have found that black sailors were not uncommon; for the first time in his life, he would *not* have been judged by his skin colour, but rather by his ability to do the job. In this more liberal environment, he saw action as a main gunner on board HMS *Polyphemus*.[18] In later life he would complain of excessive discipline in the navy; the brutal floggings of sailors in wartime evoked dark memories of what he had witnessed on the plantations of Jamaica.[19]

The precise date of Wedderburn's discharge from the navy is not known, but he was not a sailor for long. By 1779, aged seventeen or eighteen, he had arrived in London. He recalled seeing 'the remains of a rebel's skull which had been affixed over Temple Bar', but was unable to determine if it belonged to his late grandfather, Sir John. This reference suggests that

Wedderburn's relationship with his Scottish family remained of some importance to him, but he had no connection with them, and London was not an easy place for a near illiterate teenager of mixed race to make a start in a life.

In the mid-eighteenth century, London was growing at a huge pace; by 1801 it boasted a population of 1 million, twice that of Paris. Britain, meanwhile, was emerging as the world's richest and most economically dynamic nation. By the turn of the century, the wealth of the patricians could be matched by that of the mercantile and financial elites, who drove the city's consumption, built fine mansions, and secured political power. It was a troubled period of wars with France, Spain and Holland, discontent fuelled by revolution in France, and the loss of the American colonies, but despite this, the political system, underwritten by a 'paranoid government' that used censorship and prisons to silence critics, continued to sustain the interests of the newly augmented establishment, and to protect their property. The wealth of these elites was largely built on the back of impoverished labour in Britain, the expansion of empire and the embracing of slave labour abroad.[20] It was this abuse of power which rankled with Wedderburn as he struggled with the day-to-day challenges of life.

Although London was teeming with people, it was still possible to walk across the city in a couple of hours, and even by 1800, only few people lived south of the river. In *City of Laughter*, Vic Gatrell writes that 'streets were fog and smoke cursed;... St Paul's Cathedral so be-sooted that it seemed built of coal ... Great streets like the Strand were in bad weather foul with a dirty puddle to the height of three or four inches and shopfronts and coaches were caked in mud.' Night travel was done at personal risk, even with the assistance of 'link boys' lighting the way home with firebrands for a few pennies.[21] The wealthy retreated behind their fashionable gardens, closed to the man in the street, while the impoverished, except for beggars and street labourers, lived largely out of sight of the rich. Of these, the most desperate lived in the slums of Saffron Hill or St Giles by Covent Garden, the latter area an ever-increasing source of anxiety for the more affluent due to the level of crime it generated.

Within this wash of humanity ranging from the very rich, to the aspiring, to the destitute, came evangelical Christians who 'struggled to plant moral earnestness in London's soil'. They found allies in the aspiring middle classes and, to a lesser extent, those of the working class. The importance of this form of Christianity is best expressed by the historian Élie Halévy, who, for the period 1790 to 1832, credits Methodism with forestalling social revolution, which he deems was latent in society, by diverting that energy towards a spiritual focus and away from workplace concerns.[22]

It was into this polarised and unforgiving society that Wedderburn had to make his way with little or nothing to his name. Here he would walk among the poor through the muck-ridden squalor of congested roads overwhelmed with carts, chaises, coaches, wagons and horses. It is no surprise that before long he gravitated towards the deprivations of the St Giles rookeries, so close to the comforts of St James's and yet so far apart.[23] It was where many of his countrymen stayed, along with runaway slaves and other minorities such as Jews and Irish and Indian seamen. Collectively known as 'blackbirds', they were beggars, thieves, labourers, musicians and entertainers, relying on their wits and cunning to get by. Little racial prejudice was to be encountered in this community.[24]

In June 1780, within a year of his arrival in London, Wedderburn took part in the anti-Catholic Gordon Riots, which numbered some 40–60,000 people. As the looting and rioting spread, he witnessed the mob burn down Lord Mansfield's townhouse in Bloomsbury Square, which forced Mansfield to flee for his life. Coming amid the height of the American Wars when Britain had no allies, the riots provided a platform for protest by members of the proletariat who wanted reform. Their manner of expression unfortunately threatened anarchy, yet it was an approach for which Wedderburn would have had sympathy and little or no qualms in supporting. He was not motivated by self-improvement, but a wish for a fairer society for all, and he was not to be intimidated as he watched many of his countrymen being transported to Van Diemen's Land or Botany Bay for their participation.

Wedderburn acquired direction and structure in his life by becoming a journeyman 'flint' tailor, although it is not known how or when he was trained in this skilled trade.[25] He took pride in his craft and the status and social respect it afforded him; it enabled him to assert his belief in one's right to be financially independent. From this elevated perch, he looked down upon the semi-skilled 'dung' tailors who worked as sweated labour in dire conditions. He adopted the lifestyle of his trade and the world he inhabited, 'characterised by workshop pilfering, promiscuous sexuality and drunken conviviality'.[26]

By the end of the eighteenth century, harsh economic conditions saw Wedderburn's trade earnings being undercut by his unskilled competitors. It forced him to scratch a bare living, patching clothes and selling pamphlets from a stinking court off St Martin's Lane.[27] At some point he got married. In the ensuing deprivation, both he and his pregnant wife faced starvation. In desperation, he made the long journey to Inveresk in 1785 to try to persuade his father to help him.

By Wedderburn's own account, upon his arrival, his father James neither disclaimed paternity nor sought to belittle the good name of his mother,

Rosanna, but was nonetheless unwilling to help him, dismissing him as 'a lazy fellow'. It fell to James's cook and footman to show sympathy by offering him a beer and giving him a cracked sixpence. Without the funds to return to London, Wedderburn applied to the council of the City of Edinburgh for assistance. They provided him with 16 pennies and a travelling pass. For his boat journey home he was indebted to the captain of a Berwick smack.[28]

Such an experience, confirming Wedderburn's social relegation from proud artisan to beggar, with its attendant privations and loss of respect, would have been hard to bear. It suggests a possible reason for his step towards radicalism as a means of providing a better and fairer life for himself, his family and others caught in poverty. As for a means through which to express his cause, he found Evangelism. It offered him social acceptance and cultural integration.[29]

Wedderburn's epiphany took place one Sunday in 1786, while he was walking through London's slum district of Seven Dials by Covent Garden. His attention was drawn to a Methodist preacher lecturing a crowd. Wedderburn was ripe for a spiritual awakening and the preacher's words shone a light into his soul. He was able suddenly to make sense of his life and to understand how he could make positive use of his punishing experiences for the betterment of others, and thus escape from his own spiral of despair.

John Wesley, leader of the Methodist Church, preached about the freedom of the soul through salvation and the attainment of perfect love for God and fellow human beings through the power of the Holy Spirit.[30] Wedderburn would have recalled Methodists in Jamaica teaching slaves to read the Bible, despite the education of slaves being widely discouraged by most whites on the island. He would have known that Wesley was a fierce and vociferous opponent of slavery. The point had arrived in Wedderburn's life for him to embrace the Methodist movement and be released from what he had come to perceive as his 'life of sin', which he had conducted 'amongst reprobates' who were leading him on 'the road to everlasting ruin'. Instead, purged of his guilt and sins, he was elevated by 'receiving the grace of God'.[31] He had found his voice.

Wedderburn's first publication nine years later demonstrated his full commitment to the tenets of the Methodist doctrine.[32] In parallel, and perhaps surprisingly, he also held on to a belief in magic, still common in England at the time and, for Wedderburn, reminiscent of the beliefs expressed by his grandmother, Talkee Amy. These beginnings may have played a part in Wedderburn's writings on prophecy and dreams, the power of collective singing and the 'binding sense of congregation'. His preaching was steeped in imagery of 'blood, death, fertility, rebirth and transformation', and he stressed 'the instructive and inspirational role of song'.[33]

In the years that followed, Wedderburn became increasingly perplexed by the conflicting views expressed by different schisms within the evangelical church. He was careful to follow an independent line between them, retaining strong convictions for the end of slavery and for religious toleration, but there were signs of a drift towards a much more radical position, one which would see him develop his own idiosyncratic interpretation of the doctrines of the Christian faith.

By the late 1790s, Wedderburn had become a Unitarian. The Unitarians believe that God is one being—God the Father or Mother—and that Jesus was simply a man, not the incarnate deity. Their religious ideas are based on rational thought rather than external authority. They espouse a freedom of religious thought and encourage their members to seek truth and meaning for themselves by using intellect, conscience and experience.

Given Wedderburn's independent spirit, one can see why he might have been attracted to this more liberal approach. Sometime between 1802 and 1813, Wedderburn gained his licence as a Unitarian preacher and firmly established himself in London's 'plebeian culture of millenarianism and tavern radicalism'.[34] In this world he met Thomas Spence, shortly before the latter's death in 1814. Spence, the son of Scottish parents, was born in Newcastle in 1750, one of nineteen children whose father sold goods from a street booth. He was denied a formal education but was taught to read and encouraged to read the Bible each day. From this modest beginning, with an eager mind and through self-improvement, he qualified for a job as a clerk, and by the 1780s, had graduated to become a schoolmaster. His real interest, however, lay in educating poor adults. At five feet in height, of slight build, shabbily dressed and with a speech impediment, his choice of vocation was not an obvious one, but he made up for it with his enthusiasm and energy, at times aggressive, strengthened by his conviction that his opinions were correct. Indeed, the stubbornness of his conviction polarised how people viewed him.

Spence's life experiences led him to sympathise with the problems of the hard-working poor and to condemn the idle rich. Influenced by George Murray, a Presbyterian preacher, his ideas coalesced on the principle that all men were equal before God and had an equal claim to the same inalienable rights.[35] In seeking civil and religious liberty, he became progressively more radical in face of opposition from people whose advantages he wanted to challenge and impair. He moved to London in 1788, where he became a radical bookseller and author, promoting his demand that all land should be held by parish councils since all private land had been secured by force, fraud or theft. He envisioned that the land would be rented out to the highest bidder and the income used to eradicate poverty. While he aimed to achieve his objectives peacefully, he recognised that in recovering the land from the social elite, force might be necessary. The authorities perceived him as subversive, and arrested him on a number of occasions, sometimes keeping him incarcerated for several months without trial. His health suffered in gaol and in his later years he slipped into obscurity, during which time he was met by Robert Wedderburn.

Wedderburn was so influenced by Spence's ideas that he joined a small group of his disciples called the 'Spencean Philanthropists', who kept Spence's torch alight after his death. They were party to the Spa Field riots of 1816 and the Cato Street conspiracy of 23 February 1820.[36] Wedderburn's migration into this radical group, known for its underground connections to the revolutionary French Jacobins, may seem unexpected, but in fact it was a continuation of the path he had started on in the late 1790s, when he had felt the call to preach with 'boldness' and 'not fear the face of any man'.[37, 38] It was a time of inflation and unemployment caused by the Napoleonic wars, and Wedderburn was welcomed into a community of 'underground' alehouses in Soho, where there was singing and debate and the opportunity to engage with like-minded people. Within this environment, Spence's plan for a utopia in which land was expropriated from the rich may have seemed very attractive, but association with such ideas did not come without risk. After Spence's death, Wedderburn was initially loyal to his successor, Thomas Evans, but he was soon drawn to the more radical ideas of Arthur Thistlewood (ironically the nephew of the planter Thomas Thistlewood) and his revolutionary colleagues, who have been described collectively as ultra-radicals or 'London ultras'. This, at the mature age of fifty, led to Wedderburn's 'flirt with treason'.[39]

By 1819, Wedderburn had opened a chapel in Soho, which soon became a centre for insurrectionist propaganda. Recent poor harvests and a slump in trade had made life even harder for London's poorest, and in this unsettled political climate, Wedderburn adopted an increasingly confident stance, using fiery oratory associating the oppression of the British worker to that of enslaved black people. He prophesied that 'before six months were over there would be slaughter in England for their Liberty'.[40] Government spies reported that he was addressing up to 200 people who paid 6 pennies a head to listen to him preach 'violent sedition and [give] bitterly anti-Christian Spencean speeches'. Wedderburn was charged with seditious libel and found guilty.[41]

In August 1819, when Wedderburn was in gaol, the Peterloo Massacre took place in Manchester in which eleven people were killed by the yeomanry and hundreds wounded. The national outcry suggested that the opportunity was ripe for an armed revolt. The London ultras began plotting, while government spies secretly monitored their activities. Having been released from gaol, Wedderburn sensed that a revolt would fail, and he recommended Thistlewood to call off the mass uprising he was planning. Exasperated, Thistlewood agreed to do so, settling instead on a coup d'état. The decision culminated in a small group of conspirators congregating in a stable in Cato Street on 23 February 1820, 'to launch their ill fated assassination attempt on the Cabinet'.[42] Wedderburn almost certainly would have been among them had he not been arrested again in November 1819 on a charge of blasphemous libel for urging a throng of radicals to tear up iron palisades as a prelude to civil war. That arrest probably saved his life.[43] Four of the ultras, including Thistlewood, were found guilty of treason and executed.

In 1821, Wedderburn was again arrested, and sentenced to two years in Dorchester Prison. In his defence, he argued that his only crime had been to use the language he shared with Christ and his disciples, and if a crime had been committed, it was by the government for keeping the poor in ignorance and superstition.

The year 1824 saw the publication of Wedderburn's pamphlet, *The Horrors of Slavery*, an abolitionist autobiography, which demonstrated his extraordinary courage, undimmed in spite of his incarcerations. In this and his later publications, he entwined politics with 'his peculiar brand of "Pure Christian Diabolism"'.[44] Despite support for him gradually diminishing, he doggedly continued his campaign for freedom of speech. In 1831, at the age of sixty-eight, he was again imprisoned, this time in London's Giltspur Street Prison for brothel-keeping, having failed to convince the court that he had been keeping the premises as a refuge for destitute women.[45]

Upon his release in 1834, he left for America where, some six years after its release in England, his subversive, mocking essay, *The Holy Liturgy: Or Divine Science, upon the Principle of Pure Christian Diabolism, Most Strictly Founded upon the Sacred Scriptures* had been published by the influential, freethinking New York periodical, *The Correspondence*.[46]

Later in 1834, Wedderburn was back in London, where he was spied by an informer attending a congregation of an 'infidel preacher'.[47] The preacher was an admirer of Wedderburn, and delivered mock sermons described as 'ribald and shockingly impious'.[48] This, perhaps appropriately, is the last public record mentioning Robert Wedderburn. He died in obscurity in 1835 at the age of seventy-two and was buried in a pauper's grave.[49]

The complexity of the man and his extraordinary personal development make it difficult to do him proper justice. Arguably it is best to consider his life in the simple context of what really mattered to him. He wanted to fight injustice, which he chose to do by attacking the societal issues that lay at the root of his own negative experiences and suffering. In its simplest terms, his mission was twofold: to seek the liberation of slaves in the West Indies, and to seek the release of English working people from wage servitude, which locked so many into intractable poverty. It was a mission regarded by the ruling elite as seditious and subversive. Wedderburn was unquestionably a man of great courage. His wit, oratory and flair for the dramatic could spark hope among those who had nothing. He was an outsider in society, and chose to remain so, working with kindred spirits in pursuit of what became revolutionary ends. In the event, there was no revolution, but his actions nonetheless had a fundamental impact on the social and political structures he sought to change.

Before he died, Wedderburn may have taken some pleasure in witnessing the revival of mass radicalism in England. Many of those who gained leading positions in radical organisations were his disciples and friends.[50] These working class men carried the torch of fundamental change onto the next generation who emerged as leaders in the Chartist movement, which used mass protest to demand male suffrage; something not achieved until 1918.[51] Wedderburn lived to see a first small but important step in this process, achieved in the Reform Act of 1832, while in 1834, he witnessed the Slavery Abolition Act take effect, which emancipated slaves in the West Indies and elsewhere. It was an appropriate reward for a man who had always raised his voice on behalf of his enslaved countrymen.[52] In his personal life, Wedderburn married and had six children. Their lives on the fringes of society can have been no easier than his; indeed, they must have had precious little to inherit upon their father's death in 1835.

Wedderburn's bloodline, however, proved robust. On 20 July 1977, after a career committed to social justice, William 'Bill' Wedderburn of Charlton, a direct descendent of Robert's, took his seat as a Labour peer in the House of Lords.[53] In him, Robert Wedderburn would have seen a kindred spirit. That his descendent was able to continue pursuing the cause of social justice from the floor of an institution that he had aspired to do away with, would probably have brought a wry smile to his face. Robert Wedderburn might also have reflected that his vision for a fairer society had become a reality, though not via the destruction and rebuilding of the political system, but through its evolution. As for Bill Wedderburn, he rightly took pride in his remarkable ancestor who did so much to sow the seeds of change for greater equality in British society and the West Indies.

6

Passage to America: Peter Williamson

One night in early August 1743, a three-masted merchant ship, the *Planter*, bound for America, found itself caught in a ferocious south-easterly gale blowing through the darkness across the vast Atlantic. The timbers of the ship groaned and heaved as they were battered by unforgiving waves crashing down from above. The eleven-man crew, including the captain, Robert Ragg, believed they were a safe distance from any land, but at about midnight there came a terrifying, bone-crunching shudder as the ship hit a sandbank.

On impact, the three masts snapped and water began bursting in through the hull. It was clear that the ship was done for; the captain's thoughts turned to a single aim: to save himself and his crew. A longboat was launched into the boiling sea and each man clambered hastily aboard. The rope of the longboat was cut and the men rowed for their lives through the treacherous waters away from the doomed ship to the safety of a nearby island, just discernable in the night sky.

The abandonment of the ship cannot have been an easy decision for Ragg. It was the *Planter*'s maiden voyage, and not only that, in the hold was a valuable cargo; it amounted to a devastating loss of both capital and profit. There was something else, too. As the crew hurriedly rowed to safety, Ragg might have paused to reflect further on the loss of that cargo, prompted, perhaps, by haunting screams piercing the wind-torn air. Sixty-nine boys and two women had been left to drown in the darkness, locked in the *Planter*'s festering hold.[1]

Those sixty-nine boys had been destined for indentured servitude in Pennsylvania, but they were not black children from West Africa but white boys from Aberdeenshire, on the east coast of Scotland. Among them was

Peter Williamson, a robust thirteen year old. To tell his story, we must first return to Aberdeen where the fate of these boys was decided, not by a criminal gang, but by respected merchants and magistrates.

Aberdeen in the mid-eighteenth century had yet to emerge into the modern world. It was a situation reflected across Scotland, which remained broadly underdeveloped, being poorer and more backward than countries like England, Holland and France, with which it chose to compare itself. Hunger was a constant concern for the majority of the population; it was only in 1740 that Scotland accepted the cultivation of the potato.[2] By that year, wages had remained stagnant for 100 years, but slow economic development was starting to take place, caused in part by the benefits of the Union of 1707 and growth in the trades of linen and cattle, as well as tobacco from Virginia.[3] In Aberdeen, the early part of the century saw the city 'busy making stockings and clothing from tarred-wool'. The fires of 1741 saw the destruction of 'the wood faced houses with roofs of heather and straw' and the beginning of the use of granite as a principal building material to provide better housing.[4] Local governance was notoriously corrupt. Across the country, town councils were ruled by small cliques of interconnected families who served their own interests above all others. As this story shows, Aberdeen was no exception.[5]

It was into this world that Peter Williamson was born in February 1730 at Hirnley, near Aboyne in Aberdeenshire. His father was a reputable, if poor, tenant farmer. In 1738, he sent his son to his sister in Aberdeen where, being a bright boy, he could benefit from a better education at Aberdeen Grammar School than what he would have received at the local parish school.[6] When not in school, Peter spent his playtime at the quayside with his friends, and it was there, in 1742, that the 'rough, ragged, humble headed, long stowie, clever' boy of twelve caught the attention of two local seamen.[7] These men worked for an Aberdeen merchant, and one of their duties was to kidnap children for transportation to Pennsylvania and Virginia, where they would be sold as indentured servants.[8]

The practice of kidnapping had developed as an illegal adjunct to that of indentured servitude, which was justified as a means of ridding the Old World of undesirable citizens by placing them in the New World where they could be made use of.[9] This form of raising a labour force grew in popularity when it became clear that the indigenous people of North America and the Caribbean were not suited to the labour demanded of them. Their immediate successors were not black slaves from West Africa but white men from the British Isles. From the mid-sixteenth century onward, there was a constant traffic of indentured servants from Britain to chiefly the West Indies and Virginia, and later Pennsylvania.[10] Their deportation was a form of punishment decreed by the courts for criminal activities, including those deemed as politically or religiously subversive. Prisoners of war were also sent as forced labour. By the eighteenth century, two thirds of immigrants to Pennsylvania were white indentured servants.

The circumstances of the indentured servant should be distinguished from that of the black slave, who was a chattel for life, as were his or her children. For convicted criminals, deportation as an indentured labourer was often not regarded as a form of degradation or abuse, but rather as a passport to freedom, which would be forthcoming after the completion of a contract, which typically lasted between three and seven years. The colonists, meanwhile, who were in dire need of labour, were happy to receive any form of workforce to help establish their nascent communities; and even better for them, indentured labourers sent via the courts were paid for by the government.[11] An associated market soon emerged in which people were transported for their contracts of indenture to be auctioned to the highest bidder on arrival, with some contracts being set aside for sale by the captain as a reward for the safe delivery of his human cargo. These people might have sold themselves into service to secure a free passage to America and a new life, or they might have been minors sold by their guardian, or indeed their parents or siblings, in exchange for a sum.[12] Alternatively, they might have been kidnapped.

Inevitably, demand for indentured labour soon exceeded supply, encouraging the growth of kidnapping in cities such as London, Bristol and Aberdeen. Between 1740 and 1746, it is estimated over 600 children were transported to America from Aberdeen alone. Each child could be sold for anything between £16 and £50. This was a time when a parish schoolmaster in Aberdeen was paid £16 per annum.[13] 'Agents, drummers, pipers, and recruiting sergeants were dispersed throughout the town and shire to assail the unwary with bribes, alluring promises, intoxication, and still more disgraceful temptations.'[14] More direct tactics were also used, with men patrolling the streets, seizing boys violently or even taking them from their beds at night as they slept. They were then driven through town in 'flocks ... like herds of sheep', under guard of a keeper and his whip. Rarely was any effort made by the kidnappers to hide their activities as 'they had protection at the very highest levels'.[15] Pending the departure of their ship the children were often held in a locked barn under guard, where a piper played to keep them quiet while they whiled away the hours playing cards. If this space was insufficient, the public workhouse was used, or even the tolbooth or prison. For such blatant abuse of the law, the rot had to start at the top, and so it was in Aberdeen. The magistrates, city officers and leading merchants were the ones orchestrating the kidnappings.[16]

One day in early January 1743, two seamen cajoled Peter Williamson into boarding their newly built ship, the *Planter*, at the quay. There, he was detained below deck in the steerage with other children pending the boat being loaded with its remaining cargo. The wait was long, and in the months that followed, Peter was moved back on shore to a locked barn. His father, who had been searching for him, discovered his location and went to the barn to rescue him, but was prevented from doing so by the guard. His failure caused him to 'shed many salt tears on that account'. Peter, with the other victims, was then taken to a guarded building beside the public workhouse. The weekly board, a modest 20*d* for each child, was paid by the kidnappers who were funded by local merchants Walter Cochran and Baillie William Fordyce. With the rest of the cargo loaded, the children were dragooned back on board the *Planter*, which sailed from Aberdeen on 12 or 13 May 1743. This was not before a great celebration had taken place, for which the ship's owners, according to one of the accomplices to the kidnapping, invited several guests on board to have supper.[17] There was much excitement about the substantial profits expected from the cargo of tables, chairs and children. All were to be sold to make way for a cargo of tobacco to be bought for the return journey.

Eleven weeks later, it seemed that all profits had been forfeited when the *Planter* collided with a sandbank in the stormy Atlantic. Overnight, however, the storm abated, and the ship did not slip free of the sandbank to breakup or sink as Captain Ragg had expected. The mystery of their location was also answered. The vessel was found to be situated off Cape May near the entrance to the mouth of the River Delaware, which leads to Philadelphia. As for the human cargo, remarkably, it had survived, even if traumatised in spirit and significantly diminished in body after the privations endured in the squalid ship's hold. With the storm spent, Captain Ragg instructed his crew to recover what they could from the wreck. This they achieved, with the rescue of all the boys, the two women, and a portion of the tables and chairs that were undamaged. The party spent the next three weeks living on meagre rations in a makeshift camp on the island's beach before they were rescued by a vessel bound for Philadelphia.

Upon his arrival, Captain Ragg wasted no time in submitting 'his villainous loading' for auction, as Peter himself recorded in his memoir, *The Life and Curious Adventures of Peter Williamson*, published in 1758. Awaiting a pre-sale inspection with the other young boys, all with heads shaved and bodies dirty and ridden with lice, Peter must have felt very alone and frightened. He would have known that any bonds of friendship he had made with the other boys on board during their ordeal were about to be forfeited. A man purchased him for £16, the same price as the rest of the boys, and for the next seven years, Peter would have to serve him.

In the event, he was very fortunate. Peter was bought by a fellow Scot, Hugh Wilson, who had been kidnapped himself as a boy from St Johnstone, then a suburb of Perth. He had no children of his own and contrary to many other masters, Peter found him 'a humane, worthy and honest man'.[18] Wilson knew what Peter had been put through and could empathise with him. He preferred to care for Peter's welfare and fitness, initially setting him only light jobs until he was fourteen and ready for more onerous work. At that age, inspired by watching other servants spending their spare time reading and writing, Peter secured his master's permission to receive a formal education in exchange for extending his contract from seven years to eight. His study took place in wintertime, with Peter chafing for that season to arrive while learning what he could in his spare time. His ambition was matched by his energy and intellect, while physically, he grew into a strapping young man.

Peter Williamson's contract ended much earlier than expected with his master's death. As proof of the affection in which he held him, Wilson bequeathed him £150, his best horse, saddle and all of his clothes. Williamson had secured his freedom in its fullest sense. He spent the next seven years working for various employers, free to do as he pleased. Once he felt he had amassed sufficient capital, he decided to marry and 'applied' for the hand of the daughter of a wealthy plantation owner. The offer was accepted and the marriage followed, with his father-in-law gifting Williamson a tract of land measuring 200 acres, 30 of which was cleared, on which sat a 'good house and barn'. Williamson invested his savings in livestock, furniture and farm implements, and settled into a happy married life as he built up his holding. The farm was situated near the forks of the Delaware, in Berkshire County due north of Philadelphia.

On 2 October 1754, Williamson's wife left the farm for the day to visit some of her relations. Staying up late, waiting for her to return, he heard the sudden sound of war hoops close by: 'woach, coach, ha, ha, hach, woach'.[19] It turned his blood cold. His farm lay on the frontier between the province of Pennsylvania and the territory of New France, occupied by the French. The sounds were the war cries of Indians of the hostile Delaware tribe; Williamson knew he was under attack.[20]

In October 1754, a state of war existed between Britain and France, with Pennsylvania being one of the flashpoints. The province was one of thirteen colonies (plus Nova Scotia) held by Britain, which ran from the Atlantic coast to the Appalachian Mountains, beyond which lay New France, a huge expanse of land that comprised Louisiana, the Ohio River valley, Quebec (known as Canada) and the Cape Breton and St Jean islands. The frontier between British and French-held territory was ill-defined and unmapped, and violent disputes were not uncommon, even before the region was sucked into the wider, pan-European conflict of the Seven Years' War.[21]

Hostilities along the frontier were also the result of a century of land grabs by both the British and the French on the eastern side of the North American continent. These extensive gains were achieved at the expense of the native Indians who witnessed mostly British settlers, with their government's approval, moving west and north from the coast, clearing vast sections of land for farms and plantations until coming up against the disputed boundaries with New France.

The French had managed to gain their vast territory with the support of a mere 75,000 settlers, which compared unfavourably with the 1.5 million British settlers on their colonies. As a result, the French offered a lesser threat to the imperilled Indian tribes, who grew increasingly hostile towards the British settlers encroaching onto their land.

This volatile situation was exacerbated by the competing imperial ambitions of the British and French. The tipping point for outright conflict occurred on 27 May 1754 when a twenty-two-year-old George Washington ambushed French Canadian troops in the Ohio valley in Virginia at what became known as the battle of Jumonville Glen.[22] It proved to be the first action in what became known as the French and Indian War, in which the French began strongly, making good use of their allied Indian tribes who excelled in fighting in dense woodland. As the scale of the conflict began to mount from June onwards, Williamson would have started to feel more and more vulnerable in his farm on the frontier. On that fateful evening in October, peering out of a window of his house, he knew that his life was on the line.

Williamson counted twelve intruders trying to force an entry into his home. Armed only with a single loaded gun, his resistance would be limited to one shot. He shouted 'What do you want?' No answer was forthcoming as the locked door continued to judder under a welter of blows. He threatened to kill his aggressors if they didn't withdraw, but he knew from stories he had heard that he would face a bloody and painful death if he resisted. The door was sturdy and a cry came back declaring that if he didn't surrender, they would burn him to death inside his house, but if he came out he would be spared.

Williamson decided to take his chances and surrender. He came out of the house still carrying his gun in his hand, whereupon 'they rushed on [him] like so many tigers'. Once disarmed, the Indians tied him to a nearby tree. They then entered the house, seizing everything of value, before setting it and the barn alight. Williamson listened to the squeals of his trapped livestock as they were burned alive, watching in misery as all he had worked for was reduced to ash.[23]

A tomahawk brandished in his face brought him back to the immediate question of his survival. He was untied from the tree and, with the party of Indians, forced to carry his appropriated belongings on an all-night trek through the forest, fretting all the while over what had become of his wife. At daybreak, camp was struck and he was again tied to a tree. His captors then lit a fire close to where he was tethered and he rightly suspected he was about to be tortured. Exhausted from the march and emotionally shattered from the destruction of his farm and concern for his wife, he knew that what was to follow would be a grim test of his physical and mental strength.

The Indians performed a menacing dance around Williamson to frighten him. Burning coals and flaming sticks were held close to his face, eyes, hands, head and feet, burning his skin, while his captors taunted him. Throughout the ordeal, they warned him of the grisly fate that awaited him should he so much as whimper from the pain. He proved equal to the task, although he had no idea how. Afterwards, the Indians settled to eat, offering Williamson some of what remained, though he had little appetite and hid what he could not eat in the bark of the tree to which he remained tied. When the sun set, the fire was put out and leaves were placed over the ashes. They were to travel once more by night.

In the days and weeks that followed, leading towards winter, they travelled up the River Susquehanna staying within the frontier lands. Williamson soon realised that, compared to other settlers, he had been lucky—at least so far. The attacks on families were brutal and murderous. A neighbour, Joseph Snider, was scalped along with his wife and five children. Their house was plundered and they were left within it, still alive, as it burned to the ground. The Indians stood by to ensure no one escaped whilst 'rejoicing and echoing back in their diabolical manner' the hysterical cries coming from within the burning house.

Snider's young servant was spared in order to carry the plunder, like Williamson had been. However, it soon became clear that he was not cut of the same cloth and could not cope with his load or the harsh treatment. Williamson tried to console the youth as he weakened tearfully, complaining that he had had enough. His failing resolve was spotted by a warrior and within an instant, the boy was killed with a sharp blow to his head and then scalped. Williamson stood rooted to the ground, shocked by the abruptness of the execution. Ruefully he reflected that it would have been a better fate for him to have gone down with the *Planter* all those years ago, and his suffering ended there.

Over the next few weeks Williamson witnessed many more atrocities. John Adams' family was butchered on his homestead with 'the old man' tortured and killed some days later. This was followed by the torture, scalping and killing of the families of John Lewis, Jacob Miller and George Folke, the latter's family being cut to pieces and fed to their swine.

Another party of Indians delivered three prisoners from an Irish settlement called Cannocojigge by the River Susquehanna. They confirmed to Williamson that what he was witnessing was typical of the wider area: the Indians were cutting a devastating swathe through the unprotected settlements of the whole region.[24] These three prisoners, although almost dead from their mistreatment, took an opportunity to escape, but without food and in unfamiliar terrain, they were soon captured and returned by a tribe allied to their captors. After being badly burnt while tied to a tree, two of the victims had their bellies slashed open and entrails removed to be burned before them. The fate of the third victim was far worse, and witnessed by Williamson. Finding himself alone once more, he struggled to retain his will to survive.[25]

With the arrival of snow, there was a greater risk of the Indians' trails being detected, so with Williamson, who was by this stage almost starving, they trekked some 200 miles from the nearest British settlements to join their families in winter quarters at a place called Alamingo. Over the next two months, Williamson observed with interest the domestic customs of his captors.

Despite the appalling treatment the Delaware Indians meted out to those they perceived as threatening to their future, there were elements of their culture and society that Williamson respected. The women, he wrote, 'are very chaste and constant to their husbands'. As a people, they had learned to use their environment with great skill to clothe and feed themselves. They had mastered the discipline to eat only when hungry. As warriors, they were ferocious and lethal, a lesson initially learned by inexperienced British officers to the cost of their men. However, Williamson noted that the Indians' skill in fighting in woodland was not matched by their effectiveness in open engagement, which they avoided if they could.[26]

Williamson respected the strength of the social bonds within Indian tribal society. He admired their love of liberty, for which they would rather die than surrender, and the affection they held for their neighbours, though it sat in stark contrast to the harshness and determination with which they meted out revenge. It followed that crime within their society was not tolerated; criminals were burnt to death and sometimes only allowed to die after roasting in the flames for two or three days. Williamson observed that 'other nations might be more happy, if in some circumstances they copied [the Indians] and made wise conduct, courage and personal strength the chief recommendations for war captains.'

Williamson observed the extreme cruelty dispensed by the Delaware in revenge for the death of their own, but reflected that the practice of scalping could be blamed on the governors of Massachusetts and Pennsylvania who introduced a pecuniary bounty during the French and Indian War for a male Indian scalp, and a lesser bounty 'for females and children under twelve years old'. He also recognised the corruption introduced to Indian society by outsiders, particularly through the peddling of alcohol by those 'calling themselves Christians', which rendered the Indians drunk, dangerous and unpredictably violent. Indeed, to Williamson, this was at the root of the Indians' 'barbarous behaviour'. After all, in peacetime, he reflected, it was these same people who sold their expertly crafted goods to the white plantation owners.

Other characteristics of Delaware Indian society were later recalled by Williamson in his 1758 memoir. These included their pragmatic ruthlessness towards the elderly. He recounted one case in which an ageing and physically failing member of the tribe, no longer able to earn his living by hunting or fishing, was brought before his leaders. No defence for his infirmities was offered and he was sentenced to death. The old man was tied to a tree and summarily executed by a boy who was instructed to strike the victim on the head with a tomahawk until he was dead; a task which, due to the boy's lack of physical height and strength, took him an hour to achieve. The body was then placed upright in a narrow grave. An old gun was placed in his left hand with a small powder horn and shot bag was hung around his neck. In his right hand was placed some money in a silk purse. The grave was then filled with soil. Women were dealt with in like manner, except they were put to death by young girls.

The native Indian tribes were having to respond to an existential threat caused by irreversible changes beyond their control. Williamson concluded that a lasting peace would never be established between the indigenous Indians and the British unless trust between them could be established and land set aside upon which they could settle without threat. Overall he viewed the Indians as an honourable people whose goodwill had been abused and treaties dishonoured as the balance of dependency shifted from the settler on the Indian, to the other way around.

After two months in Alamingo, the winter snow started to melt. Williamson had survived by building himself a wigwam and covering it in bark and earth for insulation, but he was weak from the cold and meagre food, and his liberty remained as distant a prospect as ever. He watched in early spring as a tribal force of about 150 men gathered in the camp, strengthened by additional tribesmen and arms supplied by the French garrison at Fort De Quesne.[27] The war party assembled, they made their way towards the British settlements at the Blue Hills near Cannocojigge, taking Williamson with them. There, the party split into sections of about twenty, each commanded by its individual leader. Williamson was not trusted to join them, and was left behind at the base camp with a group of ten Indians who were to await the return of the others.

Now back in country that he knew, Williamson cautiously planned an escape. Three days after the departure of the main group, those that remained headed into the mountains to kill game for food, leaving Williamson behind, bound up. On their return, they undid his stays before roasting two polecats they had shot. Exhausted by their day's tramp, the men soon settled down to sleep. Williamson tested his opportunity, making noises, touching their feet and walking about. The men did not react. They slept with their guns under their heads, and Williamson tried to take one, but soon gave up as he could not do so without waking them. Only too aware of the consequences if his plan failed, he hesitated to take the first step for freedom, but trusting in God, he walked a few steps before stopping to look back to ensure that all was still quiet. After creeping some 200 yards, he started to run, making for the foothills of the mountains.

A spike of sheer terror cut through him when he heard the shrieking 'woop cry' of the Indians as they became aware of his escape. Driving on with increased urgency, Williamson scraped through bushes and past rocks, over small ravines and through thick woodland, cutting his legs and feet as he went. He kept going until dawn, when he found a hollow tree where he 'lay very snug', thanking God. A few hours passed before warrior voices closed in on him, shouting out what they would do to him once they had caught him, but finding nothing, they eventually moved on. With the light of the day failing, Williamson travelled on in fear, responding to the snap of every twig that broke under his feet. He kept away from any roads or paths to conceal himself as best he could, and kept going, resting during the day, moving at night.

On the fourth night, while rustling through a carpet of leaves, Williamson nearly stumbled onto a party of Indians who, upon hearing him, jumped to their feet. Seizing their weapons, they ran into the woods to address the threat. Panic and shock swept over Williamson, but then, unexpectedly, a herd of wild pigs broke through the undergrowth, running towards the warriors. Upon spotting the pigs, they hooted with laughter and resumed their leisure by their fire. Silently tip toeing away, Williamson pressed on through the night. The next morning he climbed to the summit of a hill to see if he could identify any signs of a white man's settlement. Straining his eyes, he spotted, to his huge relief, the unmistakable dwellings of settlers in the distance. Deliverance was within his grasp!

Waiting for darkness, Williamson forced his tired and torn limbs into one final effort. By 4 a.m., he was knocking on the door of an old acquaintance, John Bell, whose wife, upon opening it and seeing him, screamed and fled into the house. Mr Bell tentatively approached the door brandishing a gun. Fortunately, before shooting, he allowed Williamson to explain himself and the reason for his native clothing and dishevelled condition. Finally Mr Bell was able to reconcile the starved and filthy person before him with the man he remembered as Peter Williamson, and he flung his arms around him.

Over the next few days, Williamson was slowly nursed back to strength. Then, wearing clothes lent to him by Mr Bell and on a borrowed horse, Williamson rode 140 miles to his father-in-law's house. His arrival on 4 January 1755, some three months after his capture, was scarcely believed.[28] The joy of this warm welcome disappeared, however, when Williamson was told of his wife's death two months earlier. The cause of her death was never recorded.

Williamson soon started drawing the attention of a wider audience who were eager to learn of his experiences. The governor of Philadelphia questioned him closely on the facts of his story and called upon him to make a sworn statement of his captivity, which was sent to London and to the assembly in Philadelphia. He was then called before the assembly where he was cross-examined by the speaker for two days. Williamson was promised 'all proper methods should be taken, not only to accommodate and reimburse all those who had suffered by the savages, but to prevent them from committing the like hostilities in the future.' But what of Williamson's own future?

Williamson's father-in-law encouraged him to resume work. The possibility of his returning to the farm was discussed, but understandably it was declined. Instead, Williamson enlisted in the army under General Shirley, who was governor of New England and commander-in-chief of Britain's land forces in North America at the onset of the French and Indian War. He then began three years of military service. His first engagement in battle took place in 1756 against a tribe that had murdered a well-known local farmer, his wife, son and nine servants. The man's daughter, who had been abducted, was later rescued by Williamson's unit unharmed, though strapped naked to a tree and in a highly distressed condition having witnessed the torture and murder of her brother. Fifty scalps were torn from the heads of the dead Indians by way of retribution.

On 14 August in the same year, Williamson was wounded and taken prisoner in the siege of Oswego after the fall of the garrison to General Montcalm.[29] He was transported to Quebec where he was held with other prisoners until returned to England on a French ship in exchange for French prisoners of war. After a six-week journey, the vessel arrived in Plymouth on 6 November, where, due to his wounds, Williamson was discharged as unfit for duty. Thus he found himself 800 miles from Aberdeen, the city from which he had been kidnapped thirteen years earlier and to which he now planned to return. However, with only 6 shillings handed to him by a nation grateful for his military service, his funds ran out in York, where the next part of his story begins.[30]

It was to address his financial shortfall that, in York, Williamson wrote his memoirs. Once he had completed a draft, he received funds for their publication by a group of wealthy city gentlemen who saw a market for the book's sale. They were proved right, with the book selling well in both York and Newcastle.[31] In June 1758, Williamson finally returned to Aberdeen, where his misadventures had first begun. There he continued to sell his book with considerable success. That success, and the allegations contained in his memoir, soon came to the attention of Aberdeen's ruling families. Williamson's books were seized by the city's officers and he was imprisoned subject to bail on a charge of peddling 'scurrilous and infamous libel, reflecting greatly upon the characters and merchants of Aberdeen ... without any ground or reason'.[32]

Williamson's landlord provided the bail pending his trial. In the local court, Williamson found himself judged by the very people who had raised the complaint. He was fined 10 shillings, imprisoned until he apologised in writing for his offence, and banished from the city. His books (which were never returned to him) had the offending pages ripped out before being publicly burnt at the Market Cross by the city's hangman.[33] The magistrates were 'at once accusers, witnesses, and condemners in their own case'.[34]

Williamson, not unnaturally, bridled at these events, and upon arriving in Edinburgh, secured the services of Alexander Crosbie, a leading advocate at the Scottish bar. Crosbie was horrified at what had happened and highly supportive of Williamson's wish for justice. It led to an action for damages being raised by Williamson *in forma pauperis* in the court of session against the culprits, Alexander Cushnie and others, magistrates of Aberdeen.[35] The lord ordinary allowed proof before answer, requiring Williamson to return to Aberdeen in September 1760, where a number of witness statements were gathered to verify Williamson's claims of kidnap, including one from a newly returned traveller from Virginia.

On 2 February 1762, the court overturned the earlier decision, finding in favour of Williamson who was awarded £100 in damages, which was to be paid personally by the named magistrates, together with the expenses of the case. A reclaiming motion by the magistrates seeking a modification of the damages was lodged but refused. One of the clinching pieces of evidence to achieve this outcome had been produced by William Cochrane, deputy town clerk of Aberdeen, who placed before the court an account due by Bailie William Fordyce & Co, one of the defendants, to James Smith, the merchants' paymaster. This showed disbursements for the half year to May 1743 amounting to £160 18s 6d. Items included 'Jan 8—a pair of stockings to Williamson Williamson, 6d; ... to five days diet, 1/3d; ... to the man that brought Williamson 1s 6d.'[36]

Not satisfied with his triumph, Williamson raised a further action for damages against the orchestrators of his kidnap, Bailie Fordyce and his accomplices. Williamson, who estimated the injuries he had suffered at £2,000, agreed to submit his claim to arbitration rather than have it heard in the court of session.[37] This might have been because of his fear that the witnesses who were to be called had been bribed or threatened.[38] What was to follow had all the elements of a farce.

The arbiter to whom the case was referred was James Forbes of Shiels, sheriff substitute of Aberdeenshire. He was known as a convivial man who was fond of a drink. Worse still, he had recently lost his mother and, at the time of the referral, was still recovering from 'a hearty dose [one assumes of alcohol] at her burial'. It exposed the arbiter's Achilles Heel, which both sides eyed as a means of securing a favourable decision for themselves.

The farce began with the proceedings commencing in a local tavern at about 11 a.m., where the sheriff was to be found 'busy at hot punch'. The first round was won by Williamson and his friends, who carried off the sheriff substitute to dinner at the New Inn where they sat 'close drinking, as is the phrase in that part of the country: Helter Skelter, that is, copiously and alternately of different liquors, until 11 o'clock at night.' Sheriff Forbes, by then 'incapable of office', was escorted home by his two maid servants. Not to be outdone, the opposition took up the challenge the next morning by dragging Forbes from his bed and carrying him off to the local 'howff' where 'a large dose of spirits, white wine, and punch were administered to him', balanced by periodic 'cooling drafts of porter'. Prodigious drinking followed of wines and spirits.

Williamson, aware of what was happening, searched for the sheriff in all the taverns in the city, but without success. His fears proved justified as, by the evening, the judge, whose sensibilities were by then severely compromised, wished to show his appreciation of the defendants' generosity. He pronounced a decree arbitral in their favour. After wending his way to bed 'very merry and jocose', he slept all the next day.

Unusually, but perhaps unsurprisingly, the findings of the arbiter were subjected to review after the decision was brought before the court of session. On 3 December 1768, Forbes's judgement was recalled and Williamson was awarded £200 in damages and 100 guineas in expenses.

Twenty-six years after his kidnap, Williamson had finally gained his revenge, albeit with the payment of damages being far less than he had claimed. In doing so, he had righted a very rotten wrong; one which was embedded in abuse of privilege and a cruel greed.

Williamson was clearly a man of unflinching will and courage, but he was also one of wit, vision and energy. Any emotional or physical scarring seems to have been set aside as he regenerated himself with a number of imaginative and innovative means of earning his living. These included staging evening re-enactments of Indian war dances and ceremonies in his lodgings, fully attired in Indian clothes. The businessman within him decreed that each performance required a minimum audience of six.

Not satisfied with the living he was making from his re-enactments, he opened a wine shop near Parliament Close and a tavern adjacent to George Heriot's goldsmith's shop on the High Street, the latter becoming a popular haunt for lawyers to do their business. With the location being close to the tollbooth, the tavern was also used as a 'sort of vestry' for magistrates who repaired there to take what was described as *deid-chack* or a light dinner, which they enjoyed after attending an execution. The tentacles of Williamson's business extended into Parliament Hall where he opened a coffee shop named *Indian Peter's* at a time when the hall was divided mid-way by a screen. The northern part, or outer house, also included the premises of two booksellers, a hardware business and a hatmaker's stall. Each of these businesses was separated from the other by a partition of brown paper.[39]

Williamson's enterprise was widened further with his increasing engagement as a bookseller and publisher, not least of his own numerous works.[40] Perhaps most intriguingly, in 1773, upon his own initiative, he published the first *Edinburgh Directory*, providing 'every householder's name, place of abode, trade and traffic within the city and suburbs'.[41] Eventually sold by Williamson in 1796, its success, along with other popular publications of the works of third parties, enabled him to cease trading as a wine merchant and focus on his love, printing. Three years later, he wrote and published a periodical similar to *The Spectator*, entitled the *Scots Spy* or *Critical Observer*, which appeared every Friday, featuring local news and information.[42]

Williamson's most visionary undertaking, however, commenced in 1776 with the establishment of a system of penny postage for letters and parcels, which he conducted for many years from 'General Penny-Post Office, Edinburgh' in the Luckenbooths beside St Giles' Cathedral. The first postal system outside of London, it proved to be a money spinner; he employed four men daily for deliveries, each of whom he paid 4s 6d a week. The business ended when the government took over this function in 1793, for which Williamson was rewarded with a small pension for his loss.

One part of Williamson's life in which he was less fortunate or successful was matrimony. His first wife died young in America while he was a captive of the Delaware Indians. A second wife, Jean Colin, daughter of a farmer at Newhaven, Edinburgh, married him on 7 September 1760. Her fate is not known, but Williamson was free to get married again on 10 November 1771 to Jean Wilson, a 'mantua maker' and the daughter of a bookseller in New Kirk Parish, Edinburgh.[43] The marriage, which produced nine children, ended in acrimonious divorce, the grounds of which were Jean's adultery. She was accused of meeting 'with lewd and wicked men to whom she gave of her body carnally and in which houses she has often got herself intoxicated with liquor'. Recriminations were returned by Jean who accused Williamson of spending his time drinking with unworthy companions late into the night and dissipating his earnings in the process. Jealousy had, in her view, also played its part, due to her 'affable and cheerful temperament'. Tawdry arguments followed on both sides with Williamson claiming he had been reduced from a comfortable living as a businessman to that of a near pauper. He was on the poor roll and forced by his wife's behaviour, or so he claimed, to find alternative lodgings. The court found in his favour without pecuniary obligation to his wife, and he was divorced on 2 March 1789. Undaunted, he married for a fourth time on 6 May in the same year in St Giles. His new wife was Agnes McGeorge.[44]

Williamson died on 19 January 1799, aged sixty-nine. He had lived a life crammed with daunting and demanding adventures and had proved equal to them. With his multifarious talents, he had played the cards thrown before him with great skill, and was rewarded with the privilege of dying in his own bed. He was laid to rest dressed, as he had directed, in his Indian costume, in an unmarked grave in Old Calton Burying Ground, Edinburgh, in a plot 'fifteen paces North East of a monument erected later to the political martyrs of the time'.[45] His body may lie without a headstone disclosing his name, but his story lives on; an outcome of which he would surely have approved.

7

Slavery in West Africa: Archibald Monteith

In Westmoreland, Jamaica, Archibald Monteith approached a mansion elegantly positioned within the grounds of a rich plantation. He was a man on a mission. On entering the hall of the grand house he was greeted by the absentee owner, none other than Andrew Wedderburn, the eldest surviving son of James Wedderburn and half-brother to the radical activist Robert Wedderburn.[1] Andrew had recently arrived from England, where he resided, for a tour of his Jamaican plantations, which he had inherited upon his father's death in 1807.[2] He had asked Archibald Monteith, a Moravian missionary, to come and see him.

Monteith was a tall man with an open and friendly manner, who carried himself with dignity; he was someone with whom Wedderburn hoped to engage on friendly terms.[3] As for Monteith, he knew why he had been summoned. After exchanging pleasantries, Wedderburn got straight to the point: 'Why did you keep my Negroes from dancing?' he asked.

The previous day, when he had visited one of his plantations, his numerous slaves had declined his invitation to come up to his mansion to dance and play before him in the customary celebration of his return to Jamaica. Monteith, who had been with them earlier, replied to him, 'Not I, but the Bible forbids it.'[4] He went on to try to persuade Wedderburn to allow him to preach Christianity to the slaves on all his plantations in the same manner as he had to those whom Wedderburn had met yesterday, who had offered to pray for him rather than celebrate his return home with rum and dancing. In support of his request, Monteith quoted Galatians chapter 5, verses 16–23, which asks the reader to be led by the Holy Spirit, to set aside the sins of the flesh and thus enjoy the fruits of the Spirit: 'love, joy, peace, patience, kindness, goodness, faithfulness, gentleness, self control: against such there is no law. And those who belong to Jesus Christ have crucified the flesh with its passions and desires.'

Andrew Wedderburn listened sceptically, pausing to reflect, when Monteith had finished, on the intent of his words. Then, rising from his chair, he extended his hand in a gesture of approval. 'Just come as often as you can and want to,' he said.[5] Thus Monteith was offered the chance to promote the Bible and Christianity to a much wider audience than he had so far enjoyed. It was a cardinal moment in his life, affirming his chosen mission.

This meeting took place in 1832, a year of far-reaching events in both London and Jamaica, which had almost certainly influenced Wedderburn's positive response to this intrusion of religion on his workforce, with its potentially disruptive consequences. There is no known record of Wedderburn's private thoughts on either the matter in hand or on the preacher before him.

Archibald Monteith was a black slave, born in around 1799, the grandson of an African prince.[6] He had been abducted some twenty years earlier from his town of Nri in the Igbo region of what is now south-eastern Nigeria, inland from the Bight of Biafra.[7] His name, given to him by his parents, was Aniaso.

The Igbo tribe had started migrating into the region of Aniaso's birth from the east of modern-day Niger since as early as the eighth century, interacting with the Edo or Bini people of Benin.[8] Operating as autonomous local communities, the Igbo lacked centralised leadership and administration, but three institutions bound them together: the ritual authority of the Nri priesthood; the trade and religious networks of the Aro peoples which spread throughout the Igbo region; and the culture of kingship in western Igbo under the kingdom of Benin. Their religion was founded on the principle of pacifism, with the shedding of blood regarded as an abomination; it followed that the Igbo had no army. Instead, villages remained autonomous. Aniaso's father, as a man of social standing, was one of the leaders of Nri. The leaders were supported in decision-making by subsidiary groups within their society including secret societies and priests. Politics was handled by consensus, with checks and balances obliging the leaders to resolve quarrels. Women had rights, though they were more limited than those enjoyed by men. Great efforts were made to maintain the social equilibrium without resorting to punishment.

With his father a member of this hereditary elite, Aniaso was to undergo an initiation ceremony reserved for the sons of aristocratic families when he became an adolescent. Called the 'festival of the tattoos', it involved substantial scarification and tattooing of the recipient's face, which was to show their exalted position in society.[9] The excruciating procedure was fatal for some, but it was nonetheless accepted as an honour, and as such, pain could not be acknowledged during it. Having witnessed this ceremony many times in his childhood, Aniaso understood its implications and looked forward to it as a rite of passage into manhood and high status. As a leader of the community, Aniaso would be an arbiter of the Igbo's religious and social values, founded on the principles of peaceful negotiation and mediation. These values would filter through his life and be his constant guide.

The Igbo, however, were not immune to the winds of change blowing through their continent. Their political domination was constricted by three main destabilising factors: shortage of manpower; problems of communication over a vast territory; and the assertive and covert enterprises of the Aro people, one of which was the capture of slaves, many of them Igbo, for trading with European slavers.[10]

In 1801, such matters would have certainly passed over the head of the nine-year-old Aniaso. He spent his days in his father's company, hardly leaving his side. He was the only son of five children, and his father's favourite. His sisters, meanwhile, were rarely permitted to leave the house, and if a male guest arrived, it was customary for them to retreat to where they could not be seen.[11] It was a protective environment that engendered a certain naivety in Aniaso's character.

One day a young man came to Aniaso's home, finding him there alone. It was one of the rare occasions when his father had left him behind. The man was a regular visitor to the family, presenting himself as a suitor to one of Aniaso's sisters. He asked the boy to come with him to the local market, and dazzled by the man's descriptions of colour and excitement awaiting him there, Aniaso willingly agreed, leaving no message behind.

After a day of travel they had still not reached the market. Aniaso and the man stayed overnight with the latter's friend and continued on their way the next day. Passers-by enquired of the man whether his young companion was going to be sold. 'No,' came the reply, 'this is the son of a great and respected man.'[12] Alarm bells still did not ring in Aniaso's trusting ears.

The intended destination finally came into view: an open expanse of water that Aniaso in his innocence took to be the ocean. Considering the length of time he had been travelling, it is more likely to have been Lake Oguta, which is connected to the River Ulasi, which leads to the sea. Traditional trade and religious networks operated within the southern Igbo region, and this trade centre on the shores of the lake presented to Aniaso rich colours and smells and bustling activity, the likes of which he had never before experienced. Transfixed, he sat under a tree as the rhythm of this extraordinary and unfamiliar world danced around him.

In particular, his innocent eyes were drawn to the water lapping onto the beach and beyond, to the masted ships anchored offshore and the boats servicing them, bobbing on the swell as they tacked their way to and from the shore.

His reverie was interrupted by a man's voice: 'Come on, my boy. Come with me and try to pilot my boat on the water.' Aniaso declined, but it was to no avail. A strong hand seized his collar and he was bundled into the boat against his will. The horror of his situation suddenly dawned on him: his companion had sold him into slavery. Aniaso could see him there on the shore, coldly observing what was happening. He called out in desperation, telling him to let his father know what had happened to him, knowing at the same time he never would. Only then did he notice the other boys in the boat, bound in chains.

The small boat pulled away from the shore, soon coming to what Aniaso later described as a 'great swimming house'. As he and his companions were loaded on board, he stared in awe at the captain of the ship who was standing there to greet them. He was a man whose face and hands were white in colour, while his feet, mystifyingly, were black and shiny, and without any toes. Only later did Aniaso learn that he was looking at polished boots.

Through the open hatches on the deck, Aniaso could see huge numbers of 'bound, moaning and crying people'. Because of his young age, he was spared joining them. Instead, he and other young boys were permitted to stay in the captain's quarters, where they ate and slept. However, they were reminded each day of the misery below when the slaves were brought on deck, out 'from their caves', to breath some fresh air.[13] The wailing which came from these chained victims, grieving for lost children, friends and homeland, greatly distressed Aniaso, as did their cruel treatment meted out by the crew.

What happened to Aniaso introduces many questions. The context of his abduction can be traced back to the late fifteenth century and the Portuguese exploration of the West African coast. In what is now Ghana, the native Akan people proved to be willing commercial partners, trading manufactured goods such as cloth and base metals for gold extracted from the Akan goldmines.[14] As a result of this trade, the region became known as the Gold Coast.

Portugal was a relatively small nation with limited resources, and so, by the close of the sixteenth century, to protect their commercial interests and prevent competition from other European powers, they had built a network of forts along the Gold Coast. This network was enlarged in tandem with their expanding trading connections into the Niger delta and the kingdom of Benin. Initially they sought to secure their trade within

Benin by converting the court of its kingdom to Christianity and thus reducing it to a satellite protectorate. However, this policy became unstuck when the monarchy of Benin successfully frustrated further infiltration; by 1520 the Portuguese were almost frozen out of Benin completely, with their trade posts limited to Sao Tomé and other islands in the Gulf of Guinea. By that stage, their business had evolved primarily to the purchase of slaves from Congo and Angola. That labour force was then taken to plantations on the Spanish and Portuguese possessions in the Atlantic, such as the Cape Verde Islands and Canary Islands, to cultivate sugarcane and other produce for the European markets.

By 1600, Portuguese influence in West Africa was wavering, though a century of intense commercial activity had left its mark on the region: new crops brought from America and elsewhere had become staples; the seeds of Christianity had been sown; and pidgin Portuguese was widely spoken, providing a language of commerce for other trading nations to use in the future.[15]

The first country to break the Portuguese monopoly on global maritime trade was Holland. By 1598, the Dutch were busy establishing a distribution network between Asia, America and Africa, the unintended consequence Phillip II of Spain's decision to ban Dutch merchants from Iberian ports as punishment for Dutch revolt against Spanish rule. By the end of the 1630s, the Dutch West India Company had destroyed the Spanish fleets in the Caribbean and established themselves as the principal suppliers and customers of the Spanish plantations in the West Indies. In Brazil they seized a plantation colony from the Portuguese.

With cheap labour needed to work these plantations, the Portuguese had begun transporting slaves across the Atlantic to Brazil from as early as 1526. The Spanish had started doing the same on a modest scale a little earlier in 1520, with a voyage to Puerto Rico, one of their Caribbean colonies. They then accelerated the trade by contracting others, principally the Portuguese, to transport the slaves for them. This was to compensate for the limited Spanish presence on the West African coast.

By the mid-1620s, the Dutch were trading slaves at an annual rate of about 10,000 a year, and demand was increasing rapidly due to the arrival on the scene of the English and the French. These nations had begun seizing the smaller Spanish possessions in the Caribbean in the wake of the latter's defeat by the Dutch. To preempt the threat posed by England and France, the Dutch consolidated their future supply of slave labour by taking possession of the remaining Portuguese forts on the Gold Coast, thus becoming, by 1642, Europe's dominant trading partner with West Africa. However, the balance of power began to shift between 1652 and 1713 with a succession of European wars between England, France and the Netherlands. During this period, the English and French looked to establish a presence on the coast of West Africa either by capturing Dutch forts or building new ones. The forts changed hands regularly.

For the native Akan people of the Gold Coast, the question was how to balance the benefits of trade and the maintenance of their independence against the ever-present threat posed by expansionist Europeans operating from their fortified coastal footholds. One solution was to lease rather than sell land to the Europeans for the construction of their forts, while withdrawing essential supplies such as food and fresh water whenever they needed to apply pressure on them. Another strategy was to develop trade with more than one nationality of European merchants to generate a rivalry between them from which they, the Akan, might benefit. This task was made easier by English and French worry over the Dutch monopoly. With the support of their respective navies, the English and French encouraged their merchant mariners to compete along the West African coast.

From 1713 until the abolition of slavery, the slave trade continued unabated, albeit with Dutch activity slowly being eliminated by their competitors. The French, north of the River Gambia, sought to develop the trade on the coast at Saint Louis in modern-day Senegal, but this attempt yielded few slaves and met with effective resistance from the local population. Forts continued to be built by the trading companies of both nations along the coast of what became known as Sierra Leone, but the principal British focus was on the Gold Coast, where society was better organised for trade with Europeans due to the prior activities of the Portuguese and Dutch. In this region, gold and slaves were the primary commodities, though gum, hides, timber and palm oil were also bought by European traders. Some thirty forts came to be built on the Gold Coast, of which the strongest remained Elmina, constructed by the Portuguese in 1482. This was still under Dutch control in 1814 when they abolished the slave trade pursuant to the Anglo-Dutch Slave Trade Treaty. It remained in their hands until 1872 when the British took control of the Dutch Gold Coast. However, Dutch dominance was being supplanted by British merchants, whose activities were bolstered significantly by the presence of the Royal Navy, long before 1814.

With the Industrial Revolution gaining pace, British merchants had access to the necessary capital with which to expand their enterprise and secure manufactured goods and supplies for trading at competitive prices. At the same time, the demand for slave labour in the Caribbean and North American colonies was ever increasing. As well as the British Gold Coast (a part of the Gulf of Guinea), where a competitive commercial atmosphere created attractive opportunities for African potentates and merchants, the Upper Guinea coast, comprising what is now eastern Guinea, Sierra Leone, Liberia and the western part of Côte d'Ivoire, offered some of the most profitable markets for European merchants. Here they exchanged cargos of manufactured goods such as guns, ammunition, mirrors, cloth and beads for cargoes of slaves, which were then transported across the Atlantic in what was known as the Middle Passage.[16]

It is estimated that some 12.5 million Africans were shipped to the New World between 1500 and 1866, of which British ships transported some 3.4 million between 1640 and 1807. At the peak of the trade in the 1780s, an average of 78,000 slaves were being transported across the Atlantic every year (with an average death rate on the voyage of 15 per cent). The British were responsible for around half this number, with their nearest rivals, France and Holland, accountable for roughly 20 per cent each.[17]

After the disruption caused by the French Revolution and Napoleonic Wars, British involvement grew to about 60 per cent, while the Portuguese accounted for 25 per cent of the trade and North American merchants about 15 per cent. At the height of the trade in the 1780s, the origins of slaves from along the coast of West Africa (thus excluding Portuguese Angola) were approximately as follows: 7 per cent from Senegambia and Sierra Leone; 20 per cent from the Gold Coast; 35 per cent from the Slave Coast and the Benin region; and 29 per cent from the Niger delta and the Cameroons. The balance came from elsewhere.

Selling slaves for transportation abroad may not have been the preferred choice of most native leaders, but as the global economy expanded, the lure of what European traders offered proved irresistible to many. The slaves were usually captured through war with neighbouring kingdoms or selected for sale by African merchants and rulers, with only a small fraction being kidnapped by Europeans. This sale and delivery of slaves by willing African vendors guaranteed a smooth and peaceful transaction, which was good for business. On the Gold Coast, the costly forts gradually became redundant and were replaced by the posts of smaller merchant traders who were willing to negotiate ad hoc terms directly with their African counterparts. It was a preferable arrangement for the latter, as the presence of the forts had always carried some threat.

The economies of the many kingdoms along the West African coast naturally benefited from this burgeoning commercial activity.[18] Powerful African merchants accumulated such wealth from the slave trade that some were able to challenge local monarchs. Many European merchants settled and intermarried, establishing new merchant empires. Local rulers gained power over their rivals. But did the demand for slaves create war between kingdoms? The conventional wisdom is that it did not; rather, as anywhere else, wars between states arose in pursuit of wealth and power.

On a continent where land was in greater supply than the labour needed to cultivate or develop it, value lay in labour, not land. To divest a rival community or kingdom of their manpower by capturing its people and either placing them into some form of domestic servitude or selling them into slavery to Europeans was a potent means of weakening that rival and strengthening oneself. The accumulation of slaves, therefore, was a means of accumulating power. Moreover, a slave, unlike land, was a tradable resource, whether for horses, armaments, gunpowder or other goods. They formed a currency of exchange, providing a ruler with a source of wealth, which he could use to strengthen his administration, his military and his economy.

Local rulers sold men and women from their own societies too: the mentally or physically handicapped (for a reduced price), criminals, debtors or those in political or social disgrace within their families or communities. Those brought from outside were usually prisoners of war or the victims of kidnap, like the unfortunate young Aniaso, the future Archibald Monteith.

The hinterland of what is now south-eastern Nigeria, where Aniaso came from, was well populated and regularly exploited by kidnappers for the slave trade. As he sat aboard the ship, waiting to depart for Jamaica, Aniaso must have feared desperately for his future. His family, meanwhile, would have been plunged into an emotional abyss, knowing for certain what his disappearance meant.[19]

In his later recollections, Aniaso did not dwell on the voyage across the Atlantic, although he mentioned his comparative good fortune in not being locked in the hold. Along with eleven other boys, he was given the freedom of the deck and the captain's cabin, where he and the others were able to sleep, eat and drink. On arrival at Kingston, the human cargo was discharged for sale, but Aniaso remained on board for six more weeks. Finally, he asked to be allowed on shore, but this was refused by the captain, who told him he intended to keep him as his cabin boy. Clearly the young boy had qualities that made him stand out. This answer was met with fierce resistance from Aniaso who threatened to throw himself overboard if he was not permitted on shore. The captain acceded to his wishes and that afternoon Aniaso was sold to the owner of Kep estate, near Carmel, Westmoreland, to which he travelled by cart with the overseer and eleven other slaves. After eight days, the new slaves were taken to meet their new master, John Monteith.

John Monteith was born in Glasgow on 7 January 1776, the eldest son of Walter Monteith. His mother, Jean, was the sister of Margaret, duchess of Douglas, and had two brothers, merchants in Jamaica and Virginia.[20] Sir Archibald Walter Monteith, John's paternal grandfather, was patriarch of the family. He had inherited an estate called Ardmore in Dunbartonshire and Kep in Stirlingshire.[21] In keeping with other members of the gentry, although comparatively few in number, Sir Archibald took up opportunities presented by the burgeoning Industrial Revolution in Scotland to further his commercial ambitions. The collective methodology of the Scottish gentry (or upper-middle landed classes), based on mutual trust, was to work closely either in direct partnership or in cooperation to create a 'web of investment and domestic and overseas agricultural activity, in shipping, banking, and domestic mining and manufacture', generating a massive expansion of interlocking investments.[22]

By the early 1770s, Sir Archibald's eldest son, Walter, took up the gauntlet by investing in a series of business ventures, starting with a partnership in Glasgow Tanwork.[23] This was soon followed by joining leading Glasgow merchants in a triangular operation from Glasgow across the Atlantic, with bases in Virginia and Antigua. The company, called Glassford, Gordon, Monteith and Company, set up a series of stores in Virginia from which goods such as 'hardware, rum, wine, sugar, salt and slaves' were a major source of revenue. But the masterstroke for Glassford was that the stores were used as collection points for tobacco leaves bound for Glasgow, representing 10 per cent of all tobacco imports to the United Kingdom.[24]

Another partnership called Ramsay, Monteith and Company, set up by Walter Monteith and others, followed a similar business plan, operating in Virginia with imported goods from England and Scotland. However, both businesses were seriously damaged by the American War of Independence, during which, mainly for commercial reasons, Glasgow merchants remained loyal to the crown. A financial crisis followed, causing many businesses to fail and Walter Monteith to face bankruptcy. Actions for compensation were raised by Scottish companies in the relevant American states to cover losses due to the war, but these were resisted.

In 1796, the US supreme court finally overruled the states, binding them to pay compensation according to the terms of the Treaty of Paris, which had been ratified by the national government in 1784. In the case of Glassford, Gordon, Monteith and Company, the sum settled was a quarter of what was claimed.[25] Delayed compensation was still being paid out in 1811, which meant that Walter was still in debt as late as 1809. His son John made provision that, should he predecease his father, none of his estate left to his father should be used to pay off creditors. Nonetheless, lines of credit remained open to Walter who, in a new business named Hill and Monteith, undertook low-key commercial activities relating to brokerage and import/export credit for companies trading between Glasgow and Ireland.

John left for Jamaica in the mid-1790s, during the aftermath of the American War of Independence. This may have been a major factor in why he chose to go to Jamaica rather than Virginia. Jamaica remained a place where fortunes could be made, and for John, it was also a place replete with family connections. Five of his father's brothers, also merchants, had chosen either to work or retire in Jamaica, and they were joined by a sixth after a career in the merchant navy.[26] They were part of a much wider network on the island, which included the substantial land-owning families of the Campbells, Douglas's and Wallaces.[27] Still, of all Walter's children, only John elected to try his luck in Jamaica, arriving there in his late teens.

By 1796, most likely with the help of his family, John had secured a position of overseer on a plantation called Mexico at St Elizabeth. There he learned bookkeeping and sales skills related to the production of rum and sugar. He then graduated to Fonthill and Hampstead estates to carry out similar duties. By 1800 he was able to start purchasing parcels of land in Westmoreland, which collectively he named Kep. The land was not a sugar plantation but a livestock farm (or pen), for which slave labour was used for domestic and stock work.[28]

John's status within the community rose and public appointments followed: he was appointed lieutenant in the St Elizabeth parish foot regiment in 1800, rising to lieutenant colonel by 1811.[29] He was also one of three commissioners of the St Elizabeth Workhouse in 1806/7, and again in 1813.[30] Lastly, he managed other estates in the area as an attorney for absentee landlords, which involved sending rum, sugar, punch and logwood to Wedderburn and Co. in London and to other businesses in America, Glasgow and Bristol.[31] By the time of his death in 1815, John's extended land holdings were worked by a total of ninety slaves.

So it was into the hands of this man that Aniaso was delivered in 1801, and given the name 'Tobi'. While others were sent to the fields to work, Tobi, as he was now called, was taken in as a house servant by the manager. Within a year he was transferred to his slave master, where he was well treated. One of his duties over the ensuing eight years was as a playmate to John's children.

John never married but had children by three black women. The first was Felicia Richardson, by whom he had a daughter, Charlotte, in 1796. His second partner was Nancy Ford, by whom he had a son, James, in 1798 and five other children. Lastly, he had a son, John, born in 1812, and a daughter, Charlotte, by Mary Wilson. John allowed all of his children to take his surname as he did his long-term partner, Nancy, with whom he lived for at least seventeen years until his death.

During Tobi's period as a house servant, his master travelled to Scotland for three years. Nancy moved to the town of Savannah La Mar for her children to attend the local church and school. This held little appeal for Tobi, who preferred instead to have 'great fun romping, dancing and jumping' with the other local children and in joining them in doing as they pleased. In 1815, not long after his return from Scotland, John Monteith died at the age of forty-four, leaving part of his heritable property and some of his slaves, of whom Tobi was one, to Nancy, his black mistress.[32]

The ownership of slaves by a free black person was respected by law, but that person would nonetheless remain exposed to the racial prejudices of the wider white community. Nancy elected to place Tobi under the management of her and John's eldest son, James Monteith. Kep was sold and the family moved to another of their estates, Dumbarton, where Tobi, by then in his early twenties and clearly trusted and valued, became an overseer, with the attendant challenges of managing his fellow black slaves.

Real change was soon to come to Tobi via his baptism into the Church of England. His decision to take this life-changing step followed an invitation from the local parish minister, who earlier on the same day had baptised Nancy's children. In the service that followed at the Black River church, Tobi was christened Archibald John Monteith. No explanation was given to him of what the ritual actually meant, beyond it allowing him to 'come into a beautiful place' when he died. He was told nothing of what he later found out for himself: that 'there is a Saviour who died for us and that we are to love and serve him'.[33]

It was some years later, in 1824, that Archibald Monteith, his name from that point on, took his next step on the path to religious maturity. By chance, he was invited by a female slave to attend a service to be given by a Mr Cook, the owner of Paynestown, an adjoining estate. The girl told him there would 'be singing and prayer' at the service. Monteith was uncertain as to why Mr Cook would allow strangers to listen, to which the girl replied, 'because [he] keeps every morning especially for [black people from the neighbourhood]'. Later on, in his dictated memoirs, Monteith recalled that these words 'went through me as though something had pierced my heart'. Even so, he had misgivings about attending. His friends thought him a fool and tried to dissuade him from going, and he feared being asked why he was there. In the event, he was welcomed by Mr and Mrs Cook as 'Archie Monteith', and for the first time in his life, he entered into morning prayer and listened to the Bible being read. 'What I felt I cannot express,' he later said. 'I felt such power, as of a chill seizing my whole body. I could say nothing but went home and told the others what I had heard and felt. "Good," they replied, "next week we will come with you."'

In striking similarity to Robert Wedderburn, Monteith experienced a specific moment in which he was touched by religion. Both men were intelligent and articulate, and both trapped in societies in which their colour and education prescribed what they might hope to achieve. Faith would not solve the problem, but it would enable them to deal with it by teaching them that in the eyes of God, black and white were exactly the same, and God was greater than Man. For Robert, his faith provided a conduit through which he could channel his anger to try to create a more equal and just society, while for Monteith, it provided structure and purpose to give him, and those who would share in it with him, self respect and dignity leading to a better and more fulfilling life.

Monteith's commitment to God continued apace. He moved to the newly built Moravian church at New Carmel with its purely black congregation. At first, he did so as a candidate for induction, during which period he attended meetings of the brethren and learned to read and write. He was then received as a member of the congregation and confirmed, before being appointed as a 'native assistant'. In this role, his evangelical fervour was given full scope for expression, and he implemented it with unremitting energy.[34]

At the start of this spiritual awakening, Monteith was made aware of the need to change his living habits. This put paid to his love of dancing. Furthermore, and much to his surprise, he discovered it was immoral to live with four women at one time as he was then doing. Both practices he discovered were sinful according to Christian teaching, although consistent with the values of his African community. It caused Monteith to reflect on the double standards of the white man, many of whom, despite being called 'gentlemen' and professing to be Christians, had more than one partner. Nonetheless, he took it all on board, electing to separate from his partner who was unable to share in his faith and its strictures. Later, he settled with a kindred spirit, Rebecca Hart, whom he married on 8 January 1826.

Archibald Monteith's spiritual awakening did not come without its problems. His plantation master, James Monteith, blamed him for things going wrong at work, claiming he was distracted by his preaching. Harsh (and probably unjust) though this was, it coincided with James falling into debt and being fearful of his slaves being seized for sale by his creditors. To address this threat, he refused to allow his slaves to leave the plantation, which forced Monteith to cancel his pastoral visits and preaching. Rather than fight the embargo, Monteith's response was to pray for deliverance—which was forthcoming.

The development of Monteith's religious ambitions coincided with an unsettled period in Jamaica, which came to a head in 1831. The progress of the abolitionist movement in London encouraged the inspirational black leader of the Baptist Church, Deacon Samuel Sharpe, a self-taught slave, to demand more free time and a better working wage for his people. His followers, after attending their regular prayer meeting, took an oath to strike from their work until the plantation owners acceded to their demands.[35] The peaceful strike began on 25 December 1831 on the Kensington estate, near Montego Bay, and was soon supported by some 60,000 slaves across the island. Violence ensued, matched by brutal suppression, and the strike escalated into a rebellion known as the Baptist War. Sugar fields, houses, chapels and plantations were set on fire, and white people fled to the towns. None of this directly affected Monteith, but he was nonetheless shocked to find that fifty soldiers had been posted at New Carmel to meet any possible dissidence in his district, though none occurred.

After eleven days, the rebellion had been quelled, although sporadic fighting followed for a further two months. Beyond the 200 slaves and fourteen whites killed, over 300 slaves were executed, with Sharpe among them. For those not executed, brutal punishments were meted out. The Christian principle for the initial strike was expressed by Deacon Sharpe who 'thought and learnt from the bible that the whites had no more right to hold back people in slavery than black people had to make white people slaves'.[36] His assertive interpretation of those words and its consequences proved to be in stark contrast to Monteith's, who, living outside the area of revolt, expressed no desire to take part.[37]

The rebellion was a manifestation of the impatience and deep anger felt by many slaves in Jamaica at what they perceived to be the unacceptable refusal of the white owners to move with the times and face up to the implications of emancipation. It was, after all, a natural sequitur to the act which had abolished the slave trade in 1807, a very long twenty-five years earlier. Even that had come thirty-five years after Lord Mansfield had presided over the landmark decision in which James Somerset was given his freedom. Choosing to bury their heads in the sand, the island's government may have thought that their ruthless suppression of the rebellion had successfully dealt with the problem; back in Britain, however, their brutality was met with complete horror. There, it had already been accepted that emancipation was inevitable.

In Jamaica, although many plantation owners and prominent white citizens were wilfully blind to the changing reality, the economic model was proving unsustainable: two inquiries into the revolt highlighted the damage the rebellion had inflicted on Jamaica's economy and the finances of the plantations.[38] After the rebellion, a growing number of slave owners allowed their slaves to attend church, withdrawing their previous resistance, though some persisted and punished those who did not comply. Such attempts to dissuade churchgoing through intimidation were largely unsuccessful, however, and attendance soared. To accommodate this surge of commitment, Monteith was co-opted by his minister to visit black people within the area, to read them the Bible and hold meetings. In doing so, he met resistance from at least one overseer who wanted to keep things as they were, but on appeal by Monteith to the inspector of this and a further seven plantations, he was given formal approval to spread the word of God to the slaves on all of the plantations as he saw fit.

Andrew Wedderburn would have been well aware of the change of tone expressed by his fellow plantation owners, consequent to the recent bloodshed of the rebellion and impending legislation by parliament on emancipation. This knowledge would have undoubtedly influenced his response to Monteith's request to preach to the slaves on his plantation that day of their meeting in 1832. It explains his relief upon listening to Monteith's approach, which rested on preaching love, joy, patience, kindness and self-control.

For Monteith, having his request approved allowed him to help those who sought his spiritual guidance and aspired for a better life through the dignity and self-respect their faith would confer upon them. For Andrew Wedderburn, it served to maintain the fragile status quo on his plantations, offering the prospect of a peaceful transition into, and beyond, emancipation. There was a general fear among the island's white population that emancipation carried the threat of recriminatory violence as slaves sought to settle scores with their owners. Monteith might have reflected that the means by which he had achieved his goal shared much in common with the customs of his Igbo ancestors which he had observed as a boy in Nri, especially the use of peaceful negotiation and mediation for mutual benefit.

In 1833, just over a year after the Baptist War, the Slavery Abolition Act was passed, conferring emancipation on some 800,000 slaves, including those in the British Caribbean. However, there remained one large fly in the ointment for Monteith. Under the provisions of the new act, in addition to compensation being paid to slave owners for their loss, the freedom of slaves was not immediate. Instead, as a sop to plantation owners' demands for labour, the slaves found their contracts under the act transmuted, without compensation, to apprenticeships, which obliged them, with the exception of children under six, to continue working for their masters (with board) for up to a further six years, until actual freedom was granted to all on 1 August 1840.[39]

This came as a bitter blow to the otherwise patient Monteith. The apprentices were to be released in two groups stages: the first after three years and the second after six. Monteith was in the second group, but he was permitted under the act to buy his apprenticeship out provided he could afford to meet the cost. He approached John Daughtrey (or Dodridge) for advice. Daughtrey was a stipendiary magistrate at Black River who, as a fellow Christian, respected Monteith for his values. He had initially tried to dissuade him from buying his freedom due to his concern that once that precious status had been secured, plantation owners might be dissuaded from giving him access to their slaves for religious conversion.

Three years passed, and by that stage, Daughtrey's advice was no longer relevant; access was already granted by men like Andrew Wedderburn. But rather than apply for freedom through the judicial process, Daughtrey recommended that Monteith should try to 'cut a deal' directly with his master, James Monteith, as it should prove the most cost-effective option.

Archibald Monteith met with his master to discuss the matter, but James told him he was too highly valued as a transmuted slave, and therefore he was reluctant to grant him early release. However, after a short delay, possibly sensitive to Monteith's disappointment, James changed his mind and said he would accept £90 in exchange for the three remaining years of his apprenticeship. But it was more than Monteith could afford and, after falling into silence, he left the meeting, devastated.

Monteith's response was not lost on James. They had, after all, grown up together. The following morning, he called on him to say that the family had reflected on his disappointment and were prepared to reduce the sum to £50, a sum Monteith was just able to raise. It was a joyous moment when his discharge papers were delivered. After his kidnap and some twenty-six years of slavery, he was finally freed on 1 June 1837. His emotions were beyond the comprehension of anyone who has not experienced slavery.

'Several remarkable and honourable offers' soon arrived for positions as overseer from different plantations, but all were refused.[40] Instead, Monteith accepted an offer from the Moravian brethren to become a helper for all the mission stations at a salary of £12 per annum. In this he found contentment. He lived on his 30-acre plot in his house at Rosehall with his wife and daughter, finding satisfaction and purpose in caring for the spiritual needs of others, who, like himself, had suffered or witnessed terrible cruelty, and who, with faith, aspired to enter Heaven.[41] He forbade his congregation from stealing the property of their masters, as was the common habit, as it was not theirs to take.[42] They might have reflected that such a theft was nothing compared to the theft of a man's liberty for enslavement. But, correctly for Monteith, the path of virtue offered a much greater prize—spiritual freedom.

The 'testimony' of Monteith's life was written and published by the Moravian brethren as a statement of his faith, focusing on his religious enlightenment. It brushes over the many cruelties and injustices which must have been imposed on him during the different stages of his life. That said, he appears to have been fortunate in his master. John Monteith's choice to live with his black 'partner' and their children, and bequeath them his estate, suggests a more progressive attitude towards race. He was, however, still a slave owner, and his slaves, like any others, were afforded no legal rights.

Unlike Robert Wedderburn, whose instincts were to fight the system from the outside in order to drive through fundamental change, Monteith's instincts were to work within the system and offer, through forgiveness, spiritual peace to the oppressed. Robert's courageous sermons actively challenging the political system contributed to the reframing of attitudes and legislative change—changes which ultimately encouraged white owners in Jamaica to allow people like Monteith to preach to their slaves; something unthinkable only a few years before. That the major plantation owner in his region proved to be Robert's half brother, Andrew Wedderburn, would no doubt have caused Robert some ironic amusement.

All this said, a thought must be spared for the parents of young Aniaso, whose only son was abducted from his home in Nri when he was an innocent child. There would be no reprieve from the guilt that would have haunted them for leaving the boy alone that fateful day, or for the endless stress of wondering if he was dead or alive, happy or in anguish. It begs an important question of whether the civil society that rewarded a man for stealing someone's child had lost its sense of right and wrong.

Monteith understood implicitly what was right and good according to the Bible's teachings. He chose to dedicate his life to empowering his fellow victims of slavery to forgive their oppressors and thus liberate themselves spiritually. He helped his congregation understand the moral choices needed for the deliverance of a better and fairer society, which would serve to enhance their long-awaited freedom. After a life dedicated to the spreading of God's word, Monteith died in Jamaica in 1864.

8

The Terrors of the Middle Passage: Sam Robinson and James Irving

Time was hanging heavily for the officers of the *Lady Neilson*, a Liverpool slaver sailing in the summer of 1800 with its cargo of goods bound for the West African coast. But for fourteen-year-old Sam Robinson from Lesmahagow, in Dumfrieshire, for whom this was his maiden voyage, it was all fresh and new. It had taken him time to familiarise himself with the thirty-five-man crew, but he had made some friends, and particularly a boy named Jem, who was slightly older. To assuage the monotony of the passage, the officers tried to pit the two boys against each other by suggesting that the other was spoiling for a fight, but seeing through the sham, the boys paid no attention. Then, one afternoon, after Sam and Jem had been cleaning the decks, Captain Ward ordered the steward to 'bring up the cat'.[1]

For no apparent reason other than to provide the officers and crew with some barbaric entertainment, Sam was ordered to give his friend a dozen lashes and not hold back. With Jem's back bare and thumbs secured in 'mizzen shrouds', Sam carried out the order as gently as he thought he could get away with.[2] All the same, the skin on Jem's back broke into welts of white and blue, and when Sam had finished, Jem was ordered to return the compliment. Afterwards, with both of them in searing pain, the cat was placed back in Sam's hand and he was ordered to give Jem another dozen lashes, this time on his raw wounds. After this, with Jem about to repeat the punishment to Sam, the steward whispered to him that a fight was all that was wanted. Taking note, Sam resisted Jem's efforts to tie him up and shoved him to the floor, but he was up in a moment and punched Sam in the eye, causing him to see 'stars like the milky way'. A lengthy fist fight followed before Jem finally gave in. After this worthy exhibition of brutality, the boys were rewarded with a glass of brandy and a night off watch duty.

Life for a cabin boy on board a slaver was harsh and unpitying. Crewmembers were often forced into service due to debt or in an attempt to escape the law. They were vulnerable to vicious punishment from the captain and to the same diseases that killed the slaves under their charge. According to a survey taken between 1784 and 1790, only a decade before the *Lady Nelson* sailed from Liverpool, mortality rates among sailors on slave ships averaged 20 per cent.

Aside from Liverpool, London and Bristol were the principal British ports for the 'triangular trade' between Britain, West Africa, the Caribbean or North America. From one of these cities, the slave ships set sail for West Africa, typically with a cargo of assorted manufactured goods, which would be traded with African merchants and rulers in exchange for slaves. The crew would then transport the slaves on the so-called Middle Passage to the Caribbean or perhaps Virginia, sell them there and take on a cargo of usually sugar or tobacco or some other commodity before returning home. In the late 1790s, such a voyage would normally take just under eleven months to complete, though it could vary by up to three months, and sometimes much more, depending on the points of departure and destination, the seamanship of the captain and crew, the vagaries of the currents, wind and weather, and the time it took to purchase the human cargo.[3]

Two different approaches were adopted for the trading of slaves. The first was to buy from a trade castle or fort situated on the coast of West Africa, to which local African rulers sold their slaves in advance. These forts included a prison for slaves and a storehouse, where a permanent supply of European goods were kept available in exchange for slaves. They were protected by European troops and often under the control of a chartered company such as the English Royal African Company, and later private companies such as Grant, Sargent and Oswald at Bunce Island. Under this arrangement, each slave had to be judged as fit for purchase from the local African chiefs or rulers by the factory surgeon before acceptance into the fort.

The second approach was to trade directly with African rulers or merchants, either on shore or on the deck of the ship, whereby local traders would bring the slaves on board to negotiate a sale directly with the captain.[4] In both cases, firearms and strong drink were key supplies traded for slaves. Either way, delays had an inevitable impact on the mortality of both the slaves and the crew.[5] In this regard, the traders were in the hands of their African counterparts and their governing elite, who were themselves dependant upon the supply of slaves from the interior.

In the course of an estimated 27,000 voyages between sixteenth and eighteenth centuries, of which 12,000 were made by British or British colonial (mainly North American) crews, some 12 million slaves, predominantly male, were transported to the Americas.[6] Of this total number, about 1.5 million failed to complete the journey. When opening the parliamentary debate on the slave trade in 1789, William Wilberforce put this at 12.5 per cent of slaves who took the Middle Passage. Mortality rates of crews were also terrible; in 1787, to take an especially bad year, average losses of sailors were put at 25 per cent.[7]

Slave ships, known as slavers, were built for speed and agility, and were relatively small compared to other merchant ships. They usually carried between 200 and 400 slaves, with the smaller ones, more often than not, suffering a lower loss of life. Notwithstanding the inhuman treatment meted out on board, it was in the captain's best interests to reach port with his human cargo in a fit and healthy condition, ready for auction. A dead slave was a financial loss on the balance sheet.

Despite this, slaves were crammed in sordid conditions into the shallow lower decks of slave ships. Men were separated from women and children by a strong partition across the width of the ship, and they were typically shackled in pairs so that movement was difficult and painful. Access to cone-shaped pots placed for sanitary use was hugely problematic for those positioned far away, and fights often broke out when people tried to reach them. This lack of access to toilet pots caused people to defecate where they lay, which gave rise to infection and illness, further reducing sanitation. The most common cause of death came from a gastrointestinal disease called 'the bloody flux'. The conditions in which slaves were forced to live and try to survive were hideous.

The Scots played their part in crewing these ships, providing, for example, 7 per cent of crews out of Liverpool between 1798 and 1807, 6 per cent out of Bristol between 1789 and 1794, and 20 per cent of the slaver captains sailing out of Liverpool between 1785 and 1807. Meanwhile, with Scottish-trained surgeons facing limited career opportunities at home, there were many who were lured by the profits of the slave trade. In the second half of the eighteenth century, an astonishing 85 per cent of all medical graduates in Britain were trained in Scottish universities; by the end of the century, around 40 per cent of them had worked in the slave trade.[8]

So it was by no means unusual for Sam Robinson, a young Scot, to set out for Liverpool and join the trade to which so many of his countrymen owed their living. However, the harshness of life on board a slaver may have been worse than what he had been expecting.

Shortly after being forced to fight with his friend Jem, Sam was in for another shock. Weary and seasick, he climbed down from the maintop gallant yard, some 70 feet above deck. It had been a gruelling three-hour watch in strong winds. His replacement was another friend and fellow Scot, Thomas Hannah, an eighteen-year-old from Wigtown, near to Sam's hometown of Barglass in the Dumfries and Galloway region. An hour later, the mast snapped, catapulting Thomas into the frothy sea. Before a boat could be lowered, the keen wind had pushed the ship out of reach of the boy, and he was left to his fate.

Many years later, in 1867, Sam Robinson published his collection of letters home from his boyhood adventures in a book entitled *A Sailor Boy's Experience Aboard a Slave Ship*. In it, he described how the ship completed its maiden voyage at Liverpool eleven months later in March 1801. Some 300 slaves, plus commodities, had been purchased in the Bight of Biafra—off shore at Rio Cestos and then from three English fortresses. Before the final leg home, the ship journeyed to Demerara where the cargo was exchanged for sugar, rum and coffee. In the course of that journey, Sam injured his ankle after a fall onto the main deck. He would never fully recover from the injury and it would have a significant impact on his life, though in some regards, to his advantage. After eighteen months in England and Scotland, he was fit enough for his next voyage, this time aboard the *Crescent*, which sailed from the Thames on 13 September 1802.[9]

Sam had been inspired to go to sea in the first place by the adventuresome tales of his uncle, a captain of a merchant ship, and his second cousin, a major ship owner in Liverpool. Now, for this second voyage aboard the *Crescent*, he would be serving under his uncle, Captain Cowan.

The *Crescent* was 260 tons and licensed to carry 272 slaves. With a brief respite in the Anglo-French Wars, the Royal Navy was no longer using press gangs to gather their crews and an abundance of sailors had become available for employment. The thirty-six men required for the *Crescent* were secured at only £1 16/- a month compared to the £6 a month paid to the crew of the *Lady Neilson* the year before.[10] Of the six boys taken, Sam was the youngest.

On 8 December 1802, the *Crescent* dropped anchor off Cape Coast Castle, a British slave fort on the Gold Coast of Africa, in present-day Ghana.[11] By chance, Captain Cowan found an African agent with whom he contracted the purchase of the desired number of slaves. The ship's cargo, which had been loaded in London, immediately began to be taken on shore on boats, each paddled by twelve local men, with Sam sitting at the helm of one of them. As a non-swimmer, Sam was initially frightened by the surf, but he was soon won round by the thrill of being surged high up onto the sandy beach. Once the cargo had been offloaded and Sam was back on board, the *Crescent* purchased provisions for the

Middle Passage. Meanwhile, Captain Cowan was confident that the slaves would be ready for boarding before the expected onslaught of the rainy season. This, however, was not the case. While they had been purchasing provisions, their agent had died and 'not a single slave was forthcoming'.[12] It fell to Sam and his crew of locals to repatriate the offloaded goods onto the ship—a much tougher task in the face of the strong Atlantic surf.

With the anticipated source of slaves denied them, the ship trawled wearily up and down the 400-mile rocky coast as far as Cape Palmas in modern-day Liberia, scanning the shore for a fire—the signal that slaves were available for sale. Whenever they saw fires and dropped anchor, as they often did, the ship was surrounded by canoes in minutes, but the vendors only ever had a handful of slaves to sell—proof that the ground had already been well tilled by other slavers.

Months passed and the rainy season descended, bringing with it tornadoes, common along the West African coast. Sam described one as lashing 'the surface of the sea into white foam, blowing so strong as to prevent the waves from rising; the water smooth as a milk basin, and of the same colour ... the rain rushes down, every drop literally as large as a gooseberry ... while at very short intervals a burst of fire ... sometimes assuming the form of a gigantic tree, whose trunk and branches are alternatively of blue and silver in stained glass ... when the thunder strikes... a combined sound is emitted of the most appalling character.'[13] The survival of both ship and men were on the line.

At Cape Lahoo, a local chief ingratiated himself with Captain Cowan, who agreed to deliver him a substantial supply of goods on the promise of slaves. But despite many visits to the ship, the chief failed to keep his end of the bargain. The captain, thinking he was being taken for a fool, sought revenge. Unaware of the threat, the chief came on board with his usual bodyguard of eight powerful men, to seek delivery of more goods. Cowan invited him with great civility into his cabin to enjoy a glass of 'grog', and there, he placed him 'fast in irons'. Upon hearing the commotion, his bodyguards dived into the sea to find safety in their three canoes, fearing they would be taken as slaves.

The kidnapping of the chief was contrary to international conventions, but regardless, Cowan weighed anchor for Cape Coast, a distance of some 200 hundred miles, anticipating that he would either secure a forced payment for the fraudulently acquired goods in return for his captive, or alternatively, keep him as a slave. The next British ship to anchor at Cape Lahoo was a Liverpool slaver. It was instantly surrounded by canoes with people demanding the release of their chief. For the sake of their own trade, the Liverpool slaver chased down the *Crescent* and eventually

Captain Cowan had no choice but to return the chief and accept the loss of his cargo.

Meanwhile, the lingering injury Sam had suffered to his ankle two years ago aboard the *Lady Neilson* had become infected. Despite the doctor cutting poison deep from the abscess, Sam weakened to such an extent that he needed help to get in and out of his hammock. Good friends on board cared for him night and day, though the steward falsely reported to Captain Cowan that Sam had made a complaint about the quantity of his rations. The captain placed Sam on reduced rations by way of punishment.[14]

A few days later they returned to Cape Coast Castle. Here, finally, slaves and fresh supplies were taken on board.[15] On 29 May 1803, after six months of cruising the coast, the *Crescent* began the Middle Passage. It was not a promising start. The south-east trade winds that were to carry the ship across the Atlantic proved elusive, and in the doldrums, an equatorial region prone to calms, the breeze disappeared altogether. Then matters worsened with an outbreak of smallpox, which was aggravated by the intense heat. The 'bloody flux' was also prevalent, killing both slaves and members of the crew. Sam, still suffering from his infected ankle, came down with this ailment. Fearing for his life, he eventually persuaded the doctor to give him an opium pill, which helped purge the illness overnight.

Further into the journey, they came across a Dutch man-of-war heading for the Cape of Good Hope. As well as taking on some welcome supplies of cheese, ham and sugar, they learned that war had once again broken out between Britain and France. On the watch from now on, eyes were peeled for the enemy.

Off the coast of Barbados, a French brig, smaller than the *Crescent*, came into view. Captain Cowan ordered his crew to catch up with her. Upon being welcomed on board, Cowan was assured by the French captain that he had no knowledge of war between their countries, and in light of this, Cowan chose to pass up the chance of taking a smaller brig captive and seizing its cargo as war bounty for himself and his crew.

The next morning, another suspicious sail was spotted on the horizon: a schooner, thought to be a French privateer. With no cannon on board the *Crescent*, nor enough arms and ammunition for the crew to defend themselves against a concerted attack, they made a run for it. In time, the faster schooner gained ground, firing cannon shot without striking, until it launched a boat, which came alongside the *Crescent*. In doing so, it was clear they were not hostile; indeed, the schooner turned out to be a British rather than French privateer. The schooner captain confirmed that war had broken out between France and Britain, and upon hearing about the French brig, he set off in pursuit, eager to claim the bounty.

After a close brush with the reefs off Barbados, which very nearly proved fatal, the *Crescent* found safe anchor at Carlisle Bay, Barbados. Fresh supplies of meat and water were taken on board, which, after a hellish voyage and near death on the reefs, provided 'a turn of fortune we durst hardly dream of,' wrote Sam. The captain's orders from the ship owners were to sail to Port Royal, St Vincent, and if they could not sell their slave cargo there, to proceed to Kingston, Jamaica.

Due to the hostilities, all British ships once in port were subject to press ganging by the Royal Navy to man the ships of war for service against the French. Upon learning that HMS *Tartar*, a Royal Navy frigate, was at Port Royal, Jamaica, most of the crew of the *Crescent* walked out of the ship in Barbados, choosing to forego their pay of eighteen months rather than face the certainty of being pressed.[16] An enraged Captain Cowan refused to allow the men to take their hammocks with them.

The *Crescent* was thus reduced to a crew of nine: the captain, two mates, the doctor, armourer, cook, steward, and two boys, one of whom was Sam, still too weak to stand. With this motley crew, they needed to sail a further 1,500 miles and deliver a cargo of some 270 slaves, less the thirty who had already died.

With only the officers and two boys able to steer the ship—in Sam's case while sitting in a chair—the *Crescent* made remarkable progress, reaching its two destinations safely with the help of fair winds. First was St Vincent, where Sam wrote of entering the harbour and seeing the 'old gibbets with the iron framework in which victims had been suspended, swinging and shrieking on their rusty hinges, the sight and sound of which made me shiver'.[17] The unfortunate men in these cages were seventeen mutineers, crew members of a British frigate, the officers of which they had murdered before attempting to take the ship to an enemy port—evidently, without success.

The *Crescent* entered the next port of Kingston several days later, on 4 August 1803. In doing so, they drifted under the stern of the *Tartar*, which was lying at anchor close to their captured war bounty, an 80-gun French frigate, *La Creole*.[18] Hailed to heave over, a lieutenant and eight men boarded the *Crescent* in order to press its sailors into the service of the Royal Navy. Having called all hands on deck, the officer was, perhaps understandably, both indignant and incredulous at the apparent absence of crew to press.

Every nook and cranny of the ship was searched, but to no avail, and the lieutenant found his choice reduced to three candidates. The first was the armourer, a thick set man of short stature, whose bow legs rendered him lame, but in spite of this, once he had shown the officer that he could walk, he was ordered into service. The second, a boy reduced to a skeleton by the flux, was also approved as fit for service. Both were sent onshore, leaving Sam as the remaining candidate. Remaining seated, he did not reply when asked 'Who are you?' but simply held up his bandaged foot. Saying no more, the lieutenant left the ship, only to return with a doctor who, thankfully for Sam, found he was unfit for service. Having relieved Captain Cowan of the back pay due to his two luckless victims, the lieutenant departed the ship bearing their worldly possessions.

Captain Cowan's attention now turned to the slaves in his hold. The healthy were taken on shore, while the sick, of whom thirty were in a 'precarious state', remained on board by order of the port authorities who were nervous about the spread of smallpox. Very soon they started to die.

When in harbour, it was forbidden to dispose of corpses overboard as was the usual practice at sea. Instead, they needed to be buried on shore in the sand of the palisade, and this unsavoury task fell to Sam, who was helped by a shipmate, Tom. Lacking the necessary strength to move the corpses, they fastened a rope around each of them, and after lowering them into the water, towed them one by one to the shore for burial in temporary pits. It moved Sam to reflect in his letters home on the waste of these lives, bringing him to say write that 'to traffic in human beings is a wicked and unjustifiable thing'. He also questioned how the lot of the slave differed from that of the soldier or sailor pressed into service, asking whether the latter was any less a slave than a 'poor African carried to the West Indies'.

> In a great many cases the balance is in favour of the African; he is well lodged, well fed, moderately wrought and ... well used in every way ... or comparatively, comfortable, while the soldier or sailor is compelled by a power he cannot resist, to imbrue his hands in the blood of those called enemies, or be butchered himself, to gratify the ambition of wicked men who make war a pastime; and, if he refuses, is flogged or shot like a rabid dog. Which of the two is the most abject subject of slavery. Well, saith the poet, "Were subjects wise, war is a game kings would not play at."[19]

In Kingston, Sam perceived a clear difference between the slave in the West Indies and those he had seen in Africa.

> At home he is a slave—stalking about in naked majesty, liable to be sacrificed on the grave of his chief to deprecate the wrath of an imaginary demon—his manner sullen and aimless; in fact a very hopeless animal for good either to himself or anyone else. When established on an estate in Jamaica, a comfortable cabin is provided for him; daily rations, with clothes suitable for his work; with a piece of land upon which he raises

vegetables and fruit, keeps a stock of pigs, goats and poultry with the whole of every Saturday to cultivate and dispose of the produce [and] in many cases [able] to purchase his freedom ... and have all the necessaries and even many of the luxuries in life.[20]

Sam also observed black men and women on the wharf and public promenades 'enjoying themselves with a buoyancy of mirth wholly their own ... free of the worn expression too often met with in the countenances and bearing of peasantry of Great Britain'. He wrote of hearing from the houses music and dancing, and seeing festivals with slaves 'caper[ing]... boisterously'. When, however, he witnessed slaves at work, he identified four 'besetting sins', namely, 'laziness, drunkenness, stealing and lying', and considered that if such bad habits could 'be got the better of', there would seldom be any need for punishment.[21]

Such opinions make difficult reading in the twenty-first century. It is possible that Sam, being young and naïve, was influenced by what others had told him—people who may have had their own reasons for distorting the truth—or himself wanted to wash over the cruelty of slavery to assuage his own guilt and create a better impression of himself for those he was writing to. He may have even have edited his letters ahead of publication in 1867, decades after the abolition of slavery, in an attempt to portray his involvement in a more favourable light. Lastly, by insisting that the lot of the slaves was in fact reasonable, if not good, he may have wanted to create a greater contrast between plight of slaves and the brutal lives of pressed servicemen, for whom he felt an affinity. The sailors he conversed with and learned from were doubtless far more scathing about the evil of press ganging, which they themselves feared, than of slavery, which they facilitated for profit.

Due to his damaged ankle, Sam was put in the care of an old lady in Rum Street, Kingston, where he stayed for several weeks sleeping in his hammock, hung in the courtyard of the house. There he conversed with people who came and went, and observed the world around him, particularly the moral code by which people lived, which shocked his Protestant sensitivities:

> With exception of those married in Europe, there is no such thing ... as marriage. Among the lower tribe prostitution is the rule in every sense of the word. In the middle classes concubinage is the order of the day.[22]

Two of his fellow boarders on Rum Street were middle-aged sisters, neither of whom had married and both of whom were amazed to learn that Sam was one of seven children born to the same parents. These ladies lived by the prostitution of their daughters, 'whom they hire out for a given time—as the case may be,' wrote Sam, 'for a consideration, and who during that time remain quite faithful to their marriage, as they call it and they believe it to be right and proper.' He added that should the period of their 'engagement' involve their 'keeper' being absent, the girls saw it as their duty to remain faithful during that absence; to fail in this would be 'to lose their caste and sink to common prostitution'. Sam's own opinions of morality were confounded by the fact that 'all act on the principle without the most distant idea that anything is wrong'.

Preparations were in hand for the *Crescent*'s return leg to England. Overall, it had been a less than successful voyage: a total of around forty slaves had been lost to smallpox and other causes—valued at about £2,000—and then, to top it off, there was an accident in the harbour involving one of the ship's boats, costing the lives of a crew member and three black men.

In place of the slaves, a cargo of mahogany, logwood, and Jamaican pepper was taken on board, but departure was delayed pending the hiring of a crew, which was quite a challenge given the efficiency of the Royal Navy's press gangs and the scores of merchant ships gathered on the same errand. In the event, recourse was made to French prisoners of war, who were happy to get closer to home by accepting a place. Six Frenchmen and a boy from the prison in Kingston were added to the *Crescent*'s roster.

Having joined a convoy of 100 merchant ships under the command of the Royal Navy's magnificent HMS *Cumberland*, the *Crescent* sailed past the 'lovely green isle of Jamaica'.[23] Later, the 'lofty mountains of St Domingo away to the south and the blue hills of Cuba to the north' dazzled Sam, providing a backdrop to the magnificent sight of the convoy, 'seldom to be seen and never to be forgotten'.[24]

Strict protocols had to be followed by each ship in the convoy. The challenge of staying together was considerable, with the threat of disruptive storms and the inability of some ships to keep pace—much to the frustration of the navy. There were other challenges, too. Except during a period of freezing weather experienced as they passed Newfoundland over Christmas 1803, the crew of the *Crescent* were given little rest from invasive critters that had inadvertently been brought on board in the West Indies. Centipedes persisted in nesting in their ears as they slept, and several people were stung by scorpions, including Sam, who needed the surgeon to souse his finger in rum as it swelled black around the nail.

There were heavy gales and relentless battles with mountainous waves. In the mid-Atlantic, Sam watched as disaster overran the beautiful *La Creole*, the French prize he had first seen in Kingston harbour. The frigate somehow caught fire and began taking on water at a rate her pumps could not repel. The dramatic scene of the ship in her death throes held Sam entranced. When the fire reached the magazine, 'a roar' rang out 'like the bellow of Mount Stromboli, while glowing fragments of *La Creole* were thrown high into the air—the waters closing over the blazing hull, looking as innocent as if nothing particular had taken place'.[25]

On 29 January 1804, two years after departing London, the *Crescent* docked once more at the capital, but only after the ship had been boarded on a number of occasions by naval officers eager to press men into service. Only too aware of this threat, sailors hid in cavities they had built on board to avoid detection. It worked for all but one, whose hiding place was discovered with the inevitable consequences.

As he parted the *Crescent*, Sam reflected that he had joined the vessel a robust and active boy of fourteen but had returned 'a poor sallow skeleton, needing a staff to enable me to crawl along the street, my hopes of following the profession of my choice blasted in the bud, and my future prospects dark indeed'. Once back in Liverpool, a doctor recommended the amputation of his foot and its replacement with a cork substitute. He also told him to give up ideas of returning to the sea. His letters, always free of self-pity, end there. Whether he did lose his foot or not is uncertain, though he wrote later that the accident ended his career.

In 1807, the Slave Trade Act became law, rendering the activities of slave ships illegal 'in accordance with the united voice of a generous and philanthropic people'.[26, 27] In his concluding editorial remarks, written in 1867, of his life on a slave ship, Sam said, 'Whether I may have viewed everything without prejudice or not, I am not a proper judge; but I have done my best to do so....' One cannot ask for much more. What is to be drawn from his record rests with the reader. Having married Margaret McFie in 1821 in Kirkinner, Wigtownshire, and had several children, Sam Robinson died in Lesmahagow in 1875 at the ripe old age of eighty-nine.

Attention now turns to another account of life on a slaver: that of James Irving, captain of the *Anna*. He departed Liverpool docks on 3 May 1789, bound for Africa. It was his first command, and not only that, it was the *Anna*'s maiden voyage.[28] Prior to his appointment, Irving had served on seven voyages, the majority in the triangle trade, as a surgeon, with his first in 1782. It was testimony to the regard in which he was held by his employers, Baker and Dawson, that he was thought ready, at the comparatively young age of twenty-nine, for the challenges demanded of a captain.[29]

The *Anna*, in keeping with most of the vessels Irving had served on, was a slave ship. It had a crew of just eight and was licensed under the Dolben Act to carry eighty slaves.[30] Under his new role as captain, albeit of a comparatively small vessel, Irving would have welcomed 'the prospect of enhanced financial reward', not least through the payment of commission from the sale of slaves.[31] If the trip was successful, his profits could provide the foundations for a comfortable life for himself and his wife of four years, Mary Tunstell.

On 27 May 1789, just over three weeks into the voyage, Irving, by now in the Atlantic, became uncertain of the ship's position. Without land in sight, he determined that they must be positioned somewhere between the Canaries and the Barbary Coast, in western Morocco. At midnight all seemed fair, but Irving was aware of strong currents at play. A short time later, without warning, the first of a series of huge breakers smashed down onto the ship, flooding its deck. In response, Irving ordered the sails set to the wind, but one heavy wave was followed by the next, and the ship bumped and thumped into the hollows of the sea. Panic began to set in among the crew. The force of the ocean was beginning to break up the ship; all unnecessary weight on the deck was hurled overboard in an effort to lighten it. There were still three hours until sunrise, when unexpectedly, the ship's belly grounded on a reef.[32] Irving considered abandoning the ship and taking their chances on a raft, but with the *Anna* stuck fast, it was decided to sweat it out until morning.

As dawn broke, to their collective relief, they found themselves in only four feet of water and a short distance from the shore. After wading onto the beach, their eyes scanned a bleak prospect of featureless flat sand, which at low tide was speckled with substantial rocks. They believed they had hit upon Tenerife, the largest of the Canary Islands. An inspection of the ship determined that, with two large holes puncturing its hull, it was beyond saving. What was possible to carry was taken from the ship, while $1,000 of currency was buried in the sand along with provisions and clothes for possible future use. As the heat of the sun began to bear down on the men, they elected to head for Santa Cruz and, hopefully, safety.

They had assumed that this part of the island was uninhabited, but this was disagreeably disproved when they spotted a human footprint, and later the prints of camels and a dog. Following the shore, tiring in the heat, the men noticed pieces of wreckage of a ship other than the *Anna*, drawn to the beach by the tide. Later, at night, armed with a blunderbuss, they corralled together around a fire, seeking warmth.

The next day, their march over this desolate landscape was resumed. Most concerning was their dwindling stock of water, which was already down to the emergency supply. They were walking along a cliff top that followed the shoreline immediately above the sea, when they spotted in the distance a flock of sheep; at the same moment, they saw three people running away from them. Mixed emotions rose within each of their stomachs—hope, fear, resolution, cowardice. Within a short time, three different 'copper coloured natives' appeared over the rise before them, 'running at full speed and shouting hideously'.[33] Several more followed shortly afterwards, armed with long knives and muskets. The shocked crew were seized by their throats, had their bundles stolen and their clothes torn off their backs. In the frenzy to secure bounty, one of the weaker and less successful of the assailants attempted to stab Irving with a long dagger. It was only thanks to one of his men coming to his rescue that he escaped without getting 'terribly mangled'.

As yet more Arabs emerged from tents situated half a mile away, the thuggery continued, until Irving and his men were stripped almost naked. They were then escorted roughly to the tents, which sat like molehills in the sand. The captives were divided up among the captors. Irving found himself alone in a tent under the charge of a woman, while the men made off to plunder what they could from the wreck. Not knowing the whereabouts of his crew, Irving reflected on his 'deplorable condition'. It is very likely that, in his misery, he thought of his wife, whom he loved dearly, in far-off Liverpool, and what he had left behind in Scotland when he had departed as a teenager so many years before.

James Irving was born in Langholm in the Scottish Borders on 15 December 1759 to John Irving, a blacksmith and innkeeper, and his wife Isobel Little.[34] These modest beginnings did not prevent James from enjoying a good education at the town's parish school, sufficient for him to enter training as a surgeon sometime after the age of fourteen. Although not certain, this training, which typically took between three to seven years, might have been undertaken in Dumfries. Alternatively, it is possible that Irvine was apprenticed to Andrew Little, possibly a relative of his mother and once a surgeon of a Liverpool ship, who latterly lived in Langholm and taught in a local private school. If so, it might explain why it was to Liverpool that Irving headed to begin his career at sea.[35] Whatever the case, he was passed as a 'Surgeon to African Ships' by the Company of Surgeons, predecessor to the Royal College of Surgeons of England, on 2 April 1779.[36]

Thus it was in the role of surgeon that, during his third voyage, the twenty-three-year-old Irving first experienced Africa, arriving with the *Vulture* at Bonny in the Bight of Benin in late 1783, 'an area known for its efficiency, rapid loading rates and the effective protection of credit through powerful centralised African authority'.[37] In the course of further slave voyages that followed, Irving struck up a friendship with John Clegg, who had been promoted from 'a seaman to one of mate'.[38] When he received his first command, Irving did not hesitate to appoint Clegg his first mate.

It was during Irving's second slaving voyage, with Captain Fargher aboard the *Jane*, commencing in 1786, that he started a correspondence with his wife, Mary, whom he had recently married. In his first letter he expressed his love and longing for her, no doubt intensified by his separation, and called upon 'The Almighty' to look after her until his return.[39] In a letter dated 4 December 1786, written to his wife from Tobago, the frustrations of being away from her boiled to the surface. He was resentful at being stuck in port awaiting 'the disposal of our very disagreeable cargo', which was delayed for a further five days pending sale. He was tired of 'this unnatural accursed trade', and reflected that if nothing changed, when the chance arose he would seek alternative work, though he noted that to do so may not be easy.[40] He ended his letter abruptly, complaining, 'our black cattle are intolerably noisy and I'm almost melted in the midst of five or six hundred of them'. The apparent contradictions of a God-fearing man who loved his wife and had trained as a surgeon for the care of the sick are manifest, but they are contradictions to which Irving himself remained blind. Instead, he conformed to the widely held prejudices of his time.

After his return to Liverpool, Irving was promoted to surgeon on *The Princess Royal*, the largest ship in the owners' fleet, capable of carrying 800 slaves. Responsibility for maintaining the health of this number, in addition to a crew of eighty-three, lay with Irving. It demonstrates the faith his employers placed in him. In his letters, however, he gave little information on his ministrations of the slaves. This suggests he had little empathy for them as his patients or indeed as fellow human beings, though in writing to his wife, he may also have wanted to spare her, and himself, the moral stigma of association with the catalogue of death and disease brought on by such manifestly cruel treatment. Rather, his comments were confined to his own welfare and that of the officers.[41] Nevertheless, Irving's medical skills and temperament impressed his captain, William Sherwood, who twice sailed with him as his surgeon. This led him to recommend Irving for the command of a slave ship, a golden opportunity for pecuniary rewards, which would enable him to establish himself as a merchant. It was well known, however, that 'five captains died in the trade for every one who attained the status of merchant'.[42]

The truth of this statistic could not have been more apparent to Irving as he sat in gloomy solitude in his captor's tent, divested of both his clothing and his dignity, not knowing where he was, though now convinced he must be somewhere on the Barbary Coast. For the next twelve days Irving survived on shellfish, seeing periodically some of his fellow crew members. When they had the opportunity to talk, they resolved to do whatever they could to keep together, accepting together whatever fate was in store for them. This was soon put to the test as the man who, said Irving, 'claim[ed] me as his property', tried to take him from the others. After being 'knocked to the ground by several blows', Irving clung to his companions, preferring to die there and then rather than be separated. In the event, the second mate and apprentice were taken away, leaving behind Irving, his cousin (also James Irving) and his chief mate, John Clegg. The rest of the crew had already been dispersed for sale.

For the next ten days, Irving and his two crew were forced on a long and arduous march that pushed them to the limits of their endurance. They walked over 'several hills of accumulated sand that kept blowing before the wind like snow', and were frequently spat upon and insulted. Occasionally Irving was 'indulged' with a ride on one of the six camels forming the caravan. Water was given to the prisoners by pouring it into their hats for them to drink. Their captors, Sunni Muslims, held a deep-rooted hostility towards Christians, and to have served them water in a dish would have contaminated the vessel for good.[43] For the same reason, they were served their rations on an old wooden plate.

They arrived at the town of Goulimine on 16 June 1789. Irving was sold to a master called Bilade, who had escorted the men for the latter part of the journey. Clegg and his cousin were taken to the 'king' known as 'Muley Abderhaman'.[44] This was Mawlay 'Abd al-Rahman, the exiled son of Sidi Muhammad, emperor of Morocco. Reduced to the status of a slave, Irving was forced to cart water while his two colleagues toiled in the fields under the intense heat of the sun. Within a matter of days of his purchase by Bilade, Irving was sold for a second time, for 135 ducats to a man called Sheikh Brahim. They then resumed their journey, trekking alongside an entourage of twelve men on horseback, led by Sheikh Brahim, in a north-easterly direction through mountainous terrain. On 24 June, they arrived at a small settlement called Tellin, some 30 miles away.

At Tellin, Irving and his two crew saw their fate before them: a pitiful group of Frenchmen were toiling in the arid fields. 'I could have died rather than devote my life to be spent in so abject a state,' Irving later said, 'bereft of all Christian society, a slave to a savage race who despised and hated me for my belief.'[45] The Frenchmen had been bound for Senegal 'with a cargo suited for the gum trade', when they had foundered on the same stretch of coastline as the *Anna* on 2 or 3 January 1789. It was pieces of their wreckage that Irving and his crew had noticed on their march along the shore. They had managed to appeal to their consul at Salé to negotiate their release, but they had little hope of it being procured.

For the British, the situation seemed equally hopeless. Although Irving and his men were of much greater value to Sheikh Brahim if they could be exchanged for a ransom, their shipwreck had occurred in an area controlled by Mawlay 'Abd al-Rahman, outside the domains of his father, the emperor of Morocco, and therefore, beyond British diplomatic influence. With a feud ongoing between father and son, and each refusing to speak to the other, the emperor would not entreat his son to return the prisoners. There was, however, a spark of hope when Irving was permitted to write to John Hutchison, the British vice consul in Mogodore (now Essaouira) on 24 June 1789.

Irving laid his heart bare, explaining to Hutchison their circumstances and imploring him to do whatever it took to extract them from 'the most intolerable slavery'. 'If we were allowed to stay here to toil and be maltreated under a vertical sun,' he wrote, 'we shall soon be lost forever to ourselves, our wives and families, our country and all we hold dear.'

A price had, in fact, been demanded for the freedom of the French crew—100 dollars per head—but to Irving's disgust, it had not been paid. Fearing this, he specified who would lay out the same sums for him and those of his crew of whose whereabouts he was cognisant, confident that it would be met.[46] It came as a rude shock to discover the ransom placed on himself and his crew was 500 dollars a head. At that level, Irving could only offer surety for himself, his cousin and the nephew of one of his employers in Liverpool.

The efforts of Hutchison and his team of civil servants were strengthened by Irving's possession of what was known as 'the Mediterranean Pass', an insurance policy issued by the British government to protect shipping from 'capture or plunder by the Barbary pirates operating off the Atlantic as well as the Mediterranean Coast of North West Africa'.[47] Although not strictly applicable since Irving and his party had been captured by a nomadic desert tribe, it was nonetheless of some help. But events moved slowly. As Hutchison tried to thread a path through the seemingly intractable problems that blocked agreement between the various competing parties, Irving struggled to adapt to his role as a servant to Aaron Debauny, a Jew with whom he had been lodged. He was only too aware of the inferior status of Jews in Moroccan society.[48] He was also troubled by the harsh treatment meted out to his crew during their daily toil in the fields, where they were beaten and starved of adequate food.

By late August, Hutchison had agreed to redeem the ransoms from Sheikh Brahim for 1,200 dollars for all nine members of the crew. However, Brahim later changed his mind and attempted to negotiate a better deal. Because of this and the need of approval from the emperor, negotiations were once again stymied. The reason for the emperor's prevarication then became clear. He wanted the consul to provide him with an English doctor to attend to one of his sons, who was almost blind, and in return he would permit the release of the British crew. The eminent William Lempriere volunteered for this duty and travelled to Taroundant, where the unfortunate prince resided and close to where the crew was being held. Upon his arrival there, seven of Irving's crew were released and sent to Marrakech, leaving only Irving and James Drachen. Tragically, Drachen died shortly afterwards. That left Irving on his own for a further month, during which he suffered a second bout of fever, a recurrence of an enfeebling bout in September from which he had only recently recovered. Once restored, Irving was rescued from his solitude by Lempriere who, after informing the prince of Irving's training as a surgeon, was authorised to enlist him as his medical assistant.

Lempriere managed to improve his patient's sight, but during the five weeks the prince was under his care, both he and Irving were overwhelmed by others seeking cures for a vast range of ailments. Still, on 26 December 1789, their work was declared complete and Irving was finally delivered to freedom by the prince upon the emperor's order. They travelled with the prince to Marrakech as part of a spectacular caravan of 300 men mounted on horses, camels and mules. There, on New Year's Eve, Irving held a reunion with his crew, during which 'the greater part of the night was spent in reciting our hardships past and present'.

Although nominally free men, Irving and his crew still required the emperor's permission to leave the country, and he was not going to be rushed into giving it. The consul facilitated their move to Mogodore, on the west coast of Morocco, to be among Christians, but months passed without their permission being granted to return home. It emerged that the emperor sought satisfaction for two further conditions: the receipt of a present (previously requested) of a cannon and a mortar, and a letter from George III, naming the individuals for release.

The demand was met with muted interest from the British due to a long-running dispute with the emperor over tariffs. Goodwill was in short supply. Some two months later, in March 1790, the emperor changed his demand to the loan of a frigate to take one of his sons to Alexandria for his pilgrimage to Mecca. The next month, just as it seemed that an agreement was about to be concluded, the emperor died.

Under the new emperor, Mawley al-Yazid, the chances of repatriation for Irving and his crew seemed even slimmer than before. Described by Mr Matra, the British consul general, as 'a great bigot and decided enemy of every religion but his own', the emperor embarked on a reign of terror, executing his father's advisors, reversing his policies, and putting the country at risk of civil war.[48] Irving and his crew were placed under tighter security, but in July 1790, the sentries were suddenly removed from their lodgings and they were given their freedom. Why this happened is not clear, but diplomatic persistence will have played its part.

The brig *Bacchus* arrived in Dartmouth in the last week of October 1790, carrying Irving and his seven crew members. It had been seventeen months since their nightmare had begun. Joyfully, Irving was reunited with his wife and his first child, James, born in his absence on 4 December 1789. However, he could not rest long at home as financial pressures pushed him to accept a fresh command aboard another slaver, the *Ellen*. Weighing 134 tons with a length of 69 feet, it was licensed to carry 253 slaves.

The vessel, with Irving at its helm and his cousin as surgeon, sailed from Liverpool on 2 January 1791. The venture got off to an inauspicious start when the third mate and two other crew members attempted to jump ship before sailing; they were only prevented by Irving's holding a pistol to the head of the mate. Already short of a carpenter, he judged it better to take the risk of having three malcontents among his crew of thirty-five, than carrying on without them.[49]

Leaving a month late, the *Ellen* reached the Bight of Benin on 5 April 1791 and began the lengthy process of trawling the coast in search of slaves. This lasted five months until eventually they secured their cargo at Anamabu on the Gold Coast. On 16 September they departed for Trinidad with 253 slaves on board, their maximum number. By the time the ship had completed the Middle Passage, forty-seven slaves had died, together with six members of the thirty-five-man crew. Captain James Irving, aged thirty-one, was among the dead.[50] In his last letter to his wife written from Benin on 14 June 1791, he said, 'That the Almighty may long preserve you, so is my daily prayer. My good, nay best of girls, will be happy when she is informed that I am healthy, a state I have been in since I left her.... May [the] heavens keep you till the day comes when your company arms shall bless.' It was not to be.

In their letters home, neither James Irving nor Sam Robinson recorded much about the needs of the slaves entombed aboard the ships they sailed, despite the slaves' welfare being central to their respective duties. The reason for this can never be known, but it may have been because they wanted to spare their correspondents from the shocking realities of their business. It is clear from their diaries that both were God-fearing men. They nonetheless believed a slave was a commodity and therefore not to be treated as a human being. This is despite Robinson's acknowledgement that 'to traffic in human beings is a wicked and unjustifiable thing'.

Irving knew first-hand the fear, hopelessness and indignity of slavery, but he was able to return to the business without apparent conscience. Even despite his damaged health, he was ready to risk all for the money it offered. He made his choice, while the slaves aboard his ship had none.

9

The Findings of a Ship's Surgeon: James Ramsay and Charles Middleton

It was a chance encounter in the mid-Atlantic between HMS *Arundel*, sailing with a fleet of the Royal Navy, and the distressed slave ship *Swift* that would change James Ramsay's life forever. In response to a desperate appeal for medical assistance from the *Swift*'s captain to the fleet's commodore, it was only Ramsay, the *Arundel*'s surgeon, who volunteered to answer it. Thus it was he, with a handful of sailors, who approached the stricken *Swift* on a small rescue boat in response to their call. Long before they boarded, Ramsay's senses were assaulted by the putrid stench of death on the humid breeze. However, it could not prepare him for what he found as he stepped below deck.

On 27 November 1759, the Royal Navy's 500-ton *Arundel* had intercepted the Bristol-registered slaver *Swift*, a vessel of 100 tons.[1,2] It was taking its cargo from Bonny in the Bight of Biafra to Antigua. Upon leaving Africa, the *Swift* had had on board thirty-five crewmen and between 280 and 300 slaves, but it had been ravaged by dysentery since then. Many of the slaves and crew, including the surgeon, had already died. When Ramsay went below deck he saw 'black men naked, emaciated, dangerously ill of fluxes; black men desperately trying to catch a breath of fresh air, but hindered by the dead partners in their chains; black men wallowing in the blood and mucus, urine and faeces of the dead and the dying....'[3]

The filth, cleaned away every morning by the crew, was 'sufficient to turn even a sailor's stomach'.[4] By simply stepping aboard the ship and going below deck, Ramsay was placing himself at great personal risk from contagious diseases. With difficulty, he established that he was attending the needs of around 100 patients. It is not recorded for how long he administered them, but before leaving the *Swift*, he provided written instructions for their ongoing treatment.[5] To Ramsay, a man of great empathy, the experience 'kindled [an] undying enmity against the slave trade and slavery'.[6]

Despite their being confined in the dark, rancid air below deck, cramped and manacled each day for between eighteen and twenty-four hours, the health of slaves was logically of great importance to every slaver captain; a dead slave equated to a loss of investment and profit. Responsibility for it lay with the ship's surgeon, who, in addition to a salary and other benefits, received a payment for each slave sold on shore.[7] But how well qualified were surgeons aboard slavers in general, and how much control did they have over the welfare of the slaves and the crew? As the death of the *Swift*'s surgeon demonstrates, it was a job taken on at considerable personal risk.

Typically, a prospective surgeon or physician was apprenticed to a practitioner for several years before completing his training at a hospital or university. Surgeons were commissioned after examination at Surgeon's Hall in London. There were some highly qualified surgeons that served aboard slave ships, but for the most part, the standards were low and the motivation was purely financial.[8] Of all the surgeons employed in the British slave trade between 1785 and 1807, 38 per cent were Scots.[9]

Upon his appointment to a slave ship, it was critical for the surgeon, in speaking to the captain and the owner, to insist upon the loading of sufficient supplies of food and medicine.[10] Such an investment saved lives and protected profits, but unfortunately this demand was often ignored, resulting in supplies, if they were not replenished in Africa, running out during the Middle Passage, which compromised the interests of all parties.[11]

Once anchored off the coast of Africa, it was the surgeon's task to check that the slaves to be purchased were both fit and free from illness. Once the slaves were on board, the surgeon had to care for them as best he could, but if he was inexperienced, the diseases he encountered were often beyond his knowledge. This imperfect situation could then be exacerbated by delays in securing a full cargo of slaves. Once on the Middle Passage, the surgeon's duty each morning was to monitor the health and welfare of the cargo. Generally the sick were taken to a separate apartment where the quality of their treatment would vary according to the skill of the surgeon.

It was understood that slave ships were so dangerous to people's health because they brought about a convergence of the lethal diseases of three continents: Africa, Europe and the Americas. The long list included dysentery, malaria, smallpox, scurvy, syphilis and leprosy. Of these, dysentery (or the bloody flux) and malaria were considered the most destructive.[12] For the slaves, compounding the dangers posed by terrible sanitation and the spread of disease, were injuries due to accidents, fighting and flogging, and the provision of an unbalanced and inadequate diet. Meals were typically given at irregular intervals and preserved with so much salt as to render them virtually inedible. If sickness took hold, it was not uncommon for slaves to refuse medication. At other times, medication was not available. Faced with these endless challenges, the surgeon's ability to discharge his primary purpose—to maintain the wellbeing of his charges—was grossly reduced.[13]

Improvements were forthcoming. The Dolben Act of 1788 required the ship's surgeon aboard slavers to keep a 'regular and true journal', recording important statistical information during the voyage. The journal had to be delivered at the first British port at which the vessel arrived after leaving Africa.[14] The introduction of the act saw a decline in slave mortality, but the tight packing of slaves on board 'like herrings in a barrel' continued as before, and there was no statutory minimum introduced for standards of food and drink.[15] All that said, the risk of illness and death was not the sole preserve of the slaves. In a report by William Wilberforce in 1787, he estimated annual losses of sailors on slave ships at 25 per cent.[16]

Returning to the mid-Atlantic and HMS *Arundel*, James Ramsay, still horrified and distracted by what he had seen on the *Swift*, fell awkwardly as he clambered back on board, fracturing his thigh bone. The injury turned out to have far reaching consequences, but no more so than his brief insight into the slave trade. It had triggered in him a determination to fight the cruelty he had witnessed in whatever way he could. From his sickbed aboard the *Arundel*, he reported what he had seen below decks on the *Swift* to his captain, Charles Middleton, who was deeply moved by what he heard.

The injury Ramsay sustained ended his Royal Navy career for the foreseeable future and left him permanently lame, but also free to pursue his chosen mission in life. At no small price to himself and his family, he would come to be recognised as a leading influence in the growing campaign to end the slave trade. On that mission, his erstwhile captain and fellow Scot, Charles Middleton, would be a profound support.

Charles Middleton was born in Leith in 1726 to a customs collector from Bo'ness, West Lothian. His mother was great-granddaughter of Sir James Dundas of Arniston, and his first cousin was Henry Dundas. His father, meanwhile, was the son and grandson of two past principals of King's College, Aberdeen, the same university from which Ramsay had obtained a bursary to study under the influential moral philosopher Dr Thomas Reid. In 1741, having completed his school education, Middleton joined the Royal Navy and there demonstrated a rare aptitude for leadership that saw him advance rapidly through the ranks. Twenty years later in the West

Indies, as captain of HMS *Emerald*, his next command after the *Arundel*, he captured sixteen French warships and several privateers, earning him the gratitude of the merchants of Barbados. At this point, despite being at the peak of his naval career, Middleton elected to step back from the navy.

In 1761, he married Margaret Gambier, whom he had first met two decades before. Two years later, they moved to a house in Teston in Kent. For the next twelve years, Middleton farmed his estate as a country gentleman. He was recalled to the navy in 1775 upon the outbreak of the American War of Independence, and in 1778, was unexpectedly appointed comptroller of the navy, a key administrative position in which he prospered for the next twelve years. He was created a baronet in 1781 and launched a political career in 1783, serving as Tory member of parliament for Rochester. He was a loyal supporter of William Pitt and Henry Dundas, and a forthright advocate for naval reform, the need of which was made evident by the navy's failings in the American War. But when, in 1790, his efforts for reform were hamstrung by an unsupportive first lord of the Admiralty and the illness of George III, he resigned from his post as comptroller. Before then, however, he had ensured that the fleet was repaired, rebuilt and ready for war. He continued to make valuable contributions to the navy's administration until his retirement in 1805, when he was appointed, aged seventy-nine, Baron Barham of Teston.

In his long and distinguished career, Charles Middleton proved that he had the courage of his convictions and was not afraid to speak his mind when it mattered. His steely ambition enabled him to modernise radically an inefficient navy, and his achievements as an administrator placed him on a par with the great Samuel Pepys.[17] These characteristics of courage, ambition and administrative talent were to be valuable assets in the fight against slavery, as were Middleton's prominent social connections. With his wife, he actively encouraged politicians and churchmen, among them Thomas Clarkson and William Wilberforce, to work with him in support of the abolitionist cause. Indeed, Middleton is credited with initiating the latter's parliamentary campaign on abolitionism.

Middleton's first public speech, given on 12 June 1788, was on the subject of the overcrowding of slave ships. The choice of topic can almost certainly be linked to that day in November 1759 aboard HMS *Arundel*, when a shocked James Ramsay, ignoring the matter of his broken leg, told him of the atrocious and unacceptable conditions he had seen aboard the *Swift*.[18] Ramsay's description crystallised in both men an abhorrence for slavery and, at the same time, planted the seeds for a lifelong friendship. For Middleton this was founded on 'the fearless humanity which Ramsay displayed', and it gave the latter 'the patronage, friendship and esteem' of a highly influential personage.[19]

James Ramsay was born in Fraserburgh, Aberdeenshire, on 25 July 1733, the only son of ship's carpenter William Ramsay and Margaret Ogilvie of Purie in Angus. From a young age he demonstrated an active, if serious, mind, possibly inherited from his mother, a woman of strong faith. This may have influenced his early ambition upon leaving his local grammar school to study to become a clergyman. In the event, a shortage of family funds prevented him from taking this course, and instead, Ramsay served an apprenticeship in surgery and pharmacy with a local surgeon, Dr Alexander Findlay. In 1749, aged sixteen, he won a bursary of £5 to study for an arts degree at King's College, Aberdeen. In itself, it was insufficient to meet the cost of his lodgings, but it was soon supplemented by a further exhibition, which he gained on scholastic merit.

It was in Aberdeen that Ramsay came under the intellectual influences of Dr Thomas Reid, with whom he became a lifelong friend, and James Beattie, both leading thinkers in the Scottish Enlightenment.[20] Ramsay's talents were unquestionable. On one occasion, he was given responsibility to treat a young female servant who had been badly gored by a bull and thought beyond saving. Through his skilful treatment of the wound, the patient recovered. The girl's employer, a judge, was so impressed that he successfully managed to secure from King's College a further bursary for Ramsay of £15.

Upon his graduation from King's College in 1753, armed with yet another grant, Ramsay travelled to London to study surgery and pharmacy under Dr George Macaulay, physician and treasurer of the British Lying-In Hospital, with whom he lived for the next two years.[21, 22] Macaulay was another Scot, Edinburgh born and educated. On passing his examination at Surgeon's Hall, Ramsay entered the Royal Navy, first as an assistant surgeon and then for the next six years as a surgeon, during which time his talents were widely admired. He was twenty-eight years old when he underwent his transformative experience aboard the *Swift* and, thanks to his broken leg, brought his immediate future in the Royal Navy to an end.

Initially, Ramsay's thoughts returned to his original ambition of entering the church. The chance seemed there for the taking when the *Arundel* docked in St Kitts where there was a shortage of clergymen. However, his friends, thinking they were acting in his best interests, had already secured for him a medical partnership with the leading practitioner in Basseterre, the capital of St Kitts. This Ramsay decided to refuse, accepting instead Captain Middleton's offer to recommend him to the bishop of London, in whose diocese was located the established church in the West Indies.

In 1762, having returned to England, Ramsay was admitted into orders by the bishop of London, enabling him to go back immediately to St Kitts. There, after an introduction by Middleton to Sir George Thomas, the island's governor, he assumed the livings of Christchurch, Nicolatown and St John Capisterre. Shortly afterwards, in 1763, he married Rebecca Akers, daughter of a local planter, by whom he had a son and three daughters.

Ramsay's egalitarian intentions soon became apparent when he invited black slaves to attend his church and offered them basic religious education at his manse. He sought to do this with the support of local slave owners, seeking their consent to allow their slaves time off for prayer at the beginning and end of each working day. Predictably, the planters responded with bitter condemnation. It marked the beginning of a long and distressing battle between Ramsay and the planters, who saw him as a threat to their livelihoods and even their security.[23]

The huge growth in African labour in the West Indies had created 'slave societies' that underpinned the existence of the white community, which was almost completely dependent on the use of forced, unpaid labour. In St Kitts, where Ramsay lived, the ratio of whites to blacks had reached about 1:13 by 1772. While the blacks were resident without choice, most whites were transient, hoping to make their fortunes and return home—though only few succeeded in this ambition. As a result, unlike the North American colonists, white settlers in the West Indies had no incentive to impose their cultural identity on island society. For instance, the Scots did not invest in schools or churches because their children were always repatriated for their schooling.[24] Meantime, plantation managers worked their slaves to the bone to accelerate financial rewards for themselves as much as for their absentee landlords.

This 'get rich quick' culture was enforced with a degree of sadistic cruelty that far outstripped what was being done to slaves even in the American plantation colonies of Virginia and Maryland. To illustrate, some twenty years before Ramsay settled in the West Indies, it was recorded that a quarter of slaves were likely to die within eighteen months of their arrival due to them being afforded insufficient time to acclimatise.[25] Until the end of the 1700s, it was considered more economical to buy blacks off the ships than to encourage reproduction from within the slave population. This mindset of unyielding exploitation, coupled with inadequate food, resulted in about half of female slaves in the British West Indies remaining childless in the mid-eighteenth century.

The pervasive system of cruelty and oppression, in which a small number of whites ruled with an iron rod over large numbers of slaves, 'generated rancorous fear and paranoia among the British planters', who dreaded retribution and rebellion.[26] This poison meant that disproportionate penalties were imposed on any slave who even slightly transgressed the draconian rules under which they lived and suffered. The barbarity of the penalties almost beggars belief. For example, in Jamaica in 1751, three black boys were captured after running away. Their leader was hanged and beheaded, with his head put on a pole on the side of a road as a warning for all to see.[27]

In this brutality, the Scots undoubtedly played their part. They had been active throughout the Caribbean since long before the 1707 Act of Union, often coming as political migrants or criminal deportees, and their position had strengthened as Britain had secured more islands within the region through war. The Scottish may have had difficulty in accessing patronage and professional employment in London, but elsewhere, they were able to exploit expanding commercial opportunities via their highly effective networks of relatives and associates. In fact, by the time that James Ramsay came to St Kitts under the patronage of Charles Middleton, his fellow Scots and, to a lesser extent, Welsh and Irishmen, were starting to dominate professional, mercantile and governing elites throughout the British empire.

In the second half of the eighteenth century, some 12,000 to 20,000 Scots emigrated to the West Indies.[28] As noted, very few of them planned to settle, but nonetheless, by 1790, the 'sugar islands had become the Clyde's premier overseas centre of trade'.[29] Thus, trade with the West Indies became a very significant factor of Scotland's industrialisation.

Among this diaspora were men drawn from all levels of society. There were Scottish planters, merchants, colonial officers, attorneys, overseers, tradesmen and doctors.[30] The services of the last of these were in great demand, particularly when slaves were acclimatising after their arrival. Having been so long neglected, the health of slaves was a matter of increasing importance in the later eighteenth century when their price rose and public support for the abolition movement gained traction. In the face of this twin threat, the island assemblies enacted new legislation to provide improvement in the health and care of slaves, and this encouraged planters to employ more doctors. Naturally, most of them came from Scotland, where, in this period, 85 per cent of all British doctors were trained. Some, like Dr William Stephen, were entrepreneurial, using their professional skills as a platform to move into more profitable business ventures. In St Kitts, Dr Stephen bought 'refuse negroes' worth little in auction, treated their illnesses, and then resold them at profit.[31]

Anybody prepared to challenge the delicately balanced status quo on the islands of the West Indies, which was maintained by legally sanctioned violence, was, in the minds of the slave owners, placing white lives and their livings at risk. Thus, James Ramsay was judged as 'a rebel convict against the interests and majesty of plantership'.[32] His plan to convert slaves to Christianity was interpreted by the owners as a ploy to make the slaves unfit for work by wasting their valuable energy on prayers. In retaliation, several parishioners declined to attend Ramsay's services. He also received direct threats. To try to recover the trust of his mutinous congregation and preserve his and his family's safety, he felt forced to withdraw a contentious prayer for the conversion of the slaves. In the West Indies, any attempt, even by a white man, to improve the lot of slaves could prove fatal.[33] Even more discouraging for Ramsay was the reality that his ambition to convert slaves was, for the most part, met with apathy by the slaves themselves.[34] The prayers of white men were not theirs, after all.

But Ramsay was not going to give up. He had an even greater aim than winning the souls of black people for God; he wanted to take on and defeat slavery itself. He weaved religious arguments into the intellectual principles he had taken from his study of moral philosophy under Professor Thomas Reid at King's College, Aberdeen. In a later published work, he set his arguments out as follows:

> The prime design of society is the extension of the operation of law, and the equal treatment and protection of the citizens. Slavery, therefore, being the negation of law, cannot arise from law, or be compatible with it. As far as slavery prevails in any community, so far must that community be defective in answering the purposes of society. And this we affirm to be in the highest degree in our colonies. Slavery, indeed, in the manner wherein it is found there, is an unnatural state of oppression on one side, and of suffering on the other; and needs only to be laid out in its native colours, to command the abhorrence and opposition of every man of feeling and sentiment.[35]

To slave owners, sitting on top of a bonfire that a single match could ignite, this was not moral philosophy but pure politics, articulated by a man who, to their mind, was offering the slaves that match. Ramsay understood this perspective and the risks he was taking. A line was being crossed which he acknowledged by reflecting 'To dub a clergyman a politician is, without enquiry, to hold him up to censure'.

In 1769, a group of planters and government officials faced financial ruin.[36] The situation presented a moral dilemma which further alienated Ramsay and infuriated his enemies. In a desperate effort to avoid their impending bankruptcy, the planters pressed the assembly for an unwarranted reduction in interest rates. The action was detrimental to the fair treatment of the honest and prudent depositor and it served to polarise opinion in St Kitts between those who favoured credit and property and those who were against debt and poverty. Unsurprisingly, almost all of the white community, including the governor, sided with the planters and officials. A few, led by Ramsay, did not, and his words were followed by actions. He applied to the colonial courts, arguing that to enjoy legitimacy, all colonial legislation had to be sanctioned by the government in London. What the planters were proposing, he said, was contrary to this principle. In the end, Ramsay succeeded, but the cost was substantial: his legal expenses amounted to 'upwards of £380' and the planters, who already hated him for his position on slave welfare, now cast him as a traitor.[37]

Ramsay stood out in stark contrast to his predecessors. They knew that to enjoy a comfortable existence, they should keep their opinions to themselves. Instead, by speaking out against the interests of the planters, Ramsay, who exhibited remarkable courage, was soon on the receiving end of offensive attacks in newspapers, and to all beyond a group of friends who shared his views, he became a social outcast. Another attack came from his vestry, the body administering the secular affairs of the parish, which, unable to prise Ramsay from his livings, refused to increase his already inadequate income. Instead, they tried unsuccessfully to cut it back by a quarter.[38] Notwithstanding this failure, they did manage to increase his parish workload, but by making a point in welcoming this, Ramsay took the sting out of their spiteful intent.

The leader of this hostility was Edward Gillard, one of the island's most powerful men. He subjected Ramsay to extended abuse from the communion table and publicly exhorted whites to boycott Ramsay's services, adding that he would send his blacks to Ramsay's church in his place as the only fit company. Not to be outdone, Ramsay took the moral high ground by saying that the soul of the most ungenerous black was not an object beneath his notice.

Ironically, the vestry's failure to provide Ramsay with an adequate living since his arrival in 1763 proved to be counterproductive to their intentions. With the support of his friends and patrons, and with no doctor in the area, Ramsay resumed working as a doctor for both white and black populations to supplement his diminished church income. This return to medicine proved crucial as it enabled him to validate his political and religious beliefs with the hard science of medical research. He sent his findings about the treatment of slaves to his superior, the bishop of London, who in turn informed politicians in Westminster.

With access to a stream of needy patients, Ramsay was able to focus more of his time and energy on establishing the condition of the slaves and how best to address their desperate privations. Time he already had in abundance. Under a custom of the West Indian slave society, he was restricted to preaching only on Sundays—and beyond this, there were some Sundays when he still was not permitted to preach.

The volume of work grew as increasing numbers of sympathetic planters offered to pay Ramsay for the care of their plantation slaves. This enabled him to learn first hand about the lives, illnesses and problems of slaves. From a medical perspective, he soon realised that there was a limit to what he could hope to achieve due to a lack of adequate nourishment and any structured programme for the maintenance of the slaves' welfare. In response, he took the bold step of drafting a memorial, or formal report, for the better government and treatment of slaves. This he distributed after securing feedback from his planter friends and establishing a solid platform of support.

Ramsay himself owned slaves. It was a fact eagerly seized upon by his enemies wishing to discredit him. However, in the opinion of his biographer, Folarin Shyllon, had he not owned slaves and not been a doctor in St Kitts, his views would have lacked credibility. His slaves were not plantation slaves but domestic ones, and the accepted view is that he treated them with fairness.[39]

The comprehensive memorial began with the household. Ramsay submitted his slaves to daily prayer and helped them to understand the scriptures. He chided those who did not apply themselves and praised those who did. The memorial continued with Ramsay outlining his findings about the daily cycle of work for plantation slaves and the problems they had to contend with. If a slave was late for work, he recorded that the individual was whipped with sufficient skill to cut 'out flakes of skin and flesh with every strike'. He continued: 'The wretch, in this mangled condition, is turned out to work in dry or wet weather, which ... bring[s] on the cramp, [and] ends his sufferings and slavery altogether.' Many more unspeakable cruelties were carefully noted by Ramsay, but he also acknowledged that both the extent and method of execution might be tempered if good judgment was applied by the manager or overseer.

Indeed, Ramsay was careful not to tar everyone with the same brush. He made it clear that there were exceptions to misgovernment and mismanagement, and he described enlightened planters who were prepared to treat their slaves with consideration and humanity. Critically, however, he made the point that, faced with inadequate clothing, housing, diet and care, disease among slaves could not be overcome.[40] His research completed, Ramsay then outlined the benefits that would ensue for the slave owners if they applied his methods.

Ramsay wanted all slaves to be emancipated, but he also wanted them to be prepared for it. This, he believed, could be best achieved through education, the teaching of Christianity, the introduction of equitable laws, and the imparting of family and social values.[41] He did not think that emancipation should mean the dissolution of the plantations. 'A sugar plantation might be cultivated to more advantage,' he wrote, 'and at much less expense, by labourers, who were free-men, [rather] than by slaves.'

> A free-man, labouring for himself, in the earnings of his wages ... who looks forward to the conveniences of life as connected with industry, will surely exert more strength, will shew more alacrity, than a starved, depressed, dispirited wretch, who drawls out his task with the whip over him.[42]

Ramsay fought passionately for the abolition of slavery and the slave trade, arguing that both were contrary to humanity and natural and moral law. He was adamant that Africans were not an inferior race to whites, but then posited, suppose they were? In which of nature's laws, he asked, was it is declared that one race of human beings shall breed slaves for the rest? He argued that such a state could not be imagined as existing under the government of God.[43]

These thoughts he shared in his letters from St Kitts to Beilby Porteus, the future bishop of Chester and London.[44] They formed the foundation of his engagement with British politicians and liberal clergymen on the subject of abolition.[45]

Ramsay's comprehensive strategy, set out in his memorial, for the improvement, religious conversion and better treatment of slaves, as a forerunner to absolution, included the following points:[46]

- the establishment of a body of clergy among the slaves, properly remunerated to teach the Christian faith;
- the provision of parish schools;
- the rendering of Africans as the objects of civil government (as part of a plan to improve the conditions of slaves and their understanding of a civil society);
- the appointment of judges independent of colonial assemblies;
- the provision of a stable footing for marriages among slaves, and their protection from the caprice of the owner;
- the introduction of a legal minimum allowance for food, clothing and shelter;
- the grant of half a day per week for their own work and the preservation of Sundays for themselves, for rest and religious instruction;
- the treatment of slaves as part of the freehold and not subject to separate sale at the owner's discretion;
- the commitment to help slaves improve their minds, to make them fair judges of the behaviour of others;
- the commitment to oblige owners to give freedom to slaves of merit with associated benefits;

– the commitment to make the yoke of slavery as bearable as possible in every feasible way.

Ramsay's memorial was widely circulated before its eventual publication in 1784 under the title *An Essay on the Treatment and Conversion of African Slaves in the British Sugar Colonies*.

From the treatment he had received in St Kitts, Ramsay was only too aware that his ideas raised fear and hostility among many of the planters who considered them threatening and radical. Over the years, this hostility took its toll on Ramsay, and one assumes on his family too. So, in 1777, after fourteen years of it, Ramsay elected to return home with a view to going back to St Kitts at some point in the future, hoping that the enmity against him might have subsided by then.

On his return to Scotland, after an absence of twenty-two years, Ramsay first visited Fraserburgh to reward all who had helped him and his mother in his early years—probably with money earned from his medical work in St Kitts. This extended to assisting his sister by adopting and paying for the education of her son, James Walker.[47]

After an introduction to Lord George Germaine, secretary of state for the American Department, he was appointed chaplain to Admiral Barrington, then about to take command of the West Indies squadron. So, having left the navy as a surgeon after being declared medically unfit to perform that job, he was back as a clergyman, a post in which his lameness was not regarded as an issue. First under Barrington and then his successor, Lord Rodney, Ramsay saw action against the French off St Lucia and then St Kitts in 1778 and 1779. He was then deployed on St Kitts to gather intelligence for Admiral Rodney for which he was highly praised for his courage and zeal.

Ramsay loved the institution of the navy, but disliked the life of a sailor and felt the need to return to his livings in St Kitts. However, once there, it was soon made clear to him that his presence was not welcome on the island. In 1781, tired of the hostility he faced on a daily basis, he returned again to Britain and resigned his livings. In the event, his career moved him in a new direction, which ultimately provided him with a platform to express his views publicly on slavery—something in which he had been considerably handicapped at St Kitts.

At this point, Ramsay's friend and erstwhile captain, Charles Middleton, became an even more important figure in his life. Spotting an opportunity, Middleton invited Ramsay to take up the livings of Neston and Nettlestead in Kent. Soon enough, he was using Ramsay as his part-time private secretary at his home at Barham Court. In this role, Middleton obtained Ramsay's input for a paper he had been preparing as comptroller of the navy, on the remodelling and updating of navy board regulations and warrants. Ramsay took this opportunity to bend the ear of both Middleton and his wife on the need for action to address the plight of West Indian slaves.

Through Charles Middleton, Ramsay was brought into an influential circle of philanthropists, intelligentsia and politicians, some of whom were shocked by his accounts of the slave trade. It was Lady Middleton who encouraged him to raise his game by putting his case to the nation. This resulted in his earlier memorial being published in 1784 under the title *An Essay on the Treatment and Conversion of African Slaves in the British Sugar Colonies*.

It received wide support, partially because it was published on the back of an advanced preview delivered the year before on 21 February 1783 in an acclaimed sermon by Ramsay's supporter Beilby Porteus, by now bishop of Chester.[48] In the sermon, the bishop took to task the planters who failed to address the 'comfort and future salvation of their slaves'. He recommended that a code of laws should be put in place for the slaves' 'protection, their security, their encouragement, their improvement and their conversion,' crediting Ramsay at the same time for his insights.[49]

The sermon so alarmed the West Indian interest comprising slave trade merchants of the slave trade and sugar planters that they tried to frustrate the publication of Ramsay's forthcoming essay by threatening him with 'merciless revenge' should he publish'; in response to which Ramsay characteristically decided 'to publish and be damned'.[50] It proved to be the first salvo in a war of wills between the two sides, which would continue over the next five years but do nothing to curb the influence of the *Essay*, which, according to the *Oxford Dictionary of National Biography*, 'is regarded as the most important event in the early history of the anti-slavery movement'.[51]

On the other side of the coin, Ramsay's *Essay* also provoked a writer in the *Monthly Review*, a leading literary journal, to wonder whether he was not in favour of slavery and the slave trade. Ramsay was understandably upset by this purist view expressed from the 'bubble' of London. He replied, justifying his gradualist approach on the pragmatic grounds 'that he had had to bear the struggle of sentiments with the selfishness of the age, and to suppress many a generous wish'.[52] In short, given the potential political and social unrest which might be unleashed by emancipation, Ramsay wanted to prepare all concerned for that eventual outcome as best he could.

In the same year, 1784, Ramsay published another essay entitled *An Inquiry into the Effects of Putting a Stop to the African Slave Trade*, in which he proposed that emancipated slaves should diversify the existing trade of tropical products for mutual profit and benefit on the African coast to permit trade with British manufactures. The work drew the admiring attention of both Prime Minister William Pitt and rising star William Wilberforce, whom Ramsay had met that year.

The publication of both essays coincided with the emergence of liberal and enlightenment values which, in March 1783, gained greater prominence and support when a horrified public read the press and court reports describing the murderously callous actions of the captain of the slave ship *Zong*.[53] Three months later, the Quakers (as a body known as the Society of Friends) presented a petition to the House of Commons against the British slave trade (which was rejected by Lord North, while he commended them for their humanity), while another group of Quakers, through a committee led by Joseph Woods, began informing the public of the evils of the slavery and the slave trade via published letters.[54] All the while, Ramsay continued his war of words with his critics, stimulating and engaging a growing audience with further publications, and more encouragement came from contemporary literary magazines. In its 1785 edition, the *English Review* concluded, 'We have been assured by some West Indian planters that the picture Mr Ramsay has drawn of the cruelties inflicted on the slaves is too highly coloured. On this occasion, however, we are inclined to give credit to the divine rather than to the planter.' The public mood was shifting, and men like Ramsay were willing it along.

In St Kitts the enraged planters condemned Ramsay as an insider who had turned against them. They retaliated with very personal attacks on his character, his alleged hypocrisy and his motives in order to discredit him. They also questioned his authority, as a cleric, to draft a civil code for the better treatment of slaves in the West Indies. But the claims asserted in Ramsay's essay were not said in isolation.

Janet Schaw, a visitor to St Kitts from Edinburgh in 1775, two years before Ramsay had left, recounted in her diary the cruelty exerted by drivers through their use of the whip, '[a] circumstance of all others the most horrid'. However, unlike Ramsay, she preferred to rationalise what she knew instinctively to be wrong, drawing on racial prejudices, and in so doing, becoming complicit in accepting this patent evil:

> However dreadful this must appear to a humane European, I will do the creoles [whites born on the island] the justice to say, they would be as averse to it as we are, could it be avoided, which has often been tried to no purpose. When one comes to be better acquainted with the nature of the Negroes, the horror of it must wear off. It is the suffering of the human mind that constitutes the greatest misery of punishment, but with them it is merely corporal. As to the brutes it inflicts no wound on their

mind, whose Natures seem made to bear it, and whose sufferings are not attended with shame or pain beyond the present moment.[55]

There were many others, however, who rejected this racist attitude and worked tirelessly to find a route towards abolition. They included the economist Dean Tucker who recognised that slavery would not be defeated until a cheaper means of producing sugar could be found.[56] Other formidable supporters emerged in the form of the youthful Thomas Clarkson and Granville Sharp, who together formed the Committee for the Abolition of the Slave Trade.[57]

Thomas Clarkson told Ramsay that he 'was ready to devote himself to the cause', and as evidence of his commitment, he enlisted the parliamentary support of twenty-four-year-old William Wilberforce, who had met Ramsay at Teston and, thereafter, had been bombarded by him with information and encouragement to end the evils of slavery.[58] The challenge was taken up by Wilberforce who was asked by his friend, Prime Minister William Pitt, to table a question on the slave trade before parliament in a campaign coordinated by both Charles Middleton and James Ramsay. An avalanche of petitions, stimulated by Ramsay's publications, was served on the House of Commons before the debate on abolition commenced on 9 May 1789. In preparation, Ramsay tutored Wilberforce and other politicians with detailed evidence to substantiate the moral arguments in support of the case. It enabled Wilberforce to deliver a four-hour-long speech to the House.

During a continuance of the debate on 21 May, a rancorous note was struck when a long-standing antagonist of Ramsay, Crisp Molineux, a plantation owner in St Kitts and a member of parliament, launched a virulent attack on him, questioning his character and reputation.[59] Middleton and others took the floor and, after a spirited defence, routed their opponent. But nonetheless, the attack took its toll on Ramsay's health. Acute abdominal pains ensued within days, followed by what proved to be a fatal gastric haemorrhage. Ramsay died at Middleton's home in London on 20 July 1789, aged fifty-five. He was buried near to his black servant, Nestor, in Teston church.[60]

Ramsay was not fortunate enough to witness his lifelong commitment come to fruition, but his role in the abolition of the slave trade and slavery should not be understated. That abolition happened at all 'probably owed more,' wrote one biographer, 'to Ramsay's personal integrity, ethical arguments, and constructive proposals than any other influence'.[61] As a rare first-hand witness to slavery both at sea and on the plantations, he was far better placed than most to expose its evils, though doing so took huge personal courage and commitment in the face of a powerful group of people set on destroying him. Through his essays and network of supporters, Ramsay was able to hold a morally bankrupt system up to the scrutiny of a public who were awakening belatedly to its crimes.

Crucially, Ramsay was able to mobilise men of distinction to the abolitionist cause—men like Charles Middleton, Beilby Porteus, Thomas Clarkson and William Wilberforce. His extraordinary contribution, through the application of reason and debate, demonstrated the triumph of enlightenment thought over evil. It was a remarkable achievement for the son of a ship's carpenter from Fraserburgh, and a testament to the qualities of the man and the values and education he absorbed in his youth.

10

The Abolition of the Slave Trade: Henry Dundas, William Pitt and William Wilberforce

Abolitionist James Ramsay must have been both flattered and excited when he received an invitation to meet Tory Prime Minister William Pitt at 10 Downing Street, London, in the spring of 1789. The purpose of his visit was to brief Pitt, himself an abolitionist, on his substantial first-hand research into the evils of slavery ahead of the forthcoming House of Commons debate on its abolition, scheduled for 9 May 1789. The grounds for this debate, the first of its kind, had been initiated when Pitt led a motion to order a privy council investigation into the slave trade in response to sustained public campaigning and petitioning of parliament. The findings of the review, published in April 1789, had opened the way for the debate, which was to be led in the House by Pitt's university friend, William Wilberforce.

Given that this debate had the backing of a prime minister, it is perhaps difficult to understand, from a modern perspective, why it took another eighteen years, until 1807, for the slave trade to be abolished, and another twenty-seven years on top of that, until 1834, for the practice itself to be outlawed. Looking back over more than two centuries, this delay appears both avoidable and unacceptable. Yet, for the abolitionists, their triumph was not measured in the time it took to achieve their daunting goal, but by their success in achieving it at all in face of so much vested interest and stubborn hostility.[1] That they achieved it comparatively quickly seems, from a twenty-first century perspective, both improbable and unacceptable. But when trying to understand the perceived 'soft peddling', it is important to keep in mind both the dominance of the West Indian trade lobby and the obstacles the abolitionists had to overcome to deliver their victory.

The huge scale and influence of the slave trade caused some leading abolitionists to conclude that the only way to defeat the entrenched opposition would be via gradual change, which implicitly involved unwanted but inevitable delay. That this situation was unsatisfactory to those involved was made clear by James Ramsay, as mentioned in the previous chapter. In response to criticism of his gradualist approach, he wrote that, regretfully, 'he had had to bear the struggle of sentiments with the selfishness of the age, and to suppress many a generous wish'.[2] This was, of course, of no consolation to the black slaves trapped in an inescapable cycle of violence and oppression. Their continued suffering through those decades of debate and incremental change should never be sidelined or forgotten, but the fact remains that during the decade of the 1780s, the slave trade was at its peak: some 300,000 slaves were transported from Africa by more than 1,000 British slave ships. Among the operators, financiers, planters and all others growing rich off the trade, there would have been few, if any, who would have thought that its future was in peril. Yet by 1807, it had been abolished by parliament. So what happened?

The work was begun by the Quakers in the mid-eighteenth century, particularly in Philadelphia, building on anti-slavery sentiments dating from much earlier. The re-emergence of this movement coincided with influential criticism against slavery being delivered by writers in Scotland, France and America. Initially, the robustness of the slave trading market and the wealth it was generating enabled these ideas to be brushed aside. The slave trade lobby was supported by a majority of churches, whose ministers and leadership regarded slavery as a part of life.

The key turning point in Britain can be traced back to the Somerset case in 1771–72, which determined that slavery was illegal in England (see Chapter 2). This decision reverberated across the Atlantic, bringing the moral and legal issues of the slave trade into sharp focus. That focus was then further intensified in 1775 with the outbreak of the American War of Independence, in which both sides sought to win the resident slaves over to their cause. Some abolitionists had hoped for the emancipation of slaves in an independent United States, but this was quickly revealed to be a vain hope. In 1787, as part of the constitutional compromise between the Northern and Southern states, it was agreed that Congress would not have the power to ban the slave trade until 1808, and that slaves fleeing the south to the north could be pursued and returned. This provision encouraged the kidnapping and return of freed slaves.[3]

Prominent in the movement for change was the dynamic Philadelphian Quaker Anthony Benezet. By maintaining visits and substantial correspondence with kindred spirits on both sides of the Atlantic, he encouraged others to confront the brutality of the slave trade and to recognise that it was immoral for European economies to rely on the labour of African slaves. The wide network he established drew in the Methodist leader Charles Wesley (younger brother of John Wesley, the founder of Methodism), who in 1774 wrote his own pamphlet entitled *Thoughts upon Slavery*, which in turn influenced the fast-growing community of Methodists. Meanwhile, Granville Sharp, who twenty years earlier had promoted the injustices suffered by blacks in Britain both in law and society, agreed with Benezet a strategy of bombarding parliament and the king with petitions from the colonies, the locus of the debate.[4] In this way, public awareness was raised in Britain of the horrendous reality of the slave trade and slavery.

In 1783, another key event occurred. The so-called '*Zong* Massacre', in which the owners of a slave ship tried to make an insurance claim for the loss of Africans thrown overboard, was brought to the public eye by Granville Sharp, causing mass outrage (see Chapter 3).[5] In the same year, Quakers petitioned both parliament and the American Continental Congress against the slave trade, and published anti-slavery literature in London. It marked the beginning of a surge of tracts and articles on the subject being published and distributed across the English-speaking world for the next fifty years. An effective propaganda campaign emerged, founded on facts and figures, reasoned argument and fierce censure, targeting first the slave trade, and once that had been abolished, slavery itself. The campaign, in its first phase, laid bare the inhumanity of the trade, its commercial inefficiencies, its immorality and its affront to Christian values.[6]

With James Ramsay's encouragement and assistance, Thomas Clarkson and William Wilberforce took up the abolitionist cause in 1784. Clarkson was a diligent researcher and indefatigable promoter of the cause across Britain, while Wilberforce was its parliamentary face—informed, resolute, articulate and supported by the resourceful Quaker national organisation. By 1787, the Society for the Abolition of the Slave Trade was formed to target the more immediate and achievable aim of ending the slave trade. Reflecting on this pragmatic decision not to include the abolition of slavery in their stated aims at this stage, Clarkson wrote, 'to aim at ending both would be to aim at too much, and ... by doing this we might lose all'.[7]

The plan rested on the simple premise that if the trade could be stopped, West Indian planters would have to treat their slaves better to maintain their stock of labour. To achieve this objective, the British public, who mostly regarded slavery as an alien and remote business, would have to be educated and converted into passionate advocates for abolition.

By 1788, in response to an initiative of the Society for the Abolition of the Slave Trade, petitions were gathered by Scottish universities, town councils and the Chamber of Commerce, and sent to parliament in Westminster, while synods (regional representatives) of the Church of Scotland weighed in for good measure.[8] Through its ministers, the Kirk played a significant role in generating public support against the slave trade in the critical period between 1788 and 1792. Among the clergymen who promoted abolition from the pulpit was William Dickson, who also toured Scotland in 1792 to secure petitions from local people.[9] In this way he performed in Scotland a role similar to that of Thomas Clarkson in England.[10] James Stephen, a skilled lawyer, was another prominent Scotsman won over to the cause.[11]

In the United States, plantation owners were no longer dependent on the slave trade because, by the 1790s, sufficient slave labour had been made available through procreation. Instead, the debate there was concentrated on how to apply the existing black labour to the differing demands generated by the contrasting economies of the various states. Thus, although there was consensus against the slave trade, the country remained deeply divided on the topic of slavery itself. The debate was aggravated in the early 1800s by the rapid expansion of the cotton industry and the concurrent increase in demand of slave labour for harvests.

The British public, unlike that of the United States, was detached from the brutal reality of colonial slavery. People were mostly unaware of the intense fear of retribution among white communities in the colonies, and the extent to which they had come to rely on slave labour. It meant that a moral position was easier to adopt, free of any direct personal consequences. Nonconformist churches in Britain joined the growing voice of protest during the 1780s and '90s to bring the slave trade to an end. This pressure resulted in the passing of the Dolben Act of 1788, which improved conditions on slave ships. However, the volume of petitions raining down on parliament from across the country did not diminish.[12] Abolitionist societies held public rallies and lectures drawing huge crowds; by 1793, the sheer success of the movement was beginning to concern the establishment who had grown fearful of civil unrest and rioting.

Across the Channel, the French Revolution had entered a dark period of recrimination against the elite, causing nervousness within the British parliament. The situation was made worse when news filtered through of a slave revolt in the French colony of Saint Domingue (later Haiti), raising the spectre of the possibility of similar uprisings in British colonies. As a result, the government began to regard abolitionist meetings as seditious and a sign of French revolutionary influence (Jacobinism). The aims of the abolitionists came under fire from the formidable West Indian lobby, which, seeking to defend its vested interests, published pamphlets in support of maintaining the status quo. But their campaign struggled against the superior force of the abolitionist movement, of which women formed a powerful sector, which continued to appeal to the public via petitions and the written word.[13]

This brings us to 9 May 1789, when at Prime Minister Pitt's request, William Wilberforce took the floor in parliament to lead the first debate on the abolition of the slave trade. In presenting his arguments, he marshalled the full breadth of his knowledge and research, drawing on all he had learned from long conversations with men like James Ramsay. The debate continued for the next two years, until the pro-abolition camp was finally defeated in 1791. Within a year of this defeat, on 2 April 1792, Wilberforce stood again in the debating chamber of the House of Commons to move once more for the immediate end and total abolition of the slave trade. Opposite him that day sat Henry Dundas, who, as home secretary, was tasked with leading the government's opposition.

Paradoxically, sixteen years earlier on 20 February 1776, it had been Dundas, as lord advocate in Edinburgh's court of session, who had pleaded successfully for the freedom of the black slave Joseph Knight from his master, James Wedderburn (see Chapter 4). Back then, during the proof, Dundas had said 'Human nature spurns any idea of slavery among any part of our species....'[14] He had been praised by James Boswell for his spirited speech in support of Knight's freedom.[15] So why, sixteen years later, was Dundas working to defeat Wilberforce's motion to abolish the slave trade?

Henry Dundas was born on 28 April 1742 near Edinburgh, the fourth son of seven children born to Robert Dundas, Lord Arniston. After attending the local grammar school in Dalkeith, he continued his education at the Royal High School, Edinburgh, and the University of Edinburgh. Three generations of Dundases had served as senators of the College of Justice, and Henry Dundas, a young man of abundant energy, was called to the bar in Edinburgh in 1763.[16] There he enthusiastically enjoyed wide interests and club life, so much so that his friends—lawyers and men of literature—formed a club known as the Feast of Tabernacles, with Dundas at its centre.[17] He was highly sociable and engaging—useful qualities for an aspiring politician.

During the early part of his legal career, work came Dundas's way, perhaps thanks to his brother Robert, who was by then lord president of the court of session. He developed friendships among the Edinburgh councillors—an early sign of his political acumen—of whose powers and privileges he would later become a staunch protector.[18] In 1764 he was elected a lay elder of the Church of Scotland, from which position he rapidly established himself as a mainstay for the moderates within the Kirk. He regularly attended the assembly, polishing his skills as a debater. Alexander Carlyle, clergyman and founder member of the Royal Society of Edinburgh, observed that Dundas engaged himself 'so warmly into the interest of his client as totally to forget himself, and to adopt all the feelings, sentiments, and interests of his employer'.[19] His biographer added that Dundas also demonstrated a gift for making 'a fair and candid statement of the question, and followed it by strong and open reasoning in support of his opinion'.[20]

In 1765, Dundas married Elizabeth Rannie, the fifteen-year-old heiress of the late Captain Rannie, who had died the year before, leaving his daughter his mansion and policies at Melville in West Lothian, and a fortune of around £100,000.[21] Dundas was then twenty-three years old and passionate and impulsive; it was a marriage based on love, but it also secured him his wife's wealth and pedigree, and brought him into her social circle. Through her connections, Dundas secured some prestigious cases, including the Douglas Cause which coincided with his first visit to London.[22] It was one of a number of appeals in which Dundas appeared before the House of Lords, and for which he received flattering reviews for his performances, raising his profile.

At the age of twenty-four, Dundas was appointed solicitor general, at least partly reflecting the influence of his family on Scottish affairs. Nonetheless, there was no question of his talent. Over the next four years, the post gave him a valuable grounding in a broad range of law, and with it, a rounded view of life in Scotland, of the people whose diverse lives he represented and of those whom he was able to observe. His career and prospects seemed to be advancing nicely, but a shock was on its way, which would mean the forfeiture of his comfortable status, achieved through his marriage, as a man of private means.

Dundas was an early investor in the Ayr Bank, founded in 1769 at a time when the subscribers' liability was unlimited. Mismanaged from the outset through ill-considered investments in speculative businesses, the bank, after suffering several runs on its capital, collapsed in June 1772, a victim of a wider commercial crisis which had begun in London.[23] It collapsed with liabilities amounting to eight or nine times its nominal capital, which for Dundas, meant that, after meeting the bank's liabilities, little of his wife's £100,000 inheritance remained. He now needed to rely on his abilities to earn a living from the law and the offices he held.[24] This sudden and traumatic experience would have emphasised to him his need to place his own interests ahead of any competing sentiments.

By 1774, a larger stage than Edinburgh beckoned the restless and ambitious Henry Dundas; London, the epicentre of the burgeoning British empire, was calling him. Britain's 1763 victory over France and its allies in the Seven Years' War had opened opportunities for Scots internationally and for Scotland. Within this context, Dundas saw a prosperous future for himself in law and public service. His first step was to find a seat in the House of Commons. Here he had the advantage of his family's effective patronage of the 'Edinburghshire' (Midlothian) seat, which they had given to the incumbent, Sir Alexander Gilmour, since 1761. Choosing to ignore Dundas's hints to stand down, Gilmour lost his seat to Dundas on 20 October 1774.[25] On 20 February the following year, Dundas gave his maiden speech in the House of Commons, and in May 1776, he became lord advocate upon the recommendation of Lord Mansfield.[26]

It was in that capacity that Dundas stood on appeal in the court of session in Edinburgh on 20 February 1776, representing the black slave Joseph Knight, to deliver his speech in favour of Knight's freedom from slavery. The case turned on a wider point of law than that taken in the Somerset case in England by addressing the question of 'whether a perpetual obligation of service to one master in any mode should be sanctified by the law of a free country'. In making his appeal to the court, Dundas responded to the solicitor general's assertion that if the practice of slavery was stopped it would ruin the West Indies trade, and if the blacks were granted their freedom it would produce a 'Code Sanguinaire'.[27] Ironically, Dundas was to utilise the same arguments, in principle if not in detail, when he opposed Wilberforce and his motion in the Commons to abolish slavery in May 1789.

Although Dundas had many friends among leading Enlightenment figures —including the economist and philosopher Adam Smith—who were against slavery, it is not known what his reasons were for accepting the instruction. What is certain is that as counsel, his personal views on slavery were irrelevant. His sole professional duty was to represent the best interests of his client.[28] This, according to the diarist John Boswell, himself pro-slavery, was something he did very effectively. Boswell was impressed by the passion and professionalism with which the lord advocate argued in favour of his client's cause. We also know that, in broad principle, Dundas followed the sentiments expressed by Lord Mansfield (whom he knew personally) six years earlier in the narrower case of Somerset v. Stewart, when Mansfield declared the state of slavery 'so odious, [that] nothing can be found to support it apart from positive law'.[29] However, in finding a pragmatic solution in law to grant Somerset his freedom in England, Mansfield was careful to avoid addressing the wider commercial and economic interests for both the nation and those whose fortunes depended on the slave trade.

It was a very different story twenty years later in the House of Commons. In the motion raised by Wilberforce to abolish the slave trade with immediate effect, both national and commercial interests were implicitly and unavoidably under threat. Finding grounds in law to grant a right of freedom for individual slaves in England and Scotland, while no less important, was a much easier issue to address than the one confronting Henry Dundas as home secretary in 1792. This was not least because Europe was in upheaval: the French Republic, after imprisoning Louis XVI, pending his execution, had declared war on Austria and Prussia. If, as an individual, Dundas was in favour of abolition, he had to set his personal views of slavery against his ministerial duty to keep his people safe and the country's borders secure. In the wider discharge of that task he had to protect Britain's colonial and domestic interests, upon which that security depended. If these competing personal and professional demands were irreconcilable, it would place him in a bind of conscience with no place to hide.

In the drama about to unfold on the parliamentary stage in 1792, Dundas was joined by the two other pivotal players: William Wilberforce and Prime Minster William Pitt. The lives of these three men had perhaps always been destined to intertwine. In February 1781, when Dundas gave his first speech on the economy to the new parliament, Pitt made his maiden speech in the same debate. During that debate, Dundas spoke adroitly on several aspects of the ongoing American War of Independence and gave a robust defence of Prime Minister North's financial measures.[30] Among those he impressed was a young William Wilberforce, who, returned as the member for Hull, was part of the new intake. Writing of Dundas a short time later, Wilberforce called him 'the first speaker on the ministerial side in the House of Commons'. He went on to say 'There is a manliness in his character which prevents him running away from the question; he grants all his adversaries' premises, and fights them upon their own ground.'[31] But it was perhaps George III who captured Dundas best when, in reference to his opposition of Wilberforce's motion in 1792, he described him as 'that able servant of the Crown'. Dundas was unquestionably a pragmatic politician who knew how best to play his cards.[32]

In June 1781, only a few months after his maiden speech, it was Pitt's turn to show his potential in a speech on the state of the American War. Afterwards, Dundas expressed an instinctive admiration for the newcomer, suggesting he was quick to spot Pitt's talents and his potential for the service of the state. It is also reasonable to assume that Dundas considered how this bright young politician could help further his own career.

In the years that followed, preceding his appointment as home secretary in 1791, Dundas aligned his career with Pitt's, sticking by him as he rode out the political upheaval following the loss of the American colonies. Dundas was a unionist from the outset, and therefore, in many ways, Pitt was a natural ally. By working together, Pitt became prime minister on 19 December 1783, enabling the two of them to address complicated administrative problems for the next fourteen years and take on war with Revolutionary France.

As Pitt's right-hand man, Dundas wielded enviable influence. Indeed, while the prime minister chose to treat his cabinet with contempt, Dundas enjoyed 'a powerful position as friend, adviser and factotum'. It also may have fuelled resentment. Dundas was a Scot with a dialect to match and therefore an outsider in Westminster, but for Pitt this was an advantage in that he could never be a rival for his power. In their complementary relationship, Pitt was the creative inspiration while Dundas dealt with the hard slog and the unpleasant tasks. Historian Michael Fry observed that 'where as [Pitt] came over as stiff and cold, Dundas always remained human, interested in those he had to deal with while entertaining no illusions about them. A master of expediency, he also knew the meaning of a fair deal.'[33]

For the ensuing eight years, from 1784 to 1791, Dundas served as treasurer to the navy, a role that allowed him to appoint his cousin and close friend, Charles Middleton, as comptroller of the navy, a key administrative position. Middleton excelled as comptroller, pushing through urgently needed reforms following defeat in the American War.[34] His support for the abolition of slavery was also hugely influential; as well as speaking on the subject himself and campaigning, he introduced his friend James Ramsay to Thomas Clarkson and William Wilberforce, and is credited with initiating the latter's parliamentary campaign on abolition.

It is reasonable to deduce from the close friendship between Middleton and Dundas, that the former's public crusade on the abolition of slavery was carried out with the latter's approval, which, irrespective of his personal views, would have been aligned to those of the prime minister. This begs the question of Pitt's attitude towards slavery at this time.

When William Pitt took office in 1784, the transatlantic slave trade formed a major part of the British economy. It may have been invisible to most Britons, but the supporting structures built around it had foundations running deep and wide. Nonetheless, Pitt wanted to see the trade abolished. His reasons lay in his view of public morality and in his sharing of the higher principles of a new generation, demonstrated by his demand for much-needed parliamentary reform. Thus, it was a matter of conscience, at least at the outset, that led him to invite Wilberforce to table a question before the Commons on the abolition of the slave trade in May 1789, in a campaign coordinated by both Charles Middleton and James Ramsay.[35]

The times had moved in favour of abolition; there was a growing propensity for enlightened thinking that imagined a diversified trade with Africa in the future, based on humanitarian principles.[36] Up to that point, beyond slavery, there had never been substantial trade with Africa.[37] The need for slavery from an economic perspective was also changing: the sugar market was no longer growing; the West Indian labour force was arguably sufficient for purpose; and the colonies in America had been forfeited. Meanwhile, other activities were taking up the slack: trade with India was expanding; growth in the fishery industry was enabling the redeployment of seamen and helping sustain livings in the slave ports; and new manufacturing towns were emerging to fill the economic void.[38] But while these evolutionary market processes were at play, the slave trade remained a major business in all its multifarious parts, and was still seen by many as a necessary evil. For those fearful of what would happen after emancipation, that question remained unanswered, while for the public at large the trade remained mostly out of sight.[39]

Pitt had become a steadfast friend of Wilberforce in London in the early 1780s when, as young men, they spent a great deal of their leisure time together. Their bond developed further when each of them won election to parliament at the same time, with Wilberforce becoming a staunch supporter of Pitt. Soon afterwards, however, Wilberforce underwent a religious conversion, something Pitt could not understand, and his interest in politics waned. The antidote to this disenchantment was the abolitionist cause, which Wilberforce adopted with gusto. Pitt was content to support his friend in this unexpected change of agenda as it allowed him to keep the cause, for which he felt sympathy, separate from government policy, to which it was only of marginal interest. Indeed, his commitment was such that he wanted the issue brought before parliament as soon as possible. The only reason for delay was that Wilberforce fell ill.

Finally, on 9 May 1789, with Wilberforce recovered from his illness and Pitt having helped him draft the resolutions, the motion 'to prevent the farther importation of slaves into the British colonies in the West Indies' was heard in the Commons. Despite thorough preparations, certain crucial questions remained unanswered: what were the expected social and economic consequences should Britain end its trade? Would competing European powers follow their example? Pitt was at the time attempting to secure the commitment of other nations to abolish the trade, but by 1790 it was clear that this had failed.[40]

These issues were sufficient to see the motion defeated on 19 April 1791 by 163 to 88, despite the support of party leaders. Undismayed, abolitionists dug deep with further petitions submitted to parliament ahead of Wilberforce's next attempt, in April 1792.[41] During the interim, however, the political landscape had changed, affecting the positions of both Pitt and Dundas.

When Henry Dundas was appointed home secretary on 8 June 1791, the responsibilities of office called on him to view the world and its affairs with a wider eye. At the same time as his appointment, Louis XVI of France was captured by revolutionary forces while attempting to flee the country, and imprisoned awaiting execution.[42] This failure to escape emphasised that in France the old order was at an end, and in its place, delivered by bloody revolution, was democracy. The people of France had elected to choose their rulers and determine their form of government. The same experiment was underway in the United States of America, but in Europe this was an entirely new principle; apart from a couple of small cantons in Switzerland, all European nations, bar France, were subject to monarchy or other forms of hereditary rule, legitimised by an established church. Generally speaking, within the parameters of this status quo, Europe had thrived in recent centuries and proved reasonably stable. Although weakened by the ideas of the Enlightenment, the systems upon which monarchies were founded endured in Europe, and new forms of government reflective of the changing times had yet to identified.[43] Thus, to outsiders observing events in France, the idea of democracy was greeted initially with amazement and wonder, but once the Revolution had degenerated into slaughter and tyranny, the reaction changed to one of fear and horror. Upon this evidence, many concluded that a democratic republic was both impractical and unworkable, and therefore, an evil to be confronted and defeated.[44]

In these turbulent times, it fell to Dundas, as home secretary, to fulfil his primary duty of maintaining constitutional and social order in Britain. Unlike in Revolutionary France, Britain was a nation underpinned by the rule of law, and at the time, the most prosperous in the world, with an economy growing rapidly on the back of the nascent Industrial Revolution.[45] But behind this glowing picture was the social cost. Value of labour had fallen. Unemployment and poverty were widespread, with many living in appalling conditions. Consequences such as these gave the ideas of the French Revolution a distinct appeal, both to liberal intellectuals and to the victims being sacrificed under the wheels of change.[46] The hardship and inequality fostered sedition and protest; just a month into his new appointment, Dundas saw this threat manifested in a riot in Birmingham, organised to celebrate the anniversary of the fall of the Bastille. He sent troops to quell the trouble, but sanctioned the use of force only in circumstances of absolute necessity. Rather, he favoured subduing the unrest by the mere presence of troops. The strategy worked, though similar threats to public order occurred in other parts of the country. Social unrest was widespread, but Dundas managed to deal with the crises effectively and proportionately.

Ireland was also on Dundas's agenda. Suppression of the Catholics continued, and he demonstrated his liberal instincts by calling on the Irish government 'to give a favourable ear to the fair claims of the Catholics', and to repeal punitive legislation which undermined their fair treatment. The spring of 1791 saw the army's presence in Jamaica strengthened following the rebellion of slaves in Saint Domingue (known as the Black Terror)—events inspired by the 'Declaration of the Rights of Man' proclaimed by their white masters in France. The perceived threats to national security and stability emanating from fear of the Saint Domingue revolt, spread to the British colonies in the Caribbean, inducing a political realignment in Britain; Whig captains of industry withdrew their support from the radical liberal democracy that had been emerging and got behind the Tory, William Pitt.[47]

Dundas, holding a diverse imperial and domestic brief, was navigating through a challenging political climate while Wilberforce pressed on with his single policy objective of having the slave trade abolished. The abolitionist efforts had been huge and effective, resulting in some 500 petitions being presented to parliament before the debate.[48] Their opponents were less active and successful with a mere five petitions being submitted. The mood of the chamber, shaken by recent events in France and Saint Domingue, had left little prospect for the achievement of immediate abolition, and the situation was aggravated by growing fears of Jacobin sentiment fomenting social unrest within Britain.[49] Much to Dundas's fury, it was inflamed by the anti-slavery lobby led by Clarkson, who through his political network had reached out to radicals who 'were showing interest in other well-meaning but increasingly suspect movements'.[50] Indeed, Wilberforce agreed with Pitt when he warned him that some of the sympathetic vote might be lost as a result. He added that 'the gale of the world' was beginning to blow and among the losers would be the blacks.[51]

Pitt, for so long a leading supporter of abolition, was so alarmed by recent events that he felt forced to reconsider. He was increasingly under pressure to take a more circumspect position; opinion within the government, the court and elsewhere had moved away from immediate abolition towards a more gradual approach at a fixed date in the future (a variation of which the Danes had effected by royal edict the month before, fixing the year 1803 for the abolition of the trade).[52] This solution was taken on board by Dundas and influenced Pitt. In early spring 1792, Dundas tried to persuade Wilberforce to moderate his motion to one that 'would almost certainly stand a better chance of success'. Although Wilberforce was also alarmed by recent events, he refused to do so.[53]

At much the same time, Dundas decided to make his position clear. Speaking in favour of abolition, he observed that the slave trade from Africa was not policy, nor was its continuation necessary to maintain trade with the West Indies. Rather, the situation could be effectively addressed through better care of the slaves which, if achieved, would serve not only to maintain their number, but facilitate their increase through procreation. Rather than effect immediate abolition, the change should be gradual with effective regulations introduced to provide the means of cultivation and growth of population, and 'to evince that all the alarms which are now entertained of danger from that measure are ill-founded'.[54]

Contrary to what might have been expected considering the wider circumstances, Pitt stayed loyal to Wilberforce. The debate commenced, and what followed was one of the great speeches delivered to parliament. In it, Pitt sought to find a balance by weaving together the moral argument for abolition with one that addressed the objections of the pragmatists. He also demonstrated a rare depth of vision when he spoke up for a new relationship with Africa judged on its own merits for its own sake, in which he hoped 'we would hear no more of the moral impossibility of civilising the Africans'. What was needed, he said, was 'an atonement for our long and cruel injustice' towards them.[55]

Despite Pitt's efforts, the mood of the chamber did not shift sufficiently, possibly because of the doubts he himself had previously expressed. The motion was defeated by 230 votes to 85. Instead, an amendment was tabled by Dundas interposing, as he had intimated, the word 'gradually' into Wilberforce's motion. This was voted upon and approved by 193 votes to 125 on 3 April 1792. On 23 April, Dundas moved a series of twelve resolutions, the first of which was to abolish the trade by degrees until bringing it to a complete end by 1800.[56] In the event, Dundas proved overcautious, and when the motion was tabled, the date was brought forward in debate to 1796, four years ahead. The motion was carried by 151 votes to 132.[57] Dundas's remaining resolutions make for uncomfortable reading to the modern eye but they were never implemented, and he withdrew from the proceedings on 28 April, when his first resolution was defeated.[58] His absence enabled Pitt to modify the resolutions and thus widen support for the bill, which passed the Commons for scrutiny by the Lords.[59]

Wilberforce was deeply unhappy with the compromise amendments; nonetheless, the result was seen by many of his supporters as 'a great reason to be thankful'.[60] After all, it had been extracted from a Commons influenced by some sixty MPs promoting the cause of the formidable West Indian lobby.[61] Their endeavours were strengthened by a majority of parliamentarians who were unwilling to commit to the deed of immediate abolition in what many felt, either in truth or for convenience, to be an increasingly unbalanced and dangerous world.[62] They did not want to be rushed, and the amendment bill offered an answer, while serving to purge the moral consciences of some, if not all.

On 3 May 1792, the bill came before the Lords who refused to proceed further without hearing the submitted evidence for themselves in the next session (mirroring a tactic previously adopted by the Commons), thereby ensuring a lengthy delay and loss of momentum.[63] In reflecting on the events of 1792, the historian John Ehrman observed that 'it was the Lords who refused to countenance any reform at all'.[64] Whichever party or parties were to be held responsible, black lives were to be sacrificed to the evil trade for another fifteen years.[65]

One of the main reasons for the loss of momentum was Holland and Britain's declaration of war on France on 11 February 1793. Political unrest swept the country for the next five years and the hearts of British people became hardened to the lot of black slaves. British lives were being lost in battle (including in Saint Domingue) and slaves in the Caribbean were purchased by British regiments (to the chagrin of planters) to be used as labour.[66] In consequence, despite Wilberforce's continued parliamentary efforts over the next four years, the abolition hearings petered out and interest waned.

In 1798, with Britain still at war, Wilberforce made another attempt to raise morale among the dejected abolitionists by placing a further abolition bill before parliament. It narrowly failed by 83 to 87 votes. Following this, he decided to suspend the campaign until circumstances had improved. The political environment was far from receptive to radical movements, as demonstrated by the government's response, implementing repressive legislation and using intimidation. National interests, for better or worse, were to be prioritised and sustained, not deconstructed.

In February 1804, with war still ongoing between Britain and France, Wilberforce tried yet again to achieve the immediate abolition of the slave trade. Despite substantial Commons support, the Lords blocked the motion once more. The result, though disappointing, stiffened the resolve of Wilberforce's Clapham Sect, an evangelical group of social reformers.[67] They toured the country garnering support, but it was not until January 1806 that the first tangible result was achieved when Pitt agreed to ban the

Henry Home, Lord Kames by David Martin, 1769. (*National Portrait Gallery of Scotland*)

Francis Hutcheson by Allan Ramsay. (*The Hunterian, University of Glasgow*)

William Murray, 1st Earl of Mansfield by John Singleton Copley, 1783. (*The National Portrait Gallery, London*)

Dido Elizabeth Belle Lindsay. Part of a portrait by John Martin, 1778. (*The Picture Art Collection/Alamy Stocks Ltd*)

Above left: John Wedderburn of Ballindean by an unknown painter. (*Alamy Stocks Ltd*)

Above right: Robert Wedderburn by an unknown artist, *c.* 1824. (*History and Art Collection/ Alamy Stocks Ltd*)

Sugarcane cultivation in Jamaica in the 1840s. (*slaveryimages.org*)

Right: Peter Williamson dressed as a member of the Delaware tribe, 1759, by an unknown artist. (*Alamy Stocks Ltd*)

Below: Shipping slaves through the surf, West-African coast. An early nineteenth-century sketch by 'a merchant on the Coast'. (*slaveryimages.org*)

SHIPPING SLAVES THROUGH THE SURF, WEST-AFRICAN COAST. A CRUISER SIGNALLED IN SIGHT.
(From a Sketch by a merchant on the Coast.)

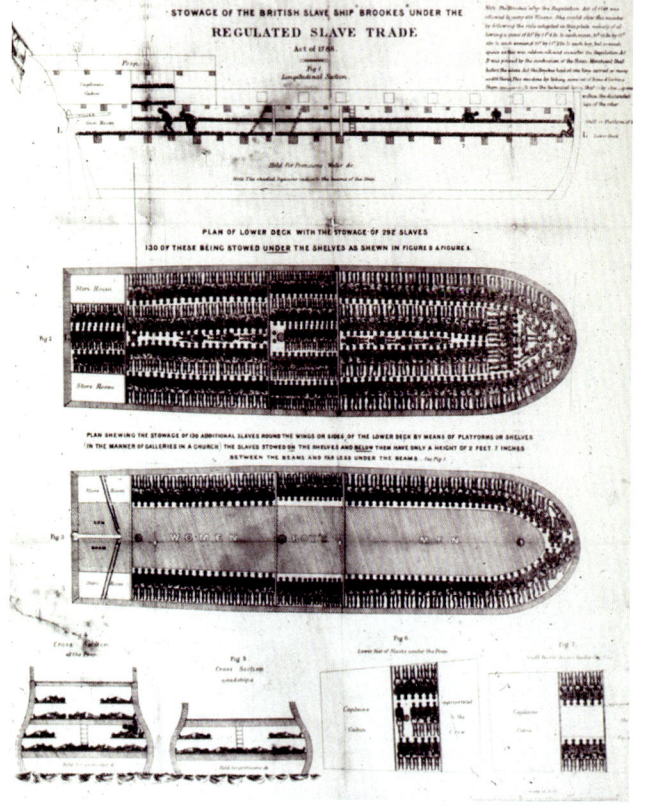

Above: Punishment aboard a slave ship, 1792. (*slaveryimages.org*)

Left: 'Stowage of the British Slave Ship *Brookes* under the Regulated Slave Trade Act of 1788'. (*slaveryimages.org*)

James Ramsay by Carl von Breda, 1789. (*National Portrait Gallery, London*)

Charles Middleton, 1st Baron Barham by Marie Anne Boulier, published 12 October 1809. (*National Portrait Gallery, London*)

Henry Dundas, 1st Viscount Melville by Sir Thomas Lawrence, c. 1810. (*National Portrait Gallery, London*)

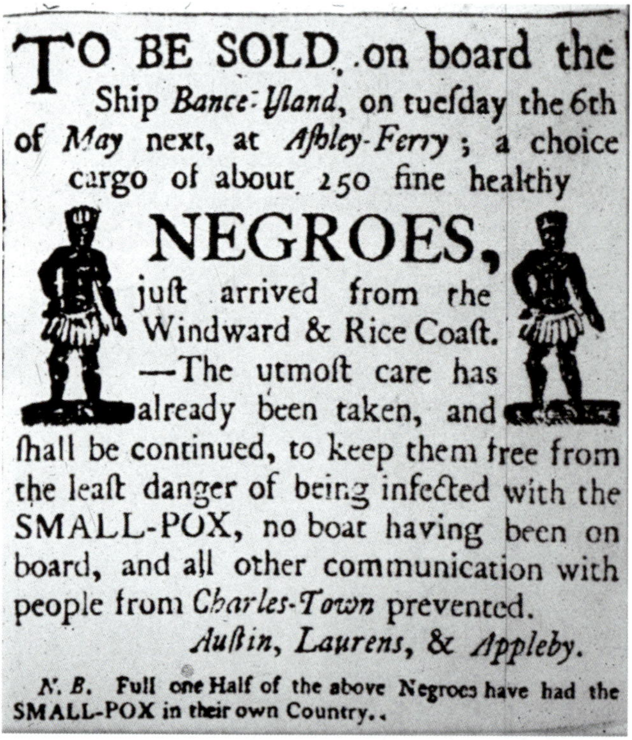

'To be sold on board the ship *Bance Island* ... a choice of about 250 fine healthy negroes.' (*slaveryimages.org*)

Bunce (here spelt 'Bense') Island, Sierra Leone, *c*. 1727. (*slaveryimages.org*)

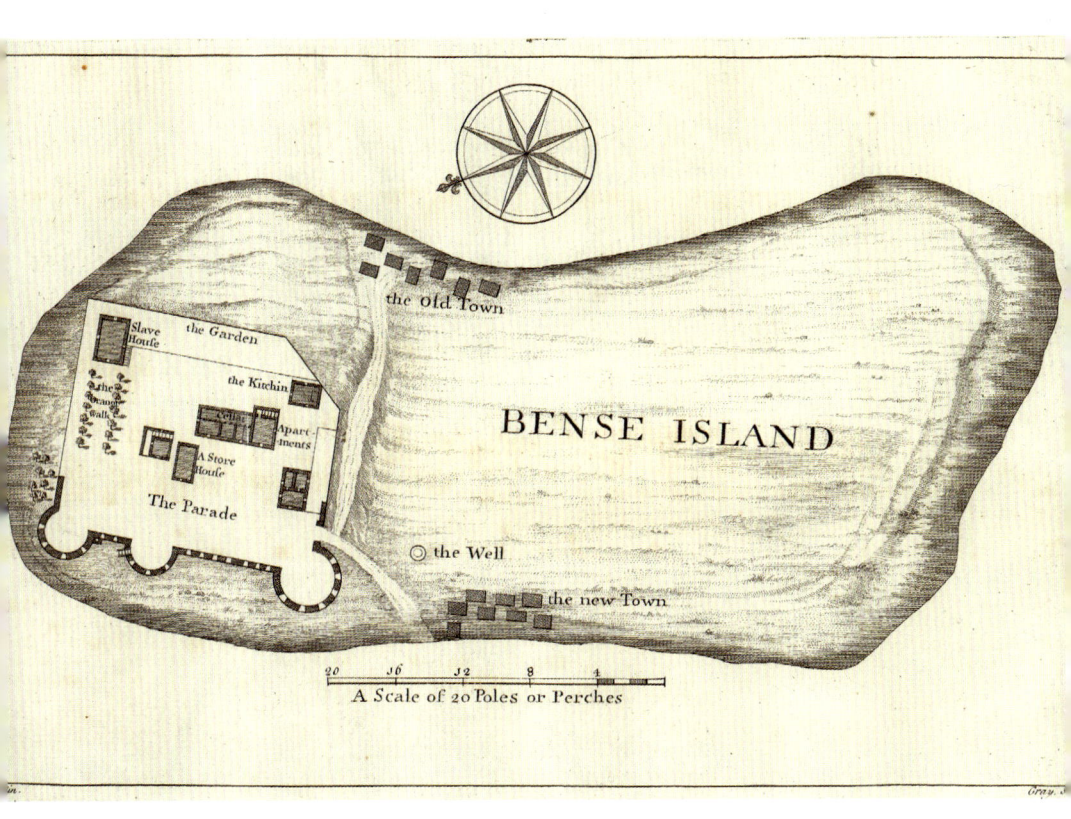

Map of Bunce (Bense) Island, illustrating the comparative size of the fort, *c*. 1727. (*slaveryimages.org*)

Metal branding irons with owners' initials. (*slaveryimages.org*)

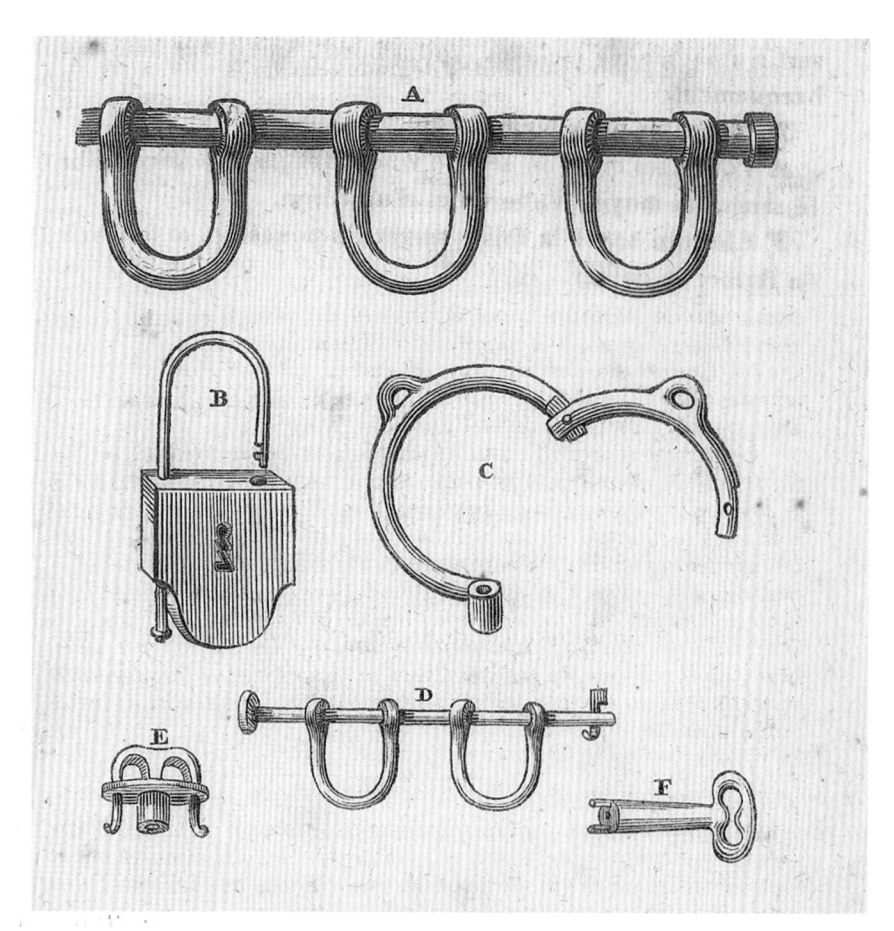

Shackles, manacles and padlocks used in the slave trade in the early nineteenth century. (*slaveryimages.org*)

A line and stipple engraving of Frances (Fanny) Wright. (*Granger Historical Picture Archive/Alamy Stocks Ltd*)

Sir John Gladstone by Thomas Gladstones, *c.* 1810. (*National Portrait Gallery, London*)

Executions in the aftermath of the slave rebellion on Demerara (British Guiana), 1823. (*slaveryimages.org*)

Interior of a boiling house, Trinidad, in the 1830s. (*slaveryimages.org*)

Head-Quarters, Montego-Bay,
St. James's, Jan. 2, 1832.

TO

THE REBELLIOUS SLAVES.

NEGROES,

YOU have taken up arms against your Masters, and have burnt and plundered their Houses and Buildings. Some wicked persons have told you that the King has made you free, and that your Masters withhold your freedom from you. In the name of the King, I come amongst you, to tell you that you are misled. I bring with me numerous Forces to punish the guilty, and all who are found with the Rebels will be put to death, without Mercy. You cannot resist the King's Troops. Surrender yourselves, and beg that your crime may be pardoned. All who yield themselves up at any Military Post *immediately*, provided they are not principals and chiefs in the burnings that have been committed, will receive His Majesty's gracious pardon. All who hold out, will meet with certain death.

WILLOUGHBY COTTON,
Maj. General Command^g.

GOD SAVE THE KING.

A warning to rebellious slaves in the Baptist War, 1832. (*slaveryimages.org*)

Heroes of the Slave Trade Abolition by an unknown artist in the mid- to late nineteenth century. (*National Portrait Gallery, London*)

Henry Brougham, 1st Baron Brougham and Vaux by James Lonsdale, 1821. (*National Portrait Gallery, London*)

Frederick Douglass by Samuel J. Millar, *c.* 1850. (*Ian Dagnall Computing/Alamy Stocks Ltd*)

Dr Thomas Chalmers by Sir John Watson Gordon, *c.* 1838. (*National Portrait Gallery of Scotland*)

Allan Pinkerton by an unknown artist, *c.* 1880. (*North Wind Picture Archives/Alamy Stocks Ltd*)

John Brown by an unknown artist, 1857. (*The Granger Collection/Alamy Stocks Ltd*)

slave trade in newly captured territories.[68] By this time, however, he had withdrawn his support for wider abolition to appease the majority of his cabinet while war raged on with the French.

Thus it was only after Pitt's death in January 1806 that the Foreign Slave Trade Act was passed in the Commons. It came in May of that year, under the new management of Prime Minister Lord Grenville's government, supported by Whig leader Charles Fox. Grenville had declared during the bill's passage 'that an event most grateful to his feelings [would be] to witness the abolition of a traffic that is an outrage to humanity, and that trampled on the rights of mankind'.[69] After a fractious General Election in which MPs had to declare their position on the issue, Grenville successfully won by a small majority. After quickly passing it through the Lords, the act finally received royal assent on 25 March 1807.

The cruel and inhuman practice of slave trading by the British had finally been abolished, though the reasons behind it are still subject to debate. For two centuries the trade had gone unchallenged, generating wealth and jobs for large numbers of people. It had made possible the settlement and development by Europeans of tropical lands ripe with economic opportunity. The reasons for its eventual demise rest on a combination of factors: a growing public awareness of the cruelty of the trade; a perception that the West Indian economy was in decline after the American War of Independence; the reduction in the trade's profitability due to an oversupply of sugar from the New World markets; the role that slaves themselves played in asserting their rights of freedom, not least those involved in the slave rebellion in modern-day Haiti; and finally, the unstinting efforts and relentless campaigning of Wilberforce, Clarkson and many other abolitionists in Britain.[70]

As for Dundas, he continued at the Home Office until 1794, when he became secretary of state for war, the same year his son, Robert, entered parliament. When Pitt's first prime ministership ended on 14 March 1801, Dundas resigned all offices, though continued to manage Scotland politically with Charles Hope. With the Peace of Amiens in 1802, Dundas was ennobled as Viscount Melville and began his editorial contribution for the *Edinburgh Review*. When war recommenced the following year, Dundas was restored under a new Pitt administration to serve as first lord of the Admiralty. Impeached in 1805 for mismanagement of naval funds, he resigned office, and although acquitted the next year, was shunned by his party for readmittance to office in government, which effectively ended his career.[71] Perhaps fittingly, his political partner, William Pitt, bowed out in the same year with his death.

In his private life, after divorcing his wife Elizabeth in 1778 on grounds of her adultery, Dundas married Lady Jane Hope, daughter of John Hope,

2nd earl of Hopetoun, in 1793. In his later years, his health began to fail and he suffered financial difficulties. He died on 28 May 1811 at the age of sixty-nine and is buried in Old Lasswade Kirkyard.

Upon his death, Dundas's political contribution was widely praised (though not by the Whigs), but over the years, his legacy has been subjected to various reviews by historians. Most recently, his handling of the abolition of the slave trade has come under particular scrutiny. How his legacy should be evaluated today, some 200 years after his death, is a matter for the reader.

11

Glasgow and London: Richard Oswald, Merchant and Entrepreneur

Following his father's death in 1725, twenty-year-old Richard Oswald left his home in Dunnet, Caithness, on the northern coast of Scotland, to join the business of his two elder cousins in Glasgow. It was a tough but inevitable decision. A living had to be earned, and despite being a son of the manse, there were few prospects in Caithness for a man of ambition.

His mode of travel is not known. If he went by horse or foot, he would have followed the ancient drove roads leading south through a landscape of under-cultivated fields and barren moors. It was a poor, undeveloped country. Accommodation overnight would likely have been in barns or, if he was lucky, modest inns. He might well have reflected that Scotland was a country in desperate need of modernisation and change. On the other hand, had he travelled by ship, he might have thought that that modernisation was well in hand.

After navigating around Cape Wrath and through the Western Isles, Oswald would have entered the Firth of Clyde from the west, sailing within the breakwaters and piers of New Port, Glasgow, in the mouth of the estuary. As his ship docked, he would have seen the activity around its newly built customs house, constructed to handle the ever-expanding trade of Glasgow merchants. Back in 1668, a tiny fishing hamlet called Newark was all that had existed here, but since then a deep-water harbour had been dredged and warehouses built. Out of New Port, before the Act of Union, Glasgow merchants had run an illegal trade with the English colonies in America and the West Indies, supplying them with Covenanters and criminals, the refuse of a politically and religiously divided Scotland, for indentured labour.[1] By the mid 1690s, the value of indentured labour faded as the demand for black labour increased. But by the early 1700s, this loss was more than compensated by the rapid and profitable growth in trade. Cargoes of American sugar, tobacco, mahogany and cotton were unloaded onto the New Port docks as well as hemp, iron and timber from the Baltic regions, which provided capital for investment in the Scottish economy.

From the port, Oswald would either have travelled along the road following the south bank of the Clyde, or taken a flat-keeled boat via shallows and sandbanks to Broomielaw Quay, 14 miles upstream. Although the quay, built in 1688, was conveniently placed not far from the city centre, river access to it was needing improvement (deep dredging was not undertaken until 1740), but being a country boy, Oswald would have been impressed by what he saw nonetheless.[2] Commercial activity was in evidence all around, and there was no mistaking the wealth and vibrancy of the city, expressed in newly constructed factories, shops and stone houses, set out in strict accordance to the city's grid iron street plan, approved by its council in 1693. Indeed, Glasgow was fast transforming 'into an entrepôt of international standing with a sophisticated financial and commercial system with a vigorous urban culture'. It was a city propelling Scotland out of economic obscurity, paving the way for the advances of the Industrial Revolution, and most impressively, doing so in the shadow of its mighty commercial competitor, England.

The secret to Glasgow's success was in the trade of tobacco, and therefore, by association, in the trade and use of slave labour. Though out of sight in Scotland, this was the basis of the country's growing economic power. Oswald, an ambitious new arrival hoping to move up in the world, wanted a part in that success. He wanted to be a merchant in the transatlantic trade, and his cousins' business, Oswald & Co., would provide the platform he needed.[3]

Oswald had not chosen an easy ambition in life. The transatlantic trade was a highly competitive environment and the preserve of a privileged few. Capital and connections were the two essential elements: without these, one couldn't hope to get started.

The amount of capital tobacco merchants needed to have at their disposal was considerable, and only a minority of those within the Glasgow business community had access to such funds. What's more, investing it came at a high risk. To manage this risk, merchants elected to work with people whom they could trust, both on a personal and commercial level. To get into the business, one either needed to be born into it, or have long-standing friends who were rich and influential.[4]

The emerging commercial elite in Glasgow was drawn mainly from the monied classes of lowland Scotland. They were below the aristocratic rank, but unlike many of their social superiors, they had access to capital from within tight family networks. Men from these merchant families grew up well tutored in the trade and with useful connections at their fingertips, but it was by no means an exclusive club. Ambitious and able men were urgently needed to cope with the rapid expansion of commerce with the American colonies, and therefore the business community in Glasgow was open to 'all comers'. It was common for young aspirants to have served indentured apprenticeships at the stores of a Glasgow merchant's house in Virginia.

In the second half of the eighteenth century, there emerged another factor for this inclusiveness: the need to replace the merchants in Glasgow whose businesses had failed. The tobacco trade remained inherently speculative, and bankruptcies still occurred in large numbers.[5] However, due to their robust networks, Scottish merchants were less affected by financial setbacks than their English counterparts.

The origins of Scottish transatlantic business networks date back to the early 1620s.[6] At this time some 2,000 Scots headed for the New World, many as indentured labourers, settling in Barbados, Jamaica and Virginia.[7] A further mass migration came shortly after 1651, during the religious and political turmoil that followed Cromwell's victory over the Covenanters. Between 1660 and 1707, some 7,000 more migrants left Scotland to take their chances in the New World, with surges happening in 1698 and 1700 following the disastrous failure of the Darien Company, which all but bankrupted the Scottish economy.[8] Of this number, about 5,000 headed for the Caribbean. It makes sense, therefore, that the first of Glasgow's sugar houses was in production before 1700.

By the time of Oswald's arrival in Glasgow in 1725, certain characteristics of the Scottish migration to the New World were beginning to become apparent. Those who had elected to settle in the mainland colonies, principally the Carolinas, Maryland, and parts of New York and Virginia, were typically drawn from a wide variety of social backgrounds ranging from sons of gentry to labourers.[9] For the most part they had settled there. In contrast, those Scots who had headed for the Caribbean had chosen not to settle, but rather to make a profit as fast as possible and return. This difference had a profound influence on outcomes. In the case of the former, the migrants had reason to invest their intellectual and moral capital, as well as their hard labour, into shaping a future for themselves. The latter, as colonial officials, planters, attorneys, doctors, overseers and merchants, never put down roots. Instead, they preferred to play their part in the ruthless drive for profit, using slave labour to work their sugar plantations as intensively as they could, using extreme brutality to attain maximum yields in the shortest time.

Both groups combined—settlers in the American colonies and non-settlers in the Caribbean—provided a close-knit network of family and associates to which the sons of Glasgow merchants were dispatched to learn their trade as apprentices. Upon their return to Glasgow, the relationships which had been developed abroad provided the foundation of trust to be built on and exploited for mutual benefit. These transatlantic relationships also provided the decision-makers in Glasgow with local market intelligence that enabled them to adapt and accommodate the ever-shifting needs and demands of the burgeoning trades of sugar and tobacco.

In this way an infrastructure of commercial opportunity, both in the West Indies and the mainland colonies, began to slip into place, assisted by Glasgow merchants eager to make it work. Two distinct operational models emerged, one after the other. The first model, which operated from the 1600s until around 1740, comprised three connected elements: the London merchant house; its factor in North America; and the planter-customer.

Put simply, the planter assigned the tobacco shipment to the merchant house's factor, an agent or broker of sorts, who sold it to a buyer in the British or Continental market. The risk remained with the planter and thus it was he who had to meet the costs of insurance, shipping, port dues and the merchants' commissions, which were all deducted from the sale price agreed. This often resulted in a net loss, with the balance due by the planter to the merchant house being carried forward from year to year. The benefit for the planter was that the credit enabled him to finance his business, which often faced rising costs, while also permitting him to expand the scale of his enterprise to reduce overheads.[10]

The second model, known as the 'store system', was developed by astute Glasgow merchants and began to be adopted in about 1740. It shifted the risk from the planter to the merchant by the latter's purchase of the tobacco outright before shipment. Scottish merchants established stores across the colonies both to collect the annual crop and to sell their settled clientele what they needed from the store on credit; in exchange, the planters undertook to sell their tobacco exclusively to the merchant's factor. As with the first model, the planter was usually unable to clear his account, which in time became a source of long-term credit to the colonists.

The attraction of this model for the Glasgow merchant, who lacked the commercial clout of his English counterparts, who themselves dealt with the wealthy Virginian planters, was that it addressed the needs of the more modest planters. For the most part, these planters lived in the rapidly expanding Chesapeake region of Virginia and operated on a scale that fell below the radar of the English merchants. Their main shortage was capital to help them expand their plantations for efficiencies of scale. The Glasgow merchants, to make their model work competitively, needed a stable pool of clients—planters whose needs they could service and respond to via their appointed resident factors. The factors secured from the planters as much tobacco crop in advance as possible, which reduced the period of turn around and thus freight costs. This, allied with the shorter sea passage between the American colonies and Glasgow compared to London, gained them an important advantage: Glasgow merchants were able to recover their capital more quickly and thereby cut costs and increase turnover.

Attractive as this system proved initially, it stoked up problems for the future. Increasingly, as planters became indebted to the merchants, they were unable to reconcile their business accounts. This unsatisfactory situation for the planters, aggravated by a lack of capital, led them to buy in more slave labour in order to match the increased demand for tobacco—something often only achieved on borrowed money. Meanwhile, the profit-hungry Glasgow merchants used their West Indian trade to supply sugar, rum and molasses to their American stores, while financially tying in their planter clients. In time, this dependency fuelled a general sense of ill-feeling and resentment among the indebted planters towards the Glasgow merchants.

The store model was also unpopular with the merchant houses of London, who found themselves progressively unable to compete with the competitive rates offered by their Glasgow rivals. Aside from issues of price and turnover, the problem faced by the London houses was that, by acting as agents for individual plantation owners, they shared a mutual interest to secure the best price for their tobacco. Their agents strove for higher prices and this approach was both more expensive and time-consuming than that of the store model.

In the international tobacco market, one of the biggest players was the French government, which imposed a national monopoly on the purchase of tobacco from foreign merchants for French consumption.[11] The French public had a preference for the flavour of the Virginian leaf, and the government wanted to secure bulk buys at competitive cost, which post-1740, was something the Scots were able to deliver under the store system.[12] To this end, they were helped by the British government, which under Prime Minister Walpole, reduced tariffs imposed for the re-exporting of goods through British entrepôts. This suited the Glasgow traders who re-exported 98 per cent of all their imports, chiefly to France, but also increasingly to Holland and Ireland.[13] This shows that, taken with a substantial increase in cargoes for sale in England, the tobacco lords did not have all their eggs in one basket.[14]

Meanwhile, as part of the enterprise, consumer goods exported from Glasgow were sold via the stores to planters. It is difficult to determine, before 1750, the extent to which the goods demanded by this trade with the

Caribbean and American colonies boosted the growth of Scottish industry, but what is known is that after 1750, almost all goods manufactured in Scotland were financed by merchants to service their colonial trade.[15]

Nothing, however, could be achieved without capital. In a country almost bankrupted by the Darien Company fiasco (see introduction), ways had to be found to provide the capital to fund the tobacco trade with its attendant risks. In a pragmatic solution that demonstrated the commercial flexibility of the tobacco barons, the Glasgow trade houses used bills of exchange, which permitted the flow of goods between parties in the knowledge that the payment would be met when the bill was presented.[16] This contractual arrangement was made possible by the mutual trust established within their international trading network.[17]

This financial instrument was not suitable to secure the long-term capital typically required to fund the ongoing credit of planters' businesses and the stores. Instead, this was funded via the reinvestment of the merchants' trading profits. Careful succession planning ensured the transfer of these accumulated profits between generations and their application to fresh business plans adapted to the evolving market. The dynastic ambitions of tobacco barons were served by arranged marriages between, for instance, a junior partner and the daughter of a senior partner. In this way, capital was consolidated within the business. Rising stars in the trade, such as Richard Oswald came to be, might seek an arranged marriage in exchange for a substantial dowry. Overall, the careful retention of huge profits within the business boosted liquidity, limiting the need for credit and other forms of debt. Indeed, most saw borrowing as the first step towards financial and moral bankruptcy, and something best avoided.[18]

Not all merchants were so fortunate, however, and some did need to go into debt to fund their short- and long-term needs, either due to trading difficulties or, post-1750, because of a wish to expand into a rapidly growing tobacco market. This need for outside capital gave rise to the foundation of the unlimited liability ventures of the Ship Bank, founded in 1752, the Glasgow Arms Bank, founded in the same year, and the Thistle Bank, founded in 1761. All three addressed the specific requests of tobacco lords and the wider commercial needs of Scottish businesses, though the majority of Glasgow merchants still preferred to draw on capital borrowed from landowners, trustees and minor investors who were prepared to take a risk on the tobacco trade.[19] Meanwhile, cash-rich merchants mostly restricted their business with banks to making cash deposits. Oswald was a case in point, maintaining modest balances sufficient for his use.[20]

The Glasgow merchants themselves were typically well educated. A high proportion attended Glasgow University, and as a result, many would have encountered Enlightenment thought under the tutelage of the hugely influential Francis Hutcheson and Adam Smith, men at 'the cutting edge of humane enquiry', and both professors of moral philosophy at the university.[21] They taught their students to open their minds to the arts and sciences, to apply reason to their mode of thinking and to seek personal improvement by conducting themselves with good manners and politeness.[22] At the same time, within an egalitarian society, they 'vigorously condemned the slave system on moral, philosophical and economic grounds'.[23]

Among students from Glasgow's merchant class, these lessons in Enlightenment ideas and values nurtured the improving aspiration to 'become a gentleman'. To achieve this aim, at least in the context of Enlightenment thought, one was expected to balance one's own interests with those of the less fortunate in society. If not already confronted, it uncovered the stark contradiction between Enlightenment values (such as all men being equal before God) and the evil of slavery, the root of the wealth which, ironically, helped facilitate the development and dissemination of Enlightenment thought.

By the time of the outbreak of the American War of Independence in 1775, the trade in Glasgow was dominated by three syndicates led by John Glassford (1715–1783), William Cunninghame (1731–1799) and Alexander Speirs (1714–1782).[24] Their personal assets included plantations, slaves and country estates, and in the case of Glassford, a fleet of merchant ships. Together, they controlled over 50 per cent of the tobacco trade. Their reliance enabled them to survive the eight-year hiatus to trade brought by the war and to invest profitably in new markets, but they were not the only ones to survive. In fact, most, if not all, the Scottish firms managed to re-establish their positions in the new United States post-1783.

Among the strata of tobacco firms immediately below the three premier syndicates were the families of Donald, Murdoch and Dunlop. The Oswalds were also among this group.[25] By 1730, five years after Richard's arrival in Glasgow, Oswald & Co. was the fifth largest tobacco firm in Glasgow, importing 300,000 pounds of leaf each year.[26]

The business Richard Oswald joined in 1725 had been set up by his two elder cousins, brothers Richard and Alexander. The last four generations of Oswalds had pursued careers as teachers, ministers and magistrates in Caithness, but these professions no longer appealed; Richard's cousins, like him, had left Caithness some years before due to the lack of opportunities there.

The elder Richard and Alexander had arrived in Glasgow in 1713, aged twenty-six and nineteen respectively, and set up an import/export business. Its growth was boosted by the elder brother's appointment as chief clerk in the New Port Glasgow Customs House. They imported tobacco from Chesapeake, sugar from the Caribbean and wine from Madeira and the Canary Islands, and with frugality and hard work, their business prospered. The younger Richard had been brought up by his Presbyterian father in much the same way as his cousins, and shared their appetite for hard work. Upon joining them in 1725, he quickly proved himself an asset to their business.[27]

During his apprenticeship, Richard would have undertaken a range of jobs within the business such as filing and storing records, examining and copying accounts, drawing bills of exchange, addressing bills for acceptance, and dealing with customs and insurance matters.[28] The work would have provided him with a solid foundation upon which to develop. After ten years, aged thirty, Richard was working as a factor mainly in Jamaica, Virginia and Carolina. His job included distributing supplies to planters, negotiating tobacco purchases, overseeing its packaging and loading, and collecting outstanding debts. He also made important connections and friendships in these places, among them Alexander Grant in Jamaica, a man with whom he would work with more closely in the future.

Appreciative of his success, the cousins brought Richard back to Glasgow in 1741 as a junior partner in their business, managing the everyday details of their joint accounts. In this position, he pressed his cousins to increase their levels of shipping activity and to embrace new trading correspondents. During the next five or six years, the firm held shares in 133 different voyages, representing a ninefold increase on their activities of the early 1730s. With operations expanding further into the Caribbean, the business was supplemented by investments in rope manufacturing, sugar refining and bottle manufacturing. This enabled Oswald & Co. to process their own imports and establish themselves as the town's supplier of wine. Meanwhile, Richard started his own account by buying shares in transatlantic trade, importing and exporting a range of goods both to and from Spain, Portugal, the Caribbean and Virginia.[29]

By 1746, Richard Oswald's ambitions to move ahead in business had begun to outgrow what he felt he could achieve in Glasgow. He decided to relocate to London, setting up a new operation from his three-storey counting house at 17 Philpot Lane. The focus of his business was in tobacco and shipping, and his success was extraordinary; within a year he had become the ninth largest London trader in tobacco. Two years later, Oswald broadened his activities, working with other expatriate Scots to expand into the slave trade through the purchase of the notorious slave-trading fort on Bunce Island in Sierra Leone. This part of Oswald's business life, which continued until his death in 1784, is dealt with later in this chapter.

Although he was enjoying great success in London, Oswald's ability to expand into the slave trade was due in no small part to his strategic marriage to Mary Ramsay, the only child of a Kingston importer/exporter from the northeast of Scotland, on 12 November 1750.[30] She was an acknowledged beauty (later painted by Zoffany) whom Richard had met during his time in Jamaica, and brought to the marriage a Jamaican estate, family ties to merchants and planters in Jamaica, and a significant dowry settled in trust and managed in London by two trustees, fellow Scots John Mill from Montrose (a co-owner with Oswald and others in the Bunce Island venture), and Robert Scott, principal owner of a major Madeira wine trading firm.[31]

Richard and Mary had much in common, sharing values such as honesty, thrift, industry and sobriety, while their mutual interests and respective connections opened up new opportunities of commercial engagement. Mary's connections enabled Richard to join a diverse group of twenty-three entrepreneurs known as the 'Associates'. They were based in London, and operated as wholesale traders primarily with the American colonies between 1735 and 1785. Oswald soon became one of the core of this group, alongside three others: Augustus Boyd, Alexander Grant and John Sargent II. The four of them together, in addition to two others, were partners in the Bunce Island venture.[32]

At the time of Oswald's arrival in London in 1746, a published guide ventured that capital of between £3,000 to £4,000 was needed to 'engage in foreign trade to any great advantage'.[33] This was at a time when a retail business or apothecary might typically need £100 to become established. In keeping with their Glasgow counterparts, the Associates in London were largely able to raise the necessary funds either from extended family networks, their previous earned profits or, like Oswald, by marriage dowries.[34] Indeed, the careers of most of the Associates followed the same pattern as Oswald's, going from apprenticeship to partnership and with marriage following later.

Like their mercantile counterparts in Glasgow, all twenty-three of these men were from the middle class, born outside London and driven by an intense ambition to move up in the world by making money. Their respective educations, values and career projections were broadly in line with Oswald's. They were men of ability, responding to the commercial opportunities of the time; about half of them traded privately in African slaves and a third of them had bought land and established plantations in colonies of Florida, Georgia, the ceded Caribbean islands and Nova Scotia. During the Seven Years' War (1756–1763), a third of them, including Oswald, served as government contractors, and most speculated in the new stocks and securities that funded the war. Significantly, they developed their businesses by seizing opportunities in London in areas where the networks of the establishment were least able to keep them out.

The Associates were men of differing temperaments, but they liked and trusted each other, and understood they would achieve greater success if they worked together, pooling their talents and resources. Although few of the twenty-three were politically active, the majority, like Oswald, operated in the shadows of government to safeguard their commercial, social and personal interests. They wanted their heirs to live comfortably and be accepted by the elite, and were thus motivated to acquire the attributes of gentlemen, defined by shared values of reason and politeness.

Oswald's business continued to expand at an astonishing pace. Oswald's cousin, James Oswald of Dunnikier, sat on the Treasury Board and through him Oswald secured a government contract to supply summer military camps in the south of England with provisions between 1756 and 1758.[35] In 1758, under a further contract, Oswald supplied the army in Germany with bread. This expanded over the period of the Seven Years' War with an additional three contracts and two separate commissions with the commissariat. It earned him a net profit of £125,000, providing him with the capital he needed to take advantage of the post-war opportunities to invest further in shipping and slavery.

Oswald acquired four plantations in the Caribbean extending to 1,566 acres, and made further investments in South Carolina and Nova Scotia where land could be acquired cheaply. In the case of the latter, a plan was devised with other planters to settle a colony, but when it became clear that it lacked direction, Oswald sold out. Instead, he directed his attention to Florida, which had been ceded to Britain by the Spanish in 1763.[36] There, in the east, he bought 30,000 acres of land, and at the head of a group of like-minded and trusted investors, he set put together a scheme to tame the wilderness.

As commissioning merchant, Oswald supplied the necessary materials and recommended the professional experts needed to manage and oversee the plantations under development. The missing link was, of course, the labour needed to make the land suitable for cultivation. In 1770, as the only slave trader among this group of Florida investors, Oswald dispatched three private ships from his slave fort at Bunce Island, Sierra Leone, with cargoes of slaves bound for Florida. Once there, he took delivery of planters' crops, mainly indigo, and managed their sale.

The American War of Independence forced Oswald to review his global strategy. In 1780 he sold his land in Virginia and began to withdraw from Florida, but earlier in response to the outbreak of war, he increased his profile in politics by submitting to British government officials detailed policy recommendations, the first sent in February 1775, on military strategy in America. This drew on his extensive knowledge of that country's geography and trade, which began with his period of residence there. In these papers, he proposed the means by which Britain retained control of its colony. During the war, Oswald was regularly consulted by Prime Minister Lord North and others in government, who valued his advice. When the peace had to be brokered in Paris 1782, the new prime minister, Lord Shelburne, selected Oswald as the best candidate to open the informal negotiations with Benjamin Franklin, with whom Oswald had already had limited dealings. Both shared the similar views on free trade and commerce, while Oswald's reflective disposition was thought likely to appeal to Franklin. After he had signed off the preliminary articles, he was recalled by parliament before the Treaty of Paris was finalised in September 1783, but in its final form it contained virtually no changes to that earlier text.[37]

Returning back to 1748, just two years after his arrival in London, Oswald made his first step into the slave trade. On a rare occasion of collective borrowing, the sextet of Augustus and John Boyd, Alexander Grant (whom Oswald had met in Jamaica), John Sargent II, John Mill and Oswald drew a loan of £4,500 to finance the operating costs of their slave fort venture at Bunce Island. The loan was drawn during their first year of ownership, and at the same time, Oswald took on a personal loan from Robert Scott, one of the trustees of his wife's dowry, to meet his share of the building's refurbishment. The partners had no way of knowing whether their venture would work, but they chose to take the gamble nonetheless to bring all the disparate elements of their supply chain under their sole control. The timing of the investment coincided with the demand for black slaves substantially increasing as new plantations for tobacco and sugar came into production in the Caribbean and the American colonies to meet the ever-growing demand for these commodities, and sugar particularly. The six partners planned to supply these new plantations as well as their own with slaves procured at the fort on Bunce Island.

The island, which sits in the estuary of the Sierra Leone River, measures 500 by 100 metres and covers 15 acres of land. Most of the island was forested, but around a quarter of its area was occupied by the fort. It was built in about 1670 by the Royal African Company (RAC), an English trading company established a decade earlier by Charles II and the merchants of the City of London to trade along the west coast of Africa. Its purpose was to house Africans in their thousands before shipment to the Americas. The commercial failure of the Royal African Company led to the fort's abandonment in 1728, following its partial destruction in a raid by Jose Lopez da Moura, a local slave trader who had wanted to challenge the RAC's monopoly in the area.

After lying neglected for ten years, the fort was bought by London slave trader George Fryer, but his venture to trade slaves and ivory from Bunce Island failed. This opened the way, in 1748, for Oswald and his five partners to buy out Fryer. Under the partnership agreement, capitalisation was divided into nine shares, with Oswald taking three and thus a commensurately greater share of the profit. Three years later, the partners secured the legal warranty in London to trade, which enabled them to attract third party finance.

These events coincided with a much-needed re-examining by the British government of how African trade was conducted. It culminated in the African Trade Act of 1750, which, along with other helpful measures for merchants, passed control of African affairs from the failed RAC to private traders. It represented a triumph for Oswald and his partners who, alongside other merchants, had lobbied parliament for change. Relieved of the threat of interference, they poured investment into the rebuilding of the fort, supervising from London as best they could, while having to see off the unwanted attention of hostile French ships in the region.[38] They managed to pull it off, and after earlier modest beginnings, slave trading began in earnest from the fort in 1755 when 304 slaves were exported. The numbers rose to a peak of well over 3,000 per annum during the years 1760–1770.

From these beginnings a flourishing entrepôt developed to match the increased demand for slave labour. Slaves were exchanged by traders or African kings for clothes, cloth, metalware, agricultural commodities and sundry items drawn from the partners' extensive international networks now spanning four continents, and all achieved without government aid or intervention.

By 1763, the end of the Seven Years' War, a further expansion of the fort had taken place to house greater quantities of slaves. The numbers needed to man the fort fluctuated, but by 1783 the total had grown to thirty-five whites and 142 free blacks, with many of the latter skilled in a trade. Of the white workforce, several were the less employable relations or friends of the six owners. They had been found jobs in that far-flung 'Scottish' outpost boasting its own two-hole golf course and tartan-clothed caddies, having failed at or sabotaged every other opportunity. The owners admitted that, as far as their relations were concerned, the settlement resembled a reformatory of sorts, though one that posed a high chance of non-return.[39]

Little information survives of the conditions in which the slaves were kept, but eighty to ninety died each year on the island.[40] Nonetheless, not a man to neglect any aspect of his business, Oswald fretted over the physical welfare of his slaves. He ordered captains to ignore international practice and forgo branding the slaves with hot irons. Instead he told them to place chequered beads around their arms. He also ordered his factors in Florida to keep families from Bunce Island on the same plantations. To the modern eye these actions do nothing to address the inherent cruelty of what Oswald and his partners were overseeing.

Whether or not Oswald was comparatively enlightened for his time, he never lost sight of the bottom line—profit—nor that the slaves were chattels. These imperatives allowed him emotionally to disconnect himself from the realities of the trade and to overlook the humanity of his slaves. By doing so, he consigned them to unspeakable cruelty and abuse, apparently without conscience. It was an attitude typical of slave merchants of the period in which productivity, rather than liberty, was king.[41] It is estimated that between the first year of trading in 1749 and 1784, 12,929 slaves were exported from the island.

The outbreak of the American War of Independence in 1775 effectively marked the end for the Bunce Island slave operation. Trading all but ceased. In 1779, the French burnt the fort to the ground, seizing all the British ships and their cargoes within the island's immediate vicinity. Efforts to rebuild were slow, and several of the partners sold their shares. By 1784 Oswald owned five-ninths of the business, at which time the fort was put up for sale. Oswald died very soon afterwards in November 1784, aged seventy-eight. His interest passed to his two nephews, John and Alexander Anderson.

Oswald had dedicated his life to attaining wealth and using it to achieve the status of 'gentleman', the meaning of which had had to adjust in the rapidly changing world of the eighteenth century. It had expanded beyond referring solely to the aristocracy, to embrace those accumulating wealth from the expanding empire as merchants or bureaucrats. Certain common characteristics included a good education, 'genteel' dress, a confident demeanour, the means to support a privileged lifestyle and the ability to express it in a refined and polite manner. By achieving these attributes, men like Oswald, born as outsiders from the middle class, could become members of this exclusive and previously unattainable club.

It was the 'Age of Improvement'. Wealthy men sought to engage in practical projects to improve the way in which they were perceived, not only by those in the higher echelons of society, but also by those beneath them on the social ladder. They invested in agriculture, transportation and industrial development. They supported charities. Some promoted an agenda of commercial and agricultural legislation in parliament.[42] The object was to help themselves in a manner that secured their status as gentlemen and, at the same time, served the interests of others in pursuit of the common good.

Oswald's activities appear to bear this out. With his initial free capital in London, he moved from his office at 17 Philpot Lane, which had doubled as his home, to a fashionable townhouse at 14 Great George Street. At roughly the same time, in keeping with the Associates, he bought the first of his several overseas plantations and a share of Bunce Island in Sierra Leone, and took on leases of country houses in both Sussex and Kent.[43] He bought two commercial tracts of land on the James River in Jamaica, a house in the City of London and, in 1764, Auchencruive Estate in Scotland, 5 miles east of Ayr. By 1782 he owned 102,678 acres in Scotland, mainly in Kirkcudbright. Oswald understood that the Scottish estates were not good investments in the conventional sense, but Auchencruive provided him with a residence where he could be the laird. From this elevated position he could dispense goodwill via projects for the benefit of himself and the wider community. Philanthropy was typically regarded by merchants like Oswald from a religious perspective, as expressed by Alexander Grant, his fellow investor in the Bunce Island fortress: 'God gave Man the earth ut operaretur [to work]', and it was incumbent on man 'to repent of his sins & improve the land', and with it the welfare of the community.[44] In this way, a landowner could enhance his standing while bringing the countryside into cultivation, permitting, as Lord Kames observed, a convergence of private and public interests.[45]

Oswald and other merchants honed their knowledge in discussion groups founded all around Scotland from 1723 onwards. Land use and management were radically modernised as more land was brought into cultivation, introducing new crops with the application of improved science and equipment.

Working with tenant farmers to whom he granted leases for fixed periods, Oswald erected march boundaries secured by good legal title.[46] He worked on comprehensive management plans, implemented to rejuvenate neglected areas by draining wetlands and introducing better fertilisers and crops.[47] He carried out other land improvements with the tenants, delegating responsibility to them wherever he could, wanting to establish productive and long-lasting relationships. They had to commit to his exacting standards, but in exchange he provided housing, training and, if necessary, leniency on rent arrears. By respecting his workforce, Oswald was demonstrating an indicator of polite status (or polished manners).[48] He understood that by helping them, they would help him.

Land improvements were natural bedfellows to improvements in infrastructure; after all, goods from farms needed to be taken to markets. The Associates, including Oswald, built roads, bridges, and to a lesser degree, canals and lighthouses in south-eastern England and in southeastern and north-eastern Scotland. The need was manifest. The roads in Ayrshire of 1750 were in a calamitous state, both impassable and dangerous in winter. Investment had failed because those responsible were cash-strapped.[49] Oswald, working with likeminded people, instituted public turnpike trusts.[50] He gave both time and money to overseeing much of this enterprise, and between 1766 and 1775, an astonishing fifty-six new roads were laid in Ayrshire. This work continued with bridges and more roads right up Oswald's death in 1784, benefitting all sections of the local community. He initiated new commercial ventures including limeworks, coal mines, salt pans and a woollen mill, creating local jobs, which he viewed as a form of poor relief. He also funded the construction of a new aisle of his local church, St Quivox, and gave to the poor of that parish annually. He was beloved by the local community and respected by his aristocratic neighbours who appreciated his endeavours and occasionally even applied for his help. For instance, the earl of Dumfries asked Oswald for his support in funding the regeneration of one of his ailing factories.

The paradox of Oswald, and others like him, was that this industrious, able and astute merchant was both a slave owner and trader. The extraordinary wealth that enabled him to raise his status so highly in British society and to fund altruistic projects in Scotland was built directly and intentionally upon the appalling suffering of thousands of Africans. It may not have been the business model with which Oswald had begun, but when the opportunity to deal directly in slaves made commercial sense, he did not hesitate.

12

Slavery and a Battle for America's Soul: Fanny Wright

On 2 September 1818, a wealthy Scotswoman named Frances (Fanny) Wright stood astride the deck of a passenger ship, the *Amity*, as it threaded its way through the Narrows between Staten Island and Brooklyn, heading for New York Bay. With her eyes straining into the 'crimson glories of the evening sky', Wright beheld the sight she had long been waiting for: New York City, a place where, she wrote, '[there is] no great proprietor, his mighty domains stretching in silent and solitary grandeur for uninterrupted miles, but thousands of little villas or thriving farms, bespeaking the residence of the easy citizen or tiller of the soil'.[1]

New York was Wright's first tangible engagement with the ideals of the republic, which she knew to be 'consecrated in freedom'. This powerful, if metaphysical image had been burnt into her mind and soul five years earlier, when as a restless seventeen-year-old she had read, in Italian, Carlo Botta's *Storia della Guerra dell'indipendenza degli Stati Uniti d'America* (1809), the history of the thirteen American colonies' fight to secure their independence from Britain. After that, Wright vowed to see the country for herself, finally departing Liverpool in early August 1818 with her younger sister, Camilla, to embark on two-year tour of the northern United States. Her expectations of this new nation were high indeed:

> Never was a national revolution conducted by greater men; by men more magnanimous, more self-devoted, and maturely wise; and these men, too, were not self elected, nor raised by chance to pilot the vessel of the state; they were called by the free voices of their fellow citizens to fill the various posts most suited to their genius.... [They formed a

community] animated with the feeling of liberty, but understanding the duties of citizens, and the nature and end of civil government.[2]

Wright later qualified these heartfelt sentiments with an admission that she had chosen not to travel to the Southern states because of the unacceptable presence of slavery there, which she blamed on British colonialism. 'The sight of slavery is revolting everywhere,' she wrote, 'but to inhale the impure breath of its pestilence in the free winds of America is odious beyond all that the imagination can conceive.'[3]

She regarded slavery as an ugly stain on the integrity of the republic that needed to be expunged. That said, she understood there were difficult issues to be addressed in American society before emancipation could or would be fully embraced. It caused her to question whether it was sufficient for the masters in the slave states to content themselves 'with idly deploring' the evil of slavery instead of 'setting their shoulders to the wheel and actively working out its remedy'.[4] Essentially, the presence of slavery in the United States presented a moral dilemma: either it was a country 'consecrated in freedom', as she believed, or it wasn't, and if the latter, she asked what could be done to rid it of this 'pestilence'?

Fanny Wright was born in Dundee on 6 September 1795 to James and Camilla Wright. Her father, the only son of a wealthy merchant, was an indifferent businessman but a dedicated political radical. He corresponded with Adam Smith, was a keen supporter of the French Revolution, and promoted the works of Thomas Paine.[5] Wright, however, never knew him or her mother. They died within three months of each other in 1797, when Fanny was just two years old. She and her two siblings, an older brother and younger sister, were parcelled off to different foster parents. Her brother Richard was placed with their uncle, James Mylne, professor of moral philosophy at Glasgow University, joining his family of five children, while her sister Camilla was left with a family in Dundee. Fanny, meanwhile, was dispatched to London to be brought up by her maternal grandfather, Major General Duncan Campbell of the Royal Marines, and his eighteen-year-old daughter Frances.

The Campbell household proved to be an unhappy one for Fanny, whose intellect and disposition were ill-suited to her guardians. Her brother Richard described his grandfather as indolent and convivial, in keeping with his social set of 'Lords and Generals', who scorned work, regarding it as shameful. Fanny bridled at this attitude and her grandfather's self-indulgent approach to life. In her memoirs, she recalled asking him why the unkempt mothers and children she had seen were so poor, to which she received the response: 'Because they were too lazy to work.' She then asked, 'Why did rich people, who do not work, not become beggars?'

He responded: 'God intended there should be poor and there should be rich.' Not satisfied, Fanny pondered whether the rich robbed the poor. Her grandfather warned her that if she adopted that way of thinking, she would have no place in good society.[6] His warning was lost on Fanny, who instead developed a strong social conscience.

In 1806, when Fanny was nine years old, her uncle, Major William Campbell, was killed in action at Saswarree in India. His death was to have significant implications for her; he had divided his substantial estate equally between his sister, Frances, and his two nieces, Fanny and Camilla. It enabled Frances to take a substantial house in Dawlish, Devon, where, in great comfort, she cared for both Fanny and Camilla, who had moved from Dundee to join them. The inheritance crucially provided both Fanny and her sister with the financial means in adulthood to do as they wished with their lives.

The loss of her parents so early in life had likely implanted within Fanny subliminal emotional insecurities. These were magnified in 1809 with the sudden deaths of her brother Richard at the hands of the French when he was on his way to India, and of her grandfather. Indeed, it is suggested that these deaths, coming on top of the loss of her parents, provoked her lifelong outrage at human suffering.[7]

At home in Dawlish, Fanny found the shallowness of drawing room conversation, in which the peak of ambition for a young lady was to find a suitor to make a 'worthy' marriage, contemptible. Nor did she make much effort to hide it. She lacked the sensitivity to charm or influence those with whom she had little in common. Later in life, she expressed this part of her character in her dogmatism and inability to empathise with others whose ideals diverged from her own, even when a concession could have benefitted her and her mission.

From a young age, Fanny Wright befriended distinguished, enlightened men who helped expand her learning in the arts and sciences. Thus, she gained a grounding in classical drama and oratory, both of which were to prove vital to her future development as a passionate public speaker. She also developed a political awareness that recognised the connection between human suffering and human causes, and 'that wealth had power in the world which age and infirmity did not'.[8] She took exception at the 'new rich' merchants in Devon clearing smallholdings to build mansions and estates for themselves while forcing the poor from the land. Social injustices like these led her to pledge to help the poor and the helpless and to redress the terrible wrongs of society.[9] At seventeen years old, she read Botta's history on the American War of Independence and within those pages saw a vision of a country which was everything that Britain was not: a utopia 'consecrated to freedom'.

By eighteen, Fanny Wright could no longer control the deep-seated contempt she felt for her unintellectual and controlling aunt, whom she believed had stifled her to an unforgiveable extent. She buried her anger and resentment by resolving to trust no one, and instead to trust only in her ideals.[10] This strength of purpose saw her and her sister move to Glasgow to stay with their uncle, Professor James Mylne. With him, they absorbed a very different environment.

The citizens of Glasgow took civic duty very seriously with continual discussions of social reform and economic improvement. Wright's uncle sat in what, only thirty-five years before, had been Adam Smith's chair at Glasgow University. A Church of Scotland minister, he extolled the virtues of reason, self-control and duty. He promoted the utilitarian principle of the greater happiness of the greater number and favoured the abolition of the slave trade. Both his nieces were embraced into a world of debate, arts and science, which served to bolster their self-confidence, and for Fanny, to polish her talent and feed her ambition. She did briefly bend to convention, becoming engaged in 1815, but when her friends persuaded her that her fiancé was not her intellectual equal, she ended the relationship.[11]

For the ensuing three years, Wright lived happily in Scotland. She befriended Robina Craig Millar, a relation of her uncle by marriage, and became so close to her that she called her 'mother'.[12] It was Millar, a radical, if anachronistic republican, who fostered in Wright the belief that America was a progressive republican utopia.[13] It was a view confirmed for Wright in the books she devoured on the new country, sourced for her by her uncle from the excellent Glasgow University library. In this rich intellectual environment, Wright wrote poetry and plays, demonstrating considerable literary ability, but this talent took second place to her sense of social justice. As demonstrated by her early conversations with her grandfather, it had been a part of her from a very young age. It came to the fore during a visit to the Highlands, where she witnessed the socially destructive effects of the Clearances.

It was a repeat by the Scottish landowners of what the rich merchants had done in Devon. Wright dismissed all landowners as being of 'a class to whom Property was becoming a sacred trust and its improvement an obligation that must take precedence over all others'. She also rebuked the Church of Scotland, with the exception of a few of their ministers, for supporting the landowners rather than their congregations, by giving 'God's authority to Improvement, and [for threatening] the more truculent of the evicted with damnation'. An incipient anger within her was beginning to find focus on the self-serving political values and religious stance of the privileged few, who exercised their power contrary to the wider interests of society, creating an imbalance that

Wright despised. It caused her to search for a way to deliver a fairer world.

At this point, Mylne's friend, Manchester textile manufacturer Robert Owen, became a significant person in Wright's life, though she was not to meet him for a few more years.[14] In 1799, after moving north, Owen, a Welshman, purchased a number of cotton spinning mills at New Lanark on the River Clyde from his father-in-law, David Dale.[15] Started by Dale and further developed by Owen, it was a visionary project which demonstrated that by improving the working and living conditions of employees, a healthy and comparatively contented workforce was mutually compatible with running a profitable business.[16] As a matter of equal importance, Owen promoted within the community the education and welfare of children, prioritising their character development.[17]

Between 1815 and 1817, Wright and her sister became familiar with the principles of Owen's work, sharing his view that the social devastation of industrialisation was unnecessary and could be reversed. They were also attracted by his model for improvement, which rested on the contentious principle that people's characters are formed for them and not by them. The model opened the way to improving the lives of many people without disadvantage to others.[18]

By 1816, Wright, now twenty-one years old, was itching to make her mark in society, which was fractured by civil unrest partly as a result of Britain's rapid industrialisation. The year before, an already inflammatory situation of social deprivation had been made worse by parliament's enacting of the protectionist Corn Laws.[19] This decision fomented extremism among the underclass, of whom Robert Wedderburn (Chapter 5) was one. Dissidents petitioned parliament for universal suffrage, and when their efforts were frustrated, rioting and economic hardship followed, ending in the public execution of ringleaders. Turning away from this bleak picture of governance, so resistant to change, Wright searched for something to inspire her. She found it in the newly born republic of the United States of America. It was time, she decided, that she and her loyal sister Camilla went there to see it for themselves.

When she disembarked at New York, Wright was overjoyed to observe nothing of the extremes between poverty and wealth which characterised England.[20] As she travelled through the north and west, meeting frontiersmen, she accepted their brusque manners as a feature of boisterous equality, and she had no complaints about the impassable roads and insect-ridden hotels. She took this lack of sophistication as a measure of virility to be set against European decadence. It was, therefore, with disappointment and distaste that, in Washington, D.C., Wright first listened to American views on slavery that were much in contrast to her own.

In 1807, when the slave trade was abolished, the United States had been receiving only about 6 per cent of African slaves sent to the New World. Distribution within the country was uneven. Just over thirty years earlier, at the start of the American War of Independence in 1775, less than 10 per cent of the 500,000 slaves in the thirteen colonies lived in the North. By 1777, most of the Northern colonies had implemented a programme of gradual emancipation, which continued during the late eighteenth and early nineteenth centuries. It was a different story in the South, where by 1820 there were approximately two white people for every black slave.[21] In Virginia, the black slave population accounted for 40.27 per cent of the total, while in Tennessee the figure was 17.02 per cent.

In Washington, Wright got involved in a debate with a group of Southerners who sought to justify the status quo by highlighting the squalor in which free blacks lived in Virginia and Maryland. This, they argued, made it clear that if their slaves were given their freedom, there was no evidence to suggest it would improve either their character or condition. While Wright had no time for this, she did recognise that if a slave was given his liberty before he understood its value, his enjoyment of that freedom might prove a burden rather than a blessing. That said, having travelled in the North, Wright knew that the blacks there enjoyed much better lives than those in the South.

This served to emphasise that the problem was not the blacks themselves but the denial to them of education and proper economic opportunity.[22] It encouraged Wright to imagine a world of total emancipation which, supported by education, would enable the white man to hire the services of the black, and for the black man in turn to sell his services to the white, making slavery a thing of the past. That lay in the future, however, because Wright believed that a slave had to be prepared for his freedom. Her reasoning was that, if freedom was received without education, it would be regarded only as a release from labour.[23]

These pithy insights are but a few of those recorded by Wright in her memoirs, published upon her return to Britain in 1821. Indeed, she recorded a wide range of perceptive thoughts on subjects including the rights of women, slavery, the treatment of the Indians and the activities of the social and political institutions of the United States.[24] The book established her name among appreciative liberals and reformers in both Britain and the Continent.[25]

Among Wright's fans was the Marquis de Lafayette, then sixty-three, a veteran of the French Revolution and the American War of Independence, and a highly respected war hero.[26] Like Wright, he had huge admiration for

America. In 1821, at his invitation, Wright visited him in Paris, where she established a close friendship with him, 'sharing the most intimate private and political confidences'.[27] Indeed, she urged Lafayette either to marry her or, oddly, to adopt her and Camilla as his daughters. Both proposals were blocked by his concerned family. This mutual admiration led to Wright's second visit to America in 1824, 'on the coat tails' of Lafayette who had been invited as guest of honour to celebrate the fiftieth anniversary of the republic for which he had fought. Lafayette introduced Wright and her sister to his friends Thomas Jefferson and James Madison, both of whom had enjoyed her books.[28] She would later spend many hours debating with them on political and economic affairs.[29]

Firm friendships followed, but not without areas of contention. Jefferson did not agree that intermarriage between blacks and whites (miscegenation) would resolve the differences of race. In fact, he had written on this subject as early as 1814, concluding that such a solution 'produces a degradation to which no lover of his country, no lover of the excellence in human character, can innocently consent'. He added sombrely that 'deep rooted prejudices entertained by the whites; ten thousand recollections by the blacks of injuries they have sustained; new provocations; the real distinctions which nature has made; and many other circumstances, divide us into parties, and produce convulsions, which will probably never end but in the extermination of one race or the other.' Jefferson's gloomy comments raised the bleak issue for Wright of whether, after emancipation, blacks would ever be able to live together as equals with whites.[30] For Jefferson, it seemed, emancipation would not bring the social harmony that Fanny anticipated.[31]

The reflections of a highly experienced, if possibly world weary, political pragmatist were not going to demoralise Wright. Indeed, her sense of resolve was to be strengthened when she finally met Robert Owen, the kindred spirit whose ideas for social reform she had so much admired through his work at New Lanark. He arrived at Washington in mid-February 1825 to speak at a public meeting, which Wright attended. In his address, Owen sought to prove, with reference to his scheme at New Lanark, that if people could learn to live communally, they could live far happier, more economic and more productive lives. It was surely, he argued, a huge improvement on 'a system which pitted one person against another, destroyed elemental decencies and was even inefficient'.[32]

To achieve what he wanted, Owen thought it necessary to change the human experience profoundly, starting with the physical environment, and he could see no better place to test his theories than in America, a land of the future. Some five months earlier, for $125,000, he had purchased, along with 20,000 acres of land, a village in Indiana called New Harmony from the Rappite community, which had settled there ten years before.[33] He was now busy inviting people to join him there. Wright, who had identified Owen as her guru, wanted to see the village for herself. This she would do on her journey to New Orleans, where she had arranged to meet Lafayette on 1 April 1825.

Before she left Washington, she learned of the American Colonisation Society, of which James Madison was a prominent member.[34] The society was promoting a scheme, heavily supported by slave owners, in which freeborn and emancipated slaves were, with their consent, to be transported to Africa. Wright regarded it disparagingly as a means of salving the moral conscience of the planters while reducing pressure to end slavery. In some cases, the American Colonisation Society and others like it bought slaves for transportation to Africa, which Wright saw as creating a market for the 'commodity'. Real change, as she saw it, would happen once blacks were able to work for wages; then they would become equal to whites and a blend of the races could be fostered.

By mid-March 1825, the Wright sisters had travelled 1,000 miles on horseback, crossing the Allegheny mountains of West Virginia before sailing up the River Ohio to arrive at New Harmony. There they found a prosperous village, with two churches, nestled among vineyards, orchards, cornfields and sheepwalks. It was still populated by some 500 Rappites. Wright observed not only cooperative workers, but others who had prospered financially through the sale of their property to Owen. She studied how the model had both been funded and worked, concluding that at its roots it depended upon perseverance, good temper and cooperation.

While at New Harmony, Wright took the opportunity to visit a nearby English farm settlement in neighbouring Illinois, where she met George Flower, a man from Herefordshire nine years her senior, who was to prove to be another important figure in her life. Though a married man, she was instantly attracted to him, both physically and intellectually, seeing in him both a square-jawed man of action and a kindred spirit with whom she could work to achieve her goals. But Flower warned her that in Illinois, whites would be resistant to her vision of an equal society. The white settlers there believed that slavery was ordained by God and that blacks were incapable of looking after themselves. So strong and united was this feeling that the settlers had changed the state constitution to legalise slavery. Flower and likeminded friends had unsuccessfully tried to prevent this. He explained that these changes had threatened to frustrate his plans to emancipate his thirty black farmworkers. In desperation, he had secured an agreement with President Jean Pierre Boyer of Haiti, a free black republic since the revolution of 1791–1804, to take his slaves, which Flower had then transported there.[35] This solution was a good outcome for Flower's slaves, and faced with the problems in Illinois, Wright acknowledged that it might be the best choice, though it was not her first.[36] For his part, seeking a change in the face of a backlash from local English settlers to his principled stand on slavery, Flower agreed to support Wright in her ambitious endeavour. He viewed the Rappite New Harmony model as one suitable for a community in which blacks could work together with whites.

While her initiative was beginning to take shape, it remained difficult for Wright to finalise any plans without having seen the slave system in action. She therefore continued her journey south, meeting slave owners in Louisiana with whom she floated her nascent plans for emancipation. Notwithstanding what she had been told, she expected to receive their support for abolition, which she thought they wanted, provided it could be done safely and without financial loss.[37] Unfortunately, possibly because of her preconceived notions, Wright misread both what the slave owners said and what they stood for. What she saw before her were men of liberal instinct who were apologetic for slavery's existence. They agreed with her that the institution of slavery was unstable and dangerous, saying that unfortunately it was the system they were stuck with. What she failed to understand was their unspoken fear that any change to the status quo could provoke a rebellion, putting them and their families at risk. It meant that, while they agreed that the present situation was far from perfect, it offered them the best security, and that was their primary concern. But Wright thought they wanted to be rid of the system before any rebellion might break out, which would endanger their lives and massively reduce the value of their estates. Such a critical misunderstanding suggests an assumption on her part that the affliction of slavery was an unwanted hangover from British colonialism. Whatever the cause, she incorrectly concluded that the slave owners were in favour of her solution of peaceful, gradual emancipation.

In New Orleans, tensions were at a peak, with white racial pride and fear riding roughshod over justice and good sense. There, as planned, Wright met Lafayette, whose patronage she continued to enjoy despite Robert Owen being her new mentor. She told him of Owen's experiment at New Harmony, which was fundamental to her plan to end slavery, the outline of which she had finally completed. It was contained in a prospectus entitled *A Plan for the Gradual Abolition of Slavery in the United States, Without Danger or Loss to the Citizens of the South*. With Lafayette's blessing, Wright initiated her campaign to raise public subscriptions and support for her experiment from leading American politicians.

To raise the funds she wanted, Wright knew that she had to convince both the subscribers and the planters that her plan to emancipate slaves could be achieved without financial loss to the planters. She had accepted that all emancipated slaves would have to be resettled outside the borders of the United States to obviate the fears of planters that freed slaves on their land would prove a source of incitement to those still in bondage. For the pilot scheme, 100 slaves were to be bought, each of whom would be debited with the cost of purchase in the bill of sale onto which would be added the cost of board and clothing. A rate of 6 per cent interest would run on that cost as a fair return on investors' capital. In turn, the slaves would be paid for their labour at the usual rates with articles provided at cost.[38] A village and school for industrial education would be built, and the land cleared and planted under a cooperative system like that pioneered by the German Rappites.[39]

Wright calculated that the produce generated by the slaves within a five-year period would cover the whole cost of the enterprise. The use of this 'united labour' would enable the slave to have saved sufficient to pay his owner a fair price for his freedom, to cover the scheme's overheads, and to transport himself, his family and his belongings to a foreign colony such as Liberia or Haiti.[40]

Wright anticipated that, with the prospect of freedom ahead of them, the slaves would prove to be high-performance workers compared with those working on ordinary farms. In this way, the cost price of their produce would be lower, enabling Wright's settlement to undercut their business competitors. Unable to compete and with their businesses failing, slave owners would be keen to send their slaves to her farm, or ones similar, to recoup their investment before the bottom fell out of the market. Wright believed that if her plan were to be implemented by others countrywide, it would achieve total emancipation, and with the free slaves resettled abroad, America would be left as the land of perfect liberty.[41] As part of this plan, slaves working in these settlements would be educated in preparation for their freedom, which once achieved, would open up their jobs to white labour.

However, in devising her plan, Wright had assumed that slavery had been imposed on America by the British against the will of a white population eager to abolish it. She also underestimated the fears of the whites, seeing the blacks, if emancipated, as the most vulnerable group due to their entrenched habits and influences—risks, she felt, to be mitigated by gradual emancipation.

Blind to her plan's flaws, Wright set about finding a location for her visionary settlement. Tennessee was seen as the best bet because the state was home to six anti-slavery societies. The site chosen was identified by General Andrew Jackson and comprised 320 acres of poor quality, uncleared land in a remote area by the Wolf River, 15 miles south-west of Memphis.[42] It took the name 'Nashoba', the Indian word for wolf.[43] Once again, Lafayette gave his approval. Success was far from guaranteed, but Fanny Wright had already made history, becoming the first woman in America to publicly oppose slavery.

Difficulties soon piled up. Despite the cajoling by Lafayette of four past and future presidents (Jefferson, Madison, Monroe and Andrew Jackson), their support was not forthcoming. Wright faced similar disappointment from the other politicians she approached, who chose to remain silent. Madison did at least give his reason why, saying that he thought Wright's plans were unachievable. The farm would do well to generate the surplus necessary to stay afloat, he said, let alone repay the purchase price. He doubted her assumption that there was a substantial advantage, measured in crop yields, of united over individual labour.[44]

The upshot was that no public funds were forthcoming. However, Wright was no more inclined to accept this market verdict on her plan than she had been to listen to the warnings of Jefferson and Madison. After refusing Lafayette's goodwill gesture of $8,000, Wright scaled back her plans, which she now undertook to fund entirely herself. Instead of purchasing 100 slaves, she settled for eight—five men and three women—plus three children.[45] A further seven slaves and their six children were bought later in February 1826. In the same month, two new men joined her community: James Richardson, a Scot from Memphis, and Richesson Whitby from New Harmony. Progress followed with the erection of rudimentary log cabins, the planting of orchards and the sowing of crops, while the backbreaking work of clearing the land continued. However, after only seven exhausting months, Wright was forced to admit that the scheme had failed.

The reasons were manifold. In the absence of donations, Wright's financial reserves had begun to dry up;[46] damaging rumours had started to circulate, particularly among anti-abolitionists, that the experiment was simply a plot to attract free labour under the guise of philanthropic emancipation; the arrival of stock and supplies was delayed; conflicts had arisen between members within the community; the slaves, who had been brought up in a world of violence, suspicion and contempt, had taken time to adapt to working productively without the threat of brutal punishment hanging over them; George Flower, who had nearly died of fever, had returned to Illinois with his wife, who had not enjoyed life at Nashoba, and their two children; and Wright, to whom George's departure was a serious blow, had nearly worked herself to death and was suffering from malaria. Her poor state of health had highlighted the risk to her experiment if she continued as sole owner of Nashoba.

It was clear that the failings at Nashoba needed to be addressed urgently and that Wright needed time to convalesce elsewhere. She refused to wind up the scheme because, at the time, she didn't have the necessary funds to transport her slaves, as freemen, overseas, as she had promised them she would do. Also, to admit defeat would be to acknowledge publicly that slavery could not be ended without cost to the slave owner—something she was not ready to concede.[47]

Crestfallen at this unhappy turn of events, she casted around for scapegoats. She blamed the politicians and other leaders for not supporting her as she had believed they would, and the many settlers who had proved hostile to her objectives. America, she concluded bitterly, was not the utopia she had thought it to be; rather, she accused it of being irrecoverably pro-slavery. But if white Americans did not want to cleanse their nation of its blemish of slavery, then she would instead focus on making Nashoba her utopia.[48]

In December 1826, Wright transferred Nashoba and its assets by deed of trust, and two supplementary documents, to ten trustees, to be held in trust for the benefit 'of the negro race'.[49] Of the trustees, five had been or still were associated with the venture at New Harmony; they included Lafayette, Richesson Whitby, James Richardson, Robert Dale Owen (the eldest son of Robert Owen) and George Flower. Wright reserved to herself the rights of trusteeship and specified two conditions: that a school for black children would always be available, and that slaves liberated by the trustees must be transported outside the United States.[50] Under the trust, the community was to be governed on a daily basis by resident trustees. As such they were responsible for all the decisions and for administering Nashoba 'for the collective benefit of the negro race'.[51]

The transfer of ownership changed Nashoba from a privately owned model farm to a utopian community, subject to strict rules of admittance put in place to see off the lazy and unfit.[52] Under this structure, the slaves were the trust's beneficiaries but not its decision makers; indeed, for as long as they were slaves they would remain technically the property of the trust unless or until they bought out their freedom as provided for under the terms of the trust prior to their departure to either Liberia and Haiti.

Under the new order, a revised set of rules and objectives was implemented.[53] These new rules included the following:

- Marriage law existing outside the community is of no force within it.
- No woman can forget her individual rights or no man can assert over her any rights or power beyond what he may exercise over her free and voluntary affections.
- Any property held by members is deemed to be gifted to the trustees.

- Religion is to occupy no place in the creed of the commune and the rule of moral practice there proposed has simply in view human happiness....
- No religious doctrines will taught in the school.
- Young people are urged to learn a trade before applying for membership and bring such tools and equipment they may have with them.[54]

These rules resolved to address within Nashoba many of America's perceived problems on issues such as women's rights, their equality with men, the imposition of formal religion, the conventional laws of marriage and the communal ownership of property.

In the spring of 1827, a downhearted Robert Dale Owen arrived at Nashoba, his father's project at New Harmony having failed due to insufficient housing and shortage of supplies to meet the demands of self-sufficiency. He hoped to find better things at Nashoba. Instead, he found a rundown enterprise working on poor land using lethargic slaves. Meanwhile, Richesson Whitby and a sickly Fanny Wright were despairing of how to manage the slaves if both she and Camilla had to leave. By May 1827, there was no question that Wright needed an urgent change of environment to rebuild her strength. With Robert Dale Owen, she left the United States, accompanying him on a visit to Lafayette near Paris.

It was not long before reports of chaotic conditions at Nashoba percolated through to Wright by letter. On her departure, she had had left behind three resident managers: her sister Camilla, Richesson Whitby and James Richardson. It was the latter who was causing the trouble. His character was described by Robert Dale Owen as 'upright, impractical and an acute metaphysician of the Thomas Brown school'.[55] His dominant nature meant that he was soon ruling the roost and making errors of judgment. One was to publish records of the Nashoba Society, which were then reported in the Ohio-based abolitionist newspaper *Genius of Universal Emancipation*. The records narrated that sexual intercourse outside of marriage was deemed acceptable on the commune.[56] It was also said that slaves were forbidden from eating at any times other than at public meals, and that trustees were entitled to remove enslaved children from the care of their uneducated parents.

Wright's supporters were shocked. Among them was Madison, who wrote to Lafayette:

[Fanny] has, I fear, created insuperable obstacles to her good fruits ... by her disregard, or rather defiance, of themes of established opinion and vivid feelings. Besides her views on amalgamation of the white and black population, so universally obnoxious, she gives an éclat to her notions on the subject of religion and marriage, the effect of which with your knowledge of this country, can readily estimate.[57]

Behind Richardson's imprudent actions lay a number of serious problems at Nashoba. Chief among them was the difficulty managers had in sourcing men and women morally and physically equipped for the work. The managers had also admitted into the community some new white people who had come without capital, some to work and others to board, creating inequality. It raised fundamental questions as to what the community was about. Was it, the trustees asked, a community in which there should be an equal work commitment by all, or was it simply a cooperative society? Should it be a society in which each member paid an annual subscription for his or her support? The trustees opted for the latter on practical grounds, which took account of illness in the unhealthy climate, by offering membership only to those who could pay a certain sum each year for their support.[58] Although further conditions of membership were issued, the trustees remained committed to facilitating the emancipation of the slaves, something the slaves could only ever achieve on the back of their own labour.[59]

Wright, after travelling to England, knew that she had to return to Nashoba to deal with all these problems. She convinced a friend, Frances Trollope, to join her, having persuaded her that it was a delightful place.[60] According to Trollope, Wright had said that she planned

> to seclude herself for life, in the deepest forest in the Western world, so that her fortune and her time and her talents might be exclusively devoted to the aid of suffering Africans. Her first object was to show that nature made no difference between white and blacks, except in complexion, and this she meant to prove by giving education perfectly equal to a class of black and white children.[61]

Thus, Frances Trollope travelled to America with her young son and two daughters in company of her friend, Fanny Wright.

Mrs Trollope's anticipated pleasure soon dissipated upon their arrival in Tennessee in January 1828. After negotiating torrential rain and travelling on poor roads—'a mass of stumps'—through a dreary forest, Nashoba finally came into view. Trollope recorded dismally, 'One glance sufficed to convince me that every idea I had formed of the place was as far as possible from the truth.' Of Wright, she said, 'I never heard or read of any enthusiasm approaching hers except in a few instances, in ages past, of religious fanaticism.'[62]

Trollope counted six log cabins erected around a square, furnished simply, and between thirty to forty slaves, including children. Although books were available, no school had been built and nothing was organised. To compound this deflating experience, there was no milk to drink, only rainwater, and to eat, a little wheat bread with no cheese or butter. Trollope shared a room with Wright, consisting of a floor of loosely fitted planks and no ceiling. Water leaked through the roof and its chimney caught fire a dozen times a day. Faced with these desolate conditions, Mrs Trollope departed the community with her children on 26 January after three long weeks.

It is probable that Wright was also distressed by what she found upon her return to Nashoba, though she put on a brave face. There is no doubt that the settlement had deteriorated during her absence. Flogging had been introduced to punish idle slaves. She found Camilla, now married to Whitby, in poor health, and when Robert Dale Owen returned at the end of January, he did so without the new recruits they had hoped for.[63] Wright's stoicism was further put to the test by having to face the anger of the wider public, inflamed during her absence by the actions of Richardson (who had left Nashoba before her return), and now also through her association with Robert Owen, who had become discredited after publicly attacking Christianity when in New Orleans in 1827.[64]

The situation was exacerbated by Wright's latest treatise, 'Explanatory Notes Respecting the Nature and Objects of the Institution of Nashoba', published in February 1828 in, among other publications, *Genius of Universal Emancipation*.[65] She had written it during her sea voyage back to America, giving weight to Nashoba's reputation as an interracial egalitarian community. The paper defended the principle of free love and attacked the institution of marriage as one damaging to human happiness. It recommended miscegenation as the solution to America's race problems, and in conclusion, it weakened Nashoba's fundamental purpose by stating that the community would no longer take on donations of slaves unless they were owned by someone who was themselves willing to join the community.[66]

In consequence, some of Wright's erstwhile friends in America disowned her, while despite the best efforts of the ever-loyal Lafayette to change their minds, no Philadelphia newspaper would agree to print Wright's inflammatory treatise. This came as a final blow. Wright now accepted that her project had failed and that her methods of dealing with the slaves and those whom she had trusted to help her, had been fatally flawed. The slaves had proved to be unproductive, and were now forced to work under the watchful eye of a repressive overseer. It was precisely the outcome Wright had wanted to avoid.

With the experiment in its death throes, Wright and the remaining three resident trustees made a final desperate attempt to transform the community by introducing a more practical capitalist model, but it failed due to the false assumptions it was based upon. It was equally apparent that Wright and her colleagues had failed to achieve the required levels of farm production. Again, Wright looked for excuses, blaming her 'then imperfect acquaintance with the character and condition of the American people' and the weakness of prices in the cotton market.[67]

Wright had invested everything into her experiment: her ambition, her health and her wealth. Defeat was, inevitably, a bitter pill to swallow, but preferring to see the positives, she concluded that the experiment had given her 'the information and the experience ... to guide the efforts of a really efficient leader of the popular mind'. It was not perhaps a view shared by many others. One can only surmise whether, in a moment of honest self-reflection, Wright felt that the price she and her sister had paid had been worth it. Publicly, she remained unrepentant. Although she accepted that her 'practical efforts at reform had begun at the wrong end', she was certain that 'with a view to the accurate comprehension of the vital interests of [America] and of the world at large ... she had begun at the right end'.[68] In brief, she had used the wrong means to achieve the right objective, and had come up short.

As for the slaves, they had to suffer and wait at Nashoba as their futures were resolved. By October 1829, Wright had finally accepted that the farmland could not support them, never mind enable them to raise the money necessary to buy themselves out of slavery. To her great credit, however, she fulfilled her moral obligation of meeting the costs, from her much-depleted personal savings, of transporting the slaves overseas to give them their freedom. She chose Haiti, 'a country free ... from the ascendancy of colour', accepting an offer of asylum made to her slaves by the Haitian secretary general. It was against her instincts to send them abroad, her natural choice being for them to remain in America where blacks had as much right to live as whites. But by then the degree of entrenched racial hatred towards the blacks—far greater than she had ever witnessed in Europe—had led her to conclude that America offered the slaves no future.

Wright travelled with her slaves to Haiti from New Orleans in January 1830, on a chartered 16-ton brig called the *John Quincy Adams*. There she was well received and banqueted as President Boyer's guest of honour—the first woman to be so honoured. Indeed, as a gesture of goodwill, President Boyer went on to settle the slaves, at his own expense, on his own rich farmland where he had provided for them cabins, gardens, water and all else that they needed. He offered them their own farms, with legal title, once they had demonstrated good conduct.[69] Meanwhile, at considerable personal, financial and emotional cost, Wright could rest assured that, at the very least, she had honoured her commitment to those men, women and children.[70]

Between 1828 and 1830, Fanny Wright edited *The Free Enquirer* with Robert Dale Owen, standing up for the victims of social and political oppression. She was the first woman since colonial times to edit a general-circulation American paper.[71] She also toured America extensively, addressing mixed-race audiences in a series of public lectures—another first for a woman in the United States. Characteristically, she defied the sartorial conventions of the time by wearing trousers and a tunic, and cut her hair short.

Both in print and in her public addresses, Wright maintained a sharp focus on issues including the corrupting power of wealth in both America and Europe, how organised religions divide and corrupt, the damaging suppression of women by men through unequal treatment of women under marital law, the prevailing attitudes on birth control and the implicit restrictions on women through the inescapable 'cult of true womanhood'. With such a radical agenda, Wright inevitably attracted criticism, finding herself condemned by some as a monster and a harlot. Surprisingly, she was even attacked by the feminist Catherine Beecher for assaulting 'the safeguards of all that is vulnerable and sacred in religion, all that is safe and wise in law, all that is pure and lovely in domestic virtue'.[72] Though none of her ideas won wide support in her day, an impartial reader may recognise that the issues about which she was most passionate remain pertinent. She is now regarded as a pioneering activist for women's rights and other important causes.

After a brief stay in New York in 1830, where she pursued various activities relating to her calling in life, she returned to Paris that same year. Over the next three years, she continued to deliver public lectures on the emancipation of slaves and women's suffrage. On 22 July 1831, at the age of thirty-five, she married Guilliume Sylvan Phiquepal-D'Arusmont, a French physician and educational reformer, whom she had met at New Harmony and by whom she had already had a daughter, Francès-Sylva. A second child followed, who died as a baby. The marriage was unhappy and the couple divorced acrimoniously in 1851, with custody of Francès-Sylva being granted to D'Arusmont.

Despite the closure of her American newspaper, *The Free Enquirer*, by 1830, Wright chose to make her home in America, while regularly visiting Europe for personal and financial reasons. Her passion for creating a fairer, better society never wavered. She found written expression in 1848 with the anonymous publication of the book *England the Civiliser: Her*

History Developed in its Principles, in which she laid out another utopian vision for a peaceful world. In it, she expounded on why the world had been made worse by men's abuse of power, which was aggravated by their domination of government, for which they had made force a positive virtue.[73] Women, on the other hand, highlighted 'the conservation, care, and happiness of the species'.[74]

Wright died in comparative obscurity in Cincinnati on 13 December 1852, aged fifty-seven. By then her strict and unbending adherence to her causes and abstract doctrines had lost her the friendship of all who had mattered in her crusades, among them Lafayette, Robert Owen and Frances Trollope. Her intellectual rigour and vision, flawed by naivety, was not matched by an empathic ability to manage people or understand the perspectives of those she needed to convert to her ideas. She struggled to compromise in order to make real progress. However, she was hugely effective in forcing people to face unpalatable truths. How can it be, she asked, that America 'declared all men "born free and equal" … with the lamentable exception, indeed, of its citizens of colour'. She argued that while there was political freedom in the country, underpinned by law, there was no moral freedom to speak out and take action without incurring the intolerance and ignorance of popular public opinion.[75] Her vital honesty and astonishing courage are to be greatly admired, and the fact that the core issues she promoted in pursuit of a better and fairer society still resonate strongly nearly 200 years later, speaks volumes for their power and relevance.

Subsequent generations of social reformers have taken inspiration from Wright's work by adapting her ideas into a more practical and pragmatic form, putting them before a society more willing to listen.[76] By speaking out at great personal cost, Wright expressed values that are now accepted as universal truths and considered essential for a better world.

The Nashoba experiment for the emancipation of slaves was a manifestation of Wright's childhood vow to help the poor and helpless and to redress society's wrongs. It was borne of her unhappiness in her childhood, which both fuelled her exceptional power and created her limitations. She may have failed in her experiment and been forced to accept that America was not the utopia she had thought it to be, but that should not distract from the importance of what she attempted. In the event, emancipation of the slaves in America was achieved by the 13th Amendment adopted by Congress on 18 December 1865, after five years of civil war.[77] That such devastating bloodshed was required to enact real change shows the strength of the forces Wright was up against.

The legacy of slavery still casts a dark shadow over America to this day. Just as Fanny Wright wrote in 1822, 'Slavery is a subject upon which it is difficult to reason because it is so easy to feel.'[78]

13

The Abolition of Slavery: John Gladstone, Zachary Macaulay and Lord Brougham

On a dark, sultry evening at Success, a plantation in Demerara (now Guyana), a slave rebellion broke out.[1] It was led by Jack Gladstone (the name given him by his slave master), who was supported by his father, Quamina, the deacon of the chapel on the neighbouring Le Resouvenir plantation, and other senior members of the Le Resouvenir chapel. The date was 18 August 1823, fifteen years after the slave trade had been abolished.

In the wake of the Slave Trade Act of 1807, the colonial assemblies and planters in the West Indies were fearful of the future, and sought to manage expectations and discourage hopes for the abolition of slavery. Meanwhile, the influence of Christian missionaries in the slave colonies was growing, as were demands for change from abolitionists and even the government in Whitehall.[2] It made for a period of intense uncertainty, misunderstanding and distrust.

Three Scotsmen were at the centre of what unfolded: John Gladstone, who was loath to relinquish the financial advantages of the slave system on his plantations and was in denial that his slaves were treated badly; Zachary Macaulay, who atoned for the actions of his earlier life by committing himself to the abolitionist cause; and Lord Brougham, who proved a shrewd political operator in parliament to help bring slavery to an end. Slavery was, of course, a practice originally sanctioned by parliament, and so therefore, it was appropriate that the same institution should deliver its extinction. The coming of this full circle, played out within Britain's constitutional epicentre, was a demonstration of power sanctioned by law and of conscience over malignant commercial interests.

Once the Slave Trade Act of 1807 had become law, the immediate response was to sit back and see what happened next, particularly in the slave islands of the Caribbean. Denied access to fresh labour from Africa, planters would have to adjust their business model. In 1811, to address difficulties in enforcing the Slave Trade Act, the Slave Trade Felony Act was introduced, making slave trading a crime punishable by transportation. A further act in 1824 made it punishable by death.[3] But despite Britain and the United States officially ceasing to trade slaves after 1807, and Britain's pressure on many other countries to do the same, or at least to limit their activity, some 3 million Africans were transported over the next fifty years, mainly to Cuba and Brazil.[4]

Post-1807, war continued to rage in Europe, ending finally with Napoleon's defeat at Waterloo in 1815. Having just outlawed the slave trade, Britain and the abolitionists were determined not to see it revived by the French.[5] It was enough to galvanise the British abolitionist movement into action, and during the talks of the Vienna Congress between 1814–1815, they raised some 1.5 million signatures for the abolition of slavery.[6] This demonstration of united feeling secured a condemnation of the trade at the congress, but little else, permitting the continuation of the trade by other nations.

At the same time, tensions were rising in the West Indies where Nonconformist missionaries were converting ever-increasing numbers of slaves to Christianity, despite the efforts of planters to stop them. Strengthened by the doctrines of their new faith, slaves were becoming bolder in challenging their servitude. The first of three slave revolts on British islands occurred in Barbados in 1816.

It was an unexpected location. Most slaves in Barbados were locally born and not brought from Africa, while the plantations there were, generally speaking, considered to be managed in a less brutal manner than those elsewhere, like Jamaica, for instance. The seed was planted the previous year with a mistaken belief among the slaves that, upon his return from a visit to Guadeloupe, James Leith, the governor of Barbados, was bringing with him a 'free paper' to liberate them.[7] The uprising, which began on Bayley's Estate in St Philip, south of Charlestown, was led by a slave called Bussa; its goal was freedom and ownership of the island.[8] It ended within a week with about 100 slaves killed. As punishment, in addition to innumerable floggings, 144 slaves were executed and 170 deported to Honduras.[9] The corresponding losses among the whites was one soldier and one civilian killed. The planters promoted the argument that the rebellion had been caused by abolitionist activity, which was encouraging unrest by raising the expectations of slaves.

Despite the abolition of the slave trade, there was still life in the pro-slavery faction. The West Indian lobby's influence in Whitehall was reducing, but it still had power to delay and obstruct the efforts of abolitionists. Meanwhile, in the cotton fields of the southern United States, an internal slave system was flourishing, generating economic growth for the benefit for the entire nation.

In response, the abolitionists tried to recreate the success of their campaigns during the 1780s and 1790s, when their revelations of the brutal treatment of slaves aboard British slave ships had scandalised the public. Now the abolitionists focused on the treatment of slaves on plantations, and through the reports of missionaries and others, there was plenty of evidence available. Critically, however, the government got involved this time by instructing a census of the slave population to provide an accurate assessment of the impact of the Slave Trade Act. On the back of a pilot scheme launched in Trinidad in 1812, a new act was introduced in 1819, establishing the Office for the Registry of Colonial Slaves in London, with the directive to register all slaves from 1820 onwards. Inevitably, the plantation owners, who hated government interference in their business affairs, tried to resist, but this time they were unable to.

Evidence was slowly collated to provide an accurate picture of the consequences of the abolition of the slave trade. While previously the abolitionists had had to make do with hearsay and anecdotal evidence, they now had at their disposal firm evidence sourced from government data. This, and the testimonies of missionaries in the West Indies, once more drove public opinion against slavery, despite the planters' arguments that interfering with the status quo would provoke violent rebellion.

The next slave rebellion of magnitude took place in Demerara in 1823. The leader was Jack Gladstone, a cooper on the Success plantation, owned by John Gladstone MP (father of four-times prime minister William Gladstone), the first of our three Scotsmen at the centre of this story.

John Gladstone, born John Gladstones on 11 December 1764, was the eldest of sixteen children of Thomas Gladstones, a merchant of Leith, and his wife Nelly.[10] At thirteen years old, John was apprenticed to Alexander Ogilvy, manager of the Edinburgh Roper and Sailcloth Company. Upon completion of the apprenticeship in 1781, John, by then a big-boned, gangly young man with large hands and feet, entered his father's thriving corn and chandlery business. During this time, as a travelling merchant, he saw 'something of the world of northern Europe'.[11] After impressing the merchant Edgar Corrie of Liverpool with his business acumen in trading grain in the Baltic, John entered into partnership with Corrie and Jackson Bradshaw on 1 May 1787, and settled in Liverpool.[12] The next year, on Corrie's advice, he changed his name to John Gladstone, without the 's'.[13]

After the firm's first successful venture, sending a merchant ship to Calcutta, they diversified into Virginian tobacco and grain to lay down the foundations of Gladstone's fortune. Despite a commercial setback between 1789 and 1791 when flying weevil ruined a shipment of grain, Gladstone's wealth rapidly grew from £40,000 in 1799 to £502,550 by 1828. In 1801, fairly early in his career, Gladstone and Corrie had an acrimonious split which resulted in Gladstone setting up a new partnership with his brother, Robert. Later, he gradually involved his other five brothers. The business expanded into shipping insurance, shipbuilding, and commercial property in Liverpool. His success was founded on ready cash, Liverpool's advantageous location during the American War of 1812, the Napoleonic Wars, and first-class market intelligence.[14]

The West Indies was a natural market for Gladstone to exploit as his partnership made greater profits from the trade of American sugar and tobacco than it did from its trade with India. They provided shipping and finance for the 'triangular trade', and by 1803, Gladstone was purchasing significant amounts of sugar and cotton, particularly from Demerara. In keeping with merchants' practice, Gladstone financed planters with short-term loans. Some planters became mired in serious debt, and their difficulties were aggravated by the economic fallout after the abolition of the slave trade in 1807. This created the opportunity for Gladstone to foreclose on their mortgages and acquire their plantations. His first in Demerara was Success, one of the largest and most profitable plantations in the colony. He initially owned half, but four years later, in 1816, he acquired legal title to the remaining share.

Gladstone made six further distressed purchases of plantations at knock-down prices during the 1820s. His partnership had supplied imported commodities to all of them and, from all of them, had transported and thereafter sold slave-produced commodities to the British market.[15] These plantations were added to others Gladstone owned in Jamaica. He bought the plantations because he was unwilling to invest in British industry and he saw them as a safe bet into which to plough his surplus capital. He was a man driven by opportunity, and as a canny businessman, he was not to be put off by winds of change pressing for the abolition of slavery.

Although Gladstone was a non-resident owner, he was active in plantation strategy. This was evident shortly after his purchase of Success, when he switched production from coffee to sugar and more than doubled the number of slaves from 160 to almost 330.[16] Elsewhere, Gladstone and his agents reallocated the slaves, livestock and the use of buildings on his properties. These sorts of adaptations were happening in most plantations, triggered by the abolition of the slave trade, which had reduced the labour available on the plantations. Settled work practices and customs were also adapted by planters to maintain their profits, and often resulted in an increased workload for the slaves, which was apt to cause upset and confusion. Among those affected were women who were given tasks previously undertaken by men, and privileged or skilled workers who were downgraded to more arduous work. Others were demoted onto the fields. In correspondence with a drop in slaves' health and wellbeing, a sense of anger and resentment began to fester.[17]

It was into this unsettled atmosphere that twenty-six-year-old Reverend John Smith arrived in Demerara with his wife in 1817.[18] He had been appointed minister of the chapel of the London Missionary Society on the Le Resouvenir plantation, some 6 miles from Georgetown, the capital of the colony.[19] There he found himself preaching to increasing numbers of slaves who were keen to hear his sermons, whose treatment on the plantations he knew to be brutal and repressive. Some of them, like Jack Gladstone's father, Quamina, became his deacons. The atmosphere was tense and Smith was warned by the planters neither to teach the slaves how to read nor to say anything that might encourage his flock to question their masters or challenge their status. In the planters' opinion, since the slaves were not emancipated, they would have to make do with the consolation of religion.[20]

By mid-1823, Smith was all too aware of where the cruelty of the plantation owners was heading. He expressed his thoughts in a letter in August to the secretary of the London Missionary Society, making it clear that the slaves were being overworked, even pregnant women, and that those who were sick were neglected and starved. He also said that punishments were frequent and severe, and slaves were given no hope of any justice, even where grievously wronged. He felt the planters were wilfully blind to the need to adjust their working practices and that they refused to take account of the slaves' wider knowledge of impending change.[21]

On 18 August 1823, rebellion erupted. The catalyst was a belief among the slaves that they were meant to be granted rights by parliament, but that the planters were withholding them.[22] This was in fact true. In May 1823, MP Thomas Fowell Buxton, successor to the abolitionist William Wilberforce, had a resolution put to parliament for the gradual abolition of slavery.[23] After the debate, the colonial secretary sent a dispatch to Demerara instructing the legislative assembly (correctly known as the court of policy) to adopt a series of resolutions to ameliorate the condition of slaves.[24] Lieutenant Governor Murray received the dispatch on 7 July, but it was not adopted by the legislature until the end of August 1823. The implicit distrust of the slaves towards their plantation masters was sufficient to induce revolt.

Jack Gladstone of Success plantation led the rebellion and was joined by a number of other slave leaders including his father, Quamina. Much like Bussa's revolt on Barbados, the Demerara rebellion lasted only a week and was limited to a 25-mile area south of Georgetown, but otherwise it was on a far greater scale. Some 13,000 slaves took part, drawn from thirty-seven of the 350 estates in Demerara. Martial law was declared by Murray and the 21st Fusiliers and 1st West India Regiment, supported by a battalion of armed militia, suppressed the inadequately armed uprising. During the revolt, white inhabitants were placed in stocks or imprisoned, and their houses were looted for arms. Only two white civilians were murdered. By comparison, some 250 slaves were killed or executed after trial. Of the latter, ten were decapitated, with their heads placed on poles by the roadside. Many others were flogged.[25] Jack Gladstone proved to be a highly articulate advocate in his own defence; his life was spared upon the order of his master, John Gladstone, writing from England. He was transported to St Lucia, while his father, Quamina, was hanged on the gibbet in front of Success plantation.[26]

In late August, a few days after he had sent his critical letter to the secretary of the London Missionary Society, Reverend Smith was arrested and charged with complicity. He was found guilty by court martial and sentenced to death. A reprieve was sent by George IV, but it arrived too late; after languishing in a damp prison cell, Smith died of consumption in February 1824.

Smith's death caused outrage in Britain and brought public attention back to the topic of slavery.[27] In the eyes of ever-increasing numbers of Britons, the slave masters had, by their own actions, condemned the very institution they wished to uphold. Especially damning for John Gladstone and Success plantation was an excerpt published from Reverend Smith's diary, dated 30 August 1817, some six years before the revolt. 'The Negroes of Success have complained to me lately,' he wrote, 'of excessive labour and very severe treatment. I told one of the overseers that I thought they would work the people to death.' It was a charge refuted strongly by Gladstone in a letter of 24 December 1824 to the London Missionary Society. He claimed that what was asked of the slaves had always been moderate, saying,

> [My] intentions have ever been to treat my people with kindness in the attention to their wants of every description, and to grant them every reasonable and practical indulgence; these instructions have been strictly adhered to by my Attorney & Manager.

In reply, the society pointed out that Smith's observations were not made to condemn Gladstone, but to prove to non-resident owners (of which

Gladstone was one) 'how little [they] can control the conduct of [their] agents....'[28]

In 1823, the year of the revolt, Gladstone, as an MP, had listened with growing concern to the speeches of Thomas Buxton and George Canning in the House of Commons, calling for the amelioration of slavery in the British Caribbean.[29] Meanwhile, in Liverpool, where Gladstone had chaired the Liverpool West Indian Association since 1809, a very personal but public debate ensued between him and leading businessman James Cropper in the *Liverpool Courier*, in which Gladstone wrote under the pseudonym 'Mercator'.[30]

Cropper, a Quaker merchant, philanthropist and abolitionist, went into detail about the diabolical maltreatment of slaves, while arguing that, if freed, former slaves would not only work more efficiently but also consume more British-made products. For his part, Gladstone, who had never visited his plantations, continued to deny the charges of maltreatment. Rather, he described the benign conditions for slaves provided on Demerara, claiming they were afforded plenty of time and opportunity to raise their own livestock for sale and to cultivate their own gardens. He acknowledged that there would always be a few wicked miscreants, among whom he included those pressing for emancipation in England and the colonies.[31]

Cropper responded by scoffing at the hypocrisy of Gladstone's position as an absentee West Indian slave owner who, as a member of the Bible Society, actively promoted the Bible's teachings.[32] He derided the contradiction of a man who sought to improve the conditions of the slaves but at the same time had declared that 'the chief ringleaders of the Demerara insurrection were from the estates where they had received the most indulgences'. Furthermore, he stated that Gladstone wanted to restrict religious instruction in Demerara to the clergy of the established church, reducing the involvement of grassroots, egalitarian missionary societies.[33]

The public acrimony between the Gladstone and Cropper, while ending their long-standing friendship, spurred further investigation into the condition of Gladstone's slaves. It fell to John MacLean, manager of Vreehenhoop, one of Gladstone's plantations, to submit a detailed letter on the subject to Alexander McDonnell, secretary of the Committee of Inhabitants of Demerara.

MacLean was one of a number of plantation managers and doctors invited to report on the treatment of slaves under their charge, the object being to prepare a general report for the colony as a whole.[34] However well intentioned, the value of a report prepared by those with a vested interest in its findings must always be questionable. There was a strong risk that the report would reflect what plantation owners, particularly those non-resident, wanted to hear, and so it proved.

John MacLean had taken the job of manager of Vreehenhoop in April 1822 with some six years of plantation management experience in Demerara behind him. He began his letter by asserting that 'no man amongst us is so callous to the sufferings of a fellow creature as to treat a sick negro with the smallest shadow of neglect'.[35] He continued by describing the living conditions of the 356 slaves at Vreehenhoop. Beyond being well housed and fed, he said the slaves had access to 200 acres of land to grow plantains, provided they did not sell them.[36] A hospital and lying in rooms were 'of the most comfortable construction with rooms for each sex all designed to help with their recovery'. The doctor was assisted by two nurses. MacLean claimed he had never witnessed a preventable death. Regarding freedom to worship, he said that slaves attended public worship as often as they wished on a Sunday, and he issued licences for them to be baptised.

Taking account of both the working conditions of the slaves and the condition of their homes, MacLean was able to conclude that the slaves before the 1823 rebellion 'had enjoyed every comfort' and that he was 'convinced that slavery was only known to them by name'. He lay blame for the insurrection on the inflammatory effect of religious teachings 'explained in language strongly calculated to impress them with the idea that their conditions ought to be better and that their masters were their enemies, inasmuch as they deprived them of supposed rights'.[37]

This letter conveniently affirmed Gladstone's views. He also heard from his attorney in Demerara, Frederick Cort, in response to his enquiry (made before the 1823 revolt) on the condition of his slaves. Cort informed Gladstone that the slaves were generally happy and content and rarely needed punishment. After the revolt, the London Missionary Society warned Gladstone that this was a deception, but Gladstone, in keeping with his previous approach, elected to side with his attorney and his other agents.

After the revolt, efforts were made to improve conditions for slaves in Demerara, which would have further strengthened Gladstone's view that there was no cause for concern. On 1 January 1826, an 'ameliorative ordinance' was effected in response to British government policy, which included the appointment of a 'protector of slaves' whose duty it was to make an official record of the punishments inflicted on slaves and to introduce reforms to make their lives less punitive.[38] In the words of historian Eric Williams, 'It was not emancipation but amelioration, not revolution but evolution. Slavery would be killed by kindness.'[39]

It was not until 1828 that Gladstone's son, Robertson, now a partner in his father's business, suggested that he should visit Demerara to inspect the plantations for himself. Gladstone agreed and Robertson set sail that year. His findings were not positive. He found the attorney Cort to be 'an idler and a deceiver', who had neglected the welfare of the slaves. All Gladstone's estates, he reported, had been mismanaged.[40] He said that Cort had been consumed by the temptations and petty politics of a slave society, and in failing to deal with the financial management, he had become idle and plausibly self-justifying.[41] Most damning was Robertson's discovery that 75 per cent of the deaths on one plantation had been caused by dysentery. He was taken by an uncooperative Cort to the water source, which he found to be unsuitable for human consumption. Cort's regrets at the consequent loss of life were muted, and he was sacked and replaced by MacLean.

Robertson Gladstone was clearly a conscientious young man. It seems he had been diligent and objective in collecting his evidence, and yet he concluded that the slaves 'were contented and happy, and will remain so, if allowed to live undisturbed by the meddling and ill disposed'.[42] This begs the question of how he arrived at this conclusion with so much evidence to the contrary. Historian S. G. Checkland suggests that he was duped by Cort and the managers by being well cared for in the 'grand house' by biddable servants on their best behaviour, who displayed good cheer under a regime of mild discipline. Meanwhile, the less receptive field slaves would have been forced into silence by fear of retribution.

The newly appointed MacLean undertook to follow Gladstone's specific instructions, but subject to one or two qualifications. Taking account of his self-claimed superior knowledge of the 'Negro character', MacLean was against rewarding slaves with comforts, saying they would only produce an 'ungrateful and discontented feeling'. In the same vein, MacLean and other managers were resistant to implementing the British government's amelioration policy, introduced in November 1831. For MacLean, the slave remained a chattel and not a person.[43]

John Gladstone came under attack again in December 1832 via the pen of Henry Grey MP, the twenty-nine-year-old son of the then prime minister, Charles Grey, 2nd Earl Grey. In campaigning for emancipation, Henry Grey focused on the records of the protector of slaves in Demerara, which disclosed 'an extraordinary increase' in punishment. The records also noted that as this practice grew, production diminished in the face of increasing slave resistance. From this cruelty, reported Grey, came the highest levels of mortality in the slave colonies.

Grey identified Vreehenhoop as a particular example, saying that between 1829 and 1832 it had produced large crops 'to the great advantage of [John Gladstone], but unhappily, at the price of a dreadful loss of life amongst the slaves'.[44] Grey attributed the high loss of life in Demerara to the high proportion of absentee landlords, whose plantations were managed by overseers and attorneys. He did not conclude that these managers were any more or less cruel than others, but that, in the absence of the owners, they were in fierce competition with one another, which encouraged them to prioritise levels of production and profit over the welfare of the slaves, and thus maintain their masters' expectations of producing the largest crop at the lowest cost.

Inevitably, Gladstone and his sons were outraged at Grey's charges against them. Indeed William Gladstone made his maiden speech in parliament in defence of his father, claiming that Vreehenhoop was no worse than other plantations. He said the high mortality rate related to slaves imported from Africa before 1807, and 'confessed great shame and pain that the cases of cruelty had existed', declaring that 'the British legislature and public should extinguish slavery in the colonies'.[45]

Tension in the British Caribbean was made worse by the delay in implementing legislation to ameliorate, or better still, end slavery. It manifested itself in the desperate responses of brave men like Jack Gladstone and in the reports of those like Reverend Smith, who described the continuing cruelty and injustice they witnessed to correspondents in England. While this served to inform an increasingly horrified British public, committed, talented men and women were needed in Britain to assemble the evidence into a coherent form and deliver it to parliament. Zachary Macaulay, our next Scotsman in this story, was one of those men. In a speech given in 1833, Thomas Fowell Buxton described him as 'the real leader of the [abolitionist] cause—the anti-slavery tutor of us all....'[46] Interestingly, Macaulay's commitment to the cause can be viewed through the prism of atonement for wrongs committed as a younger man.

Zachary Macaulay was born in Inveraray on 2 May 1768, the third son of twelve children. His father, John, was a Church of Scotland minister. In late December 1784, Zachary, by then working in Glasgow in a merchant's office, suffered from an unspecified personal embarrassment of which no details are known.[47] To escape the 'labyrinth' he found himself in, he departed, aged sixteen, for Jamaica on the suggestion of Sir Archibald Campbell, a relative and former governor of the island. There, in 1784, Macaulay took a post as bookkeeper or under-manager of a sugar plantation.

Initially, Macaulay was shocked by the savagery of the slave system he encountered. In a letter to a clergyman friend at home, he described vividly a scene in which he was 'screaming and bawling' in a cane field where slaves were being whipped. But he was determined to 'get rid of [his] squeamishness' and become 'the slave to the sport of the basest passions'. He developed a cold-hearted, uncaring attitude towards the slaves, and later reflected, '[This was] a period of [my] life of which I scarce like to speak or think. It was a period of most degrading servitude to the worst of masters.' When, in 1789, aged twenty-four, a job offer came up in London, he was so at ease with this violent world that he hesitated before accepting it.[48] In the event, his decision to go marked a turning point in his life.

Macaulay's father had died while he had been in Jamaica, so he went to live with his sister, Jean, who was married to Thomas Babington, philanthropist, politician and member of the Clapham Sect. It was he who introduced him to William Wilberforce and others in the abolitionist circle. Within a year, with little else to do, he accepted an invitation from the Clapham Sect to become the deputy governor of the first British colony in Africa, Sierra Leone.

The colony, which extended from its capital, Freetown, along a peninsula comprising a few square miles, had been founded in 1787 by the Clapham Sect in the name of the Sierra Leone Company, to provide the basis for legitimate commerce in West Africa with a colony of freed slaves.[49] It was placed in the heart of a region of concentrated slave trading activity on Africa's west coast. Originally it was designed to relocate some of London's black poor, a portion of whom were African Americans who had been granted their freedom after supporting the British during the American War of Independence. Four hundred arrived in Sierra Leone in 1787. After the failure of this settlement, a new settlement was established at Freetown in 1792, to which freed black loyalists from Nova Scotia and Afro-Caribbeans from Jamaica were sent. The company had to work with the traders—among them the slavers of Bunce Island (see Chapter 11)—in order to secure their supplies.

As deputy governor of Sierra Leone, Macaulay had to make difficult decisions occasionally. He caused horror among his directors in London, for instance, when he returned five runaway slaves to a coastal trader. However, this did not prevent him assuming the governorship of Sierra Leone in 1794, aged twenty-six. Macaulay served in the colony until 1799, including a year's leave in England, and his tenure was marked by serious challenges. Shortly after he arrived, there was a rebellion of black settlers whose expectations of freedom had not been met; there was a French invasion which ended in the looting and destruction of large parts of the capital, Freetown; and there were conflicts with the leaders of religious groups over issues of management, which Macaulay's enemies later used to discredit him.

The experience refined Macaulay's views on the abolition of slavery as well as his leadership skills. He was portrayed as a harsh and unrelenting dispenser of his appointed civil and religious mandate in the colony, but he gradually learned diplomacy, which implicitly requires the ability to listen. He worked hard at finding a balance between maintaining a productive commercial relationship with the freemen of the colony, and for the colony to remain committed to their freedom. Strikingly, in contrast to the violent suppression of the rebellions in the Caribbean, in response to a rebellion of black settlers in Sierra Leone in 1794, Macaulay granted a pardon to most of those involved, only sending the ringleaders to London for trial. He introduced black juries into the courts, one of which found a white schoolmaster guilty of cruelty for which he was expelled from the colony.[50] Freetown also grew under Macaulay's governorship into a busy trading hub of 1,200 people, which undertook substantial trading into the interior.[51]

When returning for a break to London in 1795, Macaulay decided to travel via the West Indies on a slave ship, the *Anna*, to update his knowledge of the condition of plantation slavery. He was a man of meticulous attention to detail and he had a forensic memory. He collated detailed comments and statistics in diaries, assiduously written in Greek script, almost certainly to protect against prying eyes should the diaries fall into the wrong hands.

Even after a year's break, the demands of Macaulay's post in Sierra Leone and the hostile tropical climate took a toll on his health, forcing him to return home in 1799. He recuperated for three years before dedicating himself for the next thirty to the abolitionist cause.[52]

The focus of Macaulay's work was on the collation of factual evidence and statistics; he soon became an expert on the subject of slavery in the British colonies. The respect he governed is demonstrated by his choice as representative for the British case for abolition of the slave trade in Paris in 1814, and as advisor to the duke of Wellington and Lord Castlereagh at the Congress of Vienna the following year.[53]

Between 1802 and 1816, Macaulay was editor of *The Christian Observer*, the Clapham Sect's journal. The evidence gathered and published in the journal was used by sympathetic parliamentarians to discredit the entrenched interests of the West Indian planters, who were represented in the House of Commons. But it was with the launch of the Anti-Slavery Society in 1823, of which Macaulay was a founding member, and Macaulay's founding of the *Anti-Slavery Reporter*, that the movement began to make real progress.[54] It coincided with one of the government's periodic attempts to encourage the colonies to adopt reforms, thereby generating evidence for the *Reporter*, which had a fast-growing readership.[55]

Via the *Reporter*, Macaulay promoted an effective campaign to bring the government to account. In 1826, this took the form of a thirty-page report entitled 'The Progress of Colonial Reform', with the subtitle, 'Being a Brief View of the Real Advance Made Since May 15th, 1823, in Carrying Into Effect the Recommendations of His Majesty, the Unanimous Resolutions of Parliament, and the Universal Prayer of the Nation, With Respect to Negro Slavery'. In it he detailed and contrasted, island by island, the progress made in pursuit of the hoped-for reforms. The summary disclosed that none of the islands had done anything about religious instruction and none had abolished the flogging of females, which were two of the basic requirements of the amelioration sought by the House of Commons in 1823. Macaulay concluded that 'only five of the colonies have done anything whatsoever towards carrying out the resolutions initiated [on] 15 May 1823'.[56]

This clear failure of government intent strengthened the hand of abolitionists in parliament who, with the support of growing numbers of local committees and societies, began to redefine their goal as one of achieving emancipation rather than simply ameliorating the wretched conditions endured by slaves. To this end the abolitionists demanded the termination of government subsidies afforded to British Caribbean sugar production.

By the 1820s, cheaper sugar was available on the world market. The abolitionists believed that, by exposing British firms to open competition, they would be rendered financially unviable, thereby demonstrating the inefficiencies of the slave system.[57] As the *Edinburgh Review* observed, 'There is, in fact, but one way to put down the West Indian slavery, and that is by allowing the produce raised by comparatively cheap labour to come into competition with that raised by the slaves.'[58] Crucially, it enabled the argument for abolition to expand from the moral and religious platforms to a new economic platform, which would generate wider public appeal. The West Indian lobby's foundation of resistance began to crumble from under them as their parliamentary support weakened.

In 1823, petitions, publications and lectures to packed audiences were once more cranked into action with substantial contributions by female abolitionists, but despite this, the abolitionist cause withered in parliament. Part of the reason was that an exhausted William Wilberforce had handed over leadership to Thomas Fowell Buxton in 1821, who proved a far less potent force in parliament. However, in 1832, a thrusting young group of abolitionists founded the Agency Committee, which reanimated pressure on the government for immediate emancipation. Their initiative foundered when a cholera outbreak swept through Britain, claiming the lives of 32,000 people. Amid the tragedy, however, came a fortunate side effect: many took the pandemic as a sign of divine retribution for the national sin of slavery, especially as it came just after another slave revolt, this time in Jamaica.

The 'Baptist War' as it became known, among other names, broke out on 25 December 1831 and ended on 5 January 1832. It was led by a formidable black preacher named Sam Sharpe, a man who 'thought and learned from the Bible, that whites had no more right to hold black people in slavery than black people had to make the white people slaves'.[59] The rebellion involved around 60,000 slaves who torched several estates and killed fourteen whites. As before, the suppression was brutal, ending in the deaths of 540 blacks. Word of its ruthlessness reached Britain and once again horrified the public, who soon afterwards were left reeling by the cholera outbreak. The timing of the revolt was also significant from a political perspective.

The debate for the emancipation of slaves became entwined with the wider debate on electoral rights set out in the Reform Bill, which was to receive royal assent on 7 June 1832.[60] When an election was called in August that year, abolitionists seized the opportunity to force parliamentary candidates to declare their position on emancipation. It resulted in some 200 MPs declaring in favour of the cause. The reform of parliament and those elected to represent had finally opened the door for the abolition of slavery.

The third Scot in this story, Henry Brougham, played a significant role in bringing the abolitionist movement to this final stage. Unlike Macaulay, he had no direct experience of the West Indies, but he was the only one of the abolitionists who attained high political office and consequently had access to the levers of power, though this advantage was diminished by competing demands on his time.

In many ways, Brougham's engagement with the movement reflects that of others, though there were some inconsistencies in his position on slavery. In 1830 it was held out by some that he had previously been a supporter of slavery and had thought it best to leave the planters alone.[61] Nonetheless, Wilberforce welcomed Brougham to the abolitionary cause, and the latter soon made his position clear, writing that 'however deficient in civilisation, negroes are endowed nonetheless with powers not only of body but of mind sufficient to render their improvement and high refinement a matter of absolute certainty under a proper system of management'. The lash, he added, 'led to a state of despair not industry'.[62] Contrary to Wilberforce who represented the evangelical 'saints', inspired by their religious beliefs, Brougham led the Whig abolitionists, who were motivated by Enlightenment principles.[63]

Henry Brougham was born at 28 St Andrew's Square in Edinburgh's New Town in 1778. He entered the faculty of law at the University of

Edinburgh in 1796 and was called to the Scottish bar in June 1800.[64] It soon became clear that Brougham enjoyed sparring with judges, though the feeling was not reciprocated by them, nor by potential clients—he only attracted a handful, and even then of little importance. His growing disenchantment with the law encouraged him to transfer his to attention on a more obvious stage for his talents in showmanship: politics. But a living had to made, and after toying with the idea of becoming a diplomat and then a soldier, he reluctantly committed himself to, as he perceived it, the drudgery of five years' training for the English bar. Once completed, he was admitted to Lincoln's Inn in 1807, where his debating and oratory skills soon glittered on the Northern Circuit. Less effective in the detail of the law, his theatrics dazzled juries and he began to make a name for himself. In 1811, he established his reputation in a case of seditious libel, in which he identified the core debate as one of freedom of speech. After that, he was never short of work.[65]

In 1802, when still in Edinburgh, Brougham launched the *Edinburgh Review* alongside Francis Jeffrey, Francis Horner and Sydney Smith. He used it as a platform to express his views on several causes, most prominently slavery. Over the next three decades he contributed a huge amount of copy, and after his initial exclusion from its management, came to dominate editorial policy. In keeping with his character, his style was 'iconoclastic, lively and sometimes abusive', thereby setting the tone for the *Review* and establishing its success.[66] From the outset, his position on the slave trade in the *Review* was pro-abolition.[67]

The Slave Trade Act of 1807 appeared to have brought the *Review*'s interest on slavery to a close, but not Brougham's. In February 1810, as MP for Camelford, he introduced a bill to make slave trading punishable by transportation, replacing ineffective fines. In his opinion, the men who illegally continued the trade were not to be classified as traders or merchants, but murderers. His talent as an orator was such that he was widely regarded as the parliamentary successor to Wilberforce, though, as mentioned, this mantle was in fact passed to Thomas Fowell Buxton.[68]

In 1823, when the Reverend John Smith lay languishing in a Demerara gaol, Brougham was seeking from parliament a motion of censure of the government. He argued that Smith's trial had been unconstitutional as he had been denied legal representation, and not only that, it was an assault on Christian evangelism. Although the motion of censure narrowly failed, Brougham achieved his wider objective of bringing the case to the public's attention. This helped reactivate an anti-slavery petitioning campaign, so effective in previous years in the fight to abolish the slave trade, which did not dissipate until the goal to abolish slavery was achieved.

In 1830, riding high on public feeling, Brougham issued a warning in the House of Commons:

> Let the planters beware. Let Parliament beware. The same country is once again awake—awake to the condition of negro slavery; the same indignation kindles in the bosom of the same people; the same cloud is gathering that annihilated the Slave Trade.[69]

By the time the Slavery Abolition Bill was introduced in 1833, Brougham was lord chancellor and sitting in the House of Lords. He initially tempered his support for total emancipation by backing the 'Apprenticeship System'. Under the new legislation, instead of complete freedom, slaves over the age of six were to be apprenticed for up to eight years to enable them 'to learn how to be free'.

The Slavery Abolition Act finally took effect in August 1834, but the Apprenticeship System then came into being. The length of period varied, but during it, 'freed' slaves had to work for their existing masters for three-quarters of their time, leaving the rest of the week to work for others for a small wage.[70] It proved to be little different to slavery, and when this became apparent, Brougham introduced a bill to end the system, speaking against it to large public audiences.[71] The bill failed but he had informed the public of the atrocities which were being committed under its name. His efforts proved influential in the abolition of the system in 1838, when true emancipation was finally established. Contradictory to the expectations of planters and wider colonial society, slave freedom in the Caribbean was not marked by the settling of old scores. Rather, it was met with peaceful parades and public meetings and the soaring of church attendances.

The abolition of slavery was not Brougham's only mission in life. He promoted many causes in his long political career, and his contribution to the abolitionist cause was in fact regarded by some as self-serving. However, his positive impact was indisputable. As the committed abolitionist and Tory MP James Stephen (whose work was often heavily criticised in the *Edinburgh Review*) wrote in 1826, 'The colonists would do anything to gain [Brougham] or to suppress his voice which, from his transcendent talents and commanding influence with a powerful party, cannot easily be put down.'[72]

The Slavery Abolition Act of 1833 (it took effect the following year) included a controversial provision: the award of £20 million compensation on a per capita basis, not to the slaves, but to their owners. Planters or their agents submitted a 'Claim to be Awarded [compensation] for Slaves' on each of their properties to the registrar of slaves for the district. The compensation claim for Gladstone's four plantations amounted to over £22,000. On 1 August 1834, when the act came into effect, the total number of slaves against whom Gladstone's claim was made was 1,310. A further 193 children under six were also set free.

Gladstone and his partners decided to continue their business under the new laws, applying the apprenticeship arrangements, which in the event were to run for a further four years. Reports soon reached him from Demerara that the apprenticed slaves were not proving easy to manage. In addition, Gladstone was concerned about the future availability of labour at the end of the apprenticeship period. He had learned that workers from Bengal were both cheap to employ and compliant, and after lobbying parliament for approval, he formed a partnership with his friend John Moss, a fellow non-resident planter, through agents, to transport Indians from Calcutta to Georgetown. As part of this initiative, six plantations in Demerara received 412 Indian workers before 1839, of which Gladstone's estates of Vreedenhoop and Vreedestein took a total of 100.

Very little changed on the plantations. The overseers were unable to forgo their old habits, and the workers, though nominally free, were subjected to similar mistreatments as the slaves had been. The abuse resulted in many Indians trying to escape Gladstone's plantations.

By February 1840, Gladstone was deliberating on whether or not to sell. Twelve Indian workers had died and many more had suffered greatly through illness. Upon registering a loss of £5,000 on his Vreedenhoop estate in 1840, Gladstone sold it for £53,000. Success plantation followed, and by 1849 his interest in Demerara was limited to a mortgage of £18,000 on Wales estate. While Gladstone's experiment with Indian labour had failed, it did nonetheless revive indentured Indian immigration to the Caribbean due to the continuing departure of freed slaves from the plantations at the end of the apprenticeship arrangement in 1838.[73]

The troubled story of Gladstone's plantations serves to highlight many of the problems and challenges needing to be addressed in the Caribbean and Britain to effect the final abolition of slavery. Being an absentee owner, Gladstone relied on reports from his agents, who viewed black slaves with ruthless indifference and placed the demands of maximising crop yields far above welfare. When the veracity of their reports came into question, Gladstone elected to accept them at face value. His reasons for this are not known, but it was a decision that served his commercial interests. His motivations for allowing his son Robertson to investigate the welfare of slaves on his estates in 1828, five years after the rebellion in Demerara, are unclear, but Robertson's findings, much of them contrary to what had been reported previously to Gladstone, had limited impact on the running of the estates.

For all the public controversy, Gladstone's status in society remained undamaged, as shown by his appointment as a baronet by Prime Minister Robert Peel in 1846. He died in 1851, a demanding and embittered old man, and was buried in the vault of St Andrews' Chapel, an Episcopalian chapel he had founded five years earlier in Fasque, Perthshire.[74] His choice of resting place highlights the irreconcilable contradictions of a man of strong Christian faith who donated substantial financial support initially to the Presbyterian and then the Episcopal Church, yet was an advocate of the slave system and chose to deny the claims of Reverend John Smith of grievous ill treatment on his sugar plantations.[75]

In contrast, many in Britain, like Henry Brougham and Zachary Macaulay, were tireless in securing public support for the abolitionist cause through societies, associations, churches and councils throughout the country. They were assisted invaluably by missionaries in the slave colonies, working to educate and convert slaves to Christianity, and by the slaves themselves, whose courage in rising up against their brutal masters was incomparable.

14

Slavery in America and the Free Church of Scotland: Frederick Douglass and Dr Thomas Chalmers

In September 1838, a black slave, Frederick Bailey, successfully made an escape from his slave master in Baltimore, Maryland, to the city of New York. He did so via the 'Underground Railroad', a clandestine network organised by both black and white Americans to offer safe lodgings and assist slaves escaping from the Southern states.[1]

Twenty years old at the time of his escape, Bailey had suffered the physical and emotional cruelties of slavery. He was man of extraordinary resilience, courage and intelligence, and with a remarkably dispassionate eye, he was able to identify the core issues that lay behind slavery, which by its nature debased not only those placed in servitude but also those who chose to govern under its authority. He understood the political, economic and social divisions it caused in a republic founded on the principle that 'all men are created equal'.[2] These divisions came to a climax in the American Civil War of 1861–65.

In 1838, twenty-three years before the outbreak of the war, the newly escaped Frederick Bailey needed to adjust to the new challenges of living in a free state. His existence was one of insecurity and loneliness. Fearful of kidnappers who would be rewarded for returning him to his former slave master in the South, he had to be extremely careful of whom he trusted. David Ruggles, however, a black member of the Underground Railroad born of free African American parents, was his friend.[3] He regularly housed fugitive slaves and helped them prepare for freedom. He offered Bailey secure lodging, and at a time of extreme vulnerability, Bailey was relieved to have come under his care.

On 15 September 1838, not long after his arrival in New York, Bailey married Anna Murray, with Ruggles acting as witness. Murray was from

Denton, Maryland, and unlike several of her siblings, she had been born free, her parents having been manumitted just a month before her birth. Helped by a gift from Ruggles of a $5 bill, the newlyweds travelled in secrecy to New Bedford, south of Boston, where they were housed by another member of the Underground Railroad, Nathan Johnston. It was he, a successful black businessman of New Bedford, who tutored Bailey on the duties and responsibilities of his freedom, and recommended that he changed his name. Frederick Augustus Washington Bailey became Frederick Douglass, a surname chosen by Johnston from a poem he had been reading, Sir Walter Scott's 'Lady of the Lake'.[4] The name Frederick Douglass was to become famous throughout the world, both in Douglass's lifetime and long after his death. Today, his legacy remains a constant source of inspiration for oppressed people around the world and a powerful symbol in the ongoing campaign for racial equality.

After the American War of Independence was settled by the Treaty of Paris in 1783, in the South, the new republic inherited from the British the corrosive culture and intractable problem of the slave system. During the war, both the British and the American colonists had reviewed the system of slavery for the first time. Before that, it had been challenged on moral grounds only by the Quakers and African Americans, whose efforts had been successfully resisted by the plantation owners of the Southern states, who feared losing their wealth, their rights of property and their political control. But the American War of Independence had presented new opportunities. The war demanded manpower, and to address this, leaders on both sides offered some slaves their freedom in exchange for taking up arms. Beginning in 1781 when it was clear that the war was lost, the defeated British honoured their agreement with their black recruits by shipping some 14,000 freed slaves to foreign destinations where they could live freely. In like manner, the American colonists gave freedom to their black recruits.[5] Beyond this, the disruption caused by the war enabled thousands of black men, women and children in the South to flee to the free states of the North, the first of which was Vermont (then part of New York) in 1777, followed, in some cases with gradual abolition, by Pennsylvania in 1780, and New Hampshire and Massachusetts in 1783. This migration substantially increased the number of free black people in these Northern states.[6]

In 1787, the Confederation Congress outlawed slavery in the new territories admitted to the Union and some Northern states began to initiate the process of emancipation. In the same year, delegates from the federal states met for the Constitutional Convention to review the articles of the Confederation put in place by the separate colonies during their collective revolution against the British. This was no easy task given the disparate views on slavery. The result was a trade-off which perpetuated slavery in the Southern states by agreeing the 'three-fifths compromise', the object of which was to make sure that the Southern states held enough votes in the House of Representatives to block any attempts to regulate or abolish slavery. The compromise resolved that three-fifths of the slave population would be counted to determine direct taxation and representation in the House of Representatives.[7] The effect of this was to give states where slavery was legal greater political influence over national government policies than their respective freemen populations allowed. This was because if each slave was to be counted, then 50 per cent of the seats in the House of Representatives would be held by the slave states, but if none were counted, only 41 per cent would be.

The same convention then addressed the issue of abolishing America's participation in the slave trade. Ten of the then thirteen states had already done so, but South Carolina, Georgia and North Carolina had not, and refused to do so at the convention, pushing their slogan 'No slavery—No Union'.[8] Again, compromise was brokered. The constitution was amended to give Congress the power to abolish the international slave trade, but not until 1808, which it duly did, encouraged by British abolitionists.[9] The twenty-one-year delay enabled the slave states to increase their imports to meet anticipated needs after the abolition of the trade.[10]

Also addressed at the convention was the right of owners to recover escaped slaves, an issue of increasing importance as the Northern states, which had abolished slavery, had become havens for fugitive slaves on the run from the South. It was resolved that an escaped slave who found safety in a free state would not be legally free and would remain subject to return to their owners.[11] This resolution was still in place by 1838, and was thus of material importance to Frederick Douglass.

These compromises at the Constitutional Convention of 1787 were salient among an evident sea change in attitudes towards slavery in America after independence. The language of the constitution, asserting liberty and justice, was increasingly highlighted by those seeking to end slavery, it being plain that the values of that constitutional rhetoric, and its moral importance, were in direct conflict with the institution of slavery.[12] By 1837, thirteen Northern states were 'free', leaving the thirteen Southern states subject to slavery.[13]

Freed black slaves in the North still faced prejudice and discrimination, with many in poorly paid jobs, living in inadequate housing and with limited access to education. The situation was worse in the politically oppressive South. The question of what to do with freed slaves was addressed by a number of senior statesmen in their establishment of the

American Colonisation Society in 1816, which encouraged and facilitated the migration of former slaves to the free state of Liberia in West Africa.[14] The scheme was subject to much criticism and lost support over time, not least because, by the 1820s, most of the black population in the United States had been born there.

Influenced by events and action taken in Britain, American abolitionists pressed for immediate emancipation. In 1829 the black journalist David Walker, whose father was enslaved, published his book *Walker's Appeal* to encourage his fellow African Americans to become proactive in the fight against slavery.[15] He advocated that they should set aside risk and awaken the moral conscience of white Americans to the fact that slavery was a disgraceful affront to their religious beliefs. Indeed, it was this that encouraged many white evangelical Christians to take up the abolitionist cause, fearful that their non-action amounted to sin and could lead to damnation.[16]

In 1831, within a bubbling groundswell of protest and fear, three pivotal events took place in the United States that served to intensify the activities of both abolitionists and supporters of slavery. The first event was the publishing of a new abolitionist newspaper, *The Liberator*, by William Lloyd Garrison, a white Quaker and journalist, in which he demanded immediate abolition.[17] The second and third events were both slave rebellions: a bloody uprising in Southampton County, Virginia, in August, and in December, a mass insurrection in British Jamaica, led by black preacher Sam Sharpe. The latter, recounted in the previous chapter, played its part in bringing about the Slavery Abolition Act of 1833. Petitions followed in America and anti-slavery societies flourished.[18]

These pressure groups divided American society, not only between the North and the South, but also within those regions. Slave owners and others dependent on slavery for their livings felt threatened by the growth of the movement for emancipation. Aside from economic interests, there was a fierce response from whites who regarded blacks as racially inferior, often culminating in violence directed against blacks and white abolitionists. Counterarguments to justify slavery were promoted. They presented slavery as a positive institution, providing a source of labour for whites and work for otherwise helpless blacks, which generated profit for the whole country. The Scriptures were also used to justify the natural authority of slavery.

Politically, Southerners within Congress passed an order that prohibited the House of Representatives and the Senate from accepting any anti-slavery petitions, thus undermining the potency of the abolitionist strategy. Such a response emphasised the level of fear and division permeating the country.

In New Bedford, Douglass found work; he also found his voice. On 11 August 1841, at an anti-slavery convention at Nantucket, he was unexpectedly invited to speak. His audience was taken aback by his passion and eloquence; it was clear that a new leader had emerged. For Douglass himself, the experience ushered in a new sense of liberation—the finding of the path he had been born to tread.

Frederick Douglass was born in Tuckahoe, Maryland, around the year 1818.[19] His mother was a black slave named Harriet Bailey and his father was a white man, possibly his mother's slave master, 'Captain Anthony', though this was never proved. In keeping with custom, as an infant, Frederick was separated from his mother when she was hired out to a neighbouring plantation, and placed under the charge of an old woman who was no longer fit for work. His mother endeavoured to sustain her relationship with her son whenever she could by walking, after her long day's labour, the 12 miles back to her former plantation to sleep with him. Departing from his bed in darkness to avoid detection and punishment, she had to ensure that she was back before her new day's toil began. It was an exhausting feat and she only managed it five times before she died, worn down by her hardships. To compound the tragedy, her master refused to allow her son to visit her when she was ill and dying.

At the time, Frederick was seven years old and living in the house of his master (and possibly his father), Captain Anthony. His mother's sister, Aunt Hestor, was then fifteen years old. She was, said Douglass, 'a woman of noble form ... having very few equals'. She fared better than her sister Harriet under Anthony's authority until she was caught one evening with her boyfriend, another slave called Ned, after Anthony had told her she could not visit him.

He took her to the kitchen, stripped her to the waist and bound her hands with a strong rope attached to a hook in a ceiling joist. There she stood at full stretch on the tips of her toes. Calling her a 'damned bitch', Anthony set about beating Hestor with a whip. Frederick witnessed the punishment, recalling in his memoirs many years later the 'warm red blood [that] came dripping to the floor'.[20] Fearing he could be next, he hid himself in the closet, traumatised.

Captain Anthony, who owned two or three farms and some thirty slaves in his own right, of whom Frederick was one, was superintendent or factor of the plantations owned by a Colonel Lloyd, and lived in a house on Lloyd's home estate, Home Farm. It had the appearance of a prosperous country village and supported a range of home industries such as shoemaking, weaving and coopering. Frederick stayed there for two years, observing the farming of tobacco, corn and wheat on productive soil by some 300 to 400 slaves. Aside from Home Farm, Lloyd owned a further twenty plantations.

The adult slaves received an annual supply of clothes, while the children who were too young to work in the fields were provided each year with two coarse linen shirts but no shoes.[21] When the clothing wore out, the children were left almost naked in all weathers. There were no beds, only a single blanket for men and women, but the main issue was lack of time for sleep; after a day's work, the slaves still had to attend to their own needs. Sleeping in was severely dealt with.

Captain Anthony was the final arbiter on any misdemeanours committed by slaves on all twenty-one of Lloyd's plantations. If the deed was considered too bad or the slave unmanageable, after a severe whipping, he or she was shipped to Baltimore for sale. The plantation overseers, who were accountable to Captain Anthony, came and went, and without exception they were cruel, and some of them were murderous. So long as their actions were supported by their master, no form of accountability was brought to bear.

With the threat of violence hanging over them ceaselessly, the slaves found emotional release in singing, through which they expressed both 'the highest joy and the deepest sadness'. As a child, Frederick absorbed much of the latter—an 'ineffable sadness which he carried through life'.[22] He understood that song was the only means by which slaves could cope with the hopelessness of their circumstances.

When Frederick was too young to work in the fields, he did odd jobs about the farm and carried messages. He was seldom whipped, but his biggest problem was hunger and cold; whatever the season, he was often barely clothed.

When Frederick was about eight, he was sent to live with Hugh Auld, the brother-in-law of Captain Anthony's daughter, Lucretia, in Baltimore, with his wife and young child. Before departing, a joyous Frederick was given 'a makeover' by Lucretia to clean him up. She also provided him with a new pair of trousers. Arriving with wonderment in the first town he had seen, Frederick was welcomed kindly by Mrs Auld, a weaver, who had no knowledge of how to deal with a slave and no wish to see Frederick adopt the servile habits in which he had been trained—things like crouching and never looking a master in the eye. In this environment, Frederick began to be taught how to read by Mrs Auld. However, when her husband found out, the lessons were stopped.

Auld forbade his wife to give Frederick further instruction because, he said, it was unlawful and unsafe to do so. 'A nigger should know nothing but to obey his master—to do as he is told,' he said.[23] He feared that, with an education, Frederick would become unmanageable and thus of no value to him. It was a depressing moment for young Frederick, but it taught him something of great value: that education was the key to finding freedom from slavery. In pursuit of this goal, Frederick arranged clandestine meetings with local children whom he supplied with biscuits in return for lessons. With dogged persistence, during the seven years he spent with the Auld family, he achieved his mission of learning to read.

While he was with the Aulds, Mrs Auld's attitude towards Frederick, once benign, hardened towards contempt. She began to think and act like a slave owner, likening him to a chattel, considering humane treatment wrong and dangerous. She also became violent towards him, more so than her husband. Frederick, as an insightful twelve-year-old, drew a second lesson from this change in her behaviour. He saw that, by becoming a slave owner and acting the part, Mrs Auld had forfeited something of herself—her moral sense of right and wrong. Her natural 'heavenly qualities' that Frederick had noted early on had been corrupted; he could see that it was no less damaging to her as it was to him as the recipient of her harsh treatment.

In secret, Frederick read whatever he could get hold of. He was greatly influenced by Richard Sheridan's seminal speeches on Catholic emancipation.[24] Sheridan's work was, he observed, 'a powerful vindication of human rights' and 'a bold denunciation of slavery'. As Frederick's contempt of slaveholders and 'the robbers' who had first enslaved his ancestors grew, so he recognised in himself, just as Hugh Auld had predicted, a growing dissatisfaction at the limits of his situation. With this new awareness, he felt as if he was in a pit with no ladder to help him escape. It caused him to envy his fellow slaves 'for their stupidity'.[25] His frustration at his bondage grew so powerful that he wished himself dead, but the hope of emancipation, something he had read about and could believe in, kept him going. It was around this time that the idea of escaping to the North took root, but before making an attempt, he resolved to learn to write, which he achieved despite his fear of discovery by the harsh Mrs Auld.

Meanwhile, unexpected deaths back at the Home Farm had seen off not only Colonel Anthony but his son, Richard, leaving the estate to be divided equally between the colonel's other son, Andrew, and his daughter Lucretia. Aside from the indignity of having to return to Home Farm to be valued as a piece of stock, Frederick faced the greater fear of having to serve Andrew, a sadistic and dissipated drunkard. Fate shined on Frederick as his ownership fell to Lucretia, who returned him to Hugh Auld in Baltimore once more. A short time later both Lucretia and her brother Andrew died, leaving their estates to 'strangers' who knew nothing of the family's slaves. Frederick's grandmother, who had nurtured Andrew as a child, was turned out of her house and placed in a hut in some remote woods where she was left to die.

Two years later, in March 1832, due to personal differences between Hugh Auld and his brother Thomas, husband of the late Lucretia, Frederick was taken back by Thomas to live with him at St Michael's, a town on the Miles River, near to Chesapeake Bay. Inherently mean, Thomas Auld chose to starve his slaves, forcing them to beg and steal despite there being plenty of food available. What irritated Frederick especially was how every morning his master and his new wife, both Methodists, would piously kneel and 'pray that God would bless them in basket and store'.[26] Their house became a preacher's home for brethren with prayers morning, noon and night, but while feeding his guests well, Thomas continued to starve his slaves. It was hypocritical values such as these that would inform Frederick's views of some Christians and of how they chose to use their faith.

Frederick lived with Thomas Auld for seven months before he contracted him for one year to Mr Covey, a poor farm renter aged twenty-eight, who lived with his wife and child in a dilapidated farmstead 7 miles away. Like Auld, Covey was a class leader in the Methodist Church. Covey took on difficult slave labour cheap in return for 'breaking them' for their masters. He used Frederick as a field hand, and being 'a city boy', he struggled and had his back cut into ridges under Covey's unforgiving whip. Although he fed his slaves better than Auld, Covey denied them adequate time to eat the food. Worked to the bone in all weathers, Frederick was tamed and then broken. His energy gone, his intellect languished, he felt his soul darken. His urge to escape strengthened but he felt hopeless.[27]

Matters came to a head in August 1833 when, working on the fields, Frederick fainted. Covey first kicked him in the ribs and then cut open a bloody wound in his head. He rained down heavy blows on Frederick with a hickory slat before leaving him where he lay. Once he was strong enough to stand, Frederick took his beaten body back to his slave owner, Thomas Auld, to plead for a new home. He was given neither sympathy nor food, and was returned to Covey the next day.

Upon arriving at Covey's farm, Frederick fled to the fields, anticipating another beating. But when Covey found him, to Frederick's surprise, he welcomed him back. It was just a ruse because the next day, Covey seized Frederick and tied him up with a rope. Wriggling free, Frederick decided to fight back. Covey was taken by surprise and a fight ensued lasting for two hours before Covey finally abandoned his efforts, leaving his slave the moral victor. Frederick was reborn. His confidence was restored. Covey never tried to whip him again. The reason, much pondered upon by Frederick both then and later in life, almost certainly lay in his fears of ridicule if his failure to control a sixteen-year-old slave became public knowledge. His reputation as a slave breaker would thereafter be trashed.

January 1835 saw Frederick being transferred to another local farmer, William Freeland. Freeland made no pretensions of religion and enforced his authority with extreme violence. Efforts by Frederick and two other slaves to learn about Christianity at private meetings were broken up with sticks by two white church class leaders, ironically 'calling themselves Christian', but this setback did not stop Frederick.[28] In his free time on Sundays, and sometimes on weeknights, he organised and led a Sabbath literacy school for up to forty male slaves at the house of a free coloured man. The experience gave him his first followers and nourished his soul, giving him great pleasure. He undertook this for one year, squeezing in three evening sessions each week in the winter months.

It was during this period that Frederick went unbeaten by Mr Freeland. He also made close bonds of friendship with the other slaves. With two of them he devised a plan of escape, knowing full well the consequences should he fail. After painstaking planning, the time came, but they discovered they had been betrayed. They were taken under arrest to Easton Jail and Frederick was singled out by Freeland's mother for drawing the others into his scheme. She shouted at him, 'You devil! You yellow devil!' Traders came to look them over for purchase and to scoff at their predicament. A day or two later, Freeland returned and took back Frederick's two companions, leaving him in lonely solitude to reflect on what was in store. He sunk into absolute despair.

To Frederick's surprise, a week later, his old master, Hugh Auld, came to take him back to Baltimore. There, Auld hired him out to a shipbuilder. Frederick learned to be a caulker, making boats watertight by plugging gaps in the hull.[29] He spent the next eight months helping to build two brigs of war. During this time tensions between the white carpenters and black tradesmen increased, with the whites believing the blacks were putting their jobs at risk. A strike followed and soon a vicious fight broke out in which Frederick was attacked by four white apprentices. Badly beaten up, he had to flee for his life back to the Aulds.

Explaining these events, the proof of which was shown in his beaten condition, Frederick was almost overwhelmed by the kindness he received from Mrs Auld, who had previously grown so cruel towards him. 'With a mother's tenderness,' he relates, she bandaged his wounds. He did not say the reason for this kindness, but perhaps it was simply those 'heavenly qualities' he had noted in her long before, coming through. The next day an outraged Hugh Auld sought redress for the attack, but he was unable to secure a witness to speak up for Frederick. He refused to allow Frederick to return to the shipyard and found a job for him instead as a caulker in a yard in which he was foreman. Within a year, Frederick was earning up to $7 a week, all of which he had to give to his master.

Frederick was soon finding his own work via his own contacts, but always returning to the Aulds at the end of the day and handing Hugh Auld whatever money he had earned. Compared to what it had been before, life was good, but with his strength and confidence returning, the urge for freedom also returned. The injustice of handing over his income to his master irked Frederick especially. On his initiative, an adjustment was made to the financial arrangement between the two men. It provided a better return for Auld and greater freedom to Frederick, but with Frederick proving more confident and willing to stand his ground, tensions between them were bound to rise.[30]

At this juncture of Frederick's life, he became aware of the 'Underground Railroad', a secret network comprised of both blacks and whites, which helped slaves escape along established routes to the free states in the North and to Canada. In his autobiography, published in 1845, Frederick declined to give details of his escape for fear of prejudicing the prospects of those who might follow. However, by the autumn of 1838, the network had delivered him to the safe house of Nathan Johnston. Frederick, now Frederick Douglass, a young man of about twenty years old, was ready to embark on his new life.[31]

Douglass entered that new life with two fundamental principles engraved deep in his soul: the need for social and legal equality for all men; and the need for honesty of the spirit before God. The first offered the prospect of a society in which all, regardless of colour, could enjoy justice and prosperity without fear. The second offered 'the pure, peaceable, and impartial Christianity of Christ'. This was quite distinct in Douglass's mind from the 'Christianity of this land' in which the slave states engaged in 'corrupt, slaveholding, women-whipping, cradle plundering, partial, and hypocritical Christianity'. Douglass had no doubt that this was not Christianity, and he could substantiate his position to compelling effect with stories of personal experiences. For him, Christians in America paid lip service 'to the outward forms of religion, and at the same time, neglect[ed] the weightier matters of the law, judgment, mercy and faith ... always ready to sacrifice, but seldom to show mercy'.[32]

By 1841, Douglass, his wife Anna their two children, Rosetta and Lewis, had moved to Lynn, Massachusetts. He took part in lecture tours in Ohio, Indiana, western New York State and Pennsylvania, and he wrote. Three volumes of autobiography followed, the first in 1845 with distribution in the United States and a number of European countries.[33] More than 4,500 copies were sold in four months. Serious threats to his life followed, as did the risk of capture and a return to slavery. In response, and to take the opportunity to promote his book and the abolitionist cause, Douglass undertook an acclaimed two-year tour of British cities, during which he lectured and agitated for the cause. His supporters in Britain raised $700 to buy Douglass out of slavery from his owner, Hugh Auld. It was a crucial gesture which gave him the confidence to return home without fear of losing his freedom.[34]

While in Scotland, Douglass launched a campaign to 'Send Back the Money' to get the Free Church of Scotland to repay the donations it received from plantation owners in the Southern states of America. The Free Church was closely linked to America and the Scottish immigrant families who lived there, many of whom lived in the slave states of the South. Douglass's campaign brought him into direct conflict with the eminent Dr Thomas Chalmers and others of the Free Church on a matter close to his heart: the hypocrisy of religious practice by some churches.

The Free Church of Scotland was established in 1843 upon its split from the Church of Scotland, just two years before Frederick Douglass's arrival in Scotland. However, the cause of the rift stretched back much further, to 1690 and William III's grant of a permanent guarantee for Presbyterian Church order in Scotland following the battle of the Boyne. This was preserved in the Act of Union of 1707, but with a grassroots structure (see the introduction), divisions in the Church of Scotland were never far away.

The moderate or conservative establishment, which upheld the traditions of the Kirk, soon came into conflict with an evangelical wing, which sought to bring in converts who were keenly welcomed to gospel meetings both at home and abroad. In 1712, the Patronage Act gave the crown or landowner the right to appoint ministers to parishes, a right that had previously been abolished in the settlement of 1690. It created inevitable tensions between the landowner and the congregations, with the latter eager to exercise their independence of choice without interference. Splits within the Kirk periodically threatened, but cohesion was maintained.

In 1834, in the same momentous year as parliament was reformed and the Slavery Abolition Act came into effect, a local landowner, Lord Kinnoull, presented a minister to the congregation of Auchterarder in Perthshire. He was rejected by some 80 per cent of the congregation, who requested an alternative nominee. The presbytery refused to approve Kinnoull's candidate, but in 1839, after a long period of there being no minister, the court of session, supported by the House of Lords, upheld Kinnoull's original choice. Many other parish appointments of ministers had happened in between without incident, mainly because one side or the other preferred not 'to upset the apple cart', but the fault line remained threateningly close below the surface.

Dr Chalmers, professor of divinity at Edinburgh University and moderator of the Church of Scotland in 1832, had tried to follow a cautious line in asserting the Kirk's spiritual independence from the state, but the House of Lords' decision radicalised him sufficiently to persuade the general assembly to seek from the government a separation of civic and spiritual power, under which the church would no longer be bound by the courts in respect of the temporal aspects of its business. No progress was achieved under the Whig government, and in 1841, Robert Peel, leading a new Tory government, made a determined decision to resist the demands of the church. The general assembly in 1842 responded by a statement known as the 'Claim of Rights', which reasserted what had been set out in the 1690 settlement and by the Westminster Confession of Faith, declaring the independence of the church in all things spiritual.[35] It was remitted to parliament for a decision.

Meantime, Chalmers and other ministers saw the need to make a stand; 423 ministers agreed to leave the Church of Scotland if the Claim of Rights was not approved. Preparations were put in hand both to organise and to finance what was to be the likely outcome, namely a free church. In March 1843, as expected, the Claim was resoundingly defeated.[36]

On Thursday, 18 May 1843, in St Andrew's church in Edinburgh, the general assembly of the Church of Scotland got underway. Shortly after 2.30 p.m., Dr Welsh, the retiring moderator of the Church of Scotland, led the assembled ministers and elders in prayers. He then spoke for three-quarters of an hour, during which he declared that there had been sanctioned by government and legislature, 'an infringement on the liberties of our constitution, so that we could not now constitute this court without a violation of the terms of the union between church and state in this land, as now authoritatively declared'.[37] Dr Welsh, bowed to the lord high commissioner, picked up his hat and left the church. He was followed by about 200 ministers. Accompanied by largely cheering crowds, the ministers walked down Hanover Street to the Tanfield Hall in Canonmills where many more ministers joined them. It was there that they established the Free Church of Scotland and appointed the celebrated Dr Chalmers as their first moderator.[38] For the sake of principle and conscience, 487 ministers (or one third of the total number) gave up their livings and made themselves and their families homeless. In doing so, they not only split the Church of Scotland but also Scottish society.

With so many ministers and their families to house, land to purchase and churches to be built, the urgent need for money was patently evident. This was without even starting on the funding needed for education and outreach work at home and abroad.[39] Dr Chalmers led from the front, raising funds for ministry, building, education and missions. In only two years the new church had raised £368,871 from both home and abroad. This was a remarkable achievement, but the possibility that this support might wither had to be considered. The Free Church leaders were aware that little if anything positive would be forthcoming from a jilted Church of Scotland, while the latter's landowning members might prove obstructive and endeavour to put the Free Church down. Careful advocacy was needed both in Scotland and abroad to ensure that key support was maintained and that donations continued to be made.[40]

Within months of the foundation of the new church, it was decided to send a five-man delegation to the United States. Their brief was to travel extensively and raise support for the Free Church of Scotland among the American churches, specifically those of Presbyterian persuasion. Raising funds was not an expressed objective, but it was nonetheless hoped for as a by-product of the initiative. The travelling delegates were uncertain of how they would be received, but what was not expected was the furore that would result from their acceptance of donations for their cause, particularly from church communities in the South.

Given the treatment of slaves meted out by Southern slave owners (who very often claimed to be men of religious commitment), passionately recounted by Frederick Douglass and others, it is ironic that the Free Church hoped to receive sympathy and support from their American brethren due to the cruel treatment many Scots had suffered at the hands of their chieftains. The Highland Clearances, in which clan chieftains forcibly evicted their tenants from their homes to make way for more profitable sheep farming, had exposed critical weaknesses in the Church of Scotland. The tenants under threat of eviction had turned to the Kirk to defend them in their hour of need, but with a few honourable exceptions, the Kirk failed their congregations because the livings of their ministers depended on the patronage of the offending landowners. This betrayal was not easily forgotten by those forced to migrate. That long-standing resentment of Scottish emigrants was carried to America and, in 1843, expressed in their support of the Free Church's stand against what they perceived as the tyrannical Church of Scotland.[41]

On their arrival in the United States, the Free Church representatives found a fractured Presbyterian Church, split on the issue of slavery, with the North and the South held together by fragile compromises echoed in the political system. The religious division reflected harsh Calvinist views on one side and those of enlightened Scottish 'common sense' philosophy on the other, which called for moral government. The latter group were inclined to challenge slavery and many were active abolitionists.[42]

After a brief period when four of the five delegates were together at Princeton, they separated, covering different parts of the huge country, promoting and preaching.[43] Among those to hear one of the delegates preach was a congregation of African American Methodists in Baltimore. Despite their church being a poor, they gave a generous donation, much impressing the delegate.

The two delegates working in the Southern states found what they saw of slavery uncomfortable. Indeed, one delegate, George Lewis, challenged the general assembly in Louisville, Kentucky, by asking if it was true that state governments forbade teaching African Americans to read. Upon being told that this was the case, the delegate retorted that by adhering to this, Christians were contradicting the scriptural injunction to search all the Scriptures. The obligation of the church, he said, was 'to tell the civil power to go back to its own place'.[44]

Certainly, the general attitude of American churches to slavery troubled Lewis. For him, their failure to reject a law that prohibited African Americans from reading and writing was 'a plain violation of its freedom as a church'. Within the assembly, and even at Princeton, there was a reluctance to call slavery 'a sin'. Doing so would make their Southern colleagues and Old Testament patriarchs sinners. Lewis regarded slavery as a 'foul spot' on the nation, and saw it as the duty of all Christian churches to take strong action against those that practised it. However, it became clear that his views were not shared by many of his colleagues in the Free Church back in Scotland, who had not shared Lewis's first-hand experience.[45]

On 2 April 1844, American abolitionists, led by Arthur and Lewis Tappan, wrote a letter to the Free Church delegates to promote support for their cause, but by then the delegates had all but completed their tour.[46] Indeed, Lewis had just left the slave-owning community of Charleston, a key area of support where most of the Southern donations had been made. The abolitionists, sensing that the moment had passed, instead asked the question:

> What will the enemies of the Free Church ... say if you carry home the slave holder's bounty? They would say that the Free Church ... could not swallow the bread of their Sovereign [but were prepared to] beg a pittance from the pulpits of tyrannical oppression in Washington, Charleston and New Orleans.[47]

The Free Church was urged to refuse the money, but it ignored this plea. The first salvo of what became known as the 'Send Back the Money' campaign—a slogan coined by Frederick Douglass—which divided churches, families and communities in Scotland, was fired in New York when, in April 1844, the abolitionists' letter was made public in the American press.

The funds raised on the delegates' tour of the United States amounted to £9,000, with more expected, but no mention was made of slavery in the two speeches by the Free Church to the Scottish assembly. Instead, it would remain 'the elephant in the room', though it could not be ignored for long due to the interest of the Glasgow Emancipation Society.[48]

Before the recent Free Church visit to America, the Glasgow Emancipation Society, which had been founded in 1833, had already encouraged Scottish churches to cut their association with American churches that admitted slave owners into their congregations. By doing so, the society had won international support and been brought into close contact with anti-slavery societies in the United States run by William Lloyd Garrison and the Tappan brothers.[49] On 14 March 1844, this association led to the Glasgow Emancipation Society expressing regret that the Free Church had accepted money from churches in the South in the knowledge that their church members were known to be slave owners. They called for the donations to be returned. The truth was out.

Divisions on the issue of slavery grew to such a pitch that they were in danger of splitting the Free Church. Debate widened internally and externally, highlighting long-understood contradictions between the principle of preaching the gospel of freedom and the enslavement of fellow man. In fear of alienating members within the Free Church and upsetting the American Presbyterians by taking a stance one way or the other, a committee was appointed to report on the matter. However, the committee itself soon proved to be fraught with division, with political rather than religious issues taking precedence. The report that emerged four months later on 11 September 1844 satisfied neither side. Although the committee disclaimed the evils of American slavery, it was not prepared to express 'any rule or principle which caused American churches to take action against [it]'.[50] Abolitionists were dismayed, and Southern leaders who had supported the delegation were angered by this criticism of slavery.

On 24 May 1844, Dr Thomas Smyth, a Presbyterian minister in Charleston and supporter of the Free Church, sent to Dr Thomas Chalmers a further donation of £332. Alongside it, he expressed bitter disappointment that abolitionist views within the Free Church in Scotland had allied themselves with the Glasgow Emancipation Society. By doing so, he claimed, they were trying to destroy the Southerners' way of life. He then asked a direct question: where did Dr Chalmers stand on the subject?

It was not an easy question for Dr Chalmers to answer. Indeed, after several months, Dr Smyth had to remind him to do so. So where did Chalmers' sentiments lie? Early in his career in 1814, when parish minister of Kilmany in Fife, he had secured the support of the presbytery of Cupar to press parliament to include the abolition of the French slave trade as a condition of the Treaty of Paris. In 1822, by then a minister in Glasgow, Chalmers corresponded with the Clapham Sect via William Wilberforce and Zachary Macaulay, and even tried to secure a professorship at London University for Macaulay. In 1826, Chalmers published a pamphlet on abolition, which proved naive both in what it offered by way of a solution and in the cooperation he anticipated from Southern plantation owners.[51] Politically, his general domestic opinions were against government intervention in support of poor relief, unless there was no viable alternative. He preferred self-help, which was not a concept that sat easily with the issue of slavery. He was also potentially vulnerable to accusations of hypocrisy; both his father and brother had been investors in the slave trade in the 1790s.

Chalmers found himself between a rock and a hard place, unwilling to endorse slavery, which he saw as a great evil, but attracted by the piety and order of life that the unreformed South offered. Most controversially, he did not accept that a slave owner could not be Christian, and he distinguished between the nature of slavery, which he considered evil, and the nature of the slave owner who was born within the system. He argued that such a man should not be cast out of Christian society simply because of his circumstances. Finally, while he accepted the corrupting nature of slavery, he did not accept that slaveholding was necessarily the cause of vices, but he then contradicted himself by saying that American ministers should not hold slaves lest it 'should secularise them'.[52]

Pressure continued to pile in on Chalmers from Scottish and American abolitionist societies, pressing him and the Free Church to return the Southern donations. When he argued that there was no reason to question the integrity of the funds received, the Free Church was remorselessly lampooned for the next two years. The argument was taking a toll on Chalmers' health, while separately he shouldered the burden of securing finance for the church and planning for its future. It is worth noting, however, that despite the work of the abolitionist societies within Scotland, the contentious issue of a church permitting slaveholders to be members was of limited interest to the general public. Meanwhile, the Free Church saw off opposition on all fronts, trying to suppress the controversy; but could it last?[53]

The answer came in the form of Frederick Douglass, now on the second leg of his British tour, which had begun in Ireland. His first salvo was fired in Glasgow on 11 January 1846 at a meeting organised by the Glasgow Emancipation Society. In Douglass, they had struck gold. Here was a man who could not only speak with passion and fluency to engage his audience on the horrors of slavery, but as an African American and a former slave, with the scars on his back to prove it, none could question his authority on the subject. Douglass was careful to praise those who had fought to end the slave trade and slavery in the West Indies, including the work of the Clapham Sect, but he was ruthless in criticising those whom he thought made excuses for slaveholders. He was a popular sensation who packed out numerous halls and attracted substantial media interest, and of course, given his strident criticisms of the principles of certain churches, he generated substantial hostility towards the Free Church of Scotland.

Douglass's audiences were entranced by his skills as an orator. To begin with he carefully ignited their interest and compassion, telling personal anecdotes that informed them of the cruel reality of slavery, such as the brutal punishments meted out to slaves who aspired to read the Bible and educate their children. He distinguished between the slave who was a chattel and the harsh working conditions for many in Britain. He then attacked churches for upholding the system of slavery. 'Would you belong to a church that held fellowship with slaveholders ... with the man-stealing, cradle-robbing, woman-beating American slaveholder?'[54] Here was a man who did not try to sway his audiences with fine theological arguments and self-serving scriptural distinctions, he berated them with the harsh realities of life. He understood the effectiveness of repeating a phrase rhythmically within a speech. In Dundee, after his first explicit attack on the Free Church for 'accepting money from well known thieves to build her churches and pay her ministers', he coined the slogan 'Send Back the Money'. He used it in subsequent speeches, and on each occasion it resonated around the hall, supported by cheers. Frederick Douglass was a force to be reckoned with.

One of the principal targets in his attack on the Free Church was the revered Dr Chalmers. He scorned Chalmers' argument that American slaveholders had to work within the law and, as such, could not simply release their slaves. Douglass asked if the law was to worship a false God, would that be right because it was the law? His second objection was with Chalmers' distinction between the nature of the system of slavery and the character of the slaveholder within its bind. To accept legitimately the actions of the latter was to Douglass a licence to forgive murderers, adulterers and thieves for their crimes. At the centre of Douglass's attack was Chalmers' claim that it was unjustifiable to deny a slaveholder Christian fellowship.

There were those who disagreed with Douglass's hard line, and walked out of his lectures in Dundee, Aberdeen, Edinburgh, Paisley and elsewhere during the early months of 1846. On the other hand, while many Free Church ministers, unable or unwilling to accept the truth of his words, refused to invite him to speak in their churches, there were many members of the Free Church who agreed with his views and were against forming an alliance with slaveholders. Douglass's presence was a tour de force, winning over large, supportive crowds, raising public awareness of the harsh facts of slavery and relentlessly pressing the point that any church worthy of its name should not be associated with people and organisations involved in the slave system.[55]

His approach left the Free Church with little or no room for compromise. His satirical attacks on their leadership, particularly against Dr Chalmers, ruled out the possibility of any dialogue. At the general assembly held in May 1846, the embattled leadership of the Free Church continued to supress the attacks of the abolitionist societies by preventing their memorials or submissions from reaching the floor of the assembly. The voices of representatives of local synods, who pressed for abolition, were drowned out by the debate in which Robert Candlish submitted his latest report as convenor of the Committee of American Relations.[56] In it he referred to the letter from the American Presbyterian Church of May 1845, in which that church congratulated the Free Church for breaking from state control. In doing so, the American Presbyterians were making a pointed comparison to the same break in the United States, founded on the implicit agreement that church and state would not interfere with each other, at least in regards to slavery. Rather, the primary objective of the American Presbyterian Church was to maintain unity between the Northern and Southern churches. To aid this they pointed out the precedent of slavery within the early church and that the early disciples saw nothing wrong with it. The American Presbyterian Church elected to place ecclesiastical and political priorities ahead of the abolition of slavery, though this was unlikely to be a view shared by the many black Christians in the United States, whose opinions were never sought. The compromises made within the American church stymied any action being taken to end slavery, creating a build-up of pressure in the 1850s, which contributed to the eruption of the Civil War in 1861.[57]

In the face of this unhelpful response, the Scottish minister Robert Candlish felt there was little to say beyond that his committee was not in agreement with all the expressed sentiments of the American churches. The only question for the assembly to consider was whether the Free Church was justified in continuing with its 'friendly intercourse' with its American counterpart. In reply to his own question, although deploring the American churches' position on slavery, he argued that to put pressure on them would simply entrench their position and delay emancipation. In completing a complex speech in which he observed that slave owning was a sin, he concluded tortuously that a slave owner could competently join communion, despite being a slaveholder, if he claimed that he was a slaveholder against his will, but that God in his wisdom had chosen him to be one.

Douglass's response came in September 1846. He ridiculed the stances taken by Candlish and others and mocked the Free Church for travelling to America in the name of freedom but failing to challenge the enslavement of millions of Americans and the laws that prohibited the teaching the Bible to slaves.[58] This failure and their frustration at being ignored led to dissidents within the Free Church setting up an anti-slavery society directed, in broad terms, at ending slavery. However, at the general assembly held in May 1847, the Free Church leaders dismissed the society's activities and the petitions of others challenging its position, preferring to maintain the status quo with their American counterparts.

Later that month, Thomas Chalmers died. By the time of the next general assembly in 1848, the issue of American slavery was not mentioned, though following the report of Candlish's committee, a letter to the Presbyterian Church of America was approved and sent. This drew a line under the issue of slavery as far as the Free Church was concerned, and the efforts of the Free Church Anti-Slavery Society were abandoned. No money was returned; the Free Church had not bent.

The 'Send Back the Money' campaign was rooted in an error of judgement by the 1843 Free Church delegation to America. They failed to grasp the political divisiveness of slavery in that country and the risks they were taking by associating themselves with it. By the time they became aware of the gravity of the situation, which was during their visits to Charleston and Kentucky, where the delegates were horrified by what they heard and saw, it was too late: the funds raised from the Southern slaveholders were already on their way to Scotland. The Free Church elected to sweep the ensuing furore aside, and when that proved impossible, to rely on prosaic theological distinctions to salve the moral consciences of the hard-line adherents, and more importantly, to avoid a split within the new church. That issue came first. Despite the drama created by Douglass as he toured Scotland, and his huge popularity among the Scottish, in the words of historian Iain Whyte, his campaign proved in the end to be no more than a sideshow.[59]

But what of the hero himself? From a barefoot, illiterate slave boy on a Maryland plantation, he rose to be President Lincoln's distinguished guest for discussions in the White House on emancipation. Frederick Douglass was one of the most extraordinary men of his generation. After filling the lecture halls of England and Scotland, he returned to the United States, where he founded an abolitionist paper, the *North Star*. In 1859/60 Douglass undertook a second tour of Britain. In the American Civil War, he served as a recruiter for the Unionists and his two sons fought for that cause. Among other distinguished posts, he served as minister for the

United States in Haiti from 1889 to 1891. He is venerated in his homeland and across the world to this day.

But the true greatness of the man is perhaps revealed most poignantly and tellingly in his return, as a free man, to St Michael's, on the Miles River near Chesapeake Bay, in June 1877, after an absence of forty-one years. On his arrival he found most blacks still living in shacks as they had been when he had left in 1838, despite the ending of slavery after the Civil War. An inquisitive crowd of blacks and whites trailed behind his imposing presence as he strode through the streets, some coming to shake his hand. With confidence, he entered a house on the corner of Cherry Street and Locust Lane. The round-eyed onlookers watched him with admiration and disbelief; 'it was the first time a black man had ever entered a white home in St Michaels by the front door as an honoured guest'.[60]

The house was that of Thomas Auld, by then 'sick, bedridden', his hands 'palsied,' wrote Douglass. For the next twenty minutes, an emotional reconciliation took place between the two men. Douglass was there to forgive Auld, releasing him from the guilt of his past crimes, while at the same time, finding peace within himself and release from the fearful memories that had haunted him his whole life.[61] To help him forgive, Douglass drew on his Christian faith. It was the same faith that had urged him to fight for social and racial justice, having learned from the Scriptures as a young slave that all men are equal before God.

15

Two Men Who Changed America: Allan Pinkerton and John Brown

At 4.30 a.m. on 11 March 1859, a heavy hand struck the front door of Allan Pinkerton's house in Adam Street, Chicago. He opened the door cautiously, holding a revolver in his other hand. It was his friend, John Brown, a man who would go down in history for his role in hastening the onset of the Civil War in his quest to bring about an end to slavery in America. Pinkerton welcomed Brown into his house, along with two of his colleagues and their 'freight' of eleven slaves, all on the run from Missouri.[1]

In Pinkerton, Brown had a steadfast supporter in his work to free slaves from the South. Both men, white men, were committed abolitionists, operating within the network of the Underground Railroad.[2] This illegal activity was the common thread which had forged their friendship and their lives. They lived at a time of mass migration to America and of rapid expansion of the country; the issue of slavery had never been more divisive, and the frontier lands to the west, never so lawless. These two issues, lawlessness and slavery, were the two major challenges for the Union at the time, and Pinkerton and Brown dedicated themselves to addressing them, choosing along the way which laws to abide to and which to break.

Allan Pinkerton was born in a room on the third floor of a tenement flat in Muirhead Street in the impoverished Gorbals district of Glasgow on 21 July 1819. Growing up in that environment, living in two crowded rooms, forged the hardness of his character.[3] He was one of four boys of William Pinkerton and his second wife, Isabella. His father had five other children from his first marriage, though only seven of his children survived childhood. Allan established a loving and highly protective relationship with his mother, who worked in a spinning mill. His father, a tight-lipped man of strong build, worked as a jailer in Glasgow City Jail. He was a strict disciplinarian and would impart similar characteristics onto Allan, his favourite son.

Later in life, Pinkerton would describe his parents as atheists, but he was nonetheless christened by a Baptist minister on 25 August 1819.[4] And although religion was not a part of his upbringing, from an early age he imbued the moral values of the Scottish Enlightenment, which had been fostered in his city by Professor Francis Hutcheson (see Chapter 1) some ninety years earlier.[5] These ideas formed the foundation of what, in contrast to 'old' church principles, was essentially an evangelical message that all were rendered equal before God.[6]

Allan's father died when he was eight, and in keeping with the times, he left elementary school to begin an apprenticeship as a pattern maker with Neil Murphy, a friend of his father. He collected his pennies to give to his mother, for whom he waited each evening on a street corner as she returned from her day's work at the mill. After three years of 'a dreary existence', Allan apprenticed himself to William McCauley, a cooper. In December 1837, at eighteen years old, he was awarded his journeyman's card and became a tramp cooper who travelled to find work.[7] He remained dedicated to his mother, and any spare income was given to her.

His childhood disposition of immense self-confidence, aggressiveness and energy was complimented by his development into a muscular man who could be opinionated, violent, narrow and puritanical.[8] He assiduously eschewed alcohol having grown up being appalled by the degradation it caused in the Gorbals. Above all, he was determined and ambitious.

In 1838, Pinkerton returned from his journeyman coopering to Glasgow. It was a time of social hardship and industrial change, and he was encouraged to commit to the Chartist cause.[9] Its objectives were egalitarian, focused on enfranchising the working class in a fairer political system. The Chartists presented petitions to parliament for the adoption of the People's Charter, a bill drafted in May 1838 demanding universal male suffrage, equal electoral districts, vote by ballot, annually elected parliaments, the payment of MPs and the abolition of property qualifications for parliamentary membership.[10] The movement was regarded by opponents as dangerous and revolutionary, and potentially violent; indeed, there was threat of civil unrest if provoked. This represented a lack of agreement within the movement over how their aims could or should be achieved.

Two factions emerged: the 'moral force', who were against violence, and 'the physical force', who sought insurrection. It was to the latter group that Allan Pinkerton was attracted. The Chartist cause offered the common man the aspiration of 'a good house to live in ... good clothing and ... good food and drink to make him ... feel happy'.[11] Pinkerton was soon appointed the Glasgow representative to attend the Chartists' Convention in Birmingham.

At the convention, a general strike was approved, but it failed in its aims. Then in 1839 a petition was presented by the Chartists to parliament, but it was ignored. After this, the militant wing took control, culminating later that year in 5,000 men marching on Newport in Monmouthshire to take control of the town.

Pinkerton and his coopers had journeyed from Glasgow on foot to take part, and having joined their fellow Chartists outside the town, they arrived in Newport on 4 November 1839. In the heavy rain, they made for the Westgate Hotel, where some of the Newport Chartists, who had been arrested earlier that day, had been imprisoned. When the gathering outside the hotel refused to disperse, the King's 42nd Militia, summoned from their barracks by the Lord Mayor, opened fire, killing at least twenty-two people and sending the rest fleeing. Forced to run, Pinkerton and his coopers returned to Glasgow 'more like thieves than honest workingmen'. There, for the next three years, Pinkerton remained active in this divisive political arena, supporting those best placed to promote the Chartist cause.

While in Glasgow, Pinkerton joined a singing club, and together one evening they went to a fundraising concert given by the Unitarian church choir. At the event, Pinkerton's eyes alighted upon a woman named Joan Carfrae, a bookbinder's apprentice. He asked his friend Robbie Fergus to introduce him, and he and Joan soon became inseparable. At around the same time the authorities began to close in on Pinkerton for his Chartist activities and a warrant was issued for his arrest. Having married Joan in secret on 13 March 1842, they were smuggled onto a ship on 9 April and departed for Canada, with Pinkerton working his passage as a cooper. A new life had begun for both.

The voyage was an eventful one with the ship being wrecked off the coast of Nova Scotia, but nonetheless, the couple arrived safely in Quebec. After a few months, they travelled to the small but thriving frontier town of Chicago, drawn by better employment opportunities. It was here that Pinkerton reviewed his prospects with his old friend from the Gorbals, Robbie Fergus, and other Scottish emigrants. On their advice, in the spring of 1843, he decided to move some 50 miles west of Chicago to set up a cooperage business in the small dairy town of Dundee. It was a well-placed location, and with his rigorous work ethic, Pinkerton soon established a thriving small business.

In June 1846, Pinkerton noted that his cooperage yard was short on its required supply of timber staves. They were scarce in Dundee and to save money, he poled up the Fox River on a raft to a little island a few miles from the town. There he spotted a crop of trees suitable for that use. On his arrival there, he was surprised to find evidence of others apparently camping on the island, though no one was in sight. Given the island's remote location, it aroused his suspicion—'no honest men were in the habit of occupying the place,' he later wrote. He made several more visits to the island to find the answer, and one moonlit night he observed men rowing a craft there and lighting a fire. After reporting this information to the sheriff of Kane County, he joined the sheriff and his men on a raid. This ended in the arrest of a group of men who turned out to be counterfeiters. News spread fast and, for a short time, Pinkerton became a local celebrity. The island, meanwhile, became known as 'Bogus Island'.

Interest moved on, but the episode was not forgotten. In July of the same year, a Mr Hunt, the proprietor of the general store, and another storeowner asked Pinkerton to find the identity of a counterfeiter they believed to be operating in Dundee and elsewhere, distributing valueless currency all along the frontier. George Smith, the local bank owner, was especially alarmed at the counterfeiting of his genuine bills. They suspected a man called Crane, who lived some 35 miles away at the small town of Liberty. After some hesitation, Pinkerton took on the job, and through diligence and cunning, he succeeded in bringing the counterfeiter to justice. From the limited information provided, Pinkerton gained the confidence of Crane's friend, John Craig, who was resetting the fake currency by buying counterfeit money off Crane at a discounted value. With the Cook County deputy sheriff, Pinkerton arrested Craig for trial. Pinkerton became an instant sensation, and was offered the post of deputy sheriff of Kane County, while still maintaining his cooperage.

Allan Pinkerton was not a man of the law in every sense. His upbringing in Glasgow, steeped in the values of the Scottish Enlightenment, and his passionate commitment to the egalitarian Chartist movement, had possessed him with a strong sense of moral and social justice. It made him a staunch abolitionist. He was also a keen reader of the works of Frederick Douglass. Through his contacts in Chicago, he was an agent for the outspoken abolitionist Philo Carpenter and others of the Underground Railroad, and allowed his home in Dundee, and later Chicago, to be used as a safe house for slaves escaping from the South to Canada.[12]

The issue of slavery was beginning to tug at the seams of ordered life, even in sleepy villages like Dundee. This became evident in spring 1847, when Pinkerton put himself forward as a candidate for election as the county sheriff of Kane County, on behalf of the Abolitionists. In response, a letter was published in the *Western Citizen* in which the pastor of Dundee's Baptist Chapel, which Pinkerton attended, accused him unjustly of atheism (or rather being too liberal in religious philosophy for the stricter members of his congregation) and of selling and drinking 'ardent liquors'.

Violations of the uncompromising denominational beliefs of frontier churches typically led to the accused being put on 'trial' before the community's church elders, and then either exonerated or rebuked. In Pinkerton, however, the pastor had taken on a formidable opponent. Angrily, he challenged the allegations by rallying the support of many witnesses who testified that he was a teetotaller and never had alcohol in his house. What lay behind this attack, as Pinkerton knew full well, was his attitude to slavery. In a hostile atmosphere, after weeks of argument, the jury of church elders came out in support of the pastor. Friendships were broken and many Scots left the congregation. It was a highly damaging episode for a small, interdependent community. For Pinkerton, stifled by this toxic narrow-mindedness, it was the nudge he had needed to sell his business and move to Chicago, which he did in the autumn of 1847. In the intervening four years, the city had almost doubled its population to one approaching 30,000, and had become a dynamic metropolis and booming distribution centre for the world grain market.[13] Its streets were thronged with people active in trades, professions, commerce and crime.

Pinkerton had taken up an appointment as deputy sheriff of Cook County, of which Chicago formed a part. The city had a robustness that suited him. With his intense ambition and natural assertiveness, he soon made his presence felt among the criminal class. He showed no fear, neither in using his fists, nor in confronting armed thugs, and by 1849 he had been appointed Chicago's first detective. His activities led to a number of attempts on his life, and in reporting on one of his near escapes, the *Daily Democratic Press* praised him as Chicago's 'most efficient and courageous law officer ... keeping the community free of thugs and killers who are on the run'. However, after just one year, he resigned from his post due to 'political interference'.

Pinkerton was soon appointed to the United States Post Office as an agent, and in that role solved robberies and thefts, which were blighting post offices at that time. His growing reputation meant that he was assigned more complex cases, often going undercover, taking jobs within businesses that were falling victim to criminal activity.[14]

By the early 1850s, having enjoyed continual success and established an unrivalled reputation as a detective, Pinkerton had set up his own private detective agency. There was no shortage of work. The United States was rapidly expanding across the continent into new territories, while its urban settlements were growing at an exponential rate due to a massive influx of ambitious immigrant labour. Traditional law enforcement could not keep up. In rural areas, marshals and sheriffs, with the support of part-time deputies, entrepreneurs and bounty hunters, combatted crime, but these individuals were often corrupt or inept. In the cities, police forces were under-resourced and often paid off by criminals or had political loyalties that trampled over justice. There was no central federal agency, and local district, county and state boundaries were jealously guarded by those with jurisdiction, meaning that criminals could flee over district, county or state boundaries, outside the reach of the law. The rapid expansion of railways also exacerbated this problem, with passenger trains and the iron cars of express companies (transporting bonds, cash and merchandise) becoming common targets for criminal gangs.

Pinkerton's agency, one of the first of its kind in the world, suffered no limitations of jurisdiction in its pursuit of criminals. Pinkerton built up an able team of like-minded men and it grew rapidly.[15] He promoted his agency as a profession, not a trade, and applied a code of ethics which had to be strictly observed by his 'operatives'. They had to be neat and polite, and were trained to maintain a record of clients and cases and plans of operation. In the popular culture of the time, as reported by newspapers, Pinkerton and his men were portrayed as heroes. Investigations into scandals, divorces and the morals of women were declined.

Pinkerton's ethical values were a product of the Enlightenment principles he had imbued in Glasgow in his youth. Once a criminal was in jail, '[Pinkerton's] staff had to do all in their power to elevate and enable him....'

> If criminals are treated as men, capable of moral reform ... if they were to be instructed in their duties and responsibilities—as good citizens ... and better still taught some useful handcraft whereby they might secure an honest livelihood when they return to society ... and maintain an honest and reputable character; no one can calculate the great service that would thereby render to them and to humanity.[16]

This professional and ethical approach ensured the success of Pinkerton's Detective Agency. Large businesses such as rail companies and corporations like American Express, kept the agency on an annual retainer.

All the while, Pinkerton kept up his support of the Underground Railroad. However, with him being away on business for protracted periods, it was his wife, Joan, who, aside from bringing up a young family, had to manage the hiding of runaway slaves, often in the attic or cellar of their house. When there were too many runaways for Joan to cope with, other abolitionist friends stepped in to help with hiding, feeding or clothing the runaways. Both Pinkerton and his wife helped with passing messages up and down the Underground Railroad.

Allan and Joan Pinkerton's commitment to the cause made his house a favourite stopover for leading abolitionists when they visited Chicago. Among them was the free black leader John Jones, an ex-slave who was a frequent visitor from New York and good friend of the Pinkertons, and the messengers of Frederick Douglass and the extraordinary John Brown.[17]

In some ways, John Brown's future was predestined by his family's past. Descended from New England puritans, his paternal grandfather, the Reverend Nathan Brown, had been a missionary in India and Japan, while his maternal grandfather, the Reverend Heman Humphrey, was one of the first presidents of Amherst College in Massachusetts, which had a strong affiliation with Calvinism.[18] His father, Owen Brown (1771–1856), a wealthy cattle breeder, was a Calvinist and an abolitionist who later in life became one of the earliest agents for the Underground Railroad, after the network began in the early 1830s. When John was born on 9 May 1800 in Torrington, Connecticut, it was perhaps inevitable that he would adopt his family's strict Calvinist values and abolitionist principles. Added to this was a republican fervour, which meant a demand for social rights for everybody, without exceptions. In John Brown's world, it was all or nothing.

When John was five, the family moved to Hudson, near Cleveland, Ohio, then a frontier town, where his father, aside from owning a large tannery, sought to make Western Reserve College into an anti-slavery stronghold. Later, Owen Brown encouraged the founding of Oberlin College as a racially integrated coeducational institution of higher learning, with abolition one of its founding principles.[19] He also committed his house for use as a staging post for slaves escaping from the South. Growing up in this environment, John played with the idea of becoming a clergyman; he attended a preparatory school in Connecticut as a prelude to joining a seminary, but instead chose to drop out. Oddly, considering his antecedents, he never received a good education.

By twenty, John Brown was working as a foreman in his father's tannery and was married. His wife, Dianthe Lusk, died twelve years later in 1832, having provided him with seven children, five of whom survived to maturity. A year later, aged thirty-three, he married again. His new wife, Mary Ann Day, was an illiterate sixteen-year-old. She went on to have thirteen children, of whom six survived childhood. Brown relished being a father. He gathered his children around him to sing hymns, and discussed national affairs with the older ones, instilling in them all a duty and desire to be kind to black people, to befriend them, and to be open-minded in living with them.[20]

During his early life, there was little to indicate what was to come. Brown endeavoured to earn a living to support his enormous family. This saw him move in 1825 to Western Pennsylvania, where he ran a successful tannery and acted as postmaster. Working with others to set up a school, he became a church leader and a mason. When his business failed in 1834, he moved back to Ohio, setting up a tannery in Kent. Ambitious engagement in land speculation and associated business ventures followed, but the good times were short-lived, and an economic panic in 1837 left Brown bankrupt. By 1844 he was back on his feet, farming sheep in Akron with a wealthy business partner with a view to exporting wool to England. Again, it did not last long, perhaps due to a lack of business acumen on Brown's part. Yet, due to his evident integrity, he remained well liked and respected by his creditors, despite the losses they suffered in funding his business.

Brown's true passion was not in business but in the education of blacks. Since the 1830s he had been trying to find ways of pursuing this dream, regarding it, like Frederick Douglass, as the best route to true freedom, be it literal freedom, economic or spiritual, but his efforts had been frustrated by his financial difficulties. During his time in Western Pennsylvania from 1825 to 1834, he had provided succour for needy fugitive slaves, and later, following his father's lead, he became an active agent in the Ohio Underground Railroad, harbouring and transporting fugitives at night to destination towns, despite the risk of a $1,000 fine if caught doing so.[21] By 1837, Brown was addressing abolitionists and free blacks in Cleveland, urging the repeal of discriminatory laws against free blacks.[22]

By the late 1830s, Brown saw himself as a predestined leader who, like Moses, would lead the black slaves out of bondage.[23] In pursuit of this, he persuaded his sons to commit themselves to defeat slavery by armed warfare. This commitment was demonstrated first in 1854/55, when five of Brown's sons and their families trekked to Kansas in two separate parties, some 800 miles to the west, partly to find and establish land to farm, but also to help strengthen the abolitionist movement there.[24] It was a critical moment in the history of the new territory, in which its status on the issue of slavery was being decided. At the heart of the Brown brothers' motivation for going west lay the central question of when, if and how the United States was going to apply the words of its founding principles to all its people, regardless of colour. In Kansas, they wanted to do what they could to force the issue.

The United States had been divided along a clear fault line. Between the outbreak of the American War of Independence in 1775 and the Civil War in 1861, the slave population had increased by a factor of eight, from 500,000 to 4 million. To try to address the consequent implications for representation in Congress, the Missouri Compromise passed by Congress in 1820 admitted Missouri as a slave state and Maine as a free state.[25] This ensured that the number of slave states and free states remained equal at twelve each. The Compromise also provided that all territories north of Missouri's southern boundary were to be free of slavery.[26]

The Compromise worked for thirty years, but as the United States expanded further into new territories south and west, it started to fail.[27] Tensions mounted between pro- and anti-slavery forces over whether slavery should remain proscribed by the boundaries set by the Compromise or be permitted to expand into new territories seeking entry into the Union. This matter came into sharp focus when California sought admission as a free state to the Union. If approved, its admission would upset the political balance between the free and slave states (by then both numbering fifteen), making the free states more powerful in Congress.

The situation was exacerbated when New Mexico sought admission with the apparent intention to be a free state. This further alarmed the Southern representatives as, if approved by Congress, it threatened to diminish their power. Seeking to address these dilemmas, the Compromise of 1850, among other provisions, admitted California as a free state, and had Texas cede from its territory New Mexico and Utah, both of which were recognised as territories in their own right. In neither constitution was slavery mentioned, instead leaving the territories to resolve their status by a popular vote.[28] Finally, Congress reinvigorated the Fugitive Slave Act by making the return of runaway slaves a federal, not a state responsibility.[29]

Beyond a degree of short-term relief, the Compromise of 1850 failed to diffuse tensions. The precedent it set in allowing New Mexico and Utah to vote on their status led to a demand in 1854 for a similar provision to be granted to Kansas. Meanwhile, the Fugitive Slave Act hardened moderate opinion in the North, causing many anti-slavery supporters to become strong opponents of any further extension of slavery into the new territories. It also attracted powerful new adherents to the anti-slavery movement. The strength of feeling was demonstrated in 1854 with the trial of the escaped slave Anthony Burns in Boston. The court's decision under the Fugitive Slave Act to return Burns to slavery resulted in an attempted jail break by abolitionists, and armed troops being sent by President Pierce to escort the prisoner to his ship bound for Virginia.[30]

The Kansas–Nebraska Act of 1854 repealed the Compromise of 1850, which had only deepened divisions between North and South. It ruled that, instead of the two territories being free states on their admission to the Union (as had been previously agreed), their admission should not be granted until their status on the issue of slavery had been decided by popular vote. This decision set pro- and anti-slavery forces at each other's throats as each endeavoured to populate the richly productive Kansas territory with enough of their own supporters to secure the slavery vote in their favour.[31] Pro-slavery forces gathering in Kansas in July 1854 issued a resolution pledging to expel from the state those who opposed an extension to slavery. They feared that if Kansas became a free state, Nebraska was sure to follow. Inevitably, anti-slavery settlers from the North also flooded into the territory, seeking to prevent the domination of the pro-slavery faction.[32]

This need to support the abolitionist movement in the Kansas territory was the chief stimulus for the departure of Brown's sons and their families in October 1854. Three made the initial journey, which took around six months, ending at the Osawatomie River, some 50 miles south of Kansas town.[33] Nearly at their destination, one of the youngest of the party, four-year-old Austin Brown died of cholera. They were travelling by steamer on the Missouri River at the time, and when the ship stopped at Waverly, Missouri, the Browns alighted in a thunderstorm to bury the boy. The steamboat captain, a Southerner, did not wait for them to reboard, despite their tickets having been paid for. They had to complete the rest of the journey by stages, purchasing their food from farmers along the way, who, once they heard their northern accents, would often refuse to help. They established 'Brown's Station', their camp on the Osawatomie River, in the spring of 1854, and in the early summer they were joined by two more brothers and their families.

Before his sons left, John Brown made his views on their decision plain: 'If you and any of my family are disposed to go to Kansas or Nebraska with a view to help defeat Satan and his legions in that direction, I have not a word to say.' He remained at home at North Elba where he worked and socialised with local blacks, helping them to establish their homes while continuing his work with the Underground Railroad.[34] Above all, he treated his black neighbours and those he helped escape with respect; for their part, quite unaccustomed to this, they were often confused and disorientated.[35] The difference in colour was one frontier Brown could never cross. He was not, nor ever could be, one of them.

Brown inherited a belief from his puritan ancestors that the virtuous settlers of the New World were re-enacting biblical stories. The story that resonated with him the most was that of Gideon, who was inspired to take up his sword when the angel of the Lord blew his trumpet. Under the war cry 'The sword of the Lord, and of Gideon', Gideon's warriors scattered his enemies, leaving him leader of Israel. Brown saw himself as Gideon. On 15 January 1854, he addressed a group of some forty-five blacks whom he had named the 'League of Gideadites', urging them to learn how to use weapons and to be ready to fight.[36] 'Let the first blow be the signal for all to engage,' he said, 'and when engaged do not do your work by halves, but make clean work with your enemies—and be sure you meddle not with any others.'[37] His speech was historic because it was the first time a white person had set out a strategy for blacks to undertake a pre-emptive strike against pro-slavery forces. He invited men, women and children to join his militant movement.

Brown's objective was to deliver, through what he considered as necessary violence, his country's fundamental principle of equality without exception. He was aware of the limitations of what he was contemplating, and that many in the North would be against it, but he was nonetheless invigorated and determined.[38] He began to hatch a plan for a raid on an arsenal at Harpers Ferry in Virginia, not far from the historic house of George Washington and the plantations owned by his descendent, Colonel Lewis W. Washington. The weapons in the arsenal would be essential for the slave uprising Brown hoped to ignite, but also, the colonel was in possession of the iconic sword that had been presented by Frederick the Great to George Washington in 1785. Brown saw it as an appropriate emblem for his movement.

Meanwhile, Brown's sons were becoming increasingly alarmed at the steady build-up of pro-slavery forces in their area near the Osawatomie River in Kansas. One of his sons, John Jr, predicted that 'the great drama will open here, when we will be presented the great struggle in arms of Freedom and Despotism in America. Give us the arms,' wrote he to his father, 'and we are ready for the contest.'[39] Brown began shipping them arms, and soon decided to put his Harpers Ferry plans on hold to visit his sons to see if he could assist them.[40]

John Brown arrived at Brown's Station, Osawatomie, on 7 October 1855 to find his family living in flimsy tents. Their crops had failed due to torrential rain and most of them were succumbing to illness. With indefatigable energy, despite his fifty-five years, Brown set to putting matters right, fortifying the encampment and improving morale by his work.

The territory of Kansas, meanwhile, was on the edge of anarchy. The Southerners were threatening to seize it by force. The majority of them were 'border ruffians' who had nothing to lose. Intimidation by these thugs and electoral fraud had plagued the election of Kansas delegates to Congress in 1854 and 1855. Meanwhile, the abolitionists, migrating from the east, lured by the prospect of cheap land, were described as 'men with black and poisonous hearts'. Life was dangerous and many prominent advocates for a free state had already been murdered or humiliated. As 1856 approached, the violence escalated.

On 1 December 1855, a 'drunken' militia of 1,200 pro-slavery 'ruffians' lined up on the Wakarusa River to threaten an attack on Lawrence, a town with a strong anti-slavery identity. Days later, Brown and his family arrived in Lawrence with their weapons as news spread that on 6 December, an unarmed man from Ohio had been killed coming home from work by a band of armed Missourians who formed part of the pro-slavery militia. Having been appointed a captain of the 1st Brigade of the Kansas Volunteers, Brown set out with his sons and fifteen others on a surprise night raid on the militia by way of revenge. However, having secured volunteers to join him, Brown reflected the day for action had not yet been reached.

The delicate situation tipped in early 1856 when President Pierce replaced the first territorial governor of Kansas, who had adopted abolitionism, with a pro-slavery successor. Preferring to turn a blind eye to atrocities carried out by pro-slavery thugs, Pierce proclaimed the pro-slavery legislature as legitimate and its opponents treasonable. The situation was compounded by his government's opposition to the territory's free state government, which sat in Topeka. All this suggested that Kansas had been assigned to slavery. It radicalised political opinion among the abolitionists of whom Brown was one. 'The question here is,' wrote Brown, 'shall we be freemen or Slaves?' They felt they were at war, but the free state leaders preferred negotiation to violence. Notwithstanding this, pro-slavery violence increased over the ensuing months.[41]

Events came to a head on 21 May 1856, when pro-slavery settlers entered the anti-slavery town of Lawrence.[42] Unchallenged, the Southerners ransacked the two anti-slavery newspaper offices and burned and looted homes. Brown was absent at the time, but he returned seeking violent retribution. Three days later, he and his supporters killed five Southern settlers along the Pottawatomie River, decapitating them with swords. As a contemporary journalist observed, it was John Brown more than any other 'who brought Southern tactics to the Northern side'.[43] A few months later, Brown's son, Frederick, was killed when unarmed by a pro-slavery minister who was acting as a scout for the US Army. The scout's body was later found riddled with bullets. Brown and his entourage continued for the rest of the year fighting skirmishes with pro-slavery forces.[44]

The bold stance taken up by John Brown meant that he was both revered and hated. In New England, some abolitionists, separated by distance from the realities of this civil strife, saw him as a holy crusader. Within two weeks of the bloody raid on the Pottawatomie River settlement, a play entitled *Osawatomie Brown* was showing on Broadway, in which the pro-slavery Southerners were blamed for the massacre. This publicity encouraged Brown to raise funds for his cause in Massachusetts and Connecticut in 1857. He did not make it clear that he planned to use the funds for his assault on Harpers Ferry, which he had begun planning back in 1854.

In early 1858, when a guest of Frederick Douglass, Brown drafted a provisional constitution for the revolutionary state he hoped to create. He asked Douglass to join him, but the latter refused, albeit sympathetically, regarding his plan as suicidal. In Boston, Brown informed his six financial backers of his Harpers Ferry plan and recruited more men to join him, one of whom took a job at Harpers Ferry to secure inside knowledge.[45] Meantime, he obtained a shipment of 1,000 pikes, ready for the slave uprising he hoped to spark.

At the start of 1859, Brown, having adopted the name Shubel Morgan, launched another raid, this time into Missouri. During it, one of his 'army', Aaron D. Stevens, killed a prominent elderly slave owner while liberating eleven slaves as well as the owner's stock of horses and wagons.[46] Frontiersmen were shocked at the murder. A bounty of $250 was put on Brown's head by none other than President Buchanan.[47]

The liberation of the slaves was just the beginning for Brown, who referred to his mission as 'the War into Africa'. He led the liberated slaves and his small armed posse in a wagon train from Missouri to the north, on the long road to Canada. The journey through the prairies in the middle of winter was so cold that Brown's hands and fingers froze and his shoes fell apart. Settlers formerly sympathetic to Brown's actions turned his party away upon learning they were horse thieves—an unforgivable sin on the frontier. When Brown was passing through Springdale, Utah, pro-slavery groups threatened to attack him, but they melted away when it became clear that he and his men were prepared to fight to the death in defence of the slaves they had freed. Finally, on 9 March 1859, after an exhausting journey of ten weeks, they hid in a boxcar at the railroad town of West Liberty, and with the help of one of Brown's Underground Railroad agents, they were hitched onto the Chicago train. Two days later, early on the cold morning of 11 March, John Brown was thumping on the door of Allan Pinkerton's house in Adams Street, Chicago, with a party of fugitive slaves.

Aside from seeking a safe house for himself and his party, Brown needed money to get the escaped slaves to Canada. His old friend Pinkerton agreed to raise the funds for him at the Chicago Judiciary Convention, a meeting for the selection of a candidate to be a judge on the Cook County circuit, which by chance was due to take place that day.[48] Pinkerton first visited Colonel C. G. Hammond, superintendent of Illinois Central, whom he knew to be 'a good friend of coloured people'. As Pinkerton had hoped, the superintendent agreed to have a railroad car ready at the Chicago depot for 4.45 p.m. that evening to take the liberated slaves north to Canada, provided that Pinkerton took responsibility for their provisions. Pinkerton then dispatched two messengers to the Chicago Judiciary Convention to approach potential subscribers for the funding he needed. They returned empty handed. Lacking the funds himself to cover the cost of provisions, Pinkerton resolved to make a personal appeal.

Upon his entering the hall, silence fell. Pinkerton was instantly recognised by everyone there. Seizing the moment, he strode to the platform. His address, in keeping with his character, was honest and direct. He explained that funds were needed by John Brown to secure the escape of fugitive slaves to Canada. He said he would leave the meeting immediately if he received the support he wanted, but if he did not receive it, he would 'bring John Brown to this meeting', adding, 'If any United States Marshal dare lay a hand on him he must take the consequences. I am determined to do this or have the money.'

More silence followed. Pinkerton was known for his resolve, and no one would have regarded his words as an idle threat. Then came the sound of footsteps ringing out on the wooden boards of the hall. A well-dressed man made his way to the platform where Pinkerton stood. It was John Wilson, an established Chicago politician and later a judge. He handed Pinkerton a $50 bill. Pinkerton took off his hat and placed the bill inside it before proceeding around the hall, holding his hat out to the gathering. Minutes later he left the hall, carrying between $500 and $600.[49]

By 4 p.m., Pinkerton, armed with a pistol and accompanied by two others, helped the slaves into a wagon. It then toured the city, picking up fugitives hiding in other safe houses for transport to Canada. The last stop was the house where the black leader John Jones was staying. Jones and Pinkerton shook hands with Brown, who said, as he departed, 'Friends, lay down your tobacco, cotton and sugar because I intend to raise the stakes.'[50] It was a veiled warning of his plans for Harpers Ferry.

As Pinkerton and his son William watched John Brown depart from the station with the fugitive slaves, Pinkerton turned to his son and declared: 'He is greater than Napoleon and just as great as George Washington.'[51] Six hours later, the slaves found freedom in Canada. Brown had completed their journey of 600 miles in eighty-two days in covered wagons through the bitter heart of winter. Far from an onerous trek, however, for Brown it had been the fulfilment of a spiritual crusade.[52]

Returning from Canada, Brown resumed his efforts to raise funds by holding public meetings. He described the threats and hardships he and his men had faced in the journey to Canada, and asked for help 'to prosecute the work on a larger scale'. One of those attending in Boston detected behind Brown's glass-eyed gaze 'a touch of insanity', perhaps a symptom of his implacable certainty that he was doing God's work.[53]

In June 1859, with almost $4,000 raised, Brown returned to his home in North Elba to bid his wife and daughters goodbye. He knew the risks in what he planned, as did his family. One of his sons, Salmon, declined to join him. After this he got on the march, appointing himself commander-in-chief of his 'provisional army', a very small, motley force consisting mostly of men in their twenties—Brown's sons, freed and fugitive slaves, veterans from Kansas and young abolitionists on their first campaign. His destination was Harpers Ferry, West Virginia.[54]

A month later, they rented a farm in Maryland some 7 miles from Harpers Ferry, where they awaited the arrival of more combatants. By mid-October, however, there were still only twenty-five of them. Three were to be left behind at the farmhouse to guard their supplies, leaving just twenty-two for the raid, of whom five were black. Nonetheless, on the night of 16 October, the raid to ignite a slave uprising commenced.[55]

Cutting telegraph wires, Brown and his men rapidly secured the federal armoury and then Hall's Rifle Works, a weapon manufacturer for the national government. Meanwhile, at his plantation, Colonel Lewis W. Washington was taken prisoner and forced to surrender George Washington's famous sword. At this point, Brown could have made off with the weapons in the armoury and used them for guerrilla attacks, or he could have blown up the armoury and other targets, but he decided to stay put, placing his faith in the belief that his call to his black brothers to rise up and join him would be answered.

No one came to his support. After a short while Brown offered a truce with local armed citizens, but this failed when one of his sons was shot while carrying a white flag. US marines and soldiers, called up by President James Buchanan, arrived on the 18th and stormed the buildings Brown and his men were defending. Before the siege ended, half of his force of twenty-two, including another of his sons, had been killed or mortally wounded. A further five were captured, among them Brown himself, with seven escaping north.

John Brown was badly wounded and had to be carried to the court in Charlestown, Virginia, where was tried on 27 October 1859. He was denied time for his lawyer to arrive to mount his defence, though the outcome of the trial was hardly in dispute. Brown was convicted and sentenced to death on 2 November, to be executed a month later on 2 December.[56] During that month, Pinkerton did all he could to raise funds for Brown's defence, writing to leading politicians to win a stay of execution, but to no avail.[57] Brown's actions had deepened divisions between pro-slavery Southerners and Northern abolitionists, and the authorities were eager for a hasty trial, even if it meant failing to observe the due process of law. Indeed, Brown was found guilty on a charge of treason against the state of

Virginia, but as he pointed out, since he was not a Virginian, he owed no loyalty to the state. But to many in the South, the charge against Brown and conduct of the court were irrelevant; they only wanted to see an end to this man whom they regarded as a serious threat to their society.

Regardless of the rights and wrongs of Brown's actions, to forego legal process did not come without risks. The attention of the nation rounded on the man whose 'blazing blue eyes' and thick, long beard gave him the bearing of an Old Testament prophet. His story drove fear into the hearts of many whites; while for others, his words and deeds were a powerful inspiration.[58] But how was he viewed by black Americans?

No matter how unstinting or courageous his commitment to the cause of freedom and equality for blacks, John Brown was not a black man. This was likely to be the main reason that his call at Harpers Ferry for a slave uprising went unanswered. He was an outsider seeking to lead black people into war. It was naturally very difficult for black slaves to trust him or to understand why he was doing this.[59] Whites were oppressors not liberators, and Brown, being white, would not suffer the same retribution as his black followers should a rebellion fail. The response at Harpers Ferry might have been different if the clarion call had come from a black man, but Brown either never considered this or chose to ignore it. After all, it was God to whom he was answerable, and the outcome of his actions, in accordance to his faith, was predestined.[60]

As for his fate, John Brown met it with equanimity: 'Men cannot imprison, chain or hang my soul,' he said. His contribution to the fight against slavery was perhaps best summed up by his friend, Frederick Douglass: 'If John Brown did not end the war that ended slavery, he did, at least, begin the war that ended slavery.'[61]

The presidential elections of 1860 ended in triumph for the North, with Abraham Lincoln gaining office. While some in the North regarded him as not sufficiently radical, in the South, many feared he would attempt to bring an end to slavery. The threat issued by Southern leaders at the Constitutional Convention of 1860 to disrupt the union of the federal government if it interfered with slavery became real when, upon Lincoln's inauguration, South Carolina seceded from the Union. By February 1861, it had been followed by six other states, which formed the Confederate States of America, with slavery protected in its constitution.[62]

On 12 April 1861, Fort Sumnter, a federal fort off the coast of South Carolina, was attacked by Confederate troops on the principle that it was within Confederate land and should therefore be under Confederate ownership. When Lincoln sent troops in support of the Union, four more states joined the Confederacy and the Civil War had begun.[63] Four years later, on 9 April 1865, after the loss of 750,000 lives, the Confederate

Army surrendered. On 6 December the same year, the 13th Amendment to the constitution was ratified, finally ending slavery in the United States of America.[64]

During the war, Allan Pinkerton proved himself a valuable asset to the Unionist cause. His renown as a private detective earned him the post of head of the Union Intelligence Agency, and as such he foiled a plot to assassinate President Lincoln while guarding him on his way to Washington in February 1861. His experience in going undercover also came in very useful. Under the alias 'Major E. J. Allan', Pinkerton and his men worked behind enemy lines, gathering intelligence from Confederate soldiers. In this way, Pinkerton's Detective Agency was a precursor for became the US Secret Service.

After the Civil War, Pinkerton and his men continued their detective work, pursuing train robbers including the Reno Gang from Indiana, the Molly Maguires of Philadelphia, and Jesse James. Among his many innovations in the field of criminal investigation was the tapping of telegraph lines and the collecting of photographs of criminals for the purposes of identification. These practices were soon adopted by police forces across the world. He was a legendary figure, and from 1873 onwards, he lent his name to the publication of eighteen melodramatic detective novels. By May 1877, he passed his highly successful detective agency on to his two sons, Robert and William. Today, perhaps his most recognisable legacy is in the symbol of his detective agency: an eye with the slogan 'We never sleep', which give rise to the term 'private eye'.[65]

Until his death in 1884, Pinkerton never stopped admiring his old friend John Brown. In 1882, at Farwell Hall in Chicago, a reception was held to celebrate Brown's life. His wife, Mary, by then an elderly lady, was invited as guest of honour, and though Pinkerton was unable to attend due to suffering a number of strokes, he was asked to provide his reminiscences, which were read out by Mrs Brown.

Standing in front of a huge portrait of her late husband, on a podium which bore the motto 'Resistance to Tyrants is obedience to God', Mary Brown read out Pinkerton's memories of that early morning of 11 March 1859, when Brown had banged on his front door in Adam Street, asking for help. Later, the widow of the 'free negro' John Jones recalled how her husband, Brown and Pinkerton, who were all firm friends, planned their course of action. In particular, she recollected Pinkerton's commitment in raising the money needed to send the fugitives to Canada; the *Chicago Times*, writing about the reception, named him as 'one of the engineers of the Underground Railroad'.

These speeches and others made by Chicago's leading dignitaries were met with rousing applause from the audience, and the meeting ended with a declaration that Harpers Ferry was 'one of the most decisive battles in the world'.[66] In a final tribute to their hero John Brown, as the audience slowly filed out of the hall, they spontaneously burst into a rendition of 'John Brown's Body', the most popular marching song of Union soldiers during the Civil War.[67]

In adherence to his puritan beliefs, Brown would have regarded the Union victory in the Civil War as predestined. His friend, Allan Pinkerton, an atheist, viewed it in more pragmatic terms, but with the same sense of inevitability: the just means of bringing a cruel, degrading and unnatural institution to an end for the creation of a fairer and more equitable society, fit for all. It was the dream he had always aspired to since his days growing up in the Gorbals of Glasgow, and what had drawn him to the land of opportunity forty years earlier. However, as Pinkerton almost certainly appreciated, the work needed to achieve this timeless aspiration had only just begun.

CONCLUSION

Why It Matters Now

The preceding chapters tell the stories of individual people and of how they responded to the times in which they found themselves. All had a connection in some form or another with slavery. Some were its victims, some its beneficiaries, others were challenged indirectly by its existence. The people in these stories exhibit a range of contrasting characteristics, among them fear, greed, conceit, moral conscience (or a lack of it), cruelty, ambition, bravery, resolution and complicity—characteristics manifested in their lives by good and evil deeds. Taken together, their stories reveal how slavery was for so long legitimised and sustained by law and the church in Britain and America. They also show how in Britain, morality eventually triumphed over cruelty and greed, and slavery was defeated. But today, the legacy of slavery lives on across the world, making our knowledge of its history a critical factor in helping us understand the societies in which we live, and how to safeguard them.

In Britain in the eighteenth and early nineteenth centuries, an imbalance of economic, political and moral factors allowed for the narrow interests of a minority with enormous power to take precedence over fundamental moral standards. Today there are democracies that suffer from a similar imbalance, where equality and human rights are being sacrificed for the type of economic growth that benefits only a small elite. Across the world, the gulf between rich and poor is widening, jeopardising egalitarian values of shared benefit for the common good, generating anger, disenchantment and a dangerous loss of trust in democracy. The cause, according to the late philosopher and rabbi Jonathan Sacks, is 'the failure of honesty, integrity, responsibility, transparency and accountability'.[1] In his book, *Morality*, published in 2020, Sacks argued that the role of civil society in Britain and the United States has been hollowed out in the last half century, and the vacuum filled by the state. As a result, 'rights have ceased to be restrictions on the scope of the state, and have become instead entitlements, demands for action by the state'.[2] These demands for action, the responsibility of which should properly been exercised by the individual or people working together as a civil society, are often beyond government's ability to deliver. These failures, abetted by the unfulfilled promises of politicians, have served to stoke anger among an increasingly disaffected electorate. Furthermore, due to weak government and regulation, there has been a corrosion of corporate culture, which, while creating rapid economic growth, has been used to serve the negative interests of corporations and their shareholders.

For the Scottish economist and philosopher Adam Smith, an acolyte of Francis Hutcheson and Lord Kames, writing in 1776, slavery was founded not on economic self-interest, but on man's 'love of domination and tyranny', aided and abetted by weak government. Being representative of a human characteristic, Smith regarded slavery as a perpetual stain on human society, and given the continuance of modern slavery today, 230 years after Smith's death, there is evidence to support his bleak view.

Slavery existed in societies that licenced vicious cruelty. People like Sam Robinson, a cabin boy on a slave ship, and James Irving, a slaver captain, had few qualms, if any, about earning their living from the slave trade. The merchant Richard Oswald, who exploited slavery and the slave trade in what society regarded as the fair pursuit of fortune and social prestige, was responsible for the suffering of thousands. As far as we know, he was never held to account either by his conscience or his peers, and instead he was praised as a benefactor.

It was acceptable, before the abolition of slavery, for one's moral conscience to extend only as far as one's countrymen. It was a time when European powers engaged in war to defend their borders and to control international trade routes. For those in power, nothing could compete with the importance of financing Britain's Industrial Revolution and thereby establishing the nation as an economic powerhouse beyond its rivals to fund its imperial ambitions. Yet, as this book shows, there were many individuals for whom the horror of slavery was unbearably apparent. James Ramsay and Fanny Wright dedicated their lives to ending it, while men like Archibald Monteith and Robert Wedderburn, victims themselves, selflessly sought dignity and freedom for their enslaved brethren and spiritual peace for themselves.

Although slavery offended his egalitarian values more than anything, being an economist, Adam Smith chose to look beyond the moral and legal arguments and attack slavery on economic grounds. It was a strategic choice of an angle his opponents understood and cared about. He argued that slavery cost plantation owners more than what it would cost them to pay wages, and not only that, it placed an unnecessary economic burden on the society they serviced. As a slave could expect no reward for his work, Smith reasoned that he had no incentive to work productively. Meanwhile, sugar and tobacco were traded at artificially high prices to sustain an inherently inefficient slave system, which naturally impacted the consumer.[3]

On a human level, Smith noted the moral degradation of white slave masters, saying that there was not a black African who 'does not possess a degree of magnanimity which the soul of his sordid master is too often scarce capable of conceiving'.[4] But the unpleasant topic of human suffering was continually pushed to the margins by politicians and governments striving for dominance both at home and on the global stage. The prosperity afforded by the colonies in the Caribbean and America was too valuable to risk disrupting, and as Smith noted, the politicians themselves, particularly during the European and American wars, were too invested in the status quo. Meanwhile, most planters, fearful of uprisings, used pitiless violence to subjugate their slaves, resisting any attempts to improve conditions as if their lives depended on it. For the most part, they could act with impunity; in the seventeenth century, the crown delegated law-making in America and the Caribbean islands to colonial assemblies dominated by slave owners.

From the start, the flawed economic model was only able to prosper due to political connivance. The monopoly of the Royal African Company ended with the Glorious Revolution of 1688–89, which ushered in the principle of free trade, financed by private investment.[5] The ensuing wealth generated for people in power ensured the longevity of the trade, but in time, faced with lower sugar prices from plantations in Cuba and South America, the British government's collusion in upholding protectionist tariffs became unsustainable. Real change, however, was brought by public pressure on the government.

From the 1750s onward, Enlightenment thought and values emanating from Edinburgh, Glasgow and elsewhere began to have an impact. Landmark cases like Somerset *v.* Stewart and Knight *v.* Wedderburn attracted unprecedented public interest, as did horrific news stories like the *Zong* Massacre of 1781. Alongside this, there was a rise of courageous resistance from slaves on the plantations and an amplification of the voices of Quakers, Methodists and other religious bodies and anti-slavery organisations for whom slavery was morally unacceptable. In Britain and America, public awareness at the injustice and wickedness of slavery was

Conclusion: Why It Matters Now

mobilised and the hand of government was eventually forced—in Britain through parliament, in America through the Civil War.

Returning to the present day, by focusing on the centre ground of politics, politicians with new ideas must reach out to the silent majority in pursuit of the common good through shared values of integrity, honesty and fairness to restore trust between government and the people. People must acknowledge that politics only offers limited solutions to life's problems. Notwithstanding, these limited solutions still carry real value for people. In support of this, the silent voting majority can, for example, usefully join a political party to support it. If done in sufficient numbers, financial subscriptions can reduce a party's dependence on major funders and create a much broader membership base to choose the most representative candidate at constituency level.

As Jonathan Sacks wrote, 'Morality is us, each of us within our own sphere of interaction, taking responsibility.' This means that for our lives to change we must not first wait for the world to change.[6] The regeneration of a healthy democracy can best be achieved by restoring an active civil society which, by coming together at a local level to form moral communities (such as local community or voluntary associations or social clubs), empowers people to help each other to achieve collectively what cannot be done alone or by government. This principle, if pursued with honest commitment, can deliver a just society for all, regardless of colour or religion.

This solution to injustice was understood and implemented by the anti-slavery movements in Britain and America in the eighteenth and nineteenth centuries, in the civil rights movements of the twentieth century, and in the Black Lives Matter movement of the twenty-first century.[7] However, as has been learned over the years, to achieve greatest success it is important to separate feelings from reason. Fanny Wright acknowledged this, as well as her struggle with it, when she observed that 'slavery is a subject upon which it is difficult to reason because it is so easy to feel'. Through bitter experience, she learned of the need to examine and empathise dispassionately the rationale upon which strong feelings are based. To fail in this, to lead with passion rather than reason, risks the avoidance of inconvenient truths, which in turn makes workable long-term solutions that serve to benefit the individual and the common good more difficult to achieve, while strengthening critics and alienating active and potential supporters.

Today, dispassionate examination is needed to recognise past faults and the steps that led to them, so that, with this knowledge, we can spot the incipient development of similar evils and crush them before they can take hold in society. Eric Williams, before becoming prime minister of

Trinidad and Tobago in 1962, observed that the development of the New World countries by the European powers could never have been achieved without the backbreaking toil of slaves. Their forced labour, therefore, made them unrewarded investors in the crucial wealth which Britain and America generated to facilitate their growth. This debt remains unpaid. It can only be discharged by the recognition, through action and not just words, that the heirs of African slaves in these two countries should not only enjoy equal rights in law, but respect and equal opportunity in society, free of injustice. Prejudice must surrender to fairness, blind ignorance to learning, anger to love, pride to humility. By focusing on what we have in common rather than on what divides us, society will flourish and peace and prosperity are assured. 'Morality is us,' wrote Sacks—we all bear responsibility.

A greater public understanding of the history of slavery can help contribute to this. Teaching white and black students about how modern Britain is indebted to the labour of black slaves can help shape attitudes towards race and deepen understanding to positive effect. As proved by the abolitionist movement in Britain in the eighteenth and nineteenth centuries, it is the Scottish Enlightenment values of reason, education, understanding and debate that have the power to effect change, and in so doing, align politics and economics with moral decency.

Notes and References

INTRODUCTION

1. Robinson, *A Sailor Boy's Experience Aboard a Slave Ship* (1867), letter 2, dated Liverpool, March 1800.
2. The Portuguese were the first to trade slaves in Africa in the early fifteenth century. Starting at Cueto, Morocco, they progressed down the African coast to Angola. They were followed by Spain, Holland, and later France and Britain. In 1555, William Towerson was the first Englishman to undertake slave trading in the Atlantic, with a further voyage the following year, but John Hawkins is considered to be the first English slave trader. He left England on the first of three slaving voyages in 1562, when he sold slaves to St Domingo. His last disastrous voyage was in 1567. The voyages were undertaken with the approval of Queen Elizabeth I, but were insignificant compared to the Portuguese licensed trade of that time. Britain and Portugal account for about 70 per cent of all Africans transported to the Americas. Britain was most dominant between 1640 and 1807, when the British slave trade was abolished. An estimated 3.1 million Africans (of whom 2.7 million arrived) were transported by the British to their colonies in the Caribbean, North and South America, and other countries. See Walvin, *A Short History of Slavery* (2007), pp. 36–43.
3. Herman, *The Scottish Enlightenment* (2001), p. 11.
4. Norman, *Adam Smith: What He Thought and Why It Matters* (2018), p. 42.
5. Duignan, 'Enlightenment', www.britannica.com.
6. John Knox (1513–1572) led Scotland's Protestant Reformation. John Calvin (1509–1564) was a French theologian, pastor and ecclesiastical statesman, and the most important figure in the second generation of the Reformation.
7. By 1745, when Charles Edward Stuart raised the Jacobite flag in Scotland, the percentage of Catholics in the country was reduced to 1 per cent of the population. See Norman, *Adam Smith: What He Thought and Why It Matters* (2018), p. 27.
8. Herman, *The Scottish Enlightenment* (2001), p. 16.
9. Herman, *The Scottish Enlightenment* (2001), p. 16.
10. Herman, *The Scottish Enlightenment* (2001), p. 18.
11. Herman, *The Scottish Enlightenment* (2001), p. 18.

12. Smith, *An Inquiry into the Nature and Causes of the Wealth of Nations* (1776), Vol. 1, p. 328.
13. Herman, *The Scottish Enlightenment* (2001), p. 26.
14. Herman, *The Scottish Enlightenment* (2001), pp. 23 & 26.
15. Houston, *Scotland, A Very Short Introduction* (2008), p. 101.
16. Allan, *Scotland in the Eighteenth Century* (2002), pp. 86–87.
17. Four sugar refineries devoted to colonial trade were built in Glasgow in 1667 and 1669. By 1680 they were distilling rum. Mullen, *It Wisnae Us: The Truth About Glasgow and Slavery* (2009), p. 8.
18. Herman, *The Scottish Enlightenment* (2001), pp. 29–30.
19. The Navigation Acts of 1651 and 1660 were acts of (the English) parliament intended to promote the self-sufficiency of the British empire by restricting colonial trade to England and decreasing dependence on foreign imported goods.
20. Herman, *The Scottish Enlightenment* (2001), pp. 30–31.
21. The Bank of Scotland was established with a starting capital of £100,000, compared to the Bank of England's almost £600,000.
22. The Company of Scotland Trading to Africa and the Indies, an overseas trading company, was created by an act of parliament on 26 June 1695.
23. The Darien venture cost more than 2,000 lives and over £200,000.
24. Herman, *The Scottish Enlightenment* (2002), pp. 31–34.
25. The clans included the Camerons, the Appin Stewarts, the MacLeods and the MacDonalds of Glencoe.
26. Allan, *Scotland in the Eighteenth Century* (2002), pp. 128–129.
27. Most notably the wool, linen, brewing, and paper-making industries. Excise taxes were placed on linen, paper, salt, and in 1725, on malt for brewing beer and whisky.
28. Violence began in Hamilton on 23 June 1725 and spread throughout the country.
29. Colonial merchants funded eighteen manufactories in Glasgow between 1730 and 1750, and a further twenty-one between 1780 and 1790. More than half the city's tobacco merchants had shares in industrial ventures in the eighteenth century, including in linen, cotton, sugar boiling and glassmaking, while the tobacco lords founded the city's first three banks. See Devine, *The Scottish Nation* (1999), pp. 114–115.
30. Massie, *Glasgow: Portraits of a City* (1989), pp. 25–27.
31. Mullen, *It Wisnae Us: The Truth about Glasgow and Slavery* (2009) pp. 7–9.
32. Herman, *Scottish Enlightenment* (2001), p. 61.
33. Houston, *Scotland: A Very Short Introduction* (2008), p. 70.

CHAPTER 1

1. Francis Hutcheson (1694–1746) was a philosopher born in Ulster to a family of Scottish Presbyterians. He became known as one of the founding fathers of the Scottish Enlightenment. He is remembered for his book *A System of Moral Philosophy* (1775).
2. Henry Home, Lord Kames (1696–1782) was a Scottish advocate, judge, philosopher, writer and agricultural improver. He was a central figure of the Scottish Enlightenment, a founding member of the Philosophical Society of Edinburgh, and active in the Select Society. He acted as patron to some of the most influential thinkers of the Scottish Enlightenment, including the philosopher David Hume, the economist Adam Smith, and the writer James Boswell.
3. Forbes Gray, *Some Old Scots Judges* (1914), pp. 8–10.

Notes and References

4 Herman, *The Scottish Enlightenment* (2001), p. 78.
5 Herman, *The Scottish Enlightenment* (2001), p. 60.
6 Scott, *Francis Hutcheson* (1900), p. 285.
7 Scott, *Francis Hutcheson* (1900), p. 7.
8 Herman, *The Scottish Enlightenment* (2001), p. 64.
9 Herman, *The Scottish Enlightenment* (2001), p. 64
10 Herman, *The Scottish Enlightenment* (2001), p. 67.
11 Thomas Aikenhead (1676–1697) was a Scottish student from Edinburgh, who was prosecuted and executed at the age of twenty on a charge of blasphemy under the Act against Blasphemy 1661 and Act against Blasphemy 1695. He was the last person on the island of Great Britain to be executed for blasphemy.
12 Graham, *Scottish Men of Letters in the Eighteenth Century* (1908), p. 33.
13 Robert Molesworth, 1st Viscount Molesworth PC (1656–1725) was an Irish politician and writer. Anthony Ashley Cooper, 3rd earl of Shaftesbury (1671–1713) was an English politician, philosopher and writer.
14 Herman, *The Scottish Enlightenment* (2001), p. 73.
15 Herman, *The Scottish Enlightenment* (2001), pp. 76–77.
16 Devine, *The Scottish Nation* (1999), p. 74.
17 Devine, *The Scottish Nation* (1999), p. 199.
18 Herman, *The Scottish Enlightenment* (2001), p. 79.
19 Hutcheson, *A System of Moral Philosophy* (1755), p. 201. The book was written as early as 1738, but added to and altered by Hutcheson throughout his life and published posthumously in 1755. Hutcheson qualified his strong denunciation of slavery by adding in his conclusion, 'where no public interest require it'. It is important to note that, John Millar, his follower and successor in the chair of moral philosophy at the University of Glasgow was unambiguously an opponent of slavery. See Millar, *The Origins of the Distinction of Ranks* (1806).
20 Herman, *The Scottish Enlightenment* (2001), p. 80.
21 Herman, *The Scottish Enlightenment* (2001), pp. 80–81.
22 Herman, *The Scottish Enlightenment* (2001), pp. 93–94.
23 Herman, *The Scottish Enlightenment* (2001), p. 83.
24 Graham, *Scottish Men of Letters in the Eighteenth Century* (1908), p. 173.
25 Carr, *Principles of Equity: Lord Kames* (2013), p. v.
26 Kames, *The Decisions of the Court of Session* (1741).
27 Graham, *Scottish Men of Letters in the Eighteenth Century* (1908), p. 175.
28 Herman, *The Scottish Enlightenment* (2001), p. 87. It was a time when judges' stamina was proved by their ability to drink and live long. 'A "hearty" drinker was one to respect. The judges included Lord Minto, stately and dignified, Lord Tinwald, most courteous of gentlemen as he lisped out his elegant charges in dulcet tones which earned him the name of "Sweet Lips", Lord Dalrymple, an elder of the Kirk, who drank freely, lived loosely, and attended religious ordinances and Lord Grange, the unctuous Presbyterian saint.' See Graham, *Scottish Men of Letters in the Eighteenth Century* (1908), pp. 177 & 184.
29 Graham, *Scottish Men of Letters in the Eighteenth Century* (1908), p. 177.
30 Herman, *The Scottish Enlightenment* (2001), p. 83.
31 Herman, *The Scottish Enlightenment* (2001), p. 84. George Buchanan (1506–1582) was a Scottish historian and humanist scholar.
32 Graham, *Scottish Men of Letters in the Eighteenth Century* (1908), p. 176.
33 Chambers, *Traditions of Edinburgh* (1825), Vol. 2, p. 171.
34 Herman, *The Scottish Enlightenment* (2001), p. 85.
35 Herman, *The Scottish Enlightenment* (2001), p. 95.

36 Herman, *The Scottish Enlightenment* (2001), p. 98.
37 Herman, *The Scottish Enlightenment* (2001), p. 99.
38 Herman, *The Scottish Enlightenment* (2001), pp. 97–98 & 100.
39 'The colour of the Negroes, as above observed, affords a strong presumption of their being a different species from the Whites; and I once thought, that the presumption was supported by inferiority of understanding in the former. But it appears to me doubtful, upon second thoughts, whether that inferiority may not be occasioned by their condition. A man never ripens in judgment nor in prudence but by exercising these powers. At home, the negroes have little occasion to exercise either: they live upon fruits and roots, which grow without culture: they need little clothing: and they erect houses without trouble or art. 'Abroad, they are miserable slaves, having no encouragement either to think or to act. Who can say how far they might improve in a state of freedom, were they obliged, like Europeans, to procure bread with the sweat of their brows?' See Home, *Progress of Men Independent of Society* (1778), Vol. 1.

CHAPTER 2

1 The spelling of both James Somerset and Charles Stewart varies in historical documentation, sometimes being spelt 'Somersett' and 'Steuart'.
2 Poser, *Lord Mansfield: Justice in the Age of Reason* (2013), p. 298.
3 Mansfield was a descendant of Friskinus de Moravia, who was reputed to have conquered the lands now known as Morayshire at the beginning of the twelfth century. His linear descendant, Gulielmus de Moravia, was granted a charter by King Alexander III in 1384 of the estates of Tullibardine in Perthshire, from which descended the duke of Athol, chieftain of the Murrays. Some 200 years later, David Murray, the second son of the 8th baron of Tullibody, whose family by then had little land to speak of, reversed his family's waning fortunes by becoming founder of the Stormont branch. In 1600, David Murray, as captain of King James VI's bodyguard, rescued his monarch from an attempted kidnapping and possible murder at the hands of one of his aides, the earl of Gowrie. He then rode on to defeat an associated uprising in the district. Gowrie, who subsequently died in mysterious circumstances, had his lands at Scone forfeited by the king in favour of his loyal subject, David Murray, who on 16 August 1621 was ennobled with the title of Viscount Stormont.
4 Campbell, *The Lives of the Chief Justices of England* (2012), pp. 236–37.
5 A similar observation was made by Lord Elcho (1818–1914), who after attending the Edinburgh Academy, went to Eton College. Of this, he recorded, 'In the fact of actual learning, so far as regards the books or classics I read at Eton… when speaking of The Edinburgh Academy, that during the two years of my Eton life I had made no further advance.' See Charteris, *Memories* (1912), p. 59.
6 A thonged leather strap used by schoolmasters for beating boys on the hands or bottoms.
7 In exile, James Murray was created earl of Dunbar by the exiled James Stuart.
8 Poser, *Lord Mansfield: Justice in the Age of Reason* (2013), pp. 14–18.
9 In 1723 his admission to Christ College, Oxford, noted his place of origin as Bath. When, as lord chief justice, the error was pointed out to him, he explained that 'possibly the broad pronunciation of the person who gave the description was the origin of the mistake'—recognising that the person was no less than himself, with the registrar making an incorrect assumption.

10 Campbell, *The Lives of the Chief Justices of England* (2013), p. 247.
11 Campbell, *The Lives of the Chief Justices of England* (2013), p. 250.
12 Herman, *The Scottish Enlightenment* (2001), p. 86.
13 Haakaonssen, *Principles of Equity by Henry Home, Lord Kames* (2014), p. xxiii.
14 Foss, *The Biographical Dictionary of the Justices of England (1066–1870)* (1870), p. 470.
15 Foss, *The Biographical Dictionary of the Justices of England (1066–1870)* (1870), p. 30.
16 Ryder, 'Diary 20 February 1753', *Mansfield Manuscripts* (1753), p. 20.
17 Oldham, 'William Murray, 1st Earl of Mansfield', www.oxforddnb.com (2008), accessed 19 October 2020.
18 Charles Stewart studied at Edinburgh University, undertaking his training as an apprenticed factor on the Rappahannock River in Virginia in a business owned by Robert Boyd, a Glasgow tobacco merchant. Aside from a year in Boston, he worked for a variety of mercantile and trading houses during which he built a substantial web of professional connections embracing traders, migrants and settlers, whose common interest was to try to make money with the eventual aim of establishing themselves independently at home.
19 Weiner, *New Biographical Evidence in the Somerset Case* (2012), p. 128; Cairns, *After Somerset: The Scottish Experience* (2012), pp. 291–312; and Dobson, *Scottish Emigration to Colonial America 1607–1785* (1994), p. 102.
20 Letter from J. Steuart to C. Steuart, 21 January 1772, NLS, ms 5027, folio 106.
21 Wiener, *New Biographical Evidence in the Somerset Case* (2012), pp. 122–124.
22 Cairns, 'Freeing from Slavery in Eighteenth Century Scotland' in Burrows (ed.) et al., *Judge and Jurist: Essays in Memory of Lord Rodger of Earlsferry* (2013), p. 370.
23 Cairns, *After Somerset: The Scottish Experience* (2012), p. 296.
24 Poser, *Lord Mansfield: Justice in the Age of Reason* (2013), pp. 292–293.
25 Drescher, *Abolition: A History of Slavery and Antislavery* (2009), p. 58. 'From 1660, the British crown passed various acts and granted charters to enable companies to settle, administer and exploit British interests on the West Coast of Africa and to supply slaves to the American colonies' and from time to time to receive subsidies.' See 'Britain and the Slave Trade', www.nationalarchives.gov.uk.
26 Davis, *The Problem of Slavery in the Age of Revolution* (1999), p. 495.
27 Butts *v.* Penny, 2 Lev. 201, 83 Eng. Rep. 830: 1697; Chamberlain *v.* Harvey, Carthew 397, 90 Eng. Rep. 830: 1697; Smith *v.* Gould, 2 Salkeld 667, 3 Ld. Raym. 1275, 91 Eng. Rep. 567: 1705; Signed Opinion by P. Yorke (AG) and C. Talbot (SG) 14. 11729 BM. Egerton Mss 1074 f.70 (VC); and Poser, *Lord Mansfield: Justice in the Age of Reason* (2013), p. 289.
28 Some Quakers and Methodists were slave owners and slave traders. See White, *London in the Eighteenth Century* (2012), p. 128.
29 Granville Sharp (1735–1813) was an author and abolitionist.
30 Ditchfield, 'Granville Sharp', www.oxforddnb.com (2020), accessed 28 September 2021.
31 Davis, *The Problem of Slavery in the Age of Revolution* (1999), p. 84.
32 Locke, *Two Treatises of Government* (1690).
33 Smith, *The Theory of Moral Sentiments* (1776), p. 242.
34 David Hume (1711–1776) was a philosopher, historian, economist and librarian.
35 James Beattie (1735–1793) was a poet and philosopher baptised in Laurencekirk, Kincardineshire. The quote is from Poser, *Lord Mansfield: Justice in the Age of Reason* (2013), p. 290.

36 Beattie, *An Essay on the Nature and Immutability of Truth* (1778), p. 428.
37 Others included David Garrick, Samuel Johnston and Sir Joshua Reynolds.
38 Poser, *Lord Mansfield: Justice in the Age of Reason* (2013), p. 291.
39 Oldham, *The Mansfield Manuscripts and the Growth of English Law* (1992), Vol. 2, p. 1226.
40 Poser, *Lord Mansfield: Justice in the Age of Reason* (2013), pp. 291–292.
41 Davis, *The Problem of Slavery in the Age of Revolution* (1999), p. 488.
42 While counsel for James Somerset, a team led by John Glynn acted free of charge.
43 Lofft, 'Somerset against Stewart, May 14, 1772', Trinity Term, 12 Geo. 3, *Reports of Cases Adjudged in the Court of the King's Bench* (1772), p. 509.
44 Lofft, 'Somerset against Stewart, May 14, 1772', Trinity Term, 12 Geo. 3, *Reports of Cases Adjudged in the Court of the King's Bench* (1772), pp. 505–504. The actual number of slaves in England is not definitively known and different parties determined different numbers. Mansfield's assessment was 14,000 to 15,000.
45 Lofft, 'Somerset against Stewart, May 14, 1772', Trinity Term, 12 Geo. 3, *Reports of Cases Adjudged in the Court of the King's Bench* (1772), p. 509.
46 Poser, *Lord Mansfield: Justice in the Age of Reason* (2013), pp. 295–296.
47 Lofft, 'Somerset against Stewart, May 14, 1772', Trinity Term, 12 Geo. 3, *Reports of Cases Adjudged in the Court of the King's Bench* (1772), p. 510.
48 Shyllon, *Black Slaves in Britain* (1974), p. 157.
49 Shyllon, *Black Slaves in Britain* (1974), p. 113.
50 Oldham, *The Mansfield Manuscripts and the Growth of English Law* (1992), Vol. 2, p. 1237
51 'Rex v The Inhabitants of Thomas Ditton', 4. Dougl. 299.99, Eng. Rep. 891 (1785).
52 Drescher, *Capitalism and Antislavery* (1987), p. 40.
53 Usherwood, *The Abolitionists' Debt to Lord Mansfield* (1981), p. 40.
54 Benjamin Franklin (1706–1790) was postmaster general of British America from 1753 to 1774. The quote is from Sypher, *Guinea's Captive Kings* (1942), pp. 104–105.
55 Drescher, *Capitalism and Antislavery* (1987), pp. 104–105.
56 Poser, *Lord Mansfield: Justice in the Age of Reason* (2013), pp. 299–300.

CHAPTER 3

1 Thomas Hutchinson (1711–1780), a colonial politician and historian, was born in Boston, Massachusetts, the son of a wealthy merchant. A successful merchant himself, in 1737 he entered political life as a member of the Massachusetts assembly, to which he was appointed lieutenant governor in 1758 and then chief justice of the superior court in 1760. He got on the wrong side of the political tensions between the colonists and the British, and he, like Mansfield, saw his house burned down during protests. He was forced to resign his post to leave for England in 1774. There he sought reconciliation between the patriots and the loyalists, but found himself marginalised. He was granted a pension by George III. Longing to return home and leave the arrogant British ruling class, he died suddenly in 1780 in London. See Penak, 'Thomas Hutchinson', www.oxforddnb.com (2004), accessed 12 November 2020.
2 Kenwood House, situated on high ground in Hampstead Heath with spectacular views overlooking London 4 miles to the south, was bought by Mansfield

from the earl of Bute in 1754. The house was remodelled by Robert Adam in 1764, and later by George Saunders. Both made several additions, including the library and two wings on the north side. A dairy was added to supply Kenwood with fresh milk and cheese. In 1780 the house became Mansfield's permanent residence. It remained in the Mansfield family until 1906.

3 In the latter part of the eighteenth century, dinner was typically taken by the upper classes between 3 p.m. and 5 p.m. At the end of the meal, which might take between two and three hours to complete, each guest was served a glass of wine. After the guests had finished it, the hostess would stand and a gentleman would open the dining room door through which the female guests would depart for the drawing room, leaving the men to drink and converse. Kane, 'Cultural Rules for Dining in 18th Century, England and Mealtimes in the Regency Day', www.regencyredingote.wordpress.com (2019), accessed 14 November 2020. The quote is taken from Hutchinson, *The Diary and Letters of his Excellency Thomas Hutchinson* (1775), p. 276.

4 Dido was a popular choice of name for female slaves among their owners, providing an allusion to Dido, the mythical queen and founder of Carthage who died for love of Aeneas in Virgil's epic poem *The Aeneid*.

5 By 1757, the fireship HMS *Pluto* was one of nine converted merchant ships used by the Royal Navy in the Seven Years' War (1756–1763) against the French. Filled with combustible materials they were sent into enemy lines to try to set the warships alight.

6 This sum is comparable with the net annual salary of a captain of a sixth rate frigate of £255 19s. 'An introduction to pay and prize money in Aubrey's Royal Navy', www.thedearsurprise.com.

7 Once Havana fell, huge prize money was distributed among the many involved. Each of the forty-two captains received £1,600 (about six times the net annual salary of a captain of Lindsay's rank).

8 Havana was the centre of Spanish military power in the Caribbean. From there flotillas carried silver to Spain from the South American mines. Spain abandoned its neutrality by signing a pact with France with whom Britain was already at war. It led Britain to declare war against Spain in January 1762. Spain was a signatory to the Treaty of Paris in the following year, when Havana was returned to them in exchange for ceding Florida and Menorca to Britain.

9 Beatson, *Naval and Military Memoirs of Great Britain* (1790), and Laughton, 'Sir John Lindsay', www.oxforddnb.com (2007), accessed 19 October 2020.

10 Over the ensuing five years under Lindsay's command, HMS *Trent* was engaged in a number of chases and won numerous prizes. They include engaging in a four-hour battle with *La Bellone*, which after capture, was taken and placed into service under the name *Repulse*. Added to that was the capture of a Dutch schooner near Haiti laden with indigo, a Spanish sloop, a French privateer while on patrol in the Caribbean, a 22-gun French merchant frigate *Le Bien Aime* with a cargo of sugar and coffee, and a French slave ship off the coast of Guinea-Bissau, which Lindsay took to Sierra Leone. Other ships with their cargoes followed and Lindsay's successes provided good copy in the *London Chronicle* of January 1762. The article captures the 'derring-do' of his exploits which were shared with a public eager to read of imperial success during a lengthy period of war. The pine-bottomed *Trent* was then decommissioned and scrapped, with Lindsay being appointed captain of HMS *Tartar*. *La Bellone* was, by coincidence, the French frigate in which Lord Elcho, a close supporter of Prince Charles, 'the Young Pretender', escaped to France on 28 April 1746, following the fateful battle of Culloden.

11 Byrne, *Belle* (2014), p. 15–22.
12 Byrne, *Belle* (2014), p. 24.
13 Rodger, *The Wooden World* (1988), pp. 218–219.
14 Stark, *Female Tars: Woman aboard Ship in the Age of Sail* (1996), p. 10.
15 'Regulations and Instructions Relating to His Majesty's Service at Sea', issued in 1731 and modified in 1756.
16 McMaster, '"I hate to hear of Women on Board": Women aboard War Ships', *Jane Austen Society of North America*, Vol. 36, No. 1, Winter 2015.
17 Parish register of St George's, Bloomsbury, 1766.
18 'Lord Holdernesse to Andrew Mitchell, 17 September 1756', Add. Ms 6832, fol. 90, British Library.
19 Report of the late Reginald Rawdon Hastings HMC.
20 Scott-Murray, *David, 7th Viscount Stormont and 2nd Earl of Mansfield (1727–1796)* (2008).
21 Mason, *Dido Elizabeth Belle* (2014), p. 91.
22 Mason, *Dido Elizabeth Belle* (2014), p. 68.
23 Douglas, 'Gregson v Gilbert 1783', *Douglas' King's Bench Reports* (1783), Vol. 3, pp. 629–630.
24 A British slave ship of that period would typically carry 193 slaves; the *Zong* was carrying 442 slaves. See Walvin, *The Zong* (2011), p. 27.
25 In addition to the loss of slaves, seven of the seventeen crew also died with the captain within three days of reaching port at Black River, Jamaica, after falling gravely ill during the passage.
26 Douglas, 'Gregson v Gilbert 1783', *Douglas' King's Bench Reports* (1783), Vol. 3, p. 629.
27 Granville Sharp (1735–1813) one of the first British campaigners for the abolition of the slave trade.
28 Hoare, *Memoirs of Granville Sharp* (2012), p. 241.
29 Walvin, *The Zong* (2011), pp. 89 & 97.
30 Poser, *Lord Mansfield: Justice in the Age of Reason* (2013), p. 298.
31 A law laid down by statute.
32 Hoare, *Memoirs of Granville Sharp* (2012), p. 241.
33 Rupprecht, *A Very Uncommon Case* (2007), pp. 330–331
34 One newspaper report said that Mansfield had sent Elizabeth and his wife to Kenwood before the house was attacked; another said that once the mob attacked, Sir Thomas Mills escorted Lady Mansfield to a house in Lincoln's Inn Fields. See Poser, *Lord Mansfield: Justice in the Age of Reason* (2013), p. 364.
35 Conditions in British cities were unsanitary and overcrowded, while high taxes and repressive laws fuelled discontent among the working classes. This anger erupted when Lord George Gordon called for the repeal of the Catholic Relief Act of 1778, which had itself repealed some of the less onerous provisions of the Popery Act of 1698 in exchange for Catholics swearing allegiance to the king. The act was deeply resented in Protestant England. On 2 June, Lord Gordon led a crowd of 60,000 to the House of Commons to present a petition of 'no Popery', providing the catalyst for the start of the riots. Anger was vented over many days as and many homes and buildings were attacked. See Poser, *Lord Mansfield: Justice in the Age of Reason* (2013), pp. 360–361.
36 *Gazetteer and New Daily Advertiser* of 13 June 1878, and *General Evening Post* of 13 June 1780.
37 Poser, *Lord Mansfield: Justice in the Age of Reason* (2013), pp. 169–170.
38 Chalus, *Elite Women in English Political Life 1754–1790* (2005), pp. 84 & 94.
39 'Women in History: Dido Elizabeth Belle', www.english-heritage.org.uk.

40 Mason, *Dido Elizabeth Belle* (2014), p. 91.
41 John Lindsay's obituary from the *London Chronicle*, 1788.
42 Byrne, *Belle* (2014), p. 208.
43 Sir John Lindsay's career after his Caribbean and Senegal exploits continued in the ascendency. By 1772, he was commander-in-chief in the East Indies; six years later he was serving on HMS *Victory* before commanding HMS *George* in the Ushant. Later, upon Lord Sandwich's direction, Lindsay was appointed commander-in-chief of the Mediterranean. Shortly after this, due to deteriorating health, he was obliged to return to England where he was promoted to rear admiral in 1787.
44 Major, 'Dido Elizabeth Belle: New information about her siblings', www.georgianera.wordpress.com (2018), accessed 9 October 2020.
45 In the American War of Independence, Spain took control of Florida after the 1781 battle of Pensacola. The Spanish authorities compiled a list of property owners, of which Mrs Bell was one. Florida reverted to Britain in 1783. See Major, 'Dido Elizabeth Belle: New information about her siblings', www.georgianera.wordpress.com (2018), accessed 9 October 2020.
46 Sir John Lindsay, her father, did not provide for Dido in his will. This is probably because it had been informally agreed with Mansfield that he would do so.
47 Byrne, *Belle* (2014), p. 228.
48 King, 'Belle, Dido Elizabeth', www.oxforddnb.com (2020), accessed 14 November 2020.
49 'Women in History: Dido Elizabeth Belle', www.english-heritage.org.uk.

Chapter 4

1 Parliament Hall, home of the Scottish parliament before the Act of Union of 1707, has since been used as the court of session, Scotland's supreme civil court. The hall was at this time used as the court of first instance or outer house because it led into the court of appeal, known as the inner house.
2 Sir Alexander Wedderburn of Blackness (1610–1676) married Katherine, daughter of John Scott, lord provost of Dundee. After training as an advocate, Sir Alexander became a politician and, through patronage, town clerk of Dundee. He held the latter office for no less than forty-three years from 1633.
3 The Treaty of Ripon, signed in October 1640, settled the Second Bishops' War between Charles I and the Scottish Covenanters. It signalled a loss of control for Charles who had to leave the Scots in occupation of the six northern English counties to whom he had to pay expenses of £860 a day until the peace was restored and the English parliament recalled.
4 Sir Alexander Wedderburn, 4th baronet of Blackness (1675–1741), like his father, held a lucrative office as clerk in Dundee. He forfeited the post (and living) in 1716 after joining the failed Jacobite uprising.
5 James Francis Edward Stuart (1688–1766) was son of King James II and VII of England and Scotland. His Catholic father was exiled in the Glorious Revolution of 1688, leading to the Act of Settlement of 1701, which excluded Catholics from the English throne, and in 1707, the British throne.
6 Sankey, 'Sir John Wedderburn, 5th baronet (1704–1746)', www.oxforddnb.com (2006), accessed 23 November 2020.
7 Doran, *London in the Jacobite Times* (1877).
8 Wedderburn, *The Wedderburn Book* (1896), p. 266.

9. Wedderburn, *The Wedderburn Book* (1896), pp. 201–219.
10. Wedderburn, *The Wedderburn Book* (1896), p. lxvii.
11. Wedderburn, *The Wedderburn Book* (1896), pp. 288–290.
12. Oliver, *A History of Scotland* (2010), p. 326.
13. John Wedderburn's letter to his sister, dated 24 May 1747, from Westmoreland, Jamaica.
14. Wedderburn, *The Wedderburn Book* (1896), p. 290.
15. Hamilton, *Scotland, the Caribbean and the Atlantic World 1750–1820* (2005), p. 56.
16. Hamilton, *Scotland, the Caribbean and the Atlantic World 1750–1820* (2005), pp. 55–57.
17. Graham, *The Scots Penetration of the Jamaica Plantation Business, Recovering Scotland's Slavery Past* (2015), p. 82.
18. Newspapers in Scotland advertised for carpenters, plumbers and other trades while those who had a basic education were also sought as administrative secretaries, clerks or bookkeepers on sugar plantations. See Whyte, *Scotland and the Abolition of Black Slavery 1756–1838* (2007), p. 49.
19. Fuertado, *Official and Other Personages of Jamaica from 1655 to 1790* (1896), p. 18.
20. Walvin, *A Short History of Slavery* (2007), p. 52.
21. Burnard, Trevor, '"The Countrie Continues Sicklie": White Mortality in Jamaica 1655–1780', *Social History of Medicine* (1999), Vol. 2, No. 1, p. 45.
22. Warner-Lewis, *Archibald Monteath* (2007), p. 108.
23. Peter Wedderburn (1736–1773) worked as a millwright in Westmoreland, dying in Jamaica unmarried in 1736, aged thirty-six. Alexander Wedderburn (1737–1765) lived in the Hanover area of Jamaica where he died unmarried aged twenty-eight. See Wedderburn, *The Wedderburn Book* (1896), p. 291.
24. Cairns, *After Somerset: The Scottish Experience* (2012), p. 291.
25. Oliver, *A History of Scotland* (2010), p. 349.
26. '(a)… It requires little imagination to conceive what must be the situation of man (carried off from home by violence) torn from their families, their friends and their country; (b) ignorant of the fate they are reserved for; bound with foreign letters; and during two or three months in hot climate, confined in crowds to the hold of a small vessel, without regard to rank or decency, without sympathy, refreshment, or any consolation. The consequence of this usage is that a fifth or a sixth part, often a great deal more die of grief or disease in the voyage.' MacConachie, 'Information for Joseph Knight against John Wedderburn dated April 25, 1775', SP M6:47, pp. 14–15.
27. Whyte, *Scotland and the Abolition of Black Slavery 1756–1838* (2007), p. 188.
28. Cullen, 'Additional information for John Wedderburn against Joseph Knight', 6 February 1777, pp. 1–3.
29. Cairns, 'Joseph Knight', www.oxforddnb.com (2006), accessed 19 October 2020.
30. John McLaurin, 'Additional Information for Joseph Knight against John Wedderburn, April 20 1776', SP M6:47, pp. 2–3.
31. MacConachie, 'Information for Joseph Knight against John Wedderburn dated April 25, 1775', SP M6:47.
32. MacConachie, 'Information for Joseph Knight against John Wedderburn dated April 25, 1775', SP M6:47, p. 1.
33. MacConachie, 'Information for Joseph Knight against John Wedderburn dated April 25, 1775', SP M6:47, p. 2.
34. Whyte, *Scotland and the Abolition of Black Slavery 1756–1838* (2007), p. 189.

35 Probably a pun on the 'Code Noir' (Black Code) drawn up in 1685. It was the name of the French code which laid down the treatment of slaves in the French Caribbean.
36 As reported in the *Caledonian Mercury*, Wednesday 21 February 1776.
37 Whyte, *Scotland and the Abolition of Black Slavery 1756–1838* (2007), p. 18.
38 Boswell, *The Life of Samuel Johnston* (1884), p. 355.
39 Herman, *The Scottish Enlightenment* (2001), p. 101.
40 Whyte, *Scotland and the Abolition of Black Slavery 1756–1838* (2007), p. 101.
41 John Wedderburn died in 1803. He failed to recover his father's baronetcy of Blackness by having the attainder withdrawn by the crown, although he styled himself Sir John, 6th baronet of Blackness both socially and in legal documents. It was only after his death that his eldest surviving son, Sir David Wedderburn, was formally raised to the baronetcy.

Chapter 5

1 John Wedderburn married Isabella Blackburn in 1807 and they had four sons and three daughters. He died in 1807 at Inveresk.
2 Wedderburn, *The Wedderburn Book* (1896), p. 305.
3 Wedderburn, *The Wedderburn Book* (1896), p. 277.
4 After the 1745 uprising, 3,463 Jacobite prisoners were taken. Of this number, 936 were transported and 348 banished. Some found themselves in life-long servitude in the West Indies, but those who signed indentures in Jamaica found their terms reduced to seven years. See Mullen, 'Scots & Caribbean Slavery – Victims and Profiteers', www.glasgowwestindies.wordpress.com (2015), accessed 14 November 2020.
5 Activities included male midwifery.
6 An entry in the diary of Thomas Thistlewood dated 19 April 1769 records him riding to Bluecastle estate to provide slaves to assist James Wedderburn with his crop at '3 bitts per diem'. At that time the estate was owned by Joseph Elletson. Ownership passed to his brother, John, in 1780, and it was not until 1802 that the estate came into the joint ownership of both brothers. This suggests that James was for some time its manager. See Hall, *In Miserable Slavery: Thomas Thistlewood in Jamaica* (1999), p. 216.
7 Plantations in Jamaica owned in whole or part by James Wedderburn included the Blackheath, Bluecastle and Glen Islay (including Grove) estates, Westmoreland.
8 Burnard, *Master, Tyranny, and Desire* (2004), p. 149.
9 'Derby was again … watched … eating canes. Had him well flogged and pickled, then made Hector shit in his mouth.' His master, Thomas Thistlewood, administered the punishment. See Hall, *In Miserable Slavery: Thomas Thistlewood in Jamaica* (1999), p. 71.
10 Thomas Thistlewood (1721–1786) went to Jamaica in 1750. He brought with him gonorrhoea and the most rakish values of Regency England. He had consorted with prostitutes in London on many occasions, while finding time to have an affair with the wives of both his best friend in Lincolnshire and his manservant. He continued to practice his perilous sexual habits which placed himself and those whom he encountered at high risk of (repeated) infection. His behaviour was typical of its time in England 'when masculinity was closely associated with sexual dominance [as opposed to femininity which] rested on a base assumption of female sexual passivity'. See Burnard and Follett, *Caribbean*

Slavery, British Anti-Slavery, and the Cultural Politics of Venereal Disease (2012), pp. 427–435.
11 Burnard and Follett, *Caribbean Slavery, British Anti-Slavery, and the Cultural Politics of Venereal Disease* (2012), pp. 432 & 435.
12 Hall, *In Miserable Slavery: Thomas Thistlewood in Jamaica* (1999), p. 218.
13 Robert Wedderburn's record of events, which historians believe to be largely accurate, was refuted by his half brother, Andrew Colvile (formerly Wedderburn), when made public on 29 February 1824. The exchange of correspondence between Robert Wedderburn and Andrew Colvile was published in *Bell's Life* in London, commencing on 29 February 1824.
14 McCalman, *Radical Underworld: Prophets, Revolutionaries and Pornographers 1745–1840* (2002), p. 53.
15 McCalman, *Radical Underworld: Prophets, Revolutionaries and Pornographers 1745–1840* (2002), p. 53.
16 McCalman, *Radical Underworld: Prophets, Revolutionaries and Pornographers 1745–1840* (2002), p. 49.
17 Between 1764 and 1782, 80 per cent of crewmen in the Royal Navy were aged under twenty-five years. See Rodger, *The Wooden World* (1988), p. 360.
18 The 64-gun third-rate ship HMS *Polyphemus* was not launched until 27 April 1782, which throws into question whether this was the ship upon which Robert sailed. See McCalman, *Robert Wedderburn: The Horrors of Slavery* (1991), pp. 71–72 and Home Office Papers 42/196, BC, 6 October 1819.
19 To maintain control on board, the Royal Navy only operated to a limited extent under a defined set of rules. Rather, the authority of the officers rested on shared values among seamen everywhere, who understood that seafaring was underpinned by a collective awareness that orders had to be obeyed for the safety of all. 'To the eyes of the modern officer,' wrote N. A. M. Rodger in *The Wooden World*, 'the discipline of the mid-eighteenth century Navy would appear lax to the point of anarchy. Insubordination ... from every rank and rating ... was a daily part of life.... Where modern officers expect to command ... officers [then] hoped to persuade.' Nonetheless, it functioned well because all parties knew they were mutually dependent on one another. Class was not divisive, although the egalitarian nature of life on board had begun to erode towards the end of the eighteenth century. It meant the breaches of discipline were seen as specific to the incident and not to something wider, such as insurrection. Disorder was tolerated, reflecting the wider attitudes of society at that time. Indeed, the Admiralty was reluctant to get involved even if an officer was attacked by ratings on duty. Officers faced the threat of personal violence against them and were frequently prosecuted by their men if a grudge was born. In short, a ship was a community that needed sound leadership and management to maintain its balance and effectiveness. A good captain would not want to resort to brutality because it threatened to shatter discipline by undermining the mutual consensus of those on board, thus creating a potentially dangerous and disordered ship. Robert Wedderburn's comments, which are specific to his personal experience, suggest his captain imposed a higher degree of violence to maintain his authority than typically used by other captains. This could vary significantly from ship to ship. Nonetheless, the Admiralty's regulations restricted the maximum number of lashes a captain could authorise to twelve. Because the process for court martials, which was limited to more serious offences, was both cumbersome and unpredictable, captains preferred to avoid them. It resulted in some serious offences being lightly punished, while at the other end of the spectrum, it meant that the

punishment for minor offences was also seldom less than twelve lashes, despite such severity not being warranted. However, this did not mean that the maximum number of lashes was not exceeded, although how widespread the practice was is not known. People of colour were not punished any differently to white sailors. See Rodger, *The Wooden World* (1988), pp. 206–207 & 218–220.

20 Vic Gatrell, *City of Laughter* (2006), pp. 4–16.
21 Vic Gatrell, *City of Laughter* (2006), p. 25.
22 Élie Halévy (1870–1937) was a French philosopher and historian who wrote studies of the British utilitarians, the book of essays *Era of Tyrannies*, and a history of Britain from 1815 to 1914.
23 'Rookery' was the word for a slum. It derived from the fact that many rooks build their nests in a single tree. See Judith Flander, *The Victorian City* (2012), p. 167.
24 McCalman, *Radical Underworld: Prophets, Revolutionaries and Pornographers 1745–1840* (2002), pp. 54–55.
25 A 'flint tailor' was a tailor who belonged to an exclusive group registered in books of trade. McCalman, *Radical Underworld: Prophets, Revolutionaries and Pornographers 1745–1840* (2002), p. 8.
26 Place, *The Autobiography of Francis Place* (1972), pp. 20–34.
27 McCalman, *Robert Wedderburn: The Horrors of Slavery* (1991), p. 8.
28 McCalman, *Robert Wedderburn: The Horrors of Slavery* (1991), p. 60.
29 McCalman, *Robert Wedderburn: The Horrors of Slavery* (1991), pp. 4, 8 & 9.
30 John Wesley (1703–1791), an English cleric, theologian and evangelist, was the leader of a revival movement within the Church of England known as Methodism, which separated from the established church in 1795.
31 McCalman, *Robert Wedderburn: The Horrors of Slavery* (1991), pp. 8–9 & 66–67.
32 McCalman, *Robert Wedderburn: The Horrors of Slavery* (1991), p. 55.
33 McCalman, *Radical Underworld: Prophets, Revolutionaries and Pornographers 1745–1840* (2002), p. 56.
34 'Millenarianism' is the belief by a religious, social, or political group or movement in the coming of a fundamental transformation of society, after which 'all things will be changed'. See Gould, *Questioning the Millennium: A Rationalist's Guide to a Precisely Arbitrary Countdown* (1997), p. 112. The quote is from Chase, 'Robert Wedderburn', www.oxforddnb.com (2004), accessed 11 August 2012.
35 Dickinson, 'Thomas Spence (1750–1815)', www.oxforddnb.com (2004), accessed 11 August 2012.
36 Dickinson, 'Thomas Spence (1750–1815)', www.oxforddnb.com (2004), accessed 11 August 2012.
37 McCalman, *Radical Underworld: Prophets, Revolutionaries and Pornographers 1745–1840* (2002), p. 60.
38 Jacobin was the most famous political group of the French Revolution. It became identified with extreme egalitarianism and violence. Its actions led to the Revolutionary government from mid-1793 to mid-1794.
39 McCalman, *Robert Wedderburn: The Horrors of Slavery* (1991), p. 13.
40 Chase, 'Robert Wedderburn', www.oxforddnb.com (2004), accessed 11 August 2012.
41 Robert Wedderburn was released on bail for £200.
42 The Cato Street Conspiracy was an attempt to overthrow the government by assassinating all the cabinet ministers and the prime minister, Lord Liverpool,

when they were dining at Lord Harrowby's home in Grosvenor Square. The quote is from McCalman, *Robert Wedderburn: The Horrors of Slavery* (1991), pp. 22–23.
43 The Six Acts of 1819 were designed to reduce disturbances and to limit the growth of radical organisations and propaganda. Robert Wedderburn's actions, which led to his arrest, had been sparked by the introduction in parliament of anti-radical legislation known as the Six Acts.
44 Chase, 'Robert Wedderburn', www.oxforddnb.com (2004), accessed 11 August 2012.
45 Robert Wedderburn had been found guilty of the same offence ten years earlier, probably because of his poverty. The practice was commonplace and typical way for financially burdened tradesmen to supplement their income.
46 Once in New York, Wedderburn raised a complaint of criminal fraud against an unnamed writer employed by him write a romance that was to be entitled *Beatrice the Bleeding Beauty*. It was reported by the *New York Evening Star* on 6 February 1834.
47 The infidel preacher was Robert Taylor of Theobolds Road Institute. See Chase, 'Robert Wedderburn', www.oxforddnb.com (2004), accessed 11 August 2012.
48 McCalman, *Robert Wedderburn: The Horrors of Slavery* (1991), p. 34.
49 McCalman, *Robert Wedderburn: The Horrors of Slavery* (1991), p. 32.
50 For example, the National Union of Working Classes and its militant successor, the London Democratic Association. See McCalman, *Robert Wedderburn: The Horrors of Slavery* (1991), p. 34.
51 The Chartist movement was a working class male suffrage movement aiming to secure male suffrage. It was active between 1838 and 1857.
52 McCalman, *Robert Wedderburn: The Horrors of Slavery* (1991), pp. 34–35.
53 Kenneth W. Wedderburn, Baron Wedderburn of Charlton QC, FBA (13 April 1927–9 March 2012), Cassel professor of Commercial Law at the London School of Economics.

CHAPTER 6

1 Memorial for Peter Williamson against Alexander Cushnie and others, 27 July 1761.
2 Graham, *The Social Life of Scotland in the Eighteenth Century* (1899), Vol. 1, p. 173.
3 Graham, *The Social Life of Scotland in the Eighteenth Century* (1899), Vol. 1, p. 183 and Smout, *A History of the Scottish People 1560–1830* (1985), p. 224.
4 Graham, *The Social Life of Scotland in the Eighteenth Century* (1899), Vol. 2, pp. 243 & 254.
5 Smout, *A History of the Scottish People 1560–1830* (1985), p. 150.
6 Memorial for Peter Williamson against Alexander Cushnie and others, 27 July 1761.
7 Translated as 'a rough, ragged, bullet headed, tall, growing, smart boy'. See Mursion, 'Peter Williamson, Vintner, from the Other World', *The Deeside Field* (1930), No. 5, p. 84.
8 An indentured servant was a person who came to America under contract, or was placed under contract there, to work for another person over a period of time, usually seven years. The practice existed mostly during the seventeenth to nineteenth centuries. Indentured servants included redemptioners, victims of religious or political persecution, persons kidnapped, convicts and paupers.

9 Haar, *White Indentured Servants in Colonial New York* (1940), p. 371.
10 Williams, *Capitalism and Slavery* (1943), pp. 8–10
11 Williams, *Capitalism and Slavery* (1941), pp. 12–13.
12 To Robert Ross, for listing his son, 'one shilling'; to Maclean, for listing his brother Donald, 'one shilling and sixpence'.
13 The schoolmaster's salary also included a modest house and a garden or croft. Mursion, 'Peter Williamson, Vintner, from the Other World', *The Deeside Field* (1930), No. 5, p. 84.
14 Robertson, *The Book of Bon Accord* (1839), pp. 87–88.
15 Skelton, *Indian Peter* (2004), p. 29.
16 Roughead, *The Fatal Countess and Other Studies* (1924), p. 132.
17 Helen Law, spouse of William Soper, a sixty-year-old wool comber, cooked 'the victuals' for those held.
18 Williamson, *The Life and Curious Adventures of Peter Williamson* (1758).
19 Williamson, *The Life and Curious Adventures of Peter Williamson* (1758), p. 15.
20 In 1754, New France comprised Louisiana, the Ohio River Valley, Quebec (known as Canada), Cape Breton and the St Jean Islands.
21 The British found an ally in Prussia, and France in Austria and Russia. See Marston, *The French-Indian War 1754–1760* (2002), p. 7.
22 This was followed by the heavy defeat of General Braddock at the battle of Monongahela on 9 July 1755 by the French and Indians in the hinterland of Pennsylvania.
23 Destroyed in the barn were 200 bushels of wheat, six cows, four horses and five sheep.
24 Jean Lowry and her children, and Titus King, a soldier in Colonel Israel Williams' Regiment, were both captured by Indians in 1755. Their experiences are recorded in Marston, *The French-Indian War 1754–1760* (2002), pp. 81–83.
25 'His arms were tide close to his body, and a hole being dug deep enough for him to stand up in, he was put therein, and earth rammed and beat in all around his body up to his neck, so that only his head appeared above the ground: they scalped him, and there let him remain for three or four more hours in the greatest of agonies: after which they made a small fire near his head, causing him to suffer the most excruciating torments imaginable, whilst the poor creature could only cry for mercy in killing him immediately, for his brains were boiling in his head: inexorable to all his complaints, they continued the fire, whilst, shocking to behold, his eyes gushed out of their sockets; and such agonising torments did the unhappy creature suffer for nearly two hours till he was quite dead.' See Williamson, *The Life and Curious Adventures of Peter Williamson* (1758), p. 65.
26 Marston, *The French-Indian War 1754–1760* (2002), p. 25.
27 Fort De Quesne developed into the city of Pittsburg.
28 The timeline is a little confusing. Williamson says it was early spring that the Indians launched their raid and he his escape, and yet his arrival at his father-in-law's house on 4 January was long before the arrival of spring.
29 Oswego, built as a fur trading establishment in 1755, was the only barrier to prevent the French taking control of Lake Ontario. After its capture by the French it was demolished.
30 Roughead, *The Fatal Countess and Other Studies* (1924), pp. 126–127.
31 At York, 1,000 copies were sold; at Newcastle 650 were sold in a fortnight. Williamson's profit on a thousand copies was £30. See Roughead, *The Fatal Countess and Other Studies* (1924), p. 127.

32. Williamson, *The Life and Curious Adventures of Peter Williamson* (1758), p. 105.
33. Skelton, *Indian Peter* (2004), p. 88.
34. Roughead, *The Fatal Countess and Other Studies* (1924), p. 128.
35. *In forma pauperis* means being represented without liability for court costs and court fees.
36. Williamson, *The Life and Curious Adventures of Peter Williamson* (1758), pp. 31–132 and 'Kidnapping – Peter Williamsons' Case', *Blackwood's Magazine* (May 1848).
37. Roughead, *The Fatal Countess and Other Studies* (1924), pp. 134–135.
38. Skelton, *Indian Peter* (2004), p. 215.
39. Roughead, *The Fatal Countess and Other Studies* (1924), pp. 134–138.
40. Some examples of Williamson's other publications: *A Brief Account of the War in North America* (1760); *Travels of Peter Williamson Amongst Different Nations and Tribes of Savage Indians in America* (1768); *The Royal Abduction of Peter Williamson, King of the Mohawks* (n.d.); and *Proposals for Penny Post* (n.d.).
41. Williamson's *Directory for the City of Edinburgh, Canongate, Leith, and Suburbs from 25 May 1773–25 May 1774*.
42. Anderson, *Peter Williamson (1730–1799)* (2004).
43. A woman's loose gown of a kind fashionable during the seventeenth and eighteenth centuries.
44. Skelton, *Indian Peter* (2004), pp. 235–238.
45. The grave plot owned by John Scott has a memorial on the site erected to an Agnes Williamson, who died on 7 February 1824, aged sixty. See Skelton, *Indian Peter* (2004), p. 251.

Chapter 7

1. Andrew Wedderburn (1779–1856) second but eldest surviving son of James Wedderburn-Colvile of Inveresk. He arrived in London in 1796 and became a partner in the West Indian House of Wedderburn and Co. He is buried in Holy Trinity churchyard, Brompton.
2. Wedderburn, *The Wedderburn Book* (1896), Vol. 1, p. 308.
3. Warner-Lewis, *Archibald Monteath* (2007), p. 3.
4. Warner-Lewis, *Archibald Monteath* (2007), p. 298.
5. Warner-Lewis, *Archibald Monteath* (2007), pp. 280–281.
6. 1799 is the birth year stated in Archibald Monteith's autobiography dictated to the Moravian Brethren. But, as explained by author Maureen Warner-Lewis on page 41 of her biography on Monteith (spelled 'Monteath' by Warner-Lewis), this date does not fit with later facts presented in the autobiography. Her suggested date of 1792 makes more sense. It is reasonable to assume that the early dates in the memoir are indicative rather than precise.
7. Warner-Lewis, *Archibald Monteath* (2007), p. 270
8. Odadike, *The Ekumeku Movement: Western Igbo Resistance to the British Conquest of Nigeria, 1883–1914* (1991), p. 21.
9. The form and design of the cutting of the face varied from town to town.
10. The Aro people are a subgroup of the Igbo. Aro merchants used 'overt and covert aggression' to further their trading enterprises, of which the dominant was supplying slaves for the Atlantic trade. Aro merchants supplied around 70 per cent of the captives of the Biafra slave trade. See Warner-Lewis, *Archibald Monteath* (2007), p. 35.

11 Warner-Lewis, *Archibald Monteath* (2007), pp. 24–33 & 269.
12 Warner-Lewis, *Archibald Monteath* (2007), p. 270, Appendix I 'Monteith's account' translated by Mark Kuck.
13 When weather and security allowed the crew to bring the Africans on deck for exercise, they did so in small groups. This was partly because of fear of violence and partly to reduce the chance of them attempting to commit suicide by jumping overboard. See Walvin, *A Short History of Slavery* (2007), p. 73.
14 Portugal's commercial expansion was hampered by the fact that it was not a manufacturing nation. Therefore, many of the goods they sold to their African partners had to be bought from elsewhere.
15 For example, maize and cassava.
16 In addition, the ships paid fees and duties to local chiefs for the privilege of access.
17 The slaves were typically aged between fifteen and thirty-five, and around two-thirds were male.
18 Slavery was a long-established practice in the region. Slaves were traded with North African and Middle Eastern merchants for manufactured goods or horses to work the salt deposits in the Sahara. However, numbers rarely exceeded 6,000–7,000 a year and the Atlantic trade had a much greater impact on local economies.
19 Archibald Monteith's story, which was recorded near the end of his life, is drawn from autobiographical accounts translated into English. They were first published in German in the Moravian religious periodical *Missions-Blatt* or *Mission Newsletter* in May and June 1846. The articles were entitled 'Erlebnisse eines ehemaligen Sclaven in Jamaica' ('Experiences of a former slave in Jamaica').
20 Both Jean and her sister were daughters of James Douglas of Mains, near Glasgow, a junior branch of the Douglas clan. James adopted the name 'Douglas' in place of his birth name 'Campbell' to take on the estate of Blythswood from his maternal grandfather, together with the Douglas coat of arms.
21 Sir Archibald Monteith (1699–*c*. 1776).
22 Devine, *The Tobacco Lords: A Study of their Activities c. 1740–1790* (1975), pp. 4 & 171.
23 Walter Monteith (1739–1817), father of John Monteith (1776–1815), attended Glasgow University.
24 The tobacco leaves were shipped back to Glasgow in a twenty-five-ship fleet owned by Ingram & Glassford, two brothers-in-law.
25 The sum claimed was £11,534 and the sum settled was £2,205.
26 One of Walter's remaining brothers, Thomas, was knighted. He was a brigadier in the Bengal army of the East India Company, fighting at Peshwar and Kabul.
27 Warner-Lewis, *Archibald Monteath* (2007), pp. 69–74.
28 For example, two years after the first land was bought, he acquired fifty-two slaves, for which he paid £4,275.
29 The regiment was a local militia on call to deal with the external threat of invasion and the internal threat of riots and uprisings, extending to raids on colonies of escaped slaves.
30 *New Jamaica Almanack and Register,* 1807, p. 181; 1808, p. 177; and 1813, p. 158.
31 Logwood was mainly used to produce a purple-black dye for silk or wool.
32 Warner-Lewis, *Archibald Monteath* (2007), pp. 74 & 80–81.
33 Warner-Lewis, *Archibald Monteath* (2007), p. 290.
34 Warner-Lewis, *Archibald Monteath* (2007), p. 294.

35 Momodu, 'The Baptist War (1831–1832)', www.blackpast.org (2017), accessed 9 October 2020.
36 Craton, *Testing the Chains: Resistance to Slavery in the British West Indies* (1982), p. 321.
37 Warner-Lewis, *Archibald Monteath* (2007), p. 296.
38 The property damage inflicted during the rebellion is estimated at £1,154,589 (or approximately £124 million in current terms). More than 100 houses were destroyed and over forty sugar works.
39 Walvin, *A Short History of Slavery* (2007), p. 211.
40 Warner-Lewis, *Archibald Monteath* (2007), pp. 84 & 299.
41 Archibald Monteith had another daughter from an earlier relationship who married. She elected to work as a teacher at one of the mission's schools.
42 Warner-Lewis, *Archibald Monteath* (2007), p. 300.

Chapter 8

1 The cat comprised six 18-inch strands of whipcord with nine knots on each strand, held by a handle of thick rope of the same length.
2 The 'mizzen shrouds' were lengths of thin rope attached to the mizzen mast or standard rigging.
3 In 1787, a typical cargo to Africa might include cotton and linen goods, scarlet cloth in grain, coarse and fine hats, worsted caps, guns, powder, shot, sabres, lead bars, iron bars, pewter basins, copper kettles and pans, iron pots, hardware of various kinds, earthen and glassware, hair and gilt leather trunks, beads of various types, silver and gold rings and ornaments, paper, line ruffled shirts and caps, and British and foreign spirits and tobaccos. Donnan, *Documents Illustrative of the History of the Slave Trade to America* (1931), Vol. 2, pp. 567–568 and Schwarz, *Slave Captain: The Career of James Irving in the Liverpool Slave Trade* (1995), pp. 21 & 23.
4 Sheridan, *Doctors and Slaves: A Medical and Demographic History of Slavery in the British West Indies 1680–1834* (1985), pp. 105–106.
5 Crews could lose up to 45 per cent of their number per month sitting off the African coast.
6 The ratio changed over time.
7 'William Wilberforce to Eden, 23 November 1789', Auckland Papers, 34227 f.123, British Museum.
8 Devine, *Recovering Scotland's Slavery Past* (2015), p. 148.
9 *Crescent*, launched at Rotherhithe in 1790, was probably initially used as a privateer. After changing hands several times, a Mr Throckmorton was recorded as the owner in the 1802 *Register of Shipping*, and her master was A. Cowan. *Crescent* made her only journey as a slave ship under Captain Cowan between 1802 and 1804. The following year the ship became a whaler. She was lost off Patagonia in 1807 on her homebound trip from that first whaling expedition.
10 The crew typically included the captain, three mates, doctor, carpenter, boatswain, gunner and steward.
11 Cape Coast Castle was one of approximately forty 'slave castles' built by European traders.
12 Robinson, *A Sailor Boy's Experience Aboard a Slave Ship* (1867), p. 77.
13 Robinson, *A Sailor Boy's Experience Aboard a Slave Ship* (1867), pp. 81–82.
14 Reduced rations consisted of one pound of brined raddled meat each day and six pounds of mouldy biscuit in seven days.

15 The supplies included as much fresh water, firewood, sheep, goats, young pigs and poultry as could be attained.
16 HMS *Tartar*, launched in 1801, was a 32-gun fifth-rate frigate. It took part in the blockade of Saint Domingue in July 1803. The ship was lost when it grounded off Estonia in 1811.
17 Robinson, *A Sailor Boy's Experience Aboard a Slave Ship* (1867), p. 100.
18 *La Creole*, launched in 1797, was a 40-gun frigate of the French Navy captured by HMS *Cumberland* at Saint Domingue on 30 June 1803. When the ship foundered in January 1804, her crew were rescued.
19 Robinson, *A Sailor Boy's Experience Aboard a Slave Ship* (1867), p. 103–104.
20 Robinson, *A Sailor Boy's Experience Aboard a Slave Ship* (1867), p. 107.
21 Robinson, *A Sailor Boy's Experience Aboard a Slave Ship* (1867), p. 109.
22 Robinson, *A Sailor Boy's Experience Aboard a Slave Ship* (1867), p. 117.
23 HMS *Cumberland*, launched in 1774, was a 74-gun third-rate ship of the line. It took part in the blockade of St Domingue in June 1803. The ship was broken up in 1804.
24 Robinson, *A Sailor Boy's Experience Aboard a Slave Ship* (1867), p. 117.
25 Robinson, *A Sailor Boy's Experience Aboard a Slave Ship* (1867), p. 123.
26 The Slave Trade Act was passed on 25 March 1807, declaring that from 1 May 1807 'all manner of dealing and reading in the purchase, sale, barter, or transfer of slaves or of persons intending to be sold, transferred, used, or dealt with as slaves, practiced or carried in, at, or from any part of the coast or countries of Africa shall be abolished, prohibited and declared to be unlawful'.
27 Robinson, *A Sailor Boy's Experience Aboard a Slave Ship* (1867), p. 6.
28 Schwarz, *Slave Captain: The Career of James Irving in the Liverpool Slave Trade* (1995), p. 51.
29 Peter Baker (1731–1796) and John Dawson (d. 1812) were the owners of the largest firm of slave traders in Britain. The firm held a contract to supply slaves to Spanish America for the Spanish government. Dawson was declared bankrupt in 1793 with debts of £500,000. See Richardson, *Liverpool and Transatlantic Slavery* (2007).
30 The Dolben Act of 1788 regulated conditions on board slave ships.
31 Alexander Falconbridge, a former surgeon on slave ships, noted 'the expected premium usually allowed to captains [was] of 6% Sterling on the produce of the negroes'. See Falconbridge, *An Account of the Slave Trade on the Coast of Africa* (1788), p. 27.
32 The ship foundered 'on the Arab coast opposite Fortaventura'. See 'Matra, James M., Consul General at Tangier, a letter to William W. Grenville at the Secretary of State's Office in London from Tangiers dated 21 July 1789', Public Records Office, FO 174/284.
33 Schwarz, *Slave Captain: The Career of James Irving in the Liverpool Slave Trade* (1995), pp. 82–84.
34 John Irving (1731–1807) and his wife, Isobel Little (1725–1791).
35 Schwarz, *Slave Captain: The Career of James Irving in the Liverpool Slave Trade* (1995), p. 12.
36 The certificate granted was an inferior qualification to that of a member of the Royal College of Surgeons of England. See Schwarz, *Slave Captain: The Career of James Irving in the Liverpool Slave Trade* (1995), p. 12. With thanks to librarian Miss Glen Jones.
37 Schwarz, *Slave Captain: The Career of James Irving in the Liverpool Slave Trade* (1995), p. 150.

38. Schwarz, *Slave Captain: The Career of James Irving in the Liverpool Slave Trade* (1995), p. 15.
39. 'Irving, James, a letter to Mary, his wife in Liverpool on 19 May 1786', Lancashire Records Office.
40. Schwarz, *Slave Captain: The Career of James Irving in the Liverpool Slave Trade* (1995), p. 112. The letter by Irving was dated 2 December 1786.
41. Schwarz, *Slave Captain: The Career of James Irving in the Liverpool Slave Trade* (1995), p. 31.
42. Behrendt, 'The Captains in the Slave Trade from 1785 to 1807', *The Historic Society of Liverpool and Cheshire* (1991), Vol. 140, pp. 112–114.
43. Schwarz, *Slave Captain: The Career of James Irving in the Liverpool Slave Trade* (1995), pp. 39–40.
44. Schwarz, *Slave Captain: The Career of James Irving in the Liverpool Slave Trade* (1995), p. 41.
45. Schwarz, *Slave Captain: The Career of James Irving in the Liverpool Slave Trade* (1995), p. 42.
46. Those Irving mentioned were his uncles in London, Joseph Smith and Captain Anthony Robinson.
47. The Mediterranean Pass number 7469 was issued to protect shipping from 'capture or plunder by the Barbary pirates operating off the Atlantic as well as the Mediterranean Coast of North West Africa'. Although not strictly applicable since Irving and his men had been captured by nomadic desert tribes, it still favourably influenced the actions taken by the consul. See Schofield, 'Slave Trade from the Lancashire and Cheshire Ports Outside Liverpool *c.* 1750–*c.* 1790', *The Historic Society of Lancashire and Cheshire* (1977), Vol. 126, p. 31.
48. Schwarz, *Slave Captain: The Career of James Irving in the Liverpool Slave Trade* (1995), p. 45.
49. Mawley al-Yazid was emperor from 1790 to 1792. See Schwarz, *Slave Captain: The Career of James Irving in the Liverpool Slave Trade* (1995), p. 60.
50. 'Irving, James, a letter to Mary, his wife dated 25 January 1791 from Cumbria', Lancashire Records Office. *Ellen* was anchored off Cumbria.

CHAPTER 9

1. The 24-gun HMS *Arundel*, captained by Charles Middleton, was launched at Chichester in 1745. It carried a crew of 160 and in November 1759 was heading to the Leeward Islands, a cluster of thirty islands including Antigua.
2. Britain and France were engaged in the Seven Years' War (1756–1763). In 1759, the British attempted to take Martinique from the French. Although this failed, an attack in 1762 succeeded.
3. Shyllon, *James Ramsay: The Unknown Abolitionist* (1977), p. 6.
4. 'Sympathy Letter' published in *The Public Advertiser*, 7 July 1788.
5. The *Swift* was thereafter taken to Antigua where it was sold for salvage. Of the original 280 to 300 slaves who boarded, only seventy were alive on arrival at the island. See 'Africa and the Eighteenth-Century Slave Trade to America: The Years of Decline 1746–1769', *Bristol Records Society Publication* (1991), Vol. XLII.
6. Shyllon, *James Ramsay: The Unknown Abolitionist* (1977), p. 6.
7. Sheridan, *Doctors and Slaves: A Medical and Demographic History of Slavery in the British West Indies 1680–1834* (1985), p. 110.

8 Sheridan, *Doctors and Slaves: A Medical and Demographic History of Slavery in the British West Indies 1680–1834* (1985), pp. 109–111.
9 Graham, *The Scots Penetration of the Jamaica Plantation Business: Recovering Scotland's Slavery Past* (2015), p. 148.
10 Aubrey, *The Sea Surgeon, or the Guinea Man's Vade Mecum* (1729).
11 Sheridan, *Doctors and Slaves: A Medical and Demographic History of Slavery in the British West Indies 1680–1834* (1985), p. 113.
12 Bryson, *Report on the Climate and Principal Diseases of the African Station* (1847).
13 Sheridan, *Doctors and Slaves: A Medical and Demographic History of Slavery in the British West Indies 1680–1834* (1985), p. 119.
14 The information included the number of slaves taken on board at the start of the voyage and the number and causes of deaths of slaves and seamen during the voyage.
15 It has been argued that the decline in slave mortality was in fact a continuation of a progressive reduction which began in the late seventeenth century. Among other factors, death rates differed depending on where the slaves embarked and of the length of sailing time. For example, slaves from the Gold Coast often had a lower death rate than slaves from the Bight of Biafra. See Sheridan, *Doctors and Slaves: A Medical and Demographic History of Slavery in the British West Indies 1680–1834* (1985), pp. 122–123.
16 'William Wilberforce to Eden, 23 November 1789', Auckland Papers, 34227 f.123, British Museum.
17 Morris, Roger, 'Charles Middleton, 1st Baron Barham (1726–1813)', www.oxforddnb.com (2008), accessed 27 May 2021.
18 Another possible factor might have been Middleton's conversion around the time of his marriage in 1761 from Presbyterianism to evangelical Anglicanism. It was an unusual decision to make and unpopular among his fellow naval officers who frequently accused him of promoting Wesleyan Methodism.
19 'Manuscript of James Ramsay concerning the abolition of the slave trade' (1787), MSS. Brit. Emp. s. 2, Bodleian Library, Oxford.
20 Thomas Reid (1710–1796), founder of the Scottish School of Common Sense and joint founder of the Royal Society of Edinburgh. James Beattie (1735–1803) professor of moral philosophy at Marischal College, Aberdeen, who delivered anti-slavery lectures to his students.
21 George Macaulay (1716–1766) was the scion of a prominent Edinburgh family. He studied at Edinburgh University and later Padova, earning a double doctorate. He spent much of his life dedicated to charitable works, serving as a surgeon and man-midwife in the first hospital in England devoted purely to obstetric services for poor women. See Cook and Cook, *Male-Midwife, Male Feminist: The Life and Times of George Macaulay M.D, Ph.D* (2006), pp. 1 & 49.
22 The British Lying in Hospital, Windmill Street, was founded in 1745 by the governors of the Middlesex Hospital. Its object was to serve three classes of needy people: disabled outpatients; unwell in-patients; and women in postpartum confinement. The medical and midwifery services were provided free of charge. See Watt, 'James Ramsay', www.oxforddnb.com (2006), accessed 2 April 2021.
23 Under the 1713 Treaty of Utrecht, the French ceded to Britain the part of St Kitts that had been occupied by them since the mid-seventeenth century, thereby giving the British complete possession of the island. Between 1720 and 1772, as the monoculture of sugar plantations intensified, the slave population on St Kitts more than doubled in size to 23,462, while the white population

fell from 4,000 to 1,900. The market was driven by an insatiable demand for sugar in Europe, and especially Britain. On average, annual consumption in Britain grew from roughly 4 lb per person in 1700 to 20 lb by 1800, partly driven by the increasing popularity of tea drinking among a growing urban population, particularly in Scotland. It resulted in a quintupling of sugar sales between 1730 and 1805. Meanwhile, prices in the home market for sugar and other tropical produce, protected by a near complete British monopoly under the laws of trade and navigation, were around 50 per cent higher than those on Continental Europe. See Devine, *Scotland's Empire* (2003), pp. 222–223.
24 Devine, *Scotland's Empire* (2003), p. 242.
25 Leslie, *History of Jamaica* (1740), p. 328.
26 Devine, *Scotland's Empire* (2003), p. 225.
27 Devine, *Scotland's Empire* (2003), pp. 224–225.
28 Hamilton, *Patronage and Profit: Scottish Networks in the British West Indies, c. 1763–1807* (1999), and Devine, *Scotland's Empire* (2003), p. 231.
29 Devine, *Scotland's Empire* (2003) p. 232.
30 Devine, *Scotland's Empire* (2003) pp. 229–230.
31 Ramsay described the slaves taken for auction off the slave ships as 'emaciated [and] sickly'. See Devine, *Scotland's Empire* (2003), p. 234.
32 Ramsay, *An Essay on the Treatment of Conversion of African Slaves in the British Sugar Colonies* (1784) pp. 178–179.
33 John Smith of the London Missionary Society was ministering in Demerara when he was held responsible for a bloody rebellion in 1823. Sentenced to death on insufficient evidence, he died before his execution.
34 Ramsay, *An Essay on the Treatment of Conversion of African Slaves in the British Sugar Colonies* (1784), p. 15.
35 Ramsay, *An Essay on the Treatment of Conversion of African Slaves in the British Sugar Colonies* (1784).
36 Watt, 'James Ramsay', www.oxforddnb.com (2006), accessed 2 April 2021.
37 Shyllon, *James Ramsay: The Unknown Abolitionist* (1977), pp. 10–11.
38 The vestry was a body in an Episcopal parish comprising the rector and elected parishioners who administered the secular affairs of the parish.
39 A further reason for Ramsay being a slave owner may have been his concern about releasing slaves from servitude without adequate preparation of how to deal with the challenges of self-determination. In this he saw Christianity as the central plank. Separate to this point, runaway slaves would come to him to ask him to mediate with their masters. See Shyllon, *James Ramsay: The Unknown Abolitionist* (1977), pp. 51 & 55–56.
40 Ramsay, *An Essay on the Treatment of Conversion of African Slaves in the British Sugar Colonies* (1784), pp. 74–75 & 77–82. Typically, slaves lived in hovels that they had to build for themselves.
41 Watt, 'James Ramsay', www.oxforddnb.com (2006), accessed 2 April 2021.
42 Ramsay, *An Essay on the Treatment of Conversion of African Slaves in the British Sugar Colonies* (1784), pp. 94–98, 107 & 113–120.
43 Shyllon, *James Ramsay: The Unknown Abolitionist* (1977), pp. 32 & 34.
44 Beilby Porteus (1731–1809) was a Church of England reformer, a leading abolitionist in England, and the first really to attack the church's position on the subject.
45 Watt, 'James Ramsay', www.oxforddnb.com (2006), accessed 2 April 2021.
46 Shyllon, *James Ramsay: The Unknown Abolitionist* (1977), pp. 34–36.
47 James Walker (1770–1841) was later to become bishop of Edinburgh and primus of the Scottish Episcopal Church.

48 It was published after the seventh draft had been approved by 'many persons of worth and judgment'.
49 Shyllon, *James Ramsay: The Unknown Abolitionist* (1977), pp. 18–19.
50 Shyllon, *James Ramsay: The Unknown Abolitionist* (1977), p. 20.
51 Watt, 'James Ramsay', www.oxforddnb.com (2006), accessed 2 April 2021.
52 Shyllon, *James Ramsay: The Unknown Abolitionist* (1977), pp. 36–40.
53 Refer to Chapter 3 for further information.
54 Joseph Woods, William Dillwyn, George Harrison, Samuel Hoare, Thomas Knowles and John Lloyd.
55 Schaw and Andrews, *Journal of a Lady of Quality: Being the Narrative of a Journey from Scotland to the West Indies, North Carolina, and Portugal, in the Years 1774 to 1776* (1921), p. 127.
56 Josiah Tucker (Dean Tucker) (1713–1799) was a Welsh churchman, economist and political writer interested in free trade, Jewish emancipation and American independence.
57 Thomas Clarkson (1760–1846) was a leading English abolitionist who contributed to the passing into law of the Slave Trade Act of 1807, which ended the British slave trade.
58 Shyllon, *James Ramsay: The Unknown Abolitionist* (1977), pp. 84 & 135.
59 Crisp Molineux (1730–1792), eldest son of Charles Molineux of St Kitts, was born in Garboldisham, Norfolk, and studied law at the Inner Temple in 1749. He became MP for Castle Rising and then King's Lynn. He died in St Kitts.
60 Watt, 'James Ramsay', www.oxforddnb.com (2006), accessed 2 April 2021.
61 Watt, 'James Ramsay', www.oxforddnb.com (2006), accessed 2 April 2021.

CHAPTER 10

1 Whyte, *Scotland and the Abolition of Black Slavery, 1756–1838* (2007) p. 1.
2 Shyllon, *James Ramsay: The Unknown Abolitionist* (1977) pp. 36–40.
3 In May 1787, fifty-five delegates from twelve states met in Philadelphia to revise the articles of Confederation. Rhode Island refused to send a delegate.
5 Walvin, *A Short History of Slavery* (2007), pp. 147–150.
6 Walvin, *A Short History of Slavery* (2007), p. 151.
7 The Society for the Abolition of the Slave Trade included Granville Sharp (as chairman) and Thomas Clarkson (both Anglicans), William Dillwyn (1743–1824) and eight Quakers.
8 Among the activists were the universities of Glasgow and Aberdeen, the town councils of Paisley and Dundee, and Edinburgh's Chamber of Commerce. The synods of Glasgow and Ayr, Merse and Teviotdale, Ross, Moray, Galloway and Dumfries also took action.
9 Whyte, *Scotland and the Abolition of Black Slavery 1756–1838* (2007), pp. 70–71.
10 William Dickson (1751–1823) was born in Moffat, Dumfriesshire. He gained a scholarship to Edinburgh University before immigrating to Barbados in 1772 to work as a civil servant. By 1785, having gone to London, Dickson took up the cause of the treatment of slaves in Barbados. Many publications followed in which he condemned slavery in principle and practice. In 1792, having befriended Wilberforce and Clarkson, Dickson toured Scotland with huge success, initiating abolitionist petitions from local people. He was awarded an honorary PhD by James Beattie, staunch abolitionist and professor of moral philosophy at Marischal College, Aberdeen. See Dickinson, 'William Dickson (1751–1823)', www.oxforddnb.com (2016), accessed 22 June 2021.

11 James Stephen (1758–1832) was born in Dorset to Scottish parents. He spent his early years with his grandparents in Aberdeenshire and studied at Marischal College under Professor James Beattie. He was converted to the abolitionist cause after witnessing the trial of a slave in Barbados, which he described as the 'reversal of every principle that I had been taught to reverence'. After an introduction to Wilberforce, he provided legal advice and legislative drafting in support of the cause. This was complimented by his political skills exercised as an MP for Tralee and then East Grinstead.

12 Among other provisions, the Dolben Act restricted the number of Africans to be carried on slave ships and ruled that a doctor needed to be on board. Financial incentives were also introduced to reduce death rates among the transported slaves.

13 Walvin, *A Short History of Slavery* (2007) pp. 156–157.

14 *Caledonian Mercury*, Wednesday, 21 February 1776.

15 Boswell, *The Life of Samuel Johnston* (1884) p. 355.

16 Robert Dundas, Lord Arniston (1685–1753) was appointed solicitor general for Scotland in 1717 and lord advocate in 1720. He was appointed lord president on 15 June 1747. As a practising advocate he was responsible for the restoration of the 'not proven' verdict still with us today.

17 The club took its name from the 'Feast of Tabernacles' which is a seven-day feast or festival commemorating the forty-year journey of the Israelites in the wilderness. See Fry, 'Henry Dundas, First Viscount Melville', www.oxforddnb.com (2021), accessed 19 November 2021.

18 In Dundas's first brief in July 1764, he secured an historic verdict against the Edinburgh City Council, making them liable for the repair of damage perpetrated by a mob.

19 Alexander Carlyle (1722–1805) was minister at Inveresk in Midlothian from 1748. In 1770 he was appointed moderator of the Church of Scotland and, in 1783, dean of the Royal Chapel. He was a founder member of the Royal Society of Edinburgh in 1783.

20 Matheson, *The Life of Henry Dundas 1742–1811* (1933), p. 22.

21 Fry, 'Henry Dundas, First Viscount Melville', www.oxforddnb.com (2021), accessed 19 November 2021.

22 Regarded as the greatest civil law suit of the century, the Douglas Cause was between the families of the dukes of Douglas and Hamilton over the inheritance of the former's fortune and title upon his death. The case began in 1762 and ended in appeal before the House of Lords in 1769.

23 Douglas, Heron & Company, known as Ayr Bank, was founded in Ayr in November 1769 with nominal capital of £150,000, of which £96,000 was immediately subscribed. See Checkland, *Scottish Banking: A History 1695–1973* (1975), p. 124.

24 Matheson, *The Life of Henry Dundas 1742–1811* (1933), pp. 29–30.

25 Dundas secured 57 of the 104 electoral votes, with Dundas voting for Gilmour.

26 Following the abolition of the office of secretary of state for Scotland in the wake of the defeat of the Jacobite Rebellion in 1746, the lord advocate became the country's chief officer of government, responsible for what remained of administrative and legislative demands. See Fry, 'Henry Dundas, First Viscount Melville', www.oxforddnb.com (2021), accessed 19 November 2021.

27 A play on the 'Code Noir' (Black Code) drawn up in 1685, the French code which laid down the treatment of slaves in the French Caribbean.

28 '[Smith] despised slavery and the slave trade, and he argued with enormous force that, far from resulting from natural liberty, both were abetted by

mercantilism and monopoly.' Norman, *Adam Smith: What He Thought and Why It Matters* (2018), p. 208.

29 Lofft, 'Somerset against Stewart, May 14, 1772', Trinity Term, 12 Geo. 3, *Reports of Cases Adjudged in the Court of the King's Bench* (1772), p. 510. Dundas had visited Mansfield in London at the latter's suggestion in March 1772. On 27 June 1772, Mansfield wrote to Dundas's brother, Robert, the lord president: 'Your bros. will certainly go far as his career can carry him; and his short visit has been of use to him. There is a great difference between being personally known, and by name only, let it sound ever so high.' Mansfield determined that since the case had been brought under a writ of habeas corpus the object of the enquiry was 'the person of the slave himself' and not whether a contract for the sale of a slave was good in England, which he confirmed it was. See Matheson, *The Life of Henry Dundas 1742–1811* (1933), p. 29.
30 Dundas also spoke on the Royal Navy and the war policy as a whole.
31 Matheson, *The Life of Henry Dundas 1742–1811* (1933), p. 68.
32 'George III, letter to Lord Stormont, dated 26 July 1781', Mansfield Papers, Scone Palace.
33 Fry, 'Henry Dundas, First Viscount Melville', www.oxforddnb.com (2021), accessed 19 November 2021.
34 Matheson, *The Life of Henry Dundas 1742–1811* (1933), p. 211.
35 Ehrman, *The Younger Pitt: The Years of Acclaim* (2004), pp. 387–388.
36 Parties included the Association for Promoting the Discovery of the Interior Parts of Africa, founded in London in 1788. Its purpose was mainly scientific but it was also linked with commercial development.
37 Other than slaves, Britain imported gum, ivory, gold, dye woods, indigo, palm oil and hides from Africa.
38 Ehrman, *The Younger Pitt: The Years of Acclaim* (2004), p. 389.
39 Ehrman, *The Younger Pitt: The Years of Acclaim* (2004), pp. 387–388.
40 The Dutch and Portuguese were disinterested; the Danes proceeded at their chosen pace; and the national assembly in France defeated their leaders' endeavours, contrary to what the British had hoped for from the Revolution.
41 Ehrman, *The Younger Pitt: The Years of Acclaim* (2004), pp. 390–401.
42 Louis XVI was executed on 21 January 1793 at Place de la Concorde, Paris.
43 Matheson, *The Life of Henry Dundas 1742–1811* (1933), p. 149.
44 It was only after 1830 that revolutionary principles began to secure general, if still incomplete, recognition.
45 Matheson, *The Life of Henry Dundas 1742–1811* (1933), pp. 150–151.
46 Revolutionary ideas were cultivated in reforming associations and political clubs, in some cases fomenting sedition.
47 Matheson, *The Life of Henry Dundas 1742–1811* (1933), pp. 152–155 & 159.
48 In his capacity as MP for Edinburgh, Dundas presented one of the petitions to the House of Commons on 2 April 1792.
49 Ehrman, *The Younger Pitt: The Years of Acclaim* (2004), p. 399.
50 'You will see Clarkson, caution him against talking of the French Revolution; it will be ruin to our cause.' A letter by Wilberforce to Lord Muncaster in October 1792, reproduced in Wilberforce, *The Life of William Wilberforce* (2012), Vol. 1, pp. 342–343.
51 Ehrman, *The Younger Pitt: The Years of Acclaim* (2004), p. 400.
52 In March 1792, Denmark proclaimed a royal edict which 'outlawed participation in the trade by the King's subjects, but deferred the effectuation of the ban for a ten year period'. The edict mentioned possible support to Danish West Indian planters who wanted to buy more slaves before 1803, and this was

followed up by a loan scheme and other incentives. Thus, the proclamation of abolition entailed a boost of Danish slave trading activities. This was intentional 'to increase the slave stock so that no further imports were needed'. See Gøbel, *The Danish Edict of 16th March 1792 to Abolish the Slave Trade* (2009), p. 335.
53 Ehrman, *The Younger Pitt: The Years of Acclaim* (2004), p. 400.
54 Fry, 'Henry Dundas, First Viscount Melville', www.oxforddnb.com (2021), accessed 19 November 2021.
55 Ehrman, *The Younger Pitt: The Years of Acclaim* (2004), pp. 400–401.
56 These included the immediate end of the British slave trade with foreign colonies; the forbidding of foreigners to import slaves to the British colonies after October 1793; the immediate demand for slavers to transport equal numbers of males and females; the ruling, on an unspecified date, that newly imported slaves be under twenty years for men and sixteen for women (to encourage planters to replenish their workforce through procreation); the ruling that no new slave ships would be permitted to enter the trade. While breach of these regulations would be punished, there would be a parliamentary inquiry into any commercial losses. Finally, negotiations would be opened with other countries for general abolition. See Fry, *The Dundas Despotism* (1992), p. 200.
57 This was only after an attempt to end the trade by 1795 had failed by 161 votes to 121.
58 The first resolution was that British involvement with the transatlantic slave trade should end on 1 January 1800. An earlier date of 1 January 1796 had been proposed by Sir E. Knatchbull.
59 Mullen, 'Henry Dundas: A "Great Delayer" of the Abolition of the Transatlantic Slave Trade', *Scottish Historical Review* (2021), p. 8.
60 A letter dated 2 April 1792 from the dean of Carlisle to William Wilberforce. See Wilberforce, *The Life of William Wilberforce* (2012), Vol. 1, p. 346.
61 In the 1790 general election, 558 MPs were elected to the Commons. Research has suggested that of these, sixty had West Indian connections. See McCahill, *The Correspondence of Stephen Fuller 1788–1795: Jamaica, The West Indies Interest at Westminster and the Campaign to Preserve the Slave Trade* (2014), pp. 47–51.
62 'Speech of Drake, William, 18 April 1788', *The Parliamentary Register* (188), Vol. 23, p. 470.
63 This was achieved by Lord Stormont's motion of proposing an investigation (with witnesses under oath) into 'African trafficking, the sugar trade and more broadly', which was passed by 63 votes to 36.
64 Ehrman, *The Younger Pitt: The Years of Acclaim* (2004), p. 401.
65 The ensuing fifteen years saw over 2,000 more slave ships leave British ports carrying some 583,000 African men, women and children. See Mullen, 'Henry Dundas: A "Great Delayer" of the Abolition of the Transatlantic Slave Trade', *Scottish Historical Review* (2021).
66 Estimated to be about 11,500 slaves bought. The war included an invasion by the British of St Domingue (Haiti) and then a slave rebellion against the French. Pitt was worried that, if successful, the slave revolt would encourage insurrection in the British slave colonies. Other reasons were also factored in, however. In the event, the British suffered heavy losses which hardened public attitudes to slaves generally. In an effort to avoid the island falling into foreign hands, France freed the slaves in St Domingue on 29 August 1793.
67 The Clapham Sect, founded by William Venn, comprised a group of evangelical Anglicans who shared common political and social opinions on the liberation

of slaves. The group was active between the 1780s and 1840s. Wilberforce and Clarkson were influential members, and were encouraged by Beilby Porteus, bishop of London.
68 This included effective boycotts of slave-grown sugar in which women played a leading role. Women also continued to be effective in the petitioning campaigns. Walvin, *A Short History of Slavery* (2007), p. 148.
69 Lord Grenville's premiership ran from February 1806 to March 1807. He surrendered his seal of office on the same day the slave trade bill received royal assent.
70 Mullen, 'Henry Dundas: A "Great Delayer" of the Abolition of the Transatlantic Slave Trade', *Scottish Historical Review* (2021), p. 9, and Walvin, *A Short History of Slavery* (2007), p. 163.
71 Dundas was impeached for alleged misappropriation of public funds when he was treasurer of the Royal Navy. He was acquitted in the House of Lords.

CHAPTER 11

1 Mullen, *It Wisnae Us: The Truth About Glasgow and Slavery* (2009), p. 7.
2 Massie, *Glasgow: Portraits of a City* (1989), p. 31.
3 Oswald & Co. was founded in 1713 by the two brothers Richard 'the elder' (1687–1763) and Alexander Oswald (1694–1766).
4 Devine, *The Tobacco Lords* (1975), pp. 3–5.
5 For an insight into the occupations of the fathers of eighteenth-century Glasgow tobacco merchants, refer to 'Table II' in Devine, *The Tobacco Lords* (1975), p. 6.
6 Nisbet, 'Early Glasgow Sugar Plantations in the Caribbean', *Scottish Archaeological Journal* (2009), Vol. 1, No. 1, p. 116.
7 Morgan, *The Black Experience in the British Empire 1680–1810* (1998), p. 402.
8 The failure of the Darien expeditions led to a small number of survivors settling in Jamaica, the most eminent of whom was Colonel John Campbell of Inverarary. By his death in 1740, he had established a huge and influential network of relatives and associates drawn from the west of Scotland, which exercised powerful influence within Jamaica throughout the eighteenth century. See Devine, *Scotland's Empire* (2003), pp. 227–229.
9 Devine, *Scotland's Empire* (2003), p. 184.
10 Devine, *The Tobacco Lords* (1975), pp. 55–58.
11 The French government monopoly was called the 'Farmers General of the French Customs'.
12 'Tobacco was not homogeneous. The two basic varieties, oronoco (strong in flavour) and sweet scented (mild) were themselves differentiated by the influence of climate, soil and level of planter skills.' Devine, *The Tobacco Lords* (1975), p. 64.
13 The tariff reductions saw the amount of tobacco purchased from Glasgow merchants by the French rise from under 10 per cent in 1730 to 52 per cent between 1757 and 1762. On a wider canvas, the French purchased 35 per cent of the crop imported by the tobacco lords during the period 1752–1772.
14 Devine, *The Tobacco Lords* (1975), p. 65.
15 This production included soap, beer, nails, shoes, saddles and many other items. See Devine, *Tobacco Lords* (1975), pp. 62–64.
16 A 'bill of exchange' is short-term negotiable financial instrument consisting of an order in writing addressed by one person (the seller of goods) to another

(the buyer) requiring the latter to pay on demand (a sight draft) or at a fixed or determinable future time (a time draft) a certain sum of money to a specified person or to the bearer of the bill.

17　Devine, *Tobacco Lords* (1975), pp. 89–92.
18　On the other hand, lending was different. It placed the lender in a position of power and influence over the borrower, and it offered profit, particularly if the borrower defaulted. The Associates usually lent in Britain at the maximum 5 per cent rate, and 6–8 per cent in the colonies. Indeed, the cycle of secured loan, default, vesting and resale was favoured by Oswald, who between 1750 and 1775, when land values in the Caribbean rose steeply, was able to procure substantial returns on his loans. The attractive benefit of flexibility on the loan would also be available if it was repayable on demand. Around 80 per cent of the people Oswald lent money to were fellow Scots; most were his neighbours to his estate, Auchencruive, in Ayrshire, or victims of the crash of the Ayr Bank. See Hancock, *Citizens of the World: London Merchants and the Integration of the British Atlantic Community* (1995), pp. 248 & 250.
19　Within this context, partnership law permitted loans to be raised both on the company's joint stock and on the person of the individual partners. The 'heritable bond' gave additional security by linking the loan to a specific part of the creditor's heritable property. In the event of insolvency, the holder of such a bond would be a preferential creditor on the bankrupt's assets. See Devine, *Tobacco Lords* (1975), pp. 97–98.
20　From 1749 to 1784, Oswald averaged a balance of £835 at the close of each year in his London bank and respective accounts with the Glasgow Arms Bank and the Ayr Bank. He applied the former to buy government securities, and the latter to pay farmworkers, seed merchants and booksellers in south-west Scotland. See Hancock, *Citizens of the World: London Merchants and the Integration of the British Atlantic Community* (1995), p. 256.
21　Devine, *Scotland's Empire* (2003), p. 177.
22　Hancock, *Citizens of the World: London Merchants and the Integration of the British Atlantic Community* (1995), p. 281.
23　Devine, *Tobacco Lords* (1975), p. 246.
24　John Glassford, considered the pre-eminent tobacco lord of his era, accumulated a fortune owning tobacco plantations and twenty-one stores in Virginia and Maryland. He lost his fortune due to gambling and the American War of Independence (1775–1783), which ruined the tobacco trade. He died in 1783 in severe debt.
25　Devine, *The Tobacco Lords* (1975), p. 4.
26　Hancock, *Citizens of the World: London Merchants and the Integration of the British Atlantic Community* (1995), pp. 60–61.
27　George Oswald (1664?–1725), Richard's father, was an ordained minister in the Presbyterian church in Caithness. During his lifetime, the Presbyterian Church was devastated by religious battles with the Episcopalian Church. George was heavily committed to the inquisition of churchgoers who opposed the new Presbyterian ministers. See Hancock, *Citizens of the World: London Merchants and the Integration of the British Atlantic Community* (1995), p. 60.
28　Hancock, *Citizens of the World: London Merchants and the Integration of the British Atlantic Community* (1995), p. 62.
29　Imported goods included prunes, cork and vinegar from Spain and Portugal, sugar, spices and cotton from the Caribbean, and tobacco from Virginia. He exported and re-exported bottles, linens, woollen and leather good, candles, iron and lead products and hardware. See Hancock, *Citizens of the World:*

London Merchants and the Integration of the British Atlantic Community (1995), p. 63.
30 Hancock, 'Richard Oswald', www.oxforddnb.com (2008), accessed 22 June 2021.
31 Mary Ramsay Oswald by Johann Zoffany (1733–1810), The National Portrait Gallery, London.
32 John Boyd and John Mills were the remaining two.
33 *Browne's General Law List* was published annually in London between 1775 and 1854. Hancock, *Citizens of the World: London Merchants and the Integration of the British Atlantic Community* (1995), p. 141.
34 In 1745 Richard Oswald received £15,000 from the sale of French ships and their cargoes after their capture by ships within the Oswald fleet. These funds financed Oswald's move to London the following year.
35 The provisions were bread, straw, wood and wagons.
36 Under the 1763 Treaty of Paris, Spain ceded Florida to Britain in exchange for Britain relinquishing control of Havana, Cuba, captured by them the year before.
37 In negotiating the 1783 Treaty of Paris, Benjamin Franklin found Oswald to be 'a wise and honest man whose moderation, prudent counsels, and sound judgment may contribute much, not only to the speedy conclusion of peace but to the framing of such a peace as may be firm and longstanding'. See Hancock, *Citizens of the World: London Merchants and the Integration of the British Atlantic Community* (1995), pp. 153–157.
38 Hancock, *Citizens of the World: London Merchants and the Integration of the British Atlantic Community* (1995), pp. 172–188.
39 Hancock, *Citizens of the World: London Merchants and the Integration of the British Atlantic Community* (1995), pp. 194 & 197–198.
40 James Low of Monymusk, Aberdeen, worked on the island from 1761 to 1762, when he died due to ill health.
41 Hancock, *Citizens of the World: London Merchants and the Integration of the British Atlantic Community* (1995), pp. 203–204.
42 Hancock, *Citizens of the World: London Merchants and the Integration of the British Atlantic Community* (1995), pp. 280–283.
43 Brightenhelmstone in Sussex and Eltham in Kent.
44 'Grant, Alexander, to Sir Archibald, 1 January 1750', National Records of Scotland, GD345/1160/31.
45 'How pleasing to think, that every step a man makes for his own good, promotes that of his country.' See Home (Lord Kames), *The Gentleman Farmer* (1776), pp. xiv, xvii, xviii & 37.
46 At Auchencruive and Cravens, Oswald granted leases to tenants of all but the home farms.
47 In 1700, Oswald's estate in Kirkcudbright had no mills, no cattle, and only two carts for hire with neither wheat nor potatoes grown. By 1750, with his improvements, the land had been recast with new tools, techniques, and new crops like turnips, the use of crop rotation and rectangular fields, trimmed hedges and better market facilities. See Hancock, *Citizens of the World: London Merchants and the Integration of the British Atlantic Community* (1995), p. 297.
48 Hancock, *Citizens of the World: London Merchants and the Integration of the British Atlantic Community* (1995), p. 300.
49 Individual landowners and justice of the peace trusts.
50 Fundraising included gifts, subscriptions, loans and income earned from tolls.

Chapter 12

1. Wright, *Views of Society and Manners in America* (1822), pp. 7–8.
2. Wright, *Views of Society and Manners in America* (1822), p. 294.
3. Wright, *Views of Society and Manners in America* (1822), p. 478.
4. Wright, *Views of Society and Manners in America* (1822), p. 478.
5. Thomas Paine (1737–1809) was an English-born American philosopher, political theorist, political activist and revolutionary whose political pamphlets provided inspiration to patriots to declare independence from Great Britain.
6. Morris, *Fanny Wright: Rebel in America* (1992), pp. 6–7.
7. *Gentleman's Magazine*, November 1809, No. 79, p. 1176.
8. Wright, *Biography, Notes, and Political Letters of Frances Wright D'Arusmont* (1844), p. 11.
9. The estates built by Drury of Harrow in the 1790s, Charles Hoare at Luscombe estate, and John Inglet Fortescue at Dawlish manor (before selling it off in parcels to the highest bidders).
10. 'Fanny Wright to Frances Campbell, 1820', Theresa Wolfson Papers, Martin P. Catherwood Library, Cornell University.
11. Morris, *Fanny Wright: Rebel in America* (1992), pp. 13–15.
12. Robina Craig Millar was related by marriage to James Mylne. In 1795, she settled in Philadelphia with her husband having fled from anti-Jacobin sentiments in Britain. She was in Benjamin Rush's circle of British expatriates but returned after her husband John's unexpected death in 1813.
13. Bederman, 'Revisiting: Nashoba, Slavery, Utopia', *American Literary History* (2005), Vol. 17, No. 3, p. 440.
14. Robert Owen (1771–1858), a Welsh manufacturer and reformer, was born in Newtown, Montgomeryshire, Wales. He pioneered a social and industrial welfare project in New Lanark mills in Scotland, which housed about 2,000 men, women and children. He attempted to do something similar in New Harmony, Indiana, USA.
15. David Dale (1739–1806) was a Glasgow banker and entrepreneur who, along with Richard Arkwright, pioneered industrial cotton spinning.
16. Owen, *Observations on the Effect of the Manufacturing System* (1963), pp. 121–122.
17. In 1799, alongside other investors including English philosopher Jeremy Bentham (1748–1832), Robert Owen purchased New Lanark for £60,000. The project sought to provide better housing and encourage order, cleanliness and thrift. A store was provided which sold goods only marginally above cost, and a village school was built in 1817 with child labour being phased to allow for education.
18. Morris, *Fanny Wright: Rebel in America* (1992), pp. 20–21.
19. The Corn Laws of 1815 imposed tariffs and regulations on imported food and corn in the wake of the Napoleonic Wars. Food prices were raised and the cost of living rose, with a concurrent growth of profits for landowners. Riots in London followed.
20. In 1819, while in New York, Wright was inspired to write a play, a tragedy entitled *Altorf*, which received several favourable reviews.
21. In 1820 there were 2,867,454 white people, 130,487 free non-whites, and 1,509,904 slaves in the Southern states. See *Historical Statistics of the United States, Colonial Times to 1957* (1970).
22. Wright, *Biography, Notes, and Political Letters of Frances Wright D'Arusmont* (1844), pp. 479–481.

23 Wright, *Biography, Notes, and Political Letters of Frances Wright D'Arusmont* (1844), pp. 480–481.
24 Winfield, 'Dreamers' Vision Frances Wright at Nashoba (1825–1830)', *Tennessee Historical Magazine* (1932), Series 2, Vol. 2, No. 2, p. 76.
25 Elliot, 'Frances Wright's Experiment with Negro Emancipation', *Indiana Magazine of History* (1939), Vol. 35, No. 2, p. 143.
26 Marquis de Lafayette (1757–1834) was a French aristocrat and soldier who fought with distinction in the American War of Independence. He assisted Thomas Jefferson in drafting the Declaration of the Rights of Man and of the Citizen.
27 The precise nature of their relationship remains ambiguous but each was attracted to the other. Nonetheless, Lafayette refused Wright's marriage proposal. See Morris, *Fanny Wright: Rebel in America* (1992), p. 75.
28 Thomas Jefferson (1743–1826), primary author of the Declaration of Independence, was the grandson of a slave trader and owned slaves himself, which he demanded the Virginian assembly allow him to free in 1773. In 1784 he failed by one vote in Congress to prohibit slavery after 1800 in any newly created state. As third president of the United States, serving between 1801 and 1809, he failed to make any significant progress towards emancipation. James Madison (1751–1836) was an American statesman and diplomat who, after making a substantial contribution to the ratification of the constitution, became known as 'the father of the constitution'. He served as fourth president of the United States between 1809 and 1817. See Morris, *Fanny Wright: Rebel in America* (1992), p. 84.
29 Elliot, 'Frances Wright's Experiment with Negro Emancipation', *Indiana Magazine of History* (1939), Vol. 35, No. 2, p. 145.
30 'Frances Wright letter to Lafayette, 27 December 1821', MSS. 304, University of Chicago.
31 Morris, *Fanny Wright: Rebel in America* (1992), p. 85.
32 Morris, *Fanny Wright: Rebel in America* (1992), p. 87.
33 The Rappites were a group of German dissenters from the Lutheran Church under the leadership of George Rapp. In 1803 the Rappites migrated to Butler County in the west of Pennsylvania where they set up their first colony, Harmonie. Mills, farms and vineyards were developed. In 1814, they moved to a new site of 30,000 acres acquired at Wabash in Indiana, also named Harmonie, where they developed the same plan in a more fertile valley.
34 The American Colonisation Society was founded in 1816 by Robert Finley, a protestant minister, with George Washington's nephew, Bushrod Washington, among others. It was dedicated to transporting freeborn and emancipated slaves to Africa. The membership was principally white, including a large number of slave owners, at a time when it was widely held that free blacks could not be integrated into white America.
35 President Jean Pierre Boyer (1776–1850) was one of the black slaves who led the successful revolt of slaves and free people of colour against the French, known as the Haitian Revolution (1789–1804), after which the country became free of slavery. Boyer was the country's president from 1818 to 1842.
36 Morris, *Fanny Wright: Rebel in America* (1992), pp. 94–95.
37 Bederman, 'Revisiting: Nashoba, Slavery, Utopia', *American Literary History* (2005), Vol. 17, No. 3, p. 447.
38 Elliot, 'Frances Wright's Experiment with Negro Emancipation', *Indiana Magazine of History* (1939), Vol. 35, No. 2, pp. 149–150.
39 The school would teach the slaves trade skills such as carpentry, cobbling, blacksmithing, sewing and weaving.

40 Liberia was established by the American Colonisation Society in 1822 for the settlement of emancipated black slaves and freeborn people of colour. Haiti was chosen because slavery had been abolished there in 1804, when the country had achieved its independence from the French after the Haitian Revolution (1791–1804).
41 Bederman, 'Revisiting: Nashoba, Slavery, Utopia', *American Literary History* (2005), Vol. 17, No. 3, pp. 447–448.
42 General Andrew Jackson (1767–1845) was an American lawyer, soldier and statesman from Tennessee, who served as seventh president of the United States from 1829 to 1837.
43 The purchase price from Jackson was $480.
44 Bederman, 'Revisiting: Nashoba, Slavery, Utopia', *American Literary History* (2005), Vol. 17, No. 3, p. 449.
45 The price for the slaves Willis, Jacob, Grandison, Redick, Henry, Nelly, Peggy and Kitty was between $400 and $600 each.
46 Jeremiah Thompson, a Quaker, donated $580 to stock the store.
47 Bederman, 'Revisiting: Nashoba, Slavery, Utopia', *American Literary History* (2005), Vol. 17, No. 3, pp. 449–450.
48 Bederman, 'Revisiting: Nashoba, Slavery, Utopia', *American Literary History* (2005), Vol. 17, No. 3, p. 451
49 Deed of Trust by Frances Wright of Nashoba to General Lafayette and nine other trustees dated 17 December 1826', *Oriental Herald and Journal of Literature* (1826).
50 Morris, *Fanny Wright: Rebel in America* (1992), p. 136.
51 Wright, Frances, 'Establishment for the Abolition of Slavery', *Genius of Universal Emancipation* (1827), p. 440.
52 Elliot, 'Frances Wright's Experiment with Negro Emancipation', *Indiana Magazine of History* (1939), Vol. 35, No. 2, p. 153.
53 The rules also included the following: 'No member is to be admitted until he or she has served a six month trial and only then with the unanimous vote of the trustees; the admission of a husband does not involve the admitting the wife, or vice versa, nor the admission of a parent include children over fourteen years. Each will be judged on their individual merit; any member not to work may pay an equivalent amount of money not exceeding $200 per annum; moral prerequisites necessary are an amiable and willing disposition, kindly affections, simple tastes and a high tone of moral feeling; Children under fourteen shall be raised and educated by the community until they are twenty; ... children of outsiders may be educated in the schools at a cost of $100 per annum.'
54 Excerpts from articles published by Wright in the *New Harmony Gazette* in January and February 1828.
55 Thomas Brown (1778–1820), born in Kirkcudbright, Scotland, was a Scottish philosopher and poet with a particular interest in metaphysical analysis. See Morris, *Fanny Wright: Rebel in America* (1992), p. 114.
56 James Richardson was also cohabiting with the teenage daughter of Mme Lalotte, a mixed race schoolteacher from New Orleans. See Heineman, 'Frances Wright', www.oxforddnb.com (2008), accessed 12 July 2021.
57 Hunt, *The Writings of James Madison* (1910), pp. 310–311.
58 $100 per annum plus meeting their expenses.
59 Extracts from the report of the Nashoba Trustees, published in the *New Harmony Gazette*, November 1828.
60 Mrs Frances Trollope (1779–1863), mother of the famous novelist Anthony Trollope, was an English writer.

61 Trollope, *Domestic Manners of the Americans* (1832), pp. 17–18, and Elliot, 'Frances Wright's Experiment with Negro Emancipation', *Indiana Magazine of History* (1939), Vol. 35, No. 2, p. 156.
62 Trollope, *Domestic Manners of the Americans* (1832), p. 38.
63 Richeson Whitby was described by Mrs Trollope as 'coarse-minded and uneducated—a surly brute who would not let Camilla be a good wife'. As for Camilla, she accepted her misery stoically.
64 Robert Owen had visited New Orleans from Liverpool and issued a challenge to anyone who would defend Christianity against his contrary views in a public debate.
65 Wright, 'Explanatory Notes Respecting the Nature and Objects of the Institution of Nashoba', *Genius of Universal Emancipation* (1828).
66 Bederman, 'Revisiting: Nashoba, Slavery, Utopia', *American Literary History* (2005), Vol. 17, No. 3, p. 453.
67 Morris, *Fanny Wright: Rebel in America* (1992), pp. 164–165.
68 Morris, *Fanny Wright: Rebel in America* (1992), p. 167.
69 Morris, *Fanny Wright: Rebel in America* (1992), pp. 207–213.
70 Estimated by Robert Dale Owen at $16,000 or half Fanny's estate.
71 The American newspaper was *The Free Enquirer*, which Wright edited with Robert Dale Owen between 1828 and 1830, standing up for the victims of social and political oppression.
72 Catherine Beecher (1800–1878) was a teacher and writer who advocated equal access for women to education and promoted their roles as teachers and mothers.
73 Heineman, 'Frances Wright', www.oxforddnb.com (2008), accessed 12 July 2021.
74 Morris, *Fanny Wright: Rebel in America* (1992), p. 279.
75 Wright, 'Explanatory Notes Respecting the Nature and Objects of the Institution of Nashoba', *Genius of Universal Emancipation* (1828), pp. 249–257.
76 Heineman, 'Frances Wright', www.oxforddnb.com (2008), accessed 12 July 2021.
77 The American Civil War lasted from 12 April 1860 to 9 May 1865.
78 Wright, *Views of Society and Manners in America* (1822), p. 478.

Chapter 13

1 Trade with Demerara was undertaken by the first Dutch West India Company in 1621, but this developed into more profitable sugar production with particular growth taking place between 1742 and 1771 under the Dutch West Indian Company. The colony was increasingly settled by British planters from Barbados and the Leeward Islands, and by 1760 they were in the majority, but their prosperity was curtailed by the abolition of the slave trade in 1807. After changing hands between the Dutch and British in 1796, 1802 and 1803, Demerara was formally ceded to Britain in 1814.
2 Walvin, *A Short History of Slavery* (2007), pp. 194–195.
3 The Slave Trade Act of 1824 was applicable throughout the British empire. The legislation achieved its purpose, and by 1837 British subjects were finally no longer engaged in the trade. See Stewart, *Henry Brougham 1778–1868: His Public Career* (1986), pp. 174–175.
4 The United States of America abolished the slave trade in 1808 when the 'Act Prohibiting Importation of Slaves' passed into law on 2 March 1802. Included

within this were Sweden in 1813, Holland in 1814, France in 1814 (with effect from 1819), and Portugal in 1820, which agreed to restrict its trade into its colonies.
5. France abolished slavery in 1794 in response to the slave rebellion in Saint Domingue (Haiti), but it was reinstated by Napoleon in 1802.
6. This was out of a population of 12 million. The parties to the Congress were Britain, Austria, Prussia, Russia and France. The primary object of reaching an agreement to realign the boundaries between states was formally achieved.
7. Walvin, *A Short History of Slavery* (2007), pp. 195–196.
8. Bayley's plantation at St Philip, working some 200 slaves, was owned by absentee landlord Reverend Alexander Scott, an Anglican clergyman. Bussa was a ranger, the head officer among the enslaved workers. He was killed in battle while leading some 400 men and women against the British troops.
9. Craton, *Proto-Peasant Revolts? The Late Rebellions in the British West Indies 1816–1832* (1979).
10. Thomas Gladstones (1732–1809).
11. Checkland, *The Gladstones: Family Biography (1761–1851)* (1971), p. 13.
12. Of the £4,000 capital invested in the business, Gladstones provided £1,500.
13. Gladstones' legal name did not change to 'Gladstone' until 10 February 1835.
14. Matthew, 'Sir John Gladstone (Gladstones) 1764–1851', www.oxforddnb.com (2016), accessed 9 April 2021.
15. The Demerara estates were Success, Wales, Waller's Delight, Covenden, Hampton Court, Vreedenhoop and Vreedestein.
16. Checkland, *The Gladstones: Family Biography (1761–1851)* (1971), p. 123.
17. Walvin, *A Short History of Slavery* (2007), pp. 202–203.
18. Reverend John Smith (1790–1824).
19. The London Missionary Society was an interdenominational evangelical missionary society founded in England in 1795. It set up its first mission in the West Indies in Tobago, in 1808 only to be abandoned due to cost in 1814. A similar experience occurred in Trinidad, in part due to hostility from the governor in 1825. 1808 saw the establishment of the Demerara mission by John Wray, who carried out substantial work with the slaves on the sugar plantations which Smith inherited on his arrival as Wray's replacement.
20. Sheridan, *Doctors and Slaves: A Medical and Demographic History of Slavery in the British West Indies 1680–1834* (1985), pp. 247.
21. Jakobsson, *Am I Not a Man and a Brother? British Missions and the Abolition of the Slave Trade and Slavery in the West Indies 1786–1834* (2009), pp. 323.
22. In his defence, Jack Gladstone explained that a mulatto servant, Joe or Joseph, belonging to Mr Simpson of Le Reduit, 5 miles from Georgetown, had written a letter to Jack and his colleagues informing them that the slaves 'were to be freed, by what he had seen of his master's papers ...; that Mr Wilberforce was doing his best for us; and that if we would wait a little, a new Governor was expected very soon; and, if he came, and would not give us what is allowed to us, that we must apply to him, and that he would inform of the regular way of getting it.' See Bryant, *Account of an Insurrection of the Negro Slaves in the Colony of Demerara* (1824), p. 74.
23. The motion was 'that the state of slavery is repugnant to the principles of the British constitution and of Christian religion, and that it ought to be abolished gradually throughout the British colonies'.
24. The dispatch prohibited the flogging of female slaves and the arbitrary use of the sound of the whip, and its use on slaves, to drive them to the fields.
25. For example, 'Louis of Porter's Hope 1000 lashes; Field of Clonbrook 1000;

Jessamin of Cucess, 1000.' Bryant, *Account of an Insurrection of the Negro Slaves in the Colony of Demerara* (1824), p. 74.
26 Bryant, *Account of an Insurrection of the Negro Slaves in the Colony of Demerara* (1824).
27 Walvin, *A Short History of Slavery* (2007), pp. 204–205.
28 A letter dated 24 December 1824 to William A. Hankey, an official of the London Missionary Society. Sheridan, *Doctors and Slaves: A Medical and Demographic History of Slavery in the British West Indies 1680–1834* (1985), pp. 248–249.
29 George Canning (1770–1827) was a Tory statesman who became prime minister briefly in 1827 for the last 118 days of his life.
30 James Cropper (1773–1840) was the founder of Cropper, Benson & Company, which imported American cotton and West Indian sugar.
31 Sheridan, *Doctors and Slaves: A Medical and Demographic History of Slavery in the British West Indies 1680–1834* (1985), pp. 250–251.
32 The Bible Society was founded on 7 March 1804.
33 Offended at Cropper's taunt, Gladstone rejected his claim that the slave population was falling due to insufficient food and forced labour; rather, he preferred to base his argument on a formal triennial report for Demerara. This provided statistics that permitted him to conclude that when the proportion of the sexes became equal, as they were in America, 'we may confidently expect an increase from natural causes and good management alone'.
34 The published report was entitled *Considerations on Negro Slavery*.
35 McDonnell, *Considerations of Negro Slavery* (1824), p. 156.
36 A plantain is a banana containing high levels of starch and little sugar. It is used as a cooked vegetable in the tropics.
37 McDonnell, *Considerations of Negro Slavery* (1824), pp. 253–254.
38 The reforms included the abolition of the whip for women and the limit of twenty-five lashes for men; the limit of working hours from 6 a.m. to 6 p.m. with a two-hour midday break; the permit of slaves to marry, acquire and own property, and to purchase their freedom.
39 Williams, *Capitalism and Slavery* (1943), p. 198.
40 Sheridan, *Doctors and Slaves: A Medical and Demographic History of Slavery in the British West Indies 1680–1834* (1985), p. 255.
41 Checkland, *The Gladstones: Family Biography (1761–1851)* (1971), p. 199.
42 Checkland, *The Gladstones: Family Biography (1761–1851)* (1971), p. 200.
43 Sheridan, *Doctors and Slaves: A Medical and Demographic History of Slavery in the British West Indies 1680–1834* (1985), p. 257.
44 McDonnell, *Considerations of Negro Slavery* (1824), p. 248.
45 Sheridan, *Doctors and Slaves: A Medical and Demographic History of Slavery in the British West Indies 1680–1834* (1985), p. 260.
46 Buxton, *Memoirs of Sir Thomas Fowell Buxton* (1850), p. 267.
47 Oldfield, 'Zachary Macaulay', www.oxforddnb.com (2009), accessed 11 August 2012.
48 Whyte, *Scotland and the Abolition of Black Slavery 1756–1838* (2007), p. 123.
49 Wolffe, 'The Clapham Sect', www.oxforddnb.com (2008), accessed 11 August 2021.
50 Whyte, *Scotland and the Abolition of Black Slavery 1756–1838* (2007), pp. 125–126.
51 Oldfield, 'Zachary Macaulay', www.oxforddnb.com (2009), accessed 11 August 2012.
52 Whyte, *Scotland and the Abolition of Black Slavery 1756–1838* (2007), pp. 125–127.

53 Oldfield, 'Zachary Macaulay', www.oxforddnb.com (2009), accessed 11 August 2012.
54 Among these accounts were those of Sancho's *Letters* of 1782, Cugoano's *Thoughts and Sentiments* of 1787, and Equiano's *Narrative* of 1789. See Walvin, *A Short History of Slavery* (2007), p. 198.
55 By the late 1820s, the print-run of the *Anti-Slavery Reporter* had risen to 20,000, which does not account for groups, committees and organisations which borrowed copies.
56 Whyte, *Scotland and the Abolition of Black Slavery 1756–1838* (2007), p. 127.
57 Walvin, *A Short History of Slavery* (2007), p. 207.
58 Walvin, *England, Slaves and Freedom 1776–1838* (1986), p. 145.
59 Walvin, *A Short History of Slavery* (2007), pp. 210–211.
60 The Reform Act of 1832 disenfranchised fifty-six boroughs in England and Wales and reduced another to having only one MP. It created a uniform franchise in the boroughs which gave the vote to some lodgers and to all householders who paid a yearly rent of £10 or more.
61 In 1830, an anonymous pamphlet claimed Brougham to be a defender of slavery. He was quoted as having said that 'Negroes are the enemies to be most dreaded by all Europeans'. See Whyte, *Scotland and the Abolition of Black Slavery 1756–1838* (2007), pp. 130–131.
62 Whyte, *Scotland and the Abolition of Black Slavery 1756–1838* (2007), p. 131.
63 The National Portrait Gallery of Scotland's narrative on the bust of Henry Peter Brougham, 1st baron of Vaux, by John Adams Acton.
64 He was admitted as a member to the Royal Society of Edinburgh in 1803.
65 Lobban, *Henry Brougham, First Baron Brougham of Vaux (1778–1868)* (2021), p. 1.
74 The three other founders were Francis Jeffrey, Francis Horner and Sydney Smith.
66 Lobban, *Henry Brougham, First Baron Brougham of Vaux (1778–1868)* (2021), p. 2.
67 Brougham wrote a pamphlet on the slave trade for the Abolition Committee, which was distributed to all members of the House of Commons in May 1804. William Pitt brandished a copy of it in the first reading of his bill on abolition.
68 Whyte, *Scotland and the Abolition of Black Slavery 1756–1838* (2007), p. 133.
69 Whyte, *Scotland and the Abolition of Black Slavery 1756–1838* (2007), p. 135.
70 Whyte, *Scotland and the Abolition of Black Slavery 1756–1838* (2007), p. 131.
71 In Antigua and Bermuda, plantation owners freed their slaves immediately, deciding it was cheaper for them to pay the slaves a small wage than to feed and house them as slaves.
72 Whyte, *Scotland and the Abolition of Black Slavery 1756–1838* (2007), p. 136.
73 Sheridan, 'The Condition of Slaves on the Sugar Plantations of Sir John Gladstone in the Colony of Demerara (1812–1832)', *New West Indian Guide* (2002), Vol. 76, No. 3/4, pp. 263–266.
74 Matthew, 'Sir John Gladstone (Gladstones) 1764–1851', www.oxforddnb.com (2016), accessed 9 April 2021.
75 Gladstone and others build a Scottish church and school in Oldham Street, Liverpool. In 1815, he founded both St Andrew's Episcopal church in Renshaw Street and St Thomas's church in Toxteth.

Chapter 14

1. The Underground Railroad was a network of people, African American as well as white, offering shelter and aid to escaped enslaved people from the South. It developed as a convergence of several different clandestine efforts. The exact dates of its existence are not known, but it operated from the late eighteenth century to the Civil War, at which point its efforts continued to undermine the Confederacy in a less-secretive fashion.
2. The Declaration of the Thirteen United States of America, passed by Congress on 4 July 1776, included that 'all men are created equal, that they are endowed by their Creator with certain inalienable Rights, that amongst these are Life, Liberty and the pursuit of happiness....'
3. David Ruggles (1810–1849) was an American journalist who resided in New York and participated in the Underground Railroad.
4. The poem by Sir Walter Scott, published on 8 May 1810, tells of the struggle between King James V and the powerful clan Douglas. It proved a huge success with 25,000 copies sold in eight months, breaking all records for the sale of poetry and spreading Scott's fame beyond Britain to the USA.
5. At the commencement of the American War of Independence in July 1775, Washington excluded the enlistment of black men, free or enslaved. This was supported by all thirteen colonies, where people were concerned by the risk of the men being permanently lost to their owners. The British enlisted some slaves on the guarantee of freedom, causing political disruption in the slave States. In December 1775, Washington began enlisting African Americans into the Continental Army. Finally approved by the Continental Congress, recruiting began towards the end of 1776, although South Carolina refused to participate. With the war lost, the British shipped some 14,000 blacks to Britain, Nova Scotia, Canada, Sierra Leone and elsewhere in West Africa. On the American side, about 5,000 black men were awarded their freedom.
6. Williams, *American Slavery* (2014), pp. 86–87.
7. Williams, *American Slavery* (2014), p. 86.
8. Williams, *American Slavery* (2014), p. 95.
9. Article 1, section 9: 'The Migration or Importation of such Persons as any of the States now existing shall think proper to admit, shall not be prohibited by the Congress prior to the Year one thousand eight hundred and eight....'
10. Williams, *American Slavery* (2014), pp. 94–95.
11. Article 4, section 2 of the Constitutional Convention.
12. Williams, *American Slavery* (2014), p. 96.
13. Free states were Maine, New Hampshire, Massachusetts, Vermont, Rhode Island, Connecticut, New Jersey, New York, Pennsylvania, Ohio, Michigan, Indiana and Illinois.
14. Less than 10,000 people immigrated to Liberia between 1820 and 1856.
15. David Walker (1796–1830), an American writer and abolitionist, was a fierce critic of the American Colonisation Society. His book, *Walker's Appeal*, was published in 1829.
16. Williams, *American Slavery* (2014), p. 99.
17. William Lloyd Garrison (1805–1879), a journalist, was born into poverty in Massachusetts. He embraced the abolition movement after being employed by a Quaker and living with a free black family in Baltimore, Maryland. It was there that he saw slavery in action.
18. Williams, *American Slavery* (2014), pp. 100–101.
19. There is no formal record of the birth date as none was made.

20 Douglass, *Narrative of the Life of Frederick Douglass: An American Slave* (2009), p. 19.
21 The yearly clothing allowance was two coarse linen shirts, one pair of linen trousers, one jacket, one pair of trousers for winter, one pair of stockings and a pair of shoes.
22 Douglass, *Narrative of the Life of Frederick Douglass: An American Slave* (2009), pp. 21–23.
23 Douglass, *Narrative of the Life of Frederick Douglass: An American Slave* (2009), p. 35.
24 The speech was given by Richard Sheridan (1751–1816) in the House of Commons on 3 January 1799.
25 Douglass, *Narrative of the Life of Frederick Douglass: An American Slave* (2009), pp. 39–40.
26 Douglass, *Narrative of the Life of Frederick Douglass: An American Slave* (2009), pp. 46–47.
27 Douglass, *Narrative of the Life of Frederick Douglass: An American Slave* (2009), pp. 54–55.
28 Douglass, *Narrative of the Life of Frederick Douglass: An American Slave* (2009), p. 65.
29 Douglass, *Narrative of the Life of Frederick Douglass: An American Slave* (2009), p. 65.
30 Douglass, *Narrative of the Life of Frederick Douglass: An American Slave* (2009), pp. 75–77.
31 Douglass, *Narrative of the Life of Frederick Douglass: An American Slave* (2009), pp. 70–79.
32 Douglass, *Narrative of the Life of Frederick Douglass: An American Slave* (2009), p. 89.
33 The book was translated into French, Dutch and German.
34 Philpott, 'Frederick Douglass (1818–1895)', www.oxforddnb.com (2020), accessed 28 September 2021.
35 The Westminster Confession of Faith of 1647 asserts the real presence in the sacrament, the supreme authority of God's Word, and the catholicity of the church, made distinctive by three characteristics: true preaching of the Word, the right administration of the sacraments, and discipline.
36 It was defeated by 221 to 76 votes, although in Scottish MPs voted 25 to 12 in favour.
37 *Proceedings of the General Assembly of the Free Church of Scotland at Edinburgh, May 1843* (1853), p. 12.
38 The Deed of Demission, which effected the final break from the Church of Scotland, was signed on 23 May 1845. See Earlsferry, *The Courts, The Church and the Constitution* (2008), p. 1.
39 Out of a total of 1,195 ministers, 474 signed the Deed of Demission from the Church of Scotland on 23 May 1843. See Earlsferry, *The Courts, The Church and the Constitution* (2008), p. 2.
40 Whyte, *Send Back the Money!* (2012), pp. 9–14.
41 Whyte, *Send Back the Money!* (2012), pp. 17–19.
42 Whyte, *Send Back the Money!* (2012), p. 18.
43 The five delegates were William Cunningham, Henry Ferguson, Robert Burns, William Chalmers and George Lewis.
44 The words of delegate George Lewis at the general assembly of the Presbyterian Church on 24 May 1844.
45 Whyte, *Send Back the Money!* (2012), p. 24.

46 The executive committee of the American and Foreign Anti-Slavery Society, which was founded in 1840 by Arthur and Lewis Tappin. The latter was a corresponding member of the Glasgow Emancipation Society.
47 Whyte, *Send Back the Money!* (2012), p. 27.
48 Whyte, *Send Back the Money!* (2012), pp. 26–27 & 33.
49 William Lloyd Garrison (1805–1879) was an American journalist who published *The Liberator* newspaper between 1831 and 1865, helping to lead the campaign for the abolition of slavery in America. Garrison chaired the American Anti-Slavery Society while the Tappan brothers chaired the American and Foreign Anti-Slavery Society.
50 Whyte, *Send Back the Money!* (2012), pp. 40–42.
51 Chalmers envisaged that slaves would buy their freedom through labour, but this would take many decades to achieve. His proposal also assumed that their owners would give them the sufficient time off work to be able to achieve it. See Chalmers, *A Few Thoughts on the Abolition of Colonial Slavery* (1826), and Whyte, *Send Back the Money!* (2012), p. 47.
52 Whyte, *Send Back the Money!* (2012), pp. 51 & 53.
53 Contrary positions were submitted by Dr John Duncan of New College, among others.
54 *Frederick Douglass Papers* (1846), Vol. 1, p. 138.
55 Whyte, *Send Back the Money!* (2012), pp. 71–84.
56 Robert S. Candlish (1806–1873).
57 Whyte, *Send Back the Money!* (2012), pp. 68–69.
58 Whyte, *Send Back the Money!* (2012), pp. 124–125.
59 Whyte, *Send Back the Money!* (2012), pp. 148–149.
60 Preston, *Young Frederick Douglass* (2018), pp. 183–184.
61 Philpott, 'Frederick Douglass (1818–1895)', www.oxforddnb.com (2020), accessed 28 September 2021.

Chapter 15

1 'Freight' was the word used by members of the Underground Railroad, and 'conductors' led their charges by various routes from the South to one of the fourteen Northern states and Canada, stopping over in safe houses or 'stations'.
2 The Underground Railroad operated in the Northern States of the United States of America before the advent of the Civil War through the operation of a network of free black and white abolitionists to enable escaped slaves find safety in either in the North or in Canada. They did so despite the Fugitive Slave Acts of 1793 and 1850, which made such action a criminal offence. It was only in Canada that the slaves were beyond the threat of slave hunters. It is estimated that between 40,000 and 100,000 slaves reached freedom this way. See 'Underground Railroad', www.britannica.com (2021), accessed 9 April 2020.
3 Davenport-Hines, 'Allan Pinkerton, (1819–1884)', www.oxforddnb.com (2008), accessed 22 January 2020.
4 Horan, *The Pinkertons: The Detective Dynasty That Made History* (1967), p. 4.
5 Hutcheson wanted Presbyterianism to present a more forgiving and encouraging face to the world with inspiration replacing fear as the message from the pulpit. A Kirk which sought to engage with the moral questions faced by their parishioners from day to day—to listen rather than to tell. 'Nothing',

according to Hutcheson, 'can change a rational creature into a piece of goods void of all rights.' His lectures, published after his death under the title, *A System of Moral Philosophy*, were an attack on all forms of slavery as well as a denial of any right to govern solely on superior abilities or riches. These sentiments would serve to inspire anti-slavery abolitionists in Scotland, England and North America. It was a vision of a free society.

6. Williams, *American Slavery* (2014), p. 60.
7. Of the Coopers of Glasgow and Suburbs Protective Association.
8. Davenport-Hines, 'Allan Pinkerton, (1819–1884)', www.oxforddnb.com (2008), accessed 22 January 2020.
9. Voting rights had been given to the property-owning middle classes in Britain in 1832, but further political reform was demanded. It found expression through Chartism, a working-class movement emerging in 1836 with the aim of gaining political rights and influence for the working classes. Its six aims were set out in the People's Charter. By 1848 the Chartist movement had failed.
10. Petitions were presented in 1839, 1842 and 1848, but all were ignored by parliament.
11. Extracted from an 1839 editorial in *The London Democrat*.
12. Philo Carpenter (1805–1886) was an abolitionist and the first pharmacist in Chicago. An elder in the First Presbyterian Church until the Civil War when it split over support for North or South, he was leader of the Chicago branch of the Anti-Slavery Society.
13. Later to become one of the most important printers and publishers in the history of the Midwest. See Horan, *The Pinkertons: The Detective Dynasty That Made History* (1967), p. 14.
14. Horan, *The Pinkertons: The Detective Dynasty That Made History* (1967), pp. 19–24.
15. Among these chosen detectives was the first female detective, Mrs Kate Warne, a widow, who infiltrated areas which men could not. She worked for Pinkerton for years 'and never let him down'. See Horan, *The Pinkertons: The Detective Dynasty That Made History* (1967), pp. 24–27.
16. Horan, *The Pinkertons: The Detective Dynasty That Made History* (1967), p. 31.
17. John W. Jones (1817–1900) was born into slavery in Leesburg, Virginia, and escaped on 3 June 1844 to Elmira New York where he received an education. By the 1850s, Jones was highly active on the Underground Railroad. See Ramsdell, 'The John Jones Story', www.johnwjonesmuseum.org (2002), and Reynolds, *John Brown: Abolitionist* (2005), pp. 22–26.
18. Amherst College was founded on 8 May 1821 and Heman Humphrey was appointed president in 1823. By the mid 1830s, it was the second largest college in the United States, behind only Yale. Officially nondenominational, it held strong affiliation to Calvinism.
19. Finkelman, 'A Look Back at John Brown', *Prologue Magazine* (2011), Vol. 43, No. 1, p. 4.
20. Reynolds, *John Brown: Abolitionist* (2005), pp. 56 & 59.
21. This was effected under the Slave Fugitive Act of 1793, which was enforced under article IV, section 2 of the US constitution. The legislation was strengthened by the Fugitive Slave Act of 1850, which served to further polarise opinion and increase the number of abolitionists. Both acts were repealed on 28 June 1864.
22. Later in 1851, Brown assisted the founding of the League of Gileadites, a mixed-race group that sought to protect fugitive slaves from slave catchers.

23 Reynolds, *John Brown: Abolitionist* (2005), p. 65.
24 Reynolds, *John Brown: Abolitionist* (2005), pp. 143–144.
25 Upon Maine's separation from Massachusetts.
26 Williams, *American Slavery* (2014), p. 104.
27 Louisiana in 1803; Florida in 1817; Maine in 1820; and land from Mexico in 1849.
28 In the event, New Mexico and Utah enacted slave codes, technically making slavery within these territories possible.
29 Under the Fugitive Slavery Act of 1850, the accused had no right to testify in their defence and the magistrate could order the alleged fugitive to be returned to slavery based only on the evidence of the alleged owner. Finally, any person who harboured or concealed a fugitive could be punished by law. See Williams, *American Slavery* (2014), pp. 104–106.
30 'Compromise of 1850', www.britannica.com (2021), accessed 5 January 2022.
31 Williams, *American Slavery* (2014), pp. 106–107.
32 Reynolds, *John Brown: Abolitionist* (2005), p. 132.
33 For their journey they took eight cattle, three horses and some belongings.
34 In response to the Fugitive Slave Act of 1850, Brown had converted his wool warehouse into a 'station' for fugitives.
35 New York author Richard Dana observed this when, by chance, he stumbled upon Brown's cabin in June 1849 in the forests near North Elba. See Reynolds, *John Brown: Abolitionist* (2005), pp. 127–128.
36 Many of this group were passing through town on the Underground Railroad.
37 Reynolds, *John Brown: Abolitionist* (2005), p. 122.
38 Reynolds, *John Brown: Abolitionist* (2005), p. 124.
39 Reynolds, *John Brown: Abolitionist* (2005), p. 135.
40 The funds for the arms (only $60) were raised by Brown at a convention of reformers known as the Radical Political Abolitionists in Syracuse on 28 June 1855.
41 Reynolds, *John Brown: Abolitionist* (2005), pp. 150–156.
42 The capital city in Shaunee County, Kansas.
43 Finkelman, 'A Look Back at John Brown', *Prologue Magazine* (2011), Vol. 43, No. 1, p. 4.
44 Reynolds, *John Brown: Abolitionist* (2005), p. 163.
45 Reverend Thomas Wentworth Higginson, Theodore Parker, George Stearns, Samuel Gridley Howe, Frank Sanborn and Gerrit Smith.
46 Aaron D. Stevens (1831–1860), an abolitionist, was executed in Charlestown, Virginia, aged twenty-nine, following the failed Harpers Ferry raid. He was convinced to the end that the raid had been just. The eleven slaves increased to twelve in number following a birth on the trail.
47 A sum matched by the Missouri legislature.
48 The wife of the 'Free Negro' John Jones with whom Brown stayed, described Brown's greeting of Pinkerton as 'warmly, more than that, brother to brother'.
49 *Chicago Times*, 1 September 1882.
50 A reference to how prices would rise once his militant activities took effect. See 'John Brown', *Chicago Tribune*, 1 September 1882.
51 Lewis, 'Pinkerton and Lincoln', *Illinois Historical Journal* (1948), p. 376.
52 Horan, *The Pinkertons: The Detective Dynasty That Made History* (1967).
53 Bronson Alcott (1799–1888), a philosopher, reformer and teacher, was described as 'a venerable Don Quixote'.
54 Horan, *The Pinkertons: The Detective Dynasty That Made History* (1967), p. 42.
55 Mackay, *Allan Pinkerton* (1996), p. 94.

56 Among the officers and soldiers present at Brown's execution were General Stonewall Jackson (1824–1863), who was to fight for the Confederates in the Civil War, and John Wilkes Booth (1838–1865), who assassinated President Lincoln.
57 Mackay, *Allan Pinkerton* (1996), p. 85.
58 Finkelman, 'A Look Back at John Brown', *Prologue Magazine* (2011), Vol. 43, No. 1, p. 6.
59 Reynolds, *John Brown: Abolitionist* (2005), p. 314.
60 Reynolds, *John Brown: Abolitionist* (2005), p. 300.
61 Reynolds, *John Brown: Abolitionist* (2005), p. ix.
62 Mississippi, Florida, Alabama, Georgia, Louisiana and Texas.
63 Virginia, North Carolina, Arkansas and Tennessee.
64 'Neither slavery nor involuntary servitude, except as a punishment for crime whereof the party shall have been duly convicted, shall exist within the United States, or any place subject to their jurisdiction.' See Williams, *American Slavery* (2014), pp. 108–114.
65 Horan, *The Pinkertons: The Detective Dynasty That Made History* (1967), p. 49.
66 'John Brown', *Chicago Tribune*, 1 September 1882.
67 'John Brown's Body' was written in 1861 by Stephen Vincent Benet.

CONCLUSION

1 Sacks, *Morality* (2021), pp. 124–125.
2 Sacks, *Morality* (2021), p. 90.
3 Norman, *Adam Smith: What He Thought and Why It Matters* (2018), pp. 209–211.
4 Smith, *The Theory of Moral Sentiments* (2002), pp. 241–242.
5 Williams, *Capitalism and Slavery* (1943), p. 32.
6 Sacks, *Morality* (2021), pp. 322–323.
7 Sacks, *Morality* (2021), p. 322.

Bibliography

Manuscript Sources

Parliamentary papers
Abolition of Slavery Act 1833, 3 & 4 William 4 c.73, www.statutes.org.uk
Home Office Papers, 42/196, BC, 6 October 1819, National Archives

Letters in archives
'Fanny Wright to Frances Campbell, 1820', Theresa Wolfson Papers, Martin P. Catherwood Library, Cornell University
'Frances Wright letter to Lafayette, 27 December 1821', MSS. 304, University of Chicago
'George III, letter to Lord Stormont, dated 26 July 1781', Mansfield Papers, Scone Palace
'Grant, Alexander, to Sir Archibald, 1 January 1750', National Records of Scotland, GD345/1160/31
'Irving, James, a letter to Mary, his wife in Liverpool on 19 May 1786', Lancashire Records Office
'Irving, James, a letter to Mary, his wife dated 25 January 1791 from Cumbria', Lancashire Records Office
'Lord Holdernesse to Andrew Mitchell, 17 September 1756', Add. Ms 6832, fol. 90, British Library
'Matra, James M., Consul General at Tangier, a letter to William W. Grenville at the Secretary of State's Office in London from Tangiers dated 21 July 1789', Public Records Office, FO 174/284
'William Wilberforce to Eden, 23 November 1789', Auckland Papers, 34227 f.123, British Museum

Legal reports
Douglas, Sylvester, 'Gregson v Gilbert 1783', *Douglas' King's Bench Reports*, Vol. 3, (London: His Majesty's Law Printers, 1783)
Lofft, Capel, 'Somerset against Stewart, May 14, 1772', Trinity Term, 12 Geo. 3, *Reports of Cases Adjudged in the Court of the King's Bench* (Dublin: James Moore, 1772)

MacConachie, Alan, 'Information for Joseph Knight against John Wedderburn dated April 25, 1775', SP M6:47, Signet Library

McLaurin, John, 'Additional Information for Joseph Knight against John Wedderburn, April 20 1776', SP M6:47, Signet Library

Unpublished dissertations

Hamilton, Douglas J., *Patronage and Profit: Scottish Networks in the British West Indies, c. 1763–1807*, Aberdeen University, 1999

PUBLISHED ARTICLES AND DOCUMENTS

In newspapers and magazines

'Extracts from the report of the Nashoba Trustees', *New Harmony Gazette*, November 1828

'John Brown', *Chicago Tribune*, 1 September 1882

'John Lindsay Obituary', *London Chronicle*, 7 June 1788

'Kidnapping – Peter Williamsons' Case', *Blackwood's Magazine*, May 1848

'Report of Henry Dundas' speech in the case of Knight v Wedderburn', *Caledonian Mercury*, No. 8573, 21 February 1776

'Sympathy Letter', *The Public Advertiser*, 7 July 1788

Wright, Frances, 'Establishment for the Abolition of Slavery', *Genius of Universal Emancipation*, 24 February 1827

Wright, Frances, 'Explanatory Notes Respecting the Nature and Objects of the Institution of Nashoba', *Genius of Universal Emancipation*, 23 February 1828

In journals

'Africa and the Eighteenth-Century Slave Trade to America: The Years of Decline 1746–1769', *Bristol Records Society Publication*, Vol. XLII, 1991

Bederman, Gail, 'Revisiting: Nashoba, Slavery, Utopia', *American Literary History*, Vol. 17, No. 3, 2005

Behrendt, Stephen D., 'The Captains in the Slave Trade from 1785 to 1807', *The Historic Society of Liverpool and Cheshire*, Vol. 140, 1991

Burnard, Trevor, '"The Countrie Continues Sicklie": White Mortality in Jamaica 1655–1780', *Social History of Medicine*, Vol. 2, No. 1, April 1999

Burnard, Trevor, and Richard Follett, 'Caribbean Slavery, British Anti-Slavery, and the Cultural Politics of Venereal Disease', *The Historical Journal*, Vol. 55, 2012

Cairns, John W., 'After Somerset: The Scottish Experience', *Journal of Legal History*, Vol. 33, No. 3, 2012

Carr, Daniel J., 'Principles of Equity: Lord Kames', *Old Studies of Scots Law*, Vol. 4, 2013

'Deed of Trust by Frances Wright of Nashoba to General Lafayette and nine other trustees dated 17 December 1826', *Oriental Herald and Journal of Literature* (London: W. Lewes, 1826)

Elliot, Helen, 'Frances Wright's Experiment with Negro Emancipation', *Indiana Magazine of History*, Vol. 35, No. 2, June 1939

Finkelman, Paul, 'A Look Back at John Brown', *Prologue Magazine*, Vol. 43, No. 1, Spring 2011

Hancock, David, 'Domestic Bubbling', *The Economic History Review*, November 1994

Lewis, Lloyd, 'Pinkerton and Lincoln', *Illinois Historical Journal*, 1948

McMaster, Rowland, '"I hate to hear of Women on Board": Women aboard War Ships', *Jane Austen Society of North America*, Vol. 36, No. 1, Winter 2015

Bibliography

Mullen, S., 'Henry Dundas: A "Great Delayer" of the Abolition of the Transatlantic Slave Trade', *Scottish Historical Review*, 7 May 2021

Murison, W., 'Peter Williamson, Vintner, from the Other World', *The Deeside Field*, No. 5, 1930

Nisbet, Stuart M., 'Early Glasgow Sugar Plantations in the Caribbean', *Scottish Archaeological Journal*, Vol. 1, No. 1, 2009

Parks, Winfield, 'Dreamers' Vision Frances Wright at Nashoba (1825–1830)', *Tennessee Historical Magazine*, Series 2, Vol. 2, No. 2, January 1932

'Peter Williamson "Indian Peter"', *Scottish Notes and Queries*, Vol. 13 (Aberdeen: John Avery & Company, 1935)

Rupprecht, Anita, 'A Very Uncommon Case', *Journal of Legal History*, 2007

Schofield, M. M., 'Slave Trade from the Lancashire and Cheshire Ports Outside Liverpool c. 1750–c. 1790', *The Historic Society of Lancashire and Cheshire*, Vol. 126, 1977

Sheridan, R. B., 'The Condition of Slaves on the Sugar Plantations of Sir John Gladstone in the Colony of Demerara (1812–1832)', *New West Indian Guide*, Vol. 76, No. 3/4, 2002

'Speech of Drake, William, 18 April 1788', *The Parliamentary Register*, Vol. 23, p. 470 (London: James Debrett, 1788)

Syrett, D., 'Siege and Capture of Havana 1762', *Navy Records Society*, Vol. 114, 1970

Usherwood, Stephen, 'The Abolitionists' Debt to Lord Mansfield', *History Today*, Vol. 31, No. 3, March 1981

Weiner, Mark S., 'New Biographical Evidence in the Somerset Case', *Journal of Legal History*, Vol. 33, No. 3, 2012

Zehedieh, Nuala, Eric Williams and William Forbes, 'Copper, Colonial Markets, and Commercial Capitalism', *The Economic History Review*, No. 74, 2021

On websites

Brain, Jessica, 'The Abolition of Slavery in Britain', www.historic-uk.com, 12 June 2019

Dickinson, H. T, 'William Dickson (1751–1823)', www.oxforddnb.com, 6 October 2016

Fry, Michael, 'Henry Dundas, First Viscount Melville', www.oxforddnb.com, 8 April 2021

Hancock, David, 'Richard Oswald', www.oxforddnb.com, 3 January 2008

Heineman, Helen, 'Frances Wright', www.oxforddnb.com, 24 May 2008

Kane, Kathryn, 'Cultural Rules for Dining in 18th Century, England and Mealtimes in the Regency Day', www.regencyredingote.wordpress.com, 2019

King, Reyhan, 'Belle, Dido Elizabeth', www.oxforddnb.com, 8 October 2020

Laughton, J. K. (revised by Clive Wilkinson), 'Sir John Lindsay', www.oxforddnb.com, 4 October 2007

Major, Joanne, 'Dido Elizabeth Belle – New information about her siblings', www.georgianera.wordpress.com, 2018

Matthew, H. C. G., 'Sir John Gladstone (Gladstones) 1764–1851', www.oxforddnb.com, 7 January 2016

Momodu, Samuel, 'The Baptist War (1831–1832)', www.blackpast.org, 2017

Morris, Roger, 'Charles Middleton, 1st Baron Barham (1726–1813)', www.oxforddnb.com, 2008

Mullen, Stephen, 'Scots & Caribbean Slavery – Victims and Profiteers', www.glasgowwestindies.wordpress.com, 2015

Oldfield, J. R., 'Zachary Macaulay', www.oxforddnb.com, 21 May 2009

Oldham, James, 'William Murray, 1st Earl of Mansfield', www.oxforddnb.com, 4 October 2008
Pencak, William, 'Thomas Hutchinson', www.oxforddnb.com, 23 September 2004
Philpott, Terry, 'Frederick Douglass (1818–1895)', www.oxforddnb.com, 8 October 2020
Power, Cathy and Sarah Murden, 'Kenwood', www.georgianera.wordpress.com, 2019
Ramsdell, Barbara S., 'The John Jones Story', www.johnwjonesmuseum.org, 2002
Sankey, Margaret D., 'Sir John Wedderburn, 5th baronet (1704–1746), www.oxforddnb.com, 25 May 2006
Scott-Murray, H. M., 'David, 7th Viscount Stormont and 2nd Earl of Mansfield (1727–1796), www.oxforddnb.com, 3 January, 2008
Watt, J., 'James Ramsay', www.oxforddnb.com, 25 May 2006
Wolffe, John, 'The Clapham Sect', www.oxforddnb.com, 24 May 2008

BOOKS

Allan, David, *Scotland in the Eighteenth Century* (London: Pearson Education Limited, 2002)
Aubrey, Thomas, *The Sea Surgeon, or the Guinea Man's Vade Mecum* (1729)
Beatson, R., *Naval and Military Memoirs of Great Britain*, 3 vols, (London: J. Strachan, 1790)
Beattie, James, *An Essay on the Nature and Immutability of Truth* (Edinburgh: William Creech, 1778)
Blight, David W., *Frederick Blight: Profit of Freedom* (London: Simon & Schuster, 2018)
Boswell, James, *The Life of Samuel Johnston* (London: James Blackwood & Co., 1884)
Bryant, Joshua, *Account of an Insurrection of the Negro Slaves in the Colony of Demerara* (Georgetown: A. Stevenson, 1824)
Bryson, Alexander, *Report on the Climate and Principal Diseases of the African Station* (London: William Clownes and Sons, 1847)
Burnard, Trevor, *Master, Tyranny, and Desire* (Kingston: University of the West Indies Press, 2004)
Buxton, Charles, *Memoirs of Sir Thomas Fowell Buxton* (London: John Murray, 1855)
Byrne, Paula, *Belle: The Slave Daughter and the Lord Chief Justice* (London: Harper Perennial, 2014)
Campbell, Lord John, *The Lives of the Chief Justices of England*, Vol. 2 (Philadelphia: Blanchard & Lea, 1853)
Chalmers, Thomas, *A Few Thoughts on the Abolition of Colonial Slavery* (Edinburgh: William Whyte & Co., 1826)
Chalus, Elaine, *Elite Women in English Political Life 1754–1790* (Oxford: Oxford University Press, 2005)
Charteris, Richard, earl of Wemyss and March, *Memories*, Vol. 1 (Edinburgh: David Douglas, 1912)
Checkland, S. G., *Scottish Banking: A History 1695–1973* (Glasgow: Collins, 1975)
Checkland, S. G., *The Gladstones: Family Biography (1761–1851)* (Cambridge: Cambridge University Press, 1971)
Cook, James Wyatt, and Barbara Collier Cook, *Male-Midwife, Male Feminist: The Life and Times of George Macaulay M.D, Ph.D* (Michigan: Michigan Publishing, 2006)

Craton, Michael, *Proto-Peasant Revolts? The Late Rebellions in the British West Indies 1816–1832* (Oxford: Oxford University Press, 1979)

Craton, Michael, *Testing the Chains: Resistance to Slavery in the British West Indies* (New York: Cornell University, 1982)

Creech, William, *Preliminary Discourse Concerning the Origins of Men and of Languages: Sketch I* (London: A. Strachan and T. Cadell, 1788)

Davis, David Brion, *The Problem of Slavery in the Age of Revolution* (Oxford: Oxford University Press, 1999)

Devine, T. M., *Recovering Scotland's Slavery Past* (Edinburgh: Edinburgh University Press, 2015)

Devine, T. M., *Scotland's Empire* (London: Penguin Books, 2003)

Devine, T. M., *The Scottish Nation* (London: Penguin Books, 1999)

Devine, T. M., *The Tobacco Lords: A Study of their Activities c. 1740–1790* (Edinburgh: John Donald, 1975)

Dobson, David, *Scottish Emigration to Colonial America 1607–1785* (Georgia: Athens, 1994)

Donnan, Elizabeth, *Documents Illustrative of the History of the Slave Trade to America*, Vol. 2 (Washington: Carnegie Institution of Washington, 1931)

Doran, Dr, *London in the Jacobite Times* (London: Richard Bentley & Son, 1877)

Douglass, Frederick, *Narrative of the Life of Frederick Douglass: An American Slave* (originally published 1845) (Oxford: Oxford University Press, 2009)

Drescher, Seymour, *Abolition: A History of Slavery and Antislavery* (Cambridge: Cambridge University Press, 2009)

Drescher, Seymour, *Capitalism and Antislavery* (Oxford: Oxford University Press, 1987)

Earlsferry, Rodger of, *The Courts, The Church and the Constitution* (Edinburgh: Edinburgh University Press, 2008)

Ehrman, John, *The Younger Pitt: The Years of Acclaim* (London: Constable, 2004)

Falconbridge, Alexander, *An Account of the Slave Trade on the Coast of Africa* (London: J. Phillips, 1788)

Flander, Judith, *The Victorian City* (London: Atlantic Books, 2012)

Forbes, William, *A Journal of the Session Containing the Decisions of the Lords of Council and Session, in the Most Important Cases, Heard and Determin'd from February 1705, till November 1713* (Edinburgh: printed by the author, 1714)

Forbes Gray, W., *Some Old Scots Judges* (London: Constable & Co, 1914)

Foss, Edward, *The Biographical Dictionary of the Justices of England (1066–1870)* (London: Spottiswoode and Company, 1870)

Fry, Michael, *The Dundas Despotism* (Edinburgh: John Donald, 1992)

Fuertado, W. A., *Official and Other Personages of Jamaica from 1655 to 1790* (Kingston: 1896)

Gatrell, Vic, *City of Laughter* (London: Atlantic Books, 2006)

Gøbel, Erik, *The Danish Edict of 16th March 1792 to Abolish the Slave Trade* (St Croix: Antilles Press, 2009)

Gould, Stephen Jay, *Questioning the Millennium: A Rationalist's Guide to a Precisely Arbitrary Countdown* (New York: Harmony Books, 1997)

Graham, Eric, *The Scots Penetration of the Jamaica Plantation Business: Recovering Scotland's Slavery Past* (Edinburgh: Edinburgh University Press, 2015)

Graham, Henry G., *Scottish Men of Letters in the Eighteenth Century* (London: Adam and Charles Black, 1908)

Graham, Henry G., *The Social Life of Scotland in the Eighteenth-Century*, Vol. 1 (London: Adam and Charles Black, 1899)

Haakaonssen, Knud (ed.), *Principles of Equity by Henry Home, Lord Kames* (Indiananapolis: Liberty Fund, 2014)

Haar, C. M., *White Indentured Servants in Colonial New York' Americans* (New York: Encylopedia Americana, 1940)

Hall, Douglas, *In Miserable Slavery: Thomas Thistlewood in Jamaica* (Kingston: University of the West Indies, 1999)

Hamilton, Douglas J., *Scotland, the Caribbean and the Atlantic World 1750–1820* (Manchester: Manchester University Press, 2005)

Hancock, David, *Citizens of the World: London Merchants and the Integration of the British Atlantic Community* (Cambridge: Cambridge University Press, 1995)

Herman, Arthur, *The Scottish Enlightenment* (London: Fourth Estate, 2001)

Heward, Edmund, *Lord Mansfield* (Chichester and London: Barry Rose, 1979)

Hoare, Prince, *Memoirs of Granville Sharp, Esq* (Online: Forgotten Books, 2012)

Home, Henry, (Lord Kames), *Progress of Men Independent of Society: Sketches of the History of Man*, Vol. 1 (Edinburgh: R. Bell, 1778)

Home, Henry, (Lord Kames), *The Gentleman Farmer* (originally published 1776) (Online: Forgotten Books, 1998)

Horan, James D., *The Pinkertons: The Detective Dynasty That Made History* (New York: Bonanza Books, 1967)

Houston, Rab, *Scotland, A Very Short Introduction* (Oxford: Oxford University Press, 2008)

Hunt, Gaillard (ed.), *The Writings of James Madison* (New York: G. P. Puttnam's Sons, 1910)

Hutcheson, Francis, *A System of Moral Philosophy*, Vol. 3 (London: Francis Hutchison, 1755)

Hutchinson, Thomas, *The Diary and Letters of his Excellency Thomas Hutchinson 1886* (Online: Forgotten Books, 2015)

Jakobsson, Stiy, *Am I Not a Man and a Brother? British Missions and the Abolition of the Slave Trade and Slavery in the West Indies 1786–1834* (Cambridge: Cambridge University Press, 2009)

Karras, Alan L., *Sojourners in the Sun: Scottish Migrants in Jamaica and Chesapeake, 1740–1800* (New York: Ithaca, 1992)

Lauber, A. W., *Indian Slavery in Colonial Times with the Present Limits of the United States* (New York: Columbia University, 1913)

Leslie, Charles, *History of Jamaica* (London: J. Hodges, 1740)

Lobban, Michael, *Henry Brougham, First Baron Brougham of Vaux (1778–1868)* (Oxford: Oxford University Press, 2021)

Locke, John, *Two Treatises of Government* (London: E. P. Dutton and Co., 1943)

Mackay, James, *Allan Pinkerton* (Edinburgh: Mainstream Publishing, 1996)

Marston, Daniel, *The French-Indian War 1754–1760* (Oxford: Osprey Publishing, 2002)

Mason, Fergus, *Dido Elizabeth Belle* (South Carolina: CreateSpace Independent Publishing, 2014)

Massie, Allan, *Glasgow: Portraits of a City* (London: Barrie & Jenkins, 1989)

Matheson, Cyril, *The Life of Henry Dundas 1742–1811* (London: Constable & Co., 1933)

McCahill, Michael, *The Correspondence of Stephen Fuller 1788–1795: Jamaica, The West Indies Interest at Westminster and the Campaign to Preserve the Slave Trade* (Oxford: Wiley, 2014)

McCalman, Iain, *Radical Underworld: Prophets, Revolutionaries and Pornographers 1745–1840* (Oxford: Oxford University Press, 2002)

McCalman, Iain, *Robert Wedderburn: The Horrors of Slavery* (Princeton: Markus Weiner, 1991)

McCalman, Iain (ed.), *The Horrors of Slavery and Other Writings by Robert Wedderburn* (Princeton: Markus Weiner, 2017)

McDonnell, Alexander, *Considerations of Negro Slavery* (London: Longman, Hurst, Rees, Orme, Browne and Green, 1824)
Morgan, Philip D., *The Black Experience in the British Empire 1680–1810* (Oxford: P. J. Marshal, 1998)
Morison, William Maxwell, *The Decisions of the Court of Session* (Edinburgh: Bell and Bradfute, 1801)
Morris, Celia, *Fanny Wright: Rebel in America* (Chicago: University of Illinois Press, 1992)
Mullen, Stephen, *It Wisnae Us: The Truth About Glasgow and Slavery* (Edinburgh: The Royal Incorporation of Architects in Scotland, 2009)
Norman, Jesse, *Adam Smith: What He Thought and Why It Matters* (London: Penguin Random House, 2018)
Odadike, Don C., *The Ekumeku Movement: Western Igbo Resistance to the British Conquest of Nigeria, 1883–1914* (Ohio: Ohio University Press, 1991)
Oldham, James, *The Mansfield Manuscripts and the Growth of English Law*, Vol. 2 (London: University of North Carolina Press, 1992)
Oliver, Neil, *A History of Scotland* (London: Phoenix, 2010)
Owen, Robert, *Observations on the Effect of the Manufacturing System* (London: Everyman's Library, 1963)
Palmer, Geoffrey, *Enlightenment Abolished* (Edinburgh, Henry Publishing, 2007)
Place, Francis, *The Autobiography of Francis Place* (Cambridge: Mary Thale, 1972)
Poser, Norman S., *Lord Mansfield: Justice in the Age of Reason* (McGill: Queen's University Press, 2013)
Preston, Dickson J., *Young Frederick Douglass* (Baltimore: John Hopkins University Press, 2018)
Ramsay, James, *An Essay on the Treatment of Conversion of African Slaves in the British Sugar Colonies* (originally published 1784) (Cambridge: Cambridge University Press, 2014)
Reynolds, David S., *John Brown: Abolitionist* (New York: Vintage Books, 2005)
Richardson, David, *Liverpool and Transatlantic Slavery* (London: University Press, 2007)
Robertson, James, *The Book of Bon Accord* (Edinburgh: Lewis Smith, 1839)
Robinson, Samuel, *A Sailor Boy's Experience Aboard a Slave Ship* (London: Hamilton, 1867)
Rodger, N. A. M., *The Wooden World* (London: Fontana Press, 1988)
Roughead, William, *The Fatal Countess and Other Studies* (Edinburgh: W. Green & Son, 1924)
Sacks, Jonathan, *Morality* (London: Hodder & Stoughton, 2021)
Schaw, Janet and E. W. Andrews, *Journal of a Lady of Quality: Being the Narrative of a Journey from Scotland to the West Indies, North Carolina, and Portugal, in the Years 1774 to 1776* (Connecticut: Yale University Press, 1921)
Seale, William, *A White House of Stone* (Washington: The White House Historical Association, 2017)
Schwarz, Suzanne (ed.), *Slave Captain: The Career of James Irving in the Liverpool Slave Trade* (Wrexham: Bridge Books, 1995)
Scott, W. R., *Francis Hutcheson* (Cambridge: Cambridge University Press, 1900)
Sheridan, Richard, *Doctors and Slaves: A Medical and Demographic History of Slavery in the British West Indies 1680–1834* (Cambridge: Cambridge University Press, 1985)
Shyllon, Follarin, *Black Slaves in Britain* (Oxford: Oxford University Press, 1974)
Shyllon, Follarin, *James Ramsay: The Unknown Abolitionist* (Edinburgh: Canongate, 1977)

Skelton, Douglas, *Indian Peter* (Edinburgh: Mainstream Publishing Company, 2004)
Smith, Adam, *An Inquiry into the Nature and Causes of the Wealth of Nations*, Vol. 1 (Edinburgh: Thomas Nelson, 1776)
Smith, Adam, *The Theory of Moral Sentiments* (Cambridge: Cambridge University Press, 2002)
Smout, T. C., *A History of the Scottish People 1560–1830* (London: Fontana Press, 1985)
Stark, Suzanne J., *Female Tars: Women Aboard Ship in the Age of Sail* (Annapolis: Naval Institute, 1996)
Stewart, Robert, *Henry Brougham 1778–1868: His Public Career* (London: The Bodley Head, 1986)
Sypher, W., *Guinea's Captive Kings* (Chapel Hill: University of North Carolina Press, 1942)
Trollope, Mrs Frances, *Domestic Manners of the Americans* (London: Treacher & Co., 1832)
Walvin, James, *A Short History of Slavery* (London: Penguin Books, 2007)
Walvin, James, *England, Slaves and Freedom 1776–1838* (London: Palgrave Macmillan, 1986)
Walvin, James, *The Zong* (Connecticut: Yale University Press, 2011)c
Warner-Lewis, Maureen, *Archibald Monteath* (Jamaica: University of the West Indies Press, 2007)
Wedderburn, Alexander, *The Wedderburn Book* (published privately, 1896)
White, Jerry, *London in the Eighteenth Century* (London: The Bodley Head, 2012)
Whyte, Iain, *Evangelism in Jamaica, Theology in Scotland: Scotland and the Abolition of Slavery 1756–1838* (Edinburgh: Edinburgh University Press, 2006)
Whyte, Iain, *Scotland and the Abolition of Black Slavery 1756–1838* (Edinburgh: Edinburgh University Press, 2007)
Whyte, Iain, *Send Back the Money!* (Cambridge: James Clarke & Co., 2012)
Wilberforce, Robert Isaac, *The Life of William Wilberforce*, Vol. 1 (Online: Forgotten Books, 2012)
Williams, Eric, *Capitalism and Slavery* (Chapel Hill: The University of North Carolina Press, 1943)
Williams, Heather Andrea, *American Slavery* (Oxford: Oxford University Press, 2014)
Williamson, Peter, *The Life and Curious Adventures of Peter Williamson* (York: J. Jackson Peter Gate, 1758)
Wright, Frances, *Biography, Notes, and Political Letters of Frances Wright D'Arusmont* (Nabu Press, 2011)
Wright, Frances, *Views of Society and Manners in America* (London: Longmont, Hurst, Rees, Orme and Brown, 1822)

WEBSITES (GENERAL)

Economic History Association: www.eh.net
Encyclopaedia Britannica: www.britannica.com
English Heritage: www.english-heritage.org.uk
National Archives online: www.archives.gov
Oxford Dictionary of National Biography: www.oxforddnb.com
The Dear Surprise: www.thedearsurprise.com
Trans-Atlantic Slave Trade Database: www.slavervoyages.org

Index

Aberdeenshire, indentured labour for US 82–3
abolition movement 43, 46, 66, 70, 77, 137, 148ff, 196, 208
   abolition in parliament 159ff, 208
   abolitionists and 1832 election 209
   growth of 144, 150
   measure passed 11
   parliamentary debate 147
   petitioning campaign 210
   post Napoleonic Wars 197, 198
   Reverend Smith case 210
   women and 151, 208
   see also various legislation
Act of Setting Schools (1696) 17
Act of Union (1707) 19, 20, 23, 32, 137, 163, 224
Adams, John 89
African Trade Act (1750) 174
'Age of Improvement' 175–6
Agency Committee 208
Akan people 100, 102
Akers, Rebecca 136
'amelioration ordinance' Demerara 203
American Civil War 214, 231, 241, 249–50
American colonies 41, 47, 64, 102, 165, 167, 171, 173, 178
   impact of Somerset case 47, 148
   Scottish settlers in 165–6
   see also American War of Independence

American Colonisation Society 185, 217
American War of Independence 47, 76, 105, 106, 134, 147, 154, 155, 161, 172, 175, 241
   and position of blacks in US 182–3
   Somerset *v.* Stewart (1772) 40, 44–5, 47, 66, 109, 169, 183, 254
   Fanny Wright 178, 183
   slavery 215
American War of 1812 199
Amity (ship) 178
Anglo-French Wars 49, 86–7, 116, 118, 160
Anglo-Dutch Slave Trade Treaty 102
Anne, Queen 25
Anna (ship) 123ff, 207
Anthony, Captain 218, 219, 220
Anthony, Hugh 220
Anthony, Lucretia 219
Anthony, Richard 220
anti-slavery lobby 42, 46, 133
Anti-Slavery Reporter 207–8
Anti-Slavery Society 207
'Apprenticeship System' 211
Arundel, HMS 131, 133, 134, 135
Associates (Scottish group) 171–2, 176, 176–7
Auchinleck, Lord 61, 69
Augustus III, king of Poland and elector of Saxony 52
Auld, Hugh 219–20, 221, 222–3, 224
Auld, Mrs 219–20, 222
Auld, Thomas 221, 232

Babington, Thomas and Jean 206
Bailey, Frederick Augustus Washington 214
  changes name to Frederick Douglass 215
Bailey, Harriet 217
Bailie William Fordyce & Co. 94
Bank of Scotland 19
Baptist War (Montego Bay) 109, 110, 209
Barbados, slave revolts 197
Barbary Coast and pirates 126, 128
Barrington, Admiral 142
Bayley's Estate, Barbados 197
Beattie, James 43, 135
Beecher, Catherine 194
Bell, John 92
Belle (Bell), Maria 49, 50, 51, 52, 55, 58
Benezet, Anthony 148–9
Benin 98, 100–1, Bight of 103, 130
Berargaard, Henrietta Frederica de 52
Bible and slavery 7–8
Bible Society 202
Bilade 127
Black Lives Matter 255
bloody flux (dysentery) 115, 118, 132
Bonny, Bight of Benin 125, 131
Boswell, James 69, 153
Botto, Carlo 178, 180
Boyd, Augustus 171, 173
Boyd, John 173
Boyer, President Jean Pierre 185, 193–4
Boyne, battle of the 224
Bradshaw, Jackson 198
Brahim, Sheikh 127, 128, 129
Braxfield, Lord 68
British colonies 23, 47, 150, 207–8
  see also American colonies, individual colonies
British government 41, 49, 128, 167, 174, 203, 254
  and reform 204, 208
Broomielaw Quay 164
Brougham, Henry, Lord Brougham 196, 209–11, 213
Brown, Austin 243
Brown, Frederick 245
Brown, John 234, 240–51
  and education of blacks 241
  family 240, 241
  and Harpers Ferry 247–9
  helps blacks 241, 243
  militant movement 243–45, 246
  and Allan Pinkerton 234, 246, 248, 250
  religion 240, 243–4
  trial 248–9
  Underground Railroad 234, 241, 243, 247
  attitudes towards 245–6
  see also Allan Pinkerton
Brown, John Jr 244
Brown, Mary 250
Brown, Owen 240
Brown, Reverend Nathan 240
Brown, Salmon 248
Brown's Station 243, 244
Buchanan, George 17, 27
Buchanan, President 246
Buchanen, President James 248
Buller, Justice 54, 56
Bunce Island 114, 170, 171, 173, 174–5, 176
  and Freetown, Sierra Leone 206
  slaves on 172, 173, 174–5, 206
Burnard, Professor Trevor 72
Burns, Anthony 242
Bussa (slave) 197
Buxton, Thomas Fowell 200, 202, 205, 208, 210

Cairns, John 41
Calvinism 16–17, 226
Campbell family, Kingston, Jamaica 74
Campbell, Archibald, Lord Islay, 4th duke of Argyll 27
Campbell, Major General Duncan 179
Campbell, Major William 180
Campbell, Sir Archibald 205
Canada 86–7
  escape of slaves to 223, 236, 237, 246–7, 250
  sea routes to 20
Candlish, Robert 231–2
Canning, George 202
Cape Coast Castle 65, 116, 118
Carfare, Joan 236
Caribbean 29, 49, 83, 119, 122, 158, 170, 254
  abolition 202, 205, 207, 211
  Indian immigration 212
  slaves in 72, 103, 110, 114, 158, 160, 197
  Scots in 64, 137–8, 165–6
  Spanish in 101
  sugar 165, 170, 173, 208, 208

Index

tobacco in 173
see also Jamaica, St Kitts, Saint Domingue
Carlyle, Alexander 152
Carpenter, Philo 237
Carstares, William 25
Castlereagh, Viscount 207
Cathcart, Louisa 57
Catholics, suppression of in UK 158
Cato Street Conspiracy 79, 80
Chalmers, Dr Thomas 214, 224, 228–9
   and slavery 229
   and Frederick Douglass 229
   and Free Church 230–1, 232
   in UK 229–30, 232
Charles Edward Stuart (Bonnie Prince Charlie, the Young Pretender) 18, 62–3
Charles II, King 173
Chartist movement 81, 235–6
   and Newport Monmouthshire rising 235
   divisions within 235
Checkland, S. G. 204
Chicago Judiciary Convention 246
Christian evangelism 42, 77210
Christian Observer, The 207
Christianity in Africa 101
Church of Scotland/Kirk 16–17, 18, 19–20, 22, 25, 70, 152, 181, 224, 225
   and abolition movement 150
City of London 173, 176
'Claim of Rights' 225
Clapham Sect 160–1, 206, 207, 229
Clarkson, Thomas 134, 145, 146, 149, 150, 158
Clegg, John 125, 127
Cochraine, William 94
Cochran, Walter 85
Colin, Jean 96
Committee for the Abolition of the Slave Trade 145
Compromise of 1850 242
Confederacy 249–50
Confederation Congress 215
Constitutional Convention 215–16, 249
Cook, Mr, owner of Paynestown, Jamaica 107
Corrie, Edgar 198, 199
Cort, Frederick 203, 204
Covey, Mr 221–2
Cowan, Captain 116, 117–18, 119, 120

Craig, John 237
Crane, Mr 237
Crescent (ship) 116, 117, 118–19, 122, 123
Cropper, James 202
Crosbie, Alexander 93
Cruikshank, Mr 73
Cuba 254
Culloden, battle of 63, 71
Cumberland, HMS 122
Cunninghame, William 169
Cushnie, Alexander 93

Dale, David 182
Dalrymple, Sir Hew, Lord President 30
Darien Company 19, 63, 165, 168
Daughtrey (or Dodridge), John 111
David, Viscount Stormont and Lord Scone (Lord Stormont) 51–2, 57, 59
   children 52
Day, Mary Ann 240
Debauny, Aaron 128
Delaware Indians 87–90
Demerara 199, 201–5, 212
   importation of Calcutta Indians 212
   slave rebellion in 198, 200, 203
Devinier, Harold Charles 59
Devinier, John 58–9
Dickson, John 30, 32
Dickson, William 150
Dolben Act (1788) 123, 133, 150
Donlop, William 25
Douglas Cause (court case) 152
Douglas, Lady 73, 74
Douglass, Frederick (Frederick Bailey) 214ff, 215, 217, 237, 241, 246
   awareness of situation 220
   and John Brown 241, 246, 249
   becomes caulker 222, 223
   and Dr Chalmers 230–1
   and Christianity 221, 222, 223
   family 223
   'Send Back the Money' campaign 227–8, 232
   tours 224
   in UK 232
   writings 223–4
Drachen, James 129
Dumfries, earl of 177
Dundas, Henry 60–1, 67–8, 133, 151ff
   and abolition 159
   divorce and remarriage 161–2
   as home secretary 157

and Joseph Knight case 153
and William Pitt 155
as Viscount Melville 161
Dundas, Robert (brother) 151
Dundas, Robert (son) 161
Dundas, Robert, Lord Arniston (father) 151
Dutch and slave trade 101
Dutch West India Company 101

Edinburgh Review 208, 210, 211
Edinburgh Roper and Sailcloth Company 198
Edinburgh University, developments in 25–6
Ehrman, John 160
Ellen (ship) 130
Elmina 102
Emerald, HMS 134
England, economic development in 18
  differences between Scottish and English law 31, 38
  question of legality of slavery in England 43–44, 46
  see also British colonies
Enlightenment, coming of 16
  perceptions of 'civilised' and 'pre-civilised' societies 34–5
  and reformist lobby 42, 157–8, 254
  Scottish 20, 21–2, 168, 235, 237
  and slavery 46
European states and Africa 101–2
Evans, Thomas 79

Fargher, Captain 125
Fergus, Robbie 236
Ferguson, James 67
Finch-Hatton, George 56, 57, 59
Findlay, Dr Alexander 135
First Reform Bill (1832) 209
Flower, George 185–6, 188, 189
Foley, Lord 38
Folke, George 89
Follett, Richard, Professor 72
Forbes of Shiels, James 94
Ford, Nancy 106, as slave owner 107
Fordyce, Baillie William 85, 94
Foreign Slave Trade Act 161
Fort Sumnter 249
Fox, Charles 161
France and Africa 102
France and tobacco market 167

Franklin, Benjamin 31, 46–7, 173
Frederick the Great 52, 244
Free Church of Scotland 214, 224ff
  and abolitionists 227, 228
  founded 224, 225
  funding 228, 229, 230
  in US 225–8, 231, 232
  see also Send Back the Money
Free Church Anti-Slavery Society 232
Free Enquirer, The 194
free trade and slavery 14
Freeland, William 222
Freetown 206, 207
French and Indian War, US 92
French Revolution 103, 150, 157–8, 179
French slave trade 229
Fry, Michael 155
Fryer, George 174
Fugitive Slave Act 242

Gambier, Margaret 134
Garrison, William Lloyd 217, 228
Gatrell, Vic 75
Genius of Universal Emancipation (newspaper) 190, 192
George III, King 43, 129, 134, 154
George IV, King 201
George, 5th earl of Nottingham 57
Germaine, Lord George 142
Gillard, Edward 139
Gilmour, Sir Alexander 152
Gladstone (Gladstones), John 196, 198–200, 201ff, 212–13
  economic expansion in West Indies 199
Gladstone, Jack 196, 198, 201, 205
Gladstone, Robert 199
Gladstone, Robertson 204, 211
Gladstone, William 198, 205
Gladstones, Thomas and Nelly 198
Glasgow 20–21, tobacco trade 21
Glasgow Arms Bank 168
Glasgow, early eighteenth century 21, 163–6
  Allan Pinkerton in 234–7
  and bills of exchange 168
  capital and business development 164, 168
  Frederick Douglass in 229
  merchants 21, 105, 106, 163–9
  and 'store system' 166, 167
  Port Glasgow 21, 163, 170
  slave trade 167, 171

Index

and transatlantic settlers 165–7
transatlantic trade 105, 164, 168, 169
see also Scotland, sugar, tobacco, West Indies
Glasgow Emancipation Society 228, 229
Glasgow Tanwork, Scotland 105
Glasgow University 25, 26, 168–9, 179, 181
   and the Enlightenment 169, 254
Glassford, John 169
Glassford, Gordon, Monteith and Company 105
Glorious Revolution 254
Gold Coast (now Ghana) 100, 101, 102, 103, 116, 130
Gordon Riots 55, 56, 76
Grant, Alexander 170, 171, 176
Grant, Sargent and Oswald, Bunce Island 114
Gregson *v.* Gilbert (*Zong* Massacre) 53ff, 144, 254
Grenville, Lord 161
Grey, Henry 204–5

Haiti (Saint Domingue) 150, 161, 185, 193, 233
Halévy, Élie 75
Hall's Rifle Works 248
Hammond, Colonel C. G. 246
Hannah, Thomas 116
Hardwicke, Lord Chancellor 41
Harpers Ferry 244, 246, 248, 249, 250
Hart, Rebecca 108
Heriot, George 95
Herman, Arthur 20, 31
Hester, Aunt (Frederick Douglass' aunt) 218, 220
Highland Clearances 64, 181, 225
Hill and Monteith (company) 106
Hill, Peter 57
Holland 75, 101, 103, 160, 167
Holt, Justice 68
Home, Henry, Lord Kames *see under* Kames, Lord
Hope, Charles 161
Hope, John, 2nd earl of Hopetown 162
Hope, Lady Jane 161
Horner, Francis 210
Hume, David 22, 29, 43
Humphrey, Reverend Heman 240
Hun, Mr 237

Hutcheson, Francis 21, 23, 24–5, 26–26, 27–8, 42, 169, 235, 253
   view on slavery 28, 69
   writings 28
   youth and family
Hutcheson, Hans 25
Hutchinson, Thomas 48
Hutchison, John 128

Igbo region (now in Nigeria) 98–9
indentured servitude
   and kidnapping, UK 83–4
   in US 85–91
Industrial Revolution 157, 164, 182, 253
   impact on slave trade 102–3, 105, 164
Ireland 158
Irving, James (cousin) 127
Irving, James 123ff, 253
   attitude towards slaves 126, 130
Irving, James (son) 130
Irving, John 125

Jackson, General Andrew 187, 188
Jacobin sentiment 79, 150, 158
Jacobite Rebellion (1715) 24, 37
Jamaica 63–4, 66, 97, 106, 171, 199
   Jacobites in 64
   laws of 68–9
   limits of legal jurisdiction 69
   Scots in 63, 64, 137, 165, 176
   slavery in 21, 45, 66, 67, 69, 70, 72, 73, 74, 120, 136–7, 158, 176
   slave education 77, 97, 112
   unrest in 108–110, 158, 209, 217
   and *Zong* incident 53
Jamaica slave revolt 208–9, 217
James Francis Edward Stuart (Old Pretender) 37, 62
James VI (and I), King 17
James II and VII, King 18, 19
James, Jesse 250
Jane (ship) 125
Jean of Wigtown (ship) 15
Jefferson, Thomas 28, 184, 188
   on blacks 184
Jeffrey, Francis 210
Jem (*Lady Neilson* crew) 113–14, 115
John Quincy Adams (brig) 193
Johnson, Samuel 69
Johnston, Nathan 215, 223

Jones, John 240, 247, 250
Jumonville Glen, battle of 87

Kames, Lord (Henry Home) 21, 23, 24, 28–9, 29ff, 42, 61, 68, 176, 253
   assessment of other cultures 35
   and slavery 46, 69
   theories of law and social development 31–5, 39
   youth, career and family 29–31
Kansas 241, 242, 244, 248
Kansas-Nebraska Act 242–3
Kansas Volunteers, 1st Brigade of 245
Kennet, Lord 67
Kep Estate, Westmoreland, Jamaica 101, 106
Kinnoull, Lord 224
Knight v. Wedderburn (1777) 46, 254
Knight, Joseph 61, 64, 65–7, 68, 70, 151, 152
   promise of freedom to 68
Knight, Robert 64–5
Knowles, John 41, 44
Knox, John 16, 17, 24, 31

La Creole (ship) 119, 122–6
Lady Neilson (ship) 15, 22, 113, 114ff
Lafayette, Marquis de 183–4, 185, 186, 188, 189, 195
Lawrence, sack of 245
Le Resouvenir plantation 200
League of Gideadites 243
Leith, James 197
Lempriere, William 128–9
Lewis, George 227
Lewis, John 89
Lewis, Thomas (former slave) 43, 44
Liberator, The (newspaper) 217
Liberia 217
Lincoln, Abraham 232
Lincoln, President Abraham 232 249, 250
Lindsay, Dido 48, 49–50, 55, 56, 58–9
   marriage and children 59
   death 59
Lindsay, Elizabeth 57, 58
Lindsay, John (junior) 57–8
Lindsay, Sir Alexander 49
Lindsay, Sir John 48, 49–50
   death 57
   illegitimate children 57
Little, Andrew 125

Liverpool West Indian Association 202
Lloyd, Colonel 218
Locke, John 42
London and 'store system' 167
London Missionary Society 200, 201
London, eighteenth-century 74–6
   Christian evangelism 75
   radicalism in 77, 79
Louis XVI of France 157
Lusk, Dianthe 240

Macaulay, Dr George 135
Macaulay, John 205
Macaulay, Zachary 196, 205–7, 213, 229
   and abolition 206–7
   and Sierra Leone 206–7
MacConachie, Allan 67
MacLean, John 202, 203, 204
Madison, James 184, 185, 188, 190–1
Mansfield, Lady (Hennrietta Frederica de Berargaard) 51, 52, 56, 59
   death 56
Mansfield, Lord (William Murray) 36ff, Chapter 3, 153
   childhood, family and education 36–7, 39
   death 56–7
   Gordon Riots 55, 76
   Thomas Hutchinson and 48
   influences on 42–3
   becomes Baron Mansfield 39
   marriage 39, 56
   impact on slavery 46
   and Dido Lindsay 48, 51, 53, 58
   legal career 38–40
   enters parliament 39
   slavery cases 53
   Somerset v. Stewart (1772) 40, 44–5, 47, 66, 109, 153–4, 254
   views on slavery 42, 54–5
   see also Zong Massacre
Mansfield, 2nd earl of (David Murray) 49
Martin, James 37
Mary II, Queen 18
Matra, Mr 129
Mawlay 'Abd al-Rahman ('Muley Abderhaman') 127–8
Mawley al-Yazid 129
McCauley, William 235
McDonnell, Alexander 202
McFie, Margaret 123

McGeorge, Agnes 96
Methodism 75, 77, 254
Middle Passage 103, 114, 115, 117, 118, 130, 132
Middleton, Charles 133, 134, 135, 137, 142–3, 146
   as abolitionist 155
   as comptroller of the navy 155
Middleton, Lady 143
Mill, John 171
Millar, Robina Craig 181
Miller, Jacob 89
Milner, Mary 57
Milner, Sir William 57
missionaries 196, 197, 198, 202, 213.
Missouri Compromise 241–2
   and impact of California and New Mexico admission 242
Molesworth, Viscount 26
Molineux, Crisp 145
Molly Maguires 250
Moncrieff v. Moncrieff (1734) 39
Monroe, President James 188
Montcalm, General 92
Monteith, Sir Archibald Walter 105
Monteith, Archibald (Aniaso, 'Tobi') 97ff, 104, 110, 253
   baptism and named Archibald John Monteith 107
   emancipation 110–11
   enslavement 100
   youth in Africa 98–100
   preaching 97, 110, 111–12
   religious experience 107–8
   and slaves 97–8
   as Tobi 106–7
Monteith, James 107, 111
Monteith, Jean 105
Monteith, John 104–6, 108, 112, 112
   family 106–7
   time in Jamaica 106
Monteith, Walter 104, 105
Moravian brethren 111 112
Moss, John 212
Moura, Lose Lopez da 174
Murphy, Neil 235
Murray, Anna 214–15
Murray, Lady Anne and Lady Margery 56
Murray, Charles 37
Murray, Lady Elizabeth 56
Murray, David, 7th Viscount Stormont, 2nd Earl Mansfield 49

Murray, Emilia (sister of Lord Mansfield) 49
Murray, George 78–9
Murray, James 37
Murray, William, *see under* Lord Mansfield
Murray, Lieutenant-Governor (Demerara) 200, 201
Mylne, James 179, 181

Napoleonic Wars 103, 197, 199
'Nashoba' 187–93, 195
Ned (slave) 218
Nestor (servant) 145
New Harmony colony 184–5, 186, 189–90
New Lanark mills 182, 184, 186
new lights (group) 25–6
Newport Monmouthshire rising 235
North Star (newspaper) 232
North, Lord 144, 154, 173

Oberlin College 240
Office for the Registry of Colonial Slaves 198
Ogilvie, Margaret 135
Ogilvy, Alexander 198
Ogilvy, Lord David 63, 65
Ogilvy, Margaret 65
Osawatomie Brown (play) 245
Oswald & Co. 164, 169, 170
Oswald of Dunnikier, James 172
Oswald, Richard 163ff, 169–70, 253
   advising government 173
   Caribbean and American colonies trade 172
   land improvement 176–7
   move to London 170
   and slave trade 170, 173–5
   supplies government 172
Oswald, Richard and Alexander 169–70, 173
Owen, Robert 182, 184–5, 195
Owen, Robert Dale 189, 190, 192, 194

Paine, Thomas 179
Paris, Treaty of 215
Paterson, Dr James 64, 72
Paterson, Mr 63
Patronage Act (1712) 224
Payne, Joseph 73
Peel, Robert 213, 225

Peterloo Massacre 79–80
Phillip II of Spain 101
Phiquepal-D'Arumont, Francès-Sylva 194
Phiquepal-D'Arumont, Guilliume Sylvan 194
Pierce, President Franklin 242, 245
Pinkerton, Allan 234ff
　as abolitionist 237, 238
　Bogus Island incident 237
　and John Brown 234, 246, 248, 250
　in Canada 236–8
　and Chartism 235–6
　goes to Chicago 236, 238
　and Civil War 250
　and liberated slaves 246–7
　sets up private detective agency 238
　religious accusations against 237–8
　as deputy sheriff and US Post Office investigator 238
　and Underground Railroad 234, 237, 239–40, 250
　youth 234–5
　see also John Brown
Pinkerton, Isabella 235
Pinkerton, Joan 239–40
Pinkerton, Robert 250
Pinkerton, William 234–5, 247, 250
Pinkerton's Detective Agency 238, 239, 250
Pitt, William 134, 144, 145, 147, 151, 154
　and abolition 159
　agrees to ban slave trade 160–1
　and Dundas 155
　as prime minister 155–6
　on War of American Independence 154
Planter (ship) 82, 85
planters 142, 149, 166, 199–200, 211
　Demerara 200–1
　Glasgow and 167–8
　moral degradation of 254
　St Kitts 138–9, 140
　Virginia 166–7
　West Indies 44, 136, 137–8, 143, 144, 149, 172,196, 197, 198, 207
　Fanny Wright and 182–3
　see also legislation
Pocock, Sir George 49
Porteous, Beilby 141, 143, 146
　on slavery 143

Porteous, John 39
Portuguese and Africa 100–1, slave trade 101
Presbyterian Church 24, 26, 27, 42, 62, 224, 225–6, 228, 231
Presbyterian Church of America 226, 231, 232
Princess Royal, The (ship) 126

Quakers 7, 42, 55, 149, 254
　and abolition 148, 149
　Clapham Sect 160
Quamina (deacon) 196, 200, 201

Radicalism:
　in England 77, 78, 81, 158, 160, 249
　in St Kitts 142
Ragg, Robert 82, 85
Ramsay, James 131ff, 151, 155, 253
　admitted to holy orders 135
　anti-slavery writings 138, 140–2
　invites slaves to church 136
　planters' attitude towards 137–9
　medical practice 139–40
　meets William Pitt 147
　preaching to slaves 139–40
　writings in UK 142–4
Ramsay, Mary 171
Ramsay, Monteith and Company 105
Ramsay, William 135
Rannie, Elizabeth 152
Rappite community 185, 187
Redno Gang 250
Reid, Dr Thomas 133, 135, 138
Richardson, Felicia 106
Richardson, James 188, 189, 190
Robertson, William 67
Robinson, Sam 15, 16, 21, 113–23, 253
　on Jamaica 121–2
　views on slavery 120–1, 130
Rockingham, Lord 39
Rodney, Lord 142
Rosanna (slave, Wedderburn plantation, Jamaica) 71, 73, 76
Royal African Company 63, 67, 114, 173, 254
Royal Navy 49, 50
　sexual activity in 50–1
　and West Indies slaves 50–1
Royal Navy press gangs 122
Royal Society of Edinburgh 152
Ruggles, David 214, 215

Sacks, Jonathan 252–3, 254
Saint Domingue/Haiti revolt 150, 158
Saint Louis, Senegal 102
Schaw, Janet 144–5
Scotland
    1745 Uprising 62–3
    abolition of privy council 23
    and Act of Union 19, 20, 137
    Catholic Church 16
    colonial trade 21
    decline of economy 161
    and development 16
    differences between Scottish and English law 31, 38, 47, 67, 69
    education in 17–18
    economy 18, 19, 23, 83
    eighteenth century 83
    literacy in 17
    lobby 151
    planters 143, 167–8
    and slave trade 16, 67
    trading links 20–1
    and West Indies 64, 137–8, 165–8
    see also Glasgow, Presbyterian Church, Church of Scotland
Scotland transatlantic business networks 165, emigration 165
Scott, Robert 171, 173
Scottish parliament 17, 18
Sergeant II, John 171, 173
Seven Years' War 49, 52, 152, 171, 174
Shaftesbury, earl of 26
Sharp, Granville 42, 43, 44, 46, 149
    and *Zong* Massacre 54, 55
Sharpe, Deacon Samuel 108, 109, 209, 217
Shelburne, Lord 173
Sheridan, Richard 220
Sherwood, William 126
Ship Bank 168
Shyllon, Folarin 140
Sidi Abderhaman 127–8
Sierra Leone 102, 103, 206, 207
    see also Bunce Island
Sierra Leone Company 206
    see also Clapham Sect
Simson, John 26
Sinkum (caddy) 32
slavery
    abolition of slave trade 156
    changing role of 199–200
    and Christianity 197

economic aspects 156
habeas corpus and 41, 43, 45
Hutcheson on 28
impact on modern world 252ff
legal arguments over 66–7
slave emancipation achieved 211
slave revolts 197, 208
Smith on moral degradation of slave masters 253
slave trade late eighteenth century 41, 114ff
    health of 137
    on Jamaica 21, 45, 66, 67, 69, 70, 72, 73, 74, 120, 136–7, 158, 176
    post 1807 197
    pro-slavery movement 42, 45–6
slave ships/slavers 115, 131–2
    medical provision on 132–3
    overcrowding 134
'slave societies' 136
Slave Trade Act (1807) 123, 196, 197, 198, 210
    impact of 199–200
Slave Trade Felony Act (1811) 197
slave trade lobby 148
slave trade, abolition of, UK (1807) 47, 109, 110, 199
Slavery Abolition Act 81, 110, 211–12, 217, 224
    compensation to planters 211–12
Smith, Adam 17, 22, 25, 27–8, 42, 153–7, 179
    on inefficiencies of slavery 253–4
Smith, George 237
Smith, James 94
Smith, Reverend John 200, 201–2, 205, 210
Smith, Sydney 210
Smyth, Dr Thomas 228
Snider, Joseph 88
Society for the Abolition of the Slave Trade 149, 150
Somerset, James (slave) 36, 40–1, 44, 46, 109
Somerset *v.* Stewart (1772) 40, 44–5, 47, 66, 109, 148, 153
Sons of Liberty 47
Spa Field Riots 79
Spain and slave trade 101
Speirs, Alexander 169
Spence, Thomas 78, 79
St Kitts 125, 136, 138, 140, 142, 144, 145

St Michael's, US 221, 233
Stapylton, Robert 43, 44
Stephen, James 150, 211
Stephen, Dr William 137
Stevens, Aaron D. 246
Stewart, Charles 36, 40, 44
'store system' 166
Stormont, Elizabeth see under Lady Mansfield
Success (plantation, Demerara) 196, 199, 201
sugar trade 16, 21, 24, 41, 64, 114, 116, 145, 156, 161, 166, 170, 253
   Glasgow 165, 167
   sugar colonies 142
   changing sugar markets 208, 254
   sugar plantations 137, 140-1, 142, 173, 205
   United States 165, 199, 247
Swift (ship) 131-2, 133, 134, 135
Swinton, Sheriff Principal 66, 68

Talkee Amy (slave) 73, 74, 77
Tappan, Arthur and Lewis 227, 228
Tartar (ship) 119
Thistle Bank 168
Thistlewood, Arthur 79, 80
Thistlewood, Thomas 72, 79
Thomas, Sir George 135-6
Thompson, Anne 66
'three-fifths compromise' 216
tobacco trade 18, 21, 41, 114, 164, 165, 166, 167, 169, 170, 247, 255, 256
   Glasgow and tobacco 105, 164, 165, 167, 168, 169, 199
Tom (*Lady Neilson* crew) 120
Treaty of Paris 229
triangular slave trade 102-3, 105, 114, 155, 174
Trinidad 198
Trollope, Frances 192, 195
Tucker, Dean 145
Tunstell, Mary 124, 126

United Kingdom and Africa 102-3, 156
   public attitude to colonial slavery 150
   slave trade 16
UK-French wars America 86-7
'Underground Railroad' 214, 215, 223, 234, 237, 240, 241, 243, 246
Union Intelligence Agency 250

Unitarianism 78
United States
   13th Amendment 250
   abolition of slavery 215
   abolition of slave trade 216
   cotton industry 150
   democracy in 157
   crime in 238-9
   and emancipation 148
   freed black slaves 216-17
   lawless and slavery pre-Civil War 234
   pressure groups slavery 217
   and slavery Chapter 12, 179, 183, 198
   and slave trade 150
   recovery of escaped slaves 216
   relations between blacks and whites 215
   House of Representatives and Senate prohibited from accepting anti-slavery petitions 217
   slave rebellions 217
   slave owners and slavery 186
   see also American Colonies, American War of Independence
Usherwood, Stephen 46
Utilitarianism 181

Vienna Congress 197, 207
Virginia 166-7
   and American War of Independence 172
   as colony 21, 40, 47, 87, 93
   indentured servants 83-4, 166
   planters 166-7
   Scottish trade in 105, 144, 166-7
   slaves in 183, 217
   and Somerset case 44, 45
   Virginia tobacco 83167, 199
   see also Harpers Ferry
Vreedestein (Demerara) 212
Vreehenhoop (Demerara) 202, 203, 204-5, 212

Walker, David 217
Walker, James 142
Walker's Appeal (book) 217
Walpole, Robert 167
Ward, Captain 113
Washington, Colonel Lewis W. 248
Washington, George 87, 244

Wedderburn, Alexander 61, 64
Wedderburn, Sir Alexander 61–2
Wedderburn, Andrew 97, 98, 110, 112
Wedderburn, David 64
Wedderburn, James 63, 64, 71–2, 76–7, 97–8
Wedderburn, John ('John Thompson') 61, 62, 63, 64–70
Wedderburn, Sir John (father) 61, 62, 71
Wedderburn, Peter 64
Wedderburn, Robert 71, 73–5, 76–81, 97, 108, 182, 253
  and Jamaica 66, 68
  in London 74–6
  joins Royal Navy 74
  becomes tailor 76
  goes to United States 80
  meets father 76–7
  radicalisation 77–9, 80
  as Unitarian 78
  writings 80
Wedderburn, Lord William 'Bill', of Charlton 81
Wellington, duke of 207
Welsh, Dr David 225
Wesley, Charles 149
Wesley, John 77
West Africa and provision of slaves 102–4, 116–17
West Indies 166
  and abolition movement 149
  parliamentary lobby 198
  planters 44, 136, 137–8, 143, 144, 149, 166, 172, 196, 197, 198, 207
  planters' attitudes towards abolition 196
  relationship between owners and slaves 136–8
  Scots in 137–8, 166–8
  trade lobby 147
Western Reserve College 240
Westminster Confession of Faith 225
Whig abolitionists 209
Whitby, Richesson 188, 189, 190, 191, 192
Whyte, Iain 69–70, 232
Wilberforce, William 15, 133, 134, 144, 145, 146, 147ff, 200, 206, 208, 229
  and Lord Brougham 209
  parliamentary debate on slave trade 151, 156–7
Willes, Justice 54
William III, King 18, 25, 224
Williams, Eric 203
Williams, Eric 255–6
Williamson, Peter Chapter 6
  kidnapping and transportation 85
  escape 91
  returns to Scotland 92–5
  postal service 95–6
  as publisher 95
  witnesses atrocities 88–9
Wilson, Hugh 86
Wilson, Jean 96
Wilson, John 247
Wilson, Mary 106
Wingate, Mr 30, 31
Woods, Joseph 144
Wright Camilla (mother) 179, 180
Wright, Camilla (sister) 178, 180, 182, 190, 192
Wright, Fanny (Frances) 47, 178ff, 253
  and America 178–9, 181, 182–3
  antagonism to slavery 179, 185–7, 255
  attitudes 181–2
  attitude towards rich and poor 179–80
  attitudes toward nouveau riche 180
  childhood 179–80
  as editor 194–5, 253
  and Highland Clearances 181
  and Lafayette 184, 186, 190, 192
  and Robert Owen 182, 184
  and social improvement 181–3
  and Frances Trollope 191–2
  and US slavery 184–7, 188, 253, 255
  goes to Haiti 193
  in New York 178
  travels 178, 185, 194
  writings 183, 184, 192, 194–5
  youth and upbringing 180–1
  see also Nashoba
Wright, James 179
Wright, Richard 179–80

Zong Massacre 53ff, 144, 149, 254